Transition to the 21st Century: Prospects and Policies for Economic and Urban-Regional Transformation

CONTEMPORARY STUDIES IN SOCIOLOGY, VOL. 2

CONTEMPORARY STUDIES IN SOCIOLOGY

Theoretical and Empirical Monographs

Editor-in-Chief: John Clark
Department of Sociology, University of Minnesota
Series Editors: Robert Althauser, *Department of Sociology, Indiana University,* John D. Kasarda, *Department of Sociology, University of North Carolina* and Clark McPhail, *Department of Sociology, University of Illinois*

Volume 1. **THE ENTREPRENEURIAL BUREAUCRACY: BIOGRAPHIES OF TWO FEDERAL PROGRAMS IN EDUCATION**
Ronald G. Corwin, Department of Sociology, Ohio State University

Volume 2. **TRANSITION TO THE 21ST CENTURY: PROSPECTS AND POLICIES FOR ECONOMIC AND URBAN-REGIONAL TRANSFORMATION**
Edited by Donald A. Hicks, School of Social Sciences, University of Texas at Dallas and Norman J. Glickman, Departments of City and Regional Planning and Regional Science, University of Pennsylvania

Volume 3. **ORGANIZATIONS AND THEIR ENVIRONMENTS: ESSAYS IN THE SOCIOLOGY OF ORGANIZATIONS**
Charles K. Warriner, Department of Sociology, University of Kansas

Volume 4. **INTERDISCIPLINARY THEORIES OF RURAL DEVELOPMENT**
Frank W. Young, Department of Rural Sociology, Cornell University

Volume 5. **CONSTRUCTING CIVILIZATIONS**
Carl J. Couch, Department of Sociology, University of Iowa

Transition to the 21st Century: Prospect and Policies for Economic and Urban-Regional Transformation

by DONALD A. HICKS
Political Economy Program
University of Texas at Dallas

NORMAN J. GLICKMAN
Regional Science Department
University of Pennsylvania

JAI PRESS INC.

Greenwich, Connecticut *London, England*

Library of Congress Cataloging in Publication Data
Main entry under title:

Transition to the 21st century.

(Contemporary studies in sociology ; v. 2)
Includes index.
1. Urban policy—United States—Addresses, essays, lectures. I. Hicks, Donald A. II. Glickman, Norman J. III. Title: Transition to the twenty-first century. IV. Series.
HT123.T67 1983 307.7'64'0973 83-301
ISBN 0-89232-321-3

36 Sherwood Place
Greenwich, Connecticut 06830

JAI PRESS INC.
3 Henrietta Place
London WC2E 8LU
England

ISBN NUMBER: 0-89232-321-3

Library of Congress Catalog Card Number: 82-81209

Manufactured in the United States of America

CONTENTS

LIST OF CONTRIBUTORS

Robert B. Bradley	Chief Legislative Analyst for the Florida Advisory Council on Intergovernmental Relations
Norman J. Glickman	Regional Science Department University of Pennsylvania
Harvey J. Graff	School of Arts and Humanities University of Texas at Dallas
Donald A. Hicks	Political Economy Program School of Social Sciences University of Texas at Dallas
John D. Kasarda	Chairman, Department of Sociology University of North Carolina
Hans Lin Li	Department of City and Regional Planning University of Pennsylvania
William J. McGill	Chairman, President's Commission for a National Agenda for the Eighties, President-Emeritus, Columbia University
R. D. Norton	Department of Economics Mt. Holyoke College
Robert L. Pallone	Regional Science Department University of Pennsylvania

John Rees — Department of Geography, Maxwell School of Public Policy, Syracuse University

Gail Garfield Schwartz — President, Garfield Schwartz Associates, Washington, D.C.

Daniel R. Vining, Jr. — Regional Science Deparment, University of Pennsylvania

John M. Wardwell — Department of Sociology, Washington State University

Chung Hsin Yang — Regional Science Department, University of Pennsylvania

FOREWORD

William J. McGill, Chairman
President's Commission for a National Agenda for the Eighties

When President Jimmy Carter invited me into the Oval Office and asked me to lead the President's Commmission for a National Agenda for the Eighties in October 1979, he had in mind a far-reaching reassessment of American federalism. The President seemed to be acutely worried—not so much about his own prospects for reelection as about the fragmentation of American society into mutually adversary special interests, all claiming entitlements without regard for the consequences to the nation as a whole. He suggested contacting the state governors, asking them to form mini-commissions, hoping, I suppose, that serious examination of the harsh prospects for the eighties would cause the states to pull together, to diminish their bitter regional rivalries, and to begin concentrating on the national interest.

I persuaded President Carter that the large-scale inquiry he sought could not be brought off successfully in the 13-month period remaining before the next Presidential election. It would take at least three months to assemble the Commission and recruit a high-quality staff. That would leave eight months to conduct our inquiry and two additional months to hammer out a final report. Vigorous disagreements about national goals were bound to arise within the Commission. Moreover, all the special interest groups harassing the President would soon launch themselves at the Commission. We would be lucky to write more than a warmed-over summary of contentions with which he was already completely familiar.

The President corrected me. He was not interested in asking us to formulate national goals. It would be presumptuous of any commission to suppose it could stamp its own vision of the future on the rest of the nation. He was interested in an *agenda*. He took that to mean a statement of the major problems facing the country in the 1980s, although he did not rule out an investigation of the adequacy of governmental institutions for solving them.

President Carter acknowledged sadly that there probably was not enough time to conduct the far-reaching evaluation of government and society that he wanted. One of the problems of politics in a democracy, he said, is that its principal object seems to be to get through each day successfully. There is never enough time for long-range planning. Neither the executive bureaucracy nor the legislative process is geared to undertake a critical examination of the adequacy of democratic institutions. Perhaps in the brief time available, the Commission might make some contribution in that area, even if it could not do all he wished. We agreed.

So the Commission set to work shortly after the Christmas holidays in 1979 with the President's promise that we would be nonpartisan and independent of his executive departments. Our task was to examine them—not vice versa. I, in turn, promised President Carter that we would not leak provocative material to the newspapers or otherwise attempt to embarrass his Administration politically during an election year.

The President kept his promise and we kept ours. By October 1980, the executive committee of the Commission was writing and editing the first draft of our final report. Even then we could see that it was going to be extremely controversial.

The sections on the economy, urban policy, and foreign policy analyzed the nation's problems in ways guaranteed to evoke dismay from the White House staff. Our analysis established that the economy was weakening, inflation was not under control, the hard decisions on economic priorities were not being made. America's energy problem was not being solved, and we did not think highly of the Administration's legislation calling for federally subsidized development of new energy sources. Our stress was on conservation and using the marketplace to develop new processes.

In the Commission's view, urban policy should be directed at *people* not *places*, despite the Administration's commitment to a contrary policy. Finally, the Carter Administration's approach to foreign relations built on America's ideals of human rights had, as the Commission saw it, led us into a welter of contradictions and not a little sanctimony. A new approach should be developed based on more ruthless judgments of the national interest and a clearer understanding of the subtle goals of diplomacy.

Fortunately for the Commission, the Washington press corps paid no attention to these deliberations, despite the fact that sunshine laws forced the Commission's executive committee to operate in public as we debated and drafted positions to submit to the full Commission. It was getting close to election time. President Carter was evidently in serious trouble, and no reporter thought of probing the Commission for material that might be related to the campaign.

The Washington Press, like the government itself, is ordinarily too taken up with the delectations of the daily political struggle to pay attention to historical issues that really count. And so the draft final report was put together quietly out of public view. For more than five weeks just prior to the election, a dozen Commissioners on the executive committee and the 25 members of the Commission's staff were living in daily apprehension that some of the explosive content in our draft report might get into the newspapers before election day. We were particularly concerned about the critical sections on economic, urban, and foreign policy, and the effect they might have on the President's chances. We were a nonpartisan Commission, but it would be gross and unjust if slanted versions of our final report were leaked out to embarrass the man who had called us together in the public interest, and who had enabled us to do our work entirely free of political pressure.

Following the election, representatives of most of the special interest groups on the Commission seemed greatly depressed by President Carter's defeat. There was little disposition to scrutinize the Commission's draft report for potentially objectionable material because there was no prospect that the Commission would be influential in shaping policy for the incoming Reagan Administration. Accordingly, the Commission's scholars and the chairman were able to produce virtually unanimous support for a report that took strong, controversial stands at variance with both the outgoing and incoming administrations. Early in December 1980, the Commission voted approval of what the executive committee had earlier labelled a "blockbuster" final report. These final actions were more or less routine. There were few dissents. Representatives of special interests were now busily concentrating on the new Administration.

When I presented the first typescript copy of the Commission's report to President Carter on December 14, 1980, the U.S. Department of Housing and Urban Development (HUD) and the White House staff finally understood and reacted to its contents. Officials in HUD took unusually severe exception to the principal recommendations on urban policy because they saw them as repudiations of Carter Administration policy. These officials decided to leak slanted versions of the still unpublished report to the press in an effort to discredit it. The resulting furor by lobbying groups and elected representatives of the so-called "snowbelt arc of crisis" from the urban Midwest to the urban Northeast made the Commission famous in a way none of us had anticipated.

John Herbers noted in *The New York Times* a month later, just as the Commission's report was about to be published:

> The reason (for the controversy) is that the report will for the first time put the presidential imprimatur on the view that cities should be allowed to shrink drastically when they can no longer generate their own wealth and jobs, and that the dispersal of people to new suburbs and beyond should be overtly encouraged.
>
> *The New York Times*, January 12, 1981

I recite this remarkable tale as a way of introducing the fascinating content of this book, but also to illustrate the caprices that develop when important new policy ideas become enmeshed with the great public relations apparatus that modern Washington has become. One would suppose that a Presidential Commission would be an ideal vehicle for advancing new policy ideas for solving America's urban problems. Certainly that was what President Carter originally sought from the Commission. But the economic stakes are so high in Washington's current political environment that lobbying groups ordinarily do their best to prevent official discussion, much less advancement of any important new ideas threatening to their constituencies.

The *President's Commission for a National Agenda for the Eighties* succeeded largely because these special interests were temporarily distracted by a national election. When they realized what was going into print, they tried to scuttle the Commission's urban policy recommendations. But it was too late. Next they sought to organize a protest against the report three weeks before it was published. The protest generated an avalanche of publicity resulting in a nationwide discussion far beyond the Commission's wildest dreams. That is not the way it should be done according to the civics books, but it is the way the system now works.

The editors of this book are Donald Hicks and Norman Glickman. Hicks was the principal staff member on the Commission's panel study of urban America in the eighties. Glickman was one of the key scholars to whom the panel turned for advice. In this volume, the reader is offered a collection of papers that examine from diverse perspectives the plight and promise facing our national settlements. Indeed, while there are many issues on which the editors themselves agree, there are at least as many issues on which they do not. Nevertheless, it has been their express intention to preserve, rather than obscure, this diversity.

The papers presented in the chapters that follow are in many cases distilled versions of larger studies authorized by or submitted to the urban policy panel of the President's Commission. Several were presented in a symposium on Urban Prospects and Policies jointly sponsored by the Commission and the National Academy of Sciences held in Washington, D.C., on June 3–4, 1980.

Taken collectively, these papers yield breathtaking, almost frightening generalizations on the massive social and population changes now transforming our cities. There is a large-scale migration toward and even beyond the suburbs. There is also a major migration toward the sunbelt. Large cities in the East and Midwest are not only losing population, their economic structures are being altered. The basic policy question is what to do about it. Do you fight it with federal programs and try to turn it around as mayors and governors demand, or do you try to devise strategies of adjustment as many urban scholars now suggest.

It is a heart-wrenching question because it involves issues that go to the very survival of millions of poor people unequipped to cope with the environment in which they find themselves in our large cities. As it happens, I am a native New Yorker, deeply attached to my home town. For 10 years between 1970 and 1980, I struggled to rebuild Columbia University following the destructive changes that had brought one of our great national institutions to the edge of the abyss in 1968. While I was so engaged, I was crying out continuously for federal assistance. I did not want to see New York City and its great institutions go down unlamented in a Darwinian struggle against newer, more economically viable and presently more attractive competitors in the South and West, built mainly with earmarked federal support. Hence the recommendations of the urban panel of the President's Commission made me distinctly uncomfortable. But we do no service to New York City or the nation by attempting to avoid facing facts on what we can expect to confront in the eighties.

This is a very important book. The scholarly contributions depict an America in transition quite at variance with popular stereotypes. The book will be read carefully by serious scholars, but I would recommend it as required reading for every educated American concerned about the future of our cities.

PREFACE

This volume includes both descriptive and prescriptive materials, most of which are abbreviated and more focused versions of larger works that were either commissioned by or otherwise contributed to the deliberations of the urban policy panel (Policies and Prospects for Metropolitan and Nonmetropolitan America) of the President's Commission for a National Agenda for the Eighties. Several of the selections were prepared for the Symposium on Urban Prospects and Policies, jointly sponsored by the Commission and the National Academy of Sciences and held in Washington, D.C., on June 3–4, 1980. The resulting urban policy report—*Urban America in the Eighties: Perspectives and Prospects*—along with the full Commission report and eight other panel reports was presented to President Jimmy Carter and the nation on January 16, 1981.

The editors express their appreciation to the contributors to this volume who made special efforts to revise their chapters which had been prepared for other purposes. While the thematic overlaps and gaps across the papers reflect the constraints of time and other resources, the editors are responsible for the structure of this collection. In addition, we would like to express our appreciation to Arlene Perazzini, of JAI Press, whose skillful sheparding of the project endured over long months. Special thanks also to Florence Cohen who tirelessly assisted in the preparation of major portions of the manuscript as they moved from the editors' desks to those of the publisher. Donald Hicks wishes to acknowledge the support of the Lincoln Institute of Land Policy, for which he serves as a Postdoctoral Fellow for 1982–1983, and to thank them for providing the time to devote to this volume. Norman Glickman wishes to thank the Netherlands Institute for Advanced Study, where he was a Fellow in 1981–1982, for providing the time and resources to allow him to participate in the editing of this volume. Lastly, we would like to thank Judy Ferguson for her skillful copy-editing.

It has been a delight to work with each of the authors who—despite resource constraints and the press of deadlines—were always cooperative. It is our hope that their and our commitment to this project is reflected in the final product.

Donald A. Hicks
Norman J. Glickman

INTRODUCTION

Donald A. Hicks and Norman J. Glickman

This nation spent the better part of the 19th century coming to her cities. The processes of urbanization and industrialization both sustained and constrained one another. As a result, throughout the history of the United States, city building has been commonly equated with nation building. In the past century, a national system of settlements has developed, providing the physical expression of the industrial era. The human and physical capital resources came to be orchestrated, along with the linking technologies of transportation and communication and the energy sources that sustained them, in a new and distinctive way.

Major urban concentrations, often more bountiful than beautiful, became social, political, and economic wholes. Land, long regarded as the backbone of a receding agrarian economy, likewise shrank in significance to mere "location" in the emerging industrial era economy. The strength of the American city during this era derived increasingly from the fact that the bulk of the resources valued by these industrial economic arrangements were gathered at common crossroads.

The city of the industrial era is best understood as a reflection of the industrialization process. And, in due time, the cities that were molded by the collective activities of humankind provided a cultural context as well as a physical setting for urban life. For a century and more, these arrangements prevailed and generated a support system composed of cultural perspectives and political infrastructure to ensure their hegemony. Yet, silently and subtlely, the older arrangements were laying the framework for new economic and matching social organizations reflecting technological advancements, market-generated "discovery" and dependence on new energy sources, and related possibilities for sorting out social differences that were considered important. Cities began to lose their grip on the building blocks of wealth, power, and innovation, which had enabled these industrial era cities to more than compensate both for growth and development in regions outside the Industrial Heartland and for the suburbanization process that was slowly beginning. Without fully realizing it, America has spent the better part of the 20th century leaving her industrial-era central cities.

Since the 1920s, urban and economic scholars have studied the development of metropolitan concentrations, particularly the central cities. While hints of the suburbanization process were visible along the tracks of commuter rail systems as early as the 1880s, it was the love-at-first-sight affair between the American public and the automobile in the 1920s which, along with other distance- and time-warping technologies, imparted momentum to the patterns of deconcentration that began to restructure the nation's settlements and the lives lived within them. Circumstances six decades later attest to the enduring decisiveness of those influences. Further, since 1900 the share of metropolitan manufacturing employment—the new backbone of the increasingly nonagricultural economy—in the nation's central cities has declined. Yet, few took much notice, and those who did largely believed that such growth dynamics were adjusting the forms, rather than the basic functions, of these metropolitan settlements.

In the past decade, the list of our larger and older industrial centers that have lost population has come to be supplemented by a list of entire metropolitan areas that report net population losses. Likewise, nonmetropolitan areas, for the first time, are growing faster than metropolitan areas. The structure of our national economy is changing as well. This process, which appears to mark our exit from the industrial era, reflects the familiar influence of technological, economic, and energy factors that marked our entry into the industrial era well over a century ago. Today, the functions as well as the forms of our settlements are being redefined by the requirements of the transforming economic system. Thus, the nation is rediscovering what has been all too easily lost sight of during the past century. Our urban areas are the physical expression of the structure of the economy and the capabilities of our technology. Through time, the patterned spatial arrangements both within and among our urban settlements have evolved accordingly.

Economic and social organization have become increasingly far-flung, long ago losing their allegiences to the relatively inflexible structure of political jurisdictions. Our industrial era cities in particular have begun to yield their roles as nerve centers for industrial era arrangements. As inadequate as the term "post-industrial" may be to describe where the nation may be headed, each day a clearer vision is emerging of what we are leaving behind. It remains for us to decide what purposive roles the several levels of government and the public, private, and voluntary sectors of the nation will play, if any, during this transit to a new era.

MAJOR PURPOSE AND THEMES

This volume has the modest goal of contributing to the debate over the role of public policy in this transformation and to the formulation of future urban, economic, science and technology, and social welfare policies. The collected essays do not attempt to present a single, consensual or coherent view of the past, much less of the future. Rather, these papers are viewed as contributions to the debates arising from varied perceptions of and proposed responses to the transformation of the economy, and the social arrangements it nourishes, accompanying the emergence of a post-industrial America as the 20th century draws to a close. We hope to draw out the implications of these changes for our national economy and its settlement patterns in order to broaden understandings of urban change and to help in the formulation of policy. Where consensus cannot be offered, an attempt has been made to sketch out carefully the issues involved in order to deepen our understanding of them.

Several crucial topics are discussed in the chapters that follow: the transformation of our local, national, and international economies; the changing role of cities in America; the dispersal of population and economic activity—jobs, capital, income, and even innovative capacity itself—within and between metropolitan areas, multistate regions, and across national borders; the increasing erosion of distinctions between central city and suburb, urban, and rural areas; and the difficulties of adjustment to the direction and pace of urban and economic changes. The potential for conflict between governmental efforts in urban revitalization and those in national economic revitalization are discussed. The role and function of a spatially sensitive national urban policy vis-à-vis a set of social and economic policies that assign only secondary importance to explicit spatial objectives for the years ahead are addressed. The implications of jobs-to-people versus people-to-jobs inner city and interregional strategies are developed, as are other matters where differential priorities are applied to "people" and "place" orientations in public policy. Some authors deal with the prospects for and the wisdom of integrating regional, sectoral, and macroeconomic policies. Finally, the merits and demerits associated with reconcentration versus dispersal and high- versus low-density development are discussed.

It is anticipated that this collection will be attractive to those interested in America's future in general, as well as to those interested in specific social, economic, and political changes unfolding in our society. The changes affecting metropolitan and nonmetropolitan America can be seen in the context of changes evident in a majority of the advanced nations in the world. Thus, those who have interests in urban affairs and urban problems and policies should find this collection useful. Students and teachers of public policy analysis, urban and regional planning, and the policy sciences are likely to find the following selections of interest. Finally, those who seek to understand how to integrate domestic and international issues, articulate social with economic policies, and orchestrate intersectoral and intergovernmental resources and strengths, should find this volume of use.

STRUCTURE OF THE VOLUME

This collection begins with a selection that has been set apart from the others. Chapter I, "Perspectives on Urban America and Key Policy Issues for the Eighties," is the summary chapter of *Urban America in the Eighties: Perspectives and Prospects,* the Report of the Panel on Policies and Prospects for Metropolitan and Nonmetropolitan America which was written by Donald Hicks for the President's Commission for a National Agenda for the Eighties. Intended as a synthesis of the urban policy recommendations of the Commission, it serves as a touchstone for the remaining chapters. The reader will easily see that this initial selection makes choices rather than simply arraying alternatives in a value-neutral fashion. In the process, the prescriptive orientation of this first chapter either explicitly or implicitly introduces for the reader the themes that are developed in the subsequent chapters of this collection.

Following this initial selection, the book is divided into three major parts. *Part I, Redistribution in Urban Society: Myths and Realities of Crisis, Decline and Renaissance,* brings together discussions of the dominant patterns of population redistribution and the implications of these dynamics for the ebb and flow of our settlement patterns and of our collective life within them. As contemporary American circumstances are placed in a series of wider spatial and temporal contexts, the reader is encouraged to reconsider alternative national urban policy responses to the demographic, cultural, and political trends that have been unfolding in recent years.

In Chapter II, John Kasarda outlines the major redistributional patterns that have shaped urban America in recent decades and offers an ecological perspective of the kind that has not had much of an impact on the intellectual foundations of national urban policymaking in recent years. The resulting interpretation challenges the reader to appreciate more fully both the building strengths of transformed central cities and the growth and apparent viability of suburbs in present and future urban settlements. Kasarda urges us to avoid misinterpreting the scale and portent of limited upgrading of central city housing stock widely interpreted as evidence of an urban residential renaissance—or "gentrification" as it is sometimes called—and to realize that the changing forms and functions of our urban areas are all too easily—and mistakenly—judged not to be in the best interests of the nation. Kasarda closes with an inventory of circumstances that generate much concern and draws from them recognitions that he believes should serve as the ingredients of future national urban policies. Throughout, his policy prescriptions are ones whose net effect would be to nurture the changes being experienced by urban America rather than oppose them.

The essays in Part I assign great significance to the resurgence of growth in nonmetropolitan areas. For the past half-century, our collective attention has been directed largely toward the powerful forces behind metropolitan concentration. Yet, in the past decade several scholars have been looking over their shoulders at a remarkable series of changes that have been working themselves out in nonmetropolitan areas. John Wardwell interprets the significance of rapid nonmetropolitan growth in Chapter III. As we try to construct a national urban policy that accommodates the changes transpiring adjacent to and remote from dominant metropolitan systems, Wardwell's chapter becomes increasingly significant. Wardwell spotlights the return of vitality to rural America—a vigor accompanied by an increasingly diversified economy developing across the nation's nonmetropolitan counties. Why this is occurring and the efficiency and equity implications of these developments for post-industrial society are addressed in this chapter. Further, the meaning of revitalization and the implications of rising energy costs in rural and other low-density settlements are explored.

Part I also seeks to help us better understand contemporary American circumstances in light of the changing spatial and structural dynamics of core regions in other economically developed nations of the world. In Chapter IV, Daniel Vining, Robert L. Pallone, Han Lin Li, and Chung Hsin Yang discuss the possibility that there may be a limit to the tendency for urban growth in developed nations. Analyzing internal migration data from 21 nations, these researchers highlight systematic international urbanization trends that transcend national idiosyncrasies. They focus on the gradual diminishment of agglomeration advantages of core regions over the past century. Throughout the developed world, the trend of migration to high-density areas that has persisted for over a century has ended. The reversal of migration patterns in the United States, then, may be viewed as an accompaniment of the transformation of industrial societies in the post-industrial era that has occurred in many advanced nations. This chapter may well cause the reader to consider the wide susceptibility of industrial nations to this trend; likewise, the apparent inevitability of this development for nations as they mark time on a technological rather than a historical timeline is worth considering. The potential for a significant reversal or alteration of this tendency through public policies is likewise worth reexamination in light of this analysis.

The expanded contemporary context in the first three chapters of this section is supplemented by an expanded historical context in the next chapter. In Chapter V, we are helped to understand how and why the images of crisis and decline accompanying urban change lend themselves so effortlessly to myths and misconceptions. Harvey Graff draws our attention to the urban culture that is tied to urban places, addressing the ease with which assertions are made concerning urban "crisis" and "decline." In this regard, Chapter V complements preceding papers that call attention to the precariousness of analyzing urban development and proposing urban policies while using standards that may themselves be time-, place-, and culture-bound. With only a relatively brief urban tradition, the United States has historically had great difficulty accommodating city-based life and change. The city has come to symbolize a variety of conflicting images (e.g., "streets paved with gold" versus the setting for untold poverty and despair). Graff warns us that we do violence to the essence of a "city" if its fate and fortunes are interpreted with linear, evolutionary, or devolutionary metaphors. The search for sensible public policy, however sensitive to contemporary political and economic circumstances, that fails to exploit historical analysis, is doomed to failure.

Finally, Part I offers an analysis of the most volatile terrain of all—the shifting bases for urban political coalitions. Patterns of population redistribution are not easily divorced from the patterns of political power and representation that influence the character and substance of debate over the ingredients of national urban policies. In Chapter VI, Robert Bradley reminds us that the demographic and economic changes that are and will continue to transform urban America have ramifications for national and subnational government, for intergovernmental relations, and for the political process whereby citizens influence governmental policies. Bradley examines the extent to which the political constituency essential to urban reform politics is being eroded by the selective outmigration of citizens from older and larger cities. Moreover, does the growing representation of suburban, small town, and rural interests doom urban revitalization initiatives? Does slow economic growth dictate that the gains of some groups come not from growth surplus but rather imply commensurate losses from other groups? Finally, this chapter illustrates the continuing significance of race in urban America—an aspect of larger urban policy questions that is in danger of being oversimplified by discussions of population and job redistribution that glide over the racial and class selectivity of outmigration from our older industrial cities.

Part II, The Implications of Economic Transformation for Urban Society, is the natural sequel to the preceding section. In this section are selections that highlight several dimensions of the structural changes besetting our nation's local, regional, and national economies. The selectivity of outmigration of jobs and people from localities and regions of historical importance has generated a rash of serious and painful circumstances that are distributed unequally. The interdependent realities of "slippery" capital and "sticky" labor, especially unskilled labor, create the likelihood of an increasingly stranded urban underclass. That not only the size of this stratum may enlarge, but also its composition may become increasingly heterogeneous in a changing economy capable of expanding without significantly enlarging the pool of employment prospects for this urban underclass is discussed.

The transformation of older industrial cities has involved selective outmigration that has altered substantially the composition of the populations left behind. In Chapter VII, R. D. Norton reminds us that in the past when we have spoken of urban policy, what we have often meant was poverty policy, a series of strategies designed to link people with economic opportunity. Here the relevance of traditional local economic development strategies designed to affect the fortunes of central city residents "left behind" is examined.

The greater concentrations of poverty in our larger and older central cities and the creation of an urban underclass are discussed in light of the linkage between distressed people and distressed political jurisdictions. Norton argues for greater openness to the possibility of mobility-based solutions to central city poverty. The goal would be to break this linkage using people-to-jobs programs instead of continuing a dependence on jobs-to-people strategies that have characterized the past 15 years of urban policy.

Varied industrial and sectoral strategies aimed at bringing about the kind of economic vitality required for the expansion of economic opportunities for all Americans are developed in the next three chapters in this section. Never far from the minds of the contributors of these next selections is the fact that in a dramatically telescoped period of time, our nation's economy, as well as the economies of its constituent regions and localities, has lost much of its insulation from the political and economic transformations under way in and beyond our hemisphere. Much attention is given to the fact that the political boundaries of the world's nation-states no longer easily coincide with those of their economies. The scale of this nation's economy, like those of other advanced and advancing nations around the world, is so increasingly far-flung that anxious tradeoffs between our national political goals and our national social and economic goals can no longer be avoided. Indeed, the clear inference from these several selections is that the very notions of nation-state and welfare, if not perhaps even work itself, are susceptible to redefinition in the years ahead.

In Chapter VIII, Norman Glickman sets out some of the changing context of economic and urban policy, reviewing the urban impacts of international trade, capital movements, and business cycles. He shows that the effects of these factors are uneven across the nation and have been changing over time. Glickman also uses econometric models and a set of long-term scenarios to make some forecasts about the future of America's cities.

In Chapter IX, John Rees employs the product-cycle model of international economics to help us understand the implications of regional economic decentralization. Rees reviews the stages of industrial growth as the capacity for innovation gradually builds and then disperses within and between geographical locations. The failure of the Industrial Heartland and its major urban centers to create new growth opportunities sufficient to compensate for the presence of declining mature industries, is a dynamic that moves the major multistate regions of the nation toward income convergence. With this background, Rees outlines how an industry policy that centers on the strategy of upgrading the capacity of regions to nurture technological innovation should become a major component of any national urban policy. Drawing on the initiatives of several western European countries, Rees' recipe for policies with substantial and beneficial urban outcomes is in some contrast to those of the past two decades.

The increasing locational disadvantages at the local level, together with the structural changes working their way through the larger economy, are highlighted by Gail Schwartz as justifications for revamping traditional approaches to urban policy. In Chapter X, Schwartz argues for national sectoral policies that concentrate on restoration of health through chains of interrelated industries. Explicit attention would be directed to allowing industry to exploit its competitive advantage within and across a variety of sectors. Such sectoral strategies, Schwartz contends, requires a much greater capacity for communication between the public and private sectors, between management and labor, and among the management officials of firms that are linked within the same sector. Further, sectoral strategies, like several of the policy proposals in preceding chapters, would explicitly recognize that outcomes for specific communities, while important, must be secondary to national economic vitality.

In *Part III, Looking Ahead: National Urban Policy Conflict, Consensus and Choice,* the two editors of this volume independently attempt to outline and synthesize the perspectives and policies each feels important to understanding and responding to the economic and urban-regional changes that are shaping the closing years of this century. The two chapters interpret the events of recent years that have so redefined the stakes in national urban policymaking. Building on these bases, the conflict and choice that will accompany national urban policy debate in the coming years are discussed. While it is safe to say that neither essay presented in Part III offers the answers that have been eluding analysts and practitioners in this domain for years, the reader can distinguish multiple points of agreement and an equal number of divergences preserved in looking at the years ahead to keep alive the spirit of debate over the substance and goals of national urban policy.

In Chapter XI, Norman Glickman, using his analysis in Chapter VIII as background, sets out some policy options for America's cities. Given slow growth and social austerity, Glickman argues that new institutions and political alliances are needed to solve many of our contemporary problems. His recommendations include efforts to broaden participation at the workplace, movements toward democratically based economic and industrial planning institutions, and community rejuvenation through programs targeted to both "places" and "people".

In Chapter XII, Donald Hicks argues that the twin transformations of the economy and the city in the late 20th century are ushering in a post-industrial era that will require redefinitions of "work" and the "city" and not simply reworked versions of older urban and economic policies built on conceptions of both that have grown obsolete through past decades. The elements of a restoration of growth in national economic productivity are already in place, though they have been masked by the necessity for economic restructuring having had to contend with the wrenching influx into the labor force of a large cohort of first-time entrants and returning women. Of greater concern is the likelihood that the new economic arrangements may not be able to accompany productivity growth with employment growth. Hicks assesses the relatively narrow "shadow" urban policy that has emerged since the election of President Ronald Reagan. With special attention to the prospects of the enterprise zone as an inner city strategy, Hicks argues against the wisdom of continuing to resort to urban policies whose success is judged by what happens in specific places. People primarily, and political jurisdictions only secondarily, should be the principal objects of urban and economic policies of the future. The growing mismatch between the scales of economic organization and our political responses to it will hobble the search for and implementation of sensible national urban and economic policies in the coming years.

Chapter I

PERSPECTIVES ON URBAN AMERICA AND KEY POLICY ISSUES FOR THE EIGHTIES

Donald A. Hicks

Until 50 years ago, the proper federal role vis-à-vis the nation's cities was easily summarized. Because the Constitution had not explicitly specified otherwise, the responsibility for cities devolved to state governments. With the onslaught of the Depression, the federal government began for the first time to consider cities as national, rather than merely state, assets. Accordingly, New Deal recovery policies included federal assistance for both distressed people and beleaguered local governments. The rationale behind this action was that "the American economy was dependent upon the health of the many urban industrial economies within it and that it was in the best interests of the federal government to aid those [local] economies" [1:110]. This national economic calamity henceforth legitimized the appropriateness of a general federal urban policy presence, even though a commitment to continuing federal involvement in the functioning of local economies was never intended.

In the past 20 years, the time-honored logic of a federal commitment to assisting people in cities has been extended to assisting the cities as well. Welfare and income maintenance programs have been supplemented by programs that emphasize physical redevelopment, local economic development, and direct fiscal aid to local governments. The transition from the War on Poverty and Great Society era of the 1960s to the New Federalism of the 1970s did much to legitimize an increasing federal emphasis on places in the country. This emergent spatial sensitivity in public policy has become particularly apparent during the past four years [1977–80], as illustrated by the dominant thrusts of the national urban policy and executive orders devoted to urban impact analysis, federal facility siting, and targeted procurement. The New Deal emphasis on helping distressed people in cities directly has evolved into an emphasis on helping distressed places (local business and government) directly for the purpose of helping people indirectly. Today most federal funds directed to urban problems go to "place" recipients rather than distressed people. In the late 1970s, a spatial sensitivity appears to have overtaken in large part a social sensitivity developed during the previous decade. Politically, this shift is justified by the assertion that aiding places with problems is easier than aiding people with problems. Economically, this shift is justified by the assertion that direct aid to local economies multiplies its impact so that benefits reverberate throughout the economy in ways that direct aid to people does not.

The 1980s may well require a new perspective on aiding distressed people in urban America. To import the 1930s rationale for a federal urban policy role across the decades may not be wise. Although the economy in the 1930s was indeed dependent on the health of local urban industrial economies in ways not fully appreciated, and it undoubtedly was in the best interest of the federal government to aid those local economies, circumstances have conspired to weaken that rationale.

Unlike a half-century ago, contemporary urban economies are no longer confined within the political jurisdictions of cities. Modern urban economies have an expanded scope that integrates central city, suburban, and nonmetropolitan economies. The deconcentration trends accompanying the arrival of a postindustrial era highlight the fact that the nation's economic vitality no longer arises from or is tied to specific types of places. It increasingly derives its strength from all kinds of places, both local political jurisdictions and beyond. Today it may be in the best interest of the nation to commit itself to the promotion of locationally neutral economic and social policies rather than spatially sensitive urban policies that either explicitly or inadvertently seek to preserve cities in their historical roles. A federal policy presence that allows places to transform and assists them in adjusting to difficult circumstances can justify shifting greater explicit emphasis to helping directly those people who are suffering from the transformation process.

Our cities are truly national assets. Hence, the federal policy presence should recognize that the health of a city, or any other settlement, is determined not by population or employment levels, but by its ability to perform vital functions for the larger society. As national assets, cities and their residents are the resources and responsibilities of us all during their adjustment to the postindustrial era. With this perspective in mind, a redefined federal policy role in urban America for the coming decade is presented.

A NATIONAL URBAN POLICY RECONSIDERED

The economic health of our nation's communities ultimately depends on the health of our nation's economy. Federal efforts to revitalize urban areas through a national urban policy concerned principally with the health of specific places will inevitably conflict with efforts to revitalize the larger economy. Federal efforts to nurture economic growth through increased productivity, expanded markets, job creation, and controlled inflation will require that settlements, their residents, and local governments adjust to changing economic realities. Accordingly, *the purpose and orientation of a "national urban policy" should be reconsidered. There are no "national urban problems," only an endless variety of local ones. Consequently, a centrally administered national urban policy that legitimizes activities inconsistent with the revitalization of the larger national economy may be ill advised.*

Priority should not be assigned to the implementation of a spatially sensitive policy effort designed to retard or reverse the emergence of new economic patterns and relationships within and among the nation's settlements. The federal government should assign greater priority to meeting the needs of the residents of the nation's communities rather than to reconciling or resolving the array of constituent intrametropolitan and interregional conflicts. The federal government should exercise its policy presence carefully so as not to exacerbate unnecessarily the circumstances facing certain localities and regions that cause them to lose population and economic vitality. *Where federal policies and programs are used to assist the transformation of local communities to achieve health and vitalty at new population levels and with restructured economic bases, such national policies should endeavor to ameliorate the undesirable impacts of these transitions on people, primarily, and on places, secondarily.*

Although no national urban problems exist, myriad problems do exist within all localities and regions of the nation. Our nation's settlements, and the households, firms, and local governments within them, exhibit a bewildering diversity of conditions that reflect the confluence of long-term demographic, economic, and governance trends and that link them to emerging patterns of metropolitan and regional change. The forces underlying these transformations are relatively persistent and immutable. However, the local and regional problems left in their wake are not uniform in cause; therefore, the urban policies proposed as remedies cannot be expected to be uniform in consequence.

It is unlikely that the federal government can act wisely on behalf of the nation as a whole if economically healthy metropolitan areas are not appreciated because their vitality is discounted or obscured by a preoccupation with transforming core areas of central cities. Neither will the nation benefit if the newly prospering regions that historically have been economically depressed are defined as inimical to historically prosperous regions that are now experiencing relative economic decline. A national urban policy cannot be enunciated and implemented when the very national focus it should assume and the national wellbeing it should foster are sacrificed to a concern for the diverse fates and fortunes among cities, among metropolitan areas, among states, and among regions.

Certainly, there is merit in anticipating the locational consequences of federal government actions, but many federal policies aimed at promoting the efficiency and productivity of the nation have unavoidable negative consequences for certain localities and regions. Knowing that spatial tilts are embedded in federal policies provides no necessary justification for weeding them out. They often may be entirely justified. Indeed, anti-industry biases in federal policies may be more pernicious than anti-urban biases, given that the health of all places is directly or indirectly dependent on the strength of the larger economy. These tradeoffs should be clearly recognized, and choices should be made consistent with the functioning of the national system of settlements and the national economy, which benefits the entire country at the risk of abiding a series of smaller scale, and often painful, subnational adjustments. A national urban policy designed to place the swirl of local and regional concerns ahead of an overall concern for the nation is both inappropriate and ill advised.

Federal urban policy can be used to channel and target the enormous, if seldom adequate, resources of the federal government and to guide or influence the flows of private sector resources. Nonetheless, despite the importance of the government resources, and the far greater weight of the private resources that at times may be influenced, problems do not yield to massive infusions of resources alone. Rather, a great proportion of urban ills stems from inevitable competition for advantage among groups within localities and between regions. The litany of urban problems is a reflection of this underlying competition in a pluralistic urban society. The very competition that dictates our urban strengths may determine the nature of our urban ills, although not the character of the solutions to those ills. An explicit national urban policy can do little more than make that irony more salient.

The limits to what a federal urban policy effort can achieve are defined by several factors. First, *recognition should be made of the near immutability of the technological, economic, social, and demographic trends that herald the emergence of a postindustrial society and that are responsible for the transformation of our nation's settlements and life within them.* These major formative trends are likely to continue not only through the coming decade, but also well into the next century. Major deflection or reversal of these broad-gauge trends is not likely to result from purposive government action. *Clearly, on the basis of these trends, a federal policy of active anticipation, accommodation, and adjustment makes more sense than efforts to retard or reverse them. The efforts to revitalize those communities whose fortunes are adversely affected principally by the inadvertent consequences of past public policies are entirely justified, but these instances are judged to be rare. It is far more judicious to recognize that the major circumstances that characterize our nation's settlements have not been and will not be significantly dependent on what the federal government does or does not do.*

REDEFINING THE FEDERAL ROLE IN URBAN POLICY

What should constitute a reasonable federal urban policy role in the light of domestic trends that are transforming this nation and transnational trends that are drawing us into closer community with the world? Policy responses to such complex and changing circumstances are inevitably difficult to conceive and develop. Not only do limits to what can be accomplished with policies and programs exist, but also in many substantive areas, the local readjustments may not require vigorous federal intervention. Accordingly, a proper federal presence in urban affairs should reflect a blend of actions to be avoided as well as actions to be taken. That powerful forces are creating multiple forms of distress in local communities and regions, and that they are not likely to be deflected or defused by public policy, do not inherently justify more or less federal urban policy. Rather, this situation serves as an argument for a different conception of what the federal urban policy role should be.

The federal government can best assure the well-being of the nation's people and the vitality of the communities in which they live by striving to create and maintain a vibrant national economy characterized by an attractive investment climate that is conducive to high rates of economic productivity and growth and defined by low rates of inflation, unemployment, and dependency. Where disadvantage and inequality are selective and cumulative, federal efforts should be expended to ameliorate these consequences in ways that are consistent with developmental trends within the society and the economy as a whole.

The federal government, in partnership with the business community and state and local governments, should carefully consider developing a policy perspective on industry in order to maintain a dynamic national economy and secure a strong role in the transforming international economy. The industrial bases of our nation's economic strength must be allowed to transform, and localities and regions should be assisted in anticipating and adjusting to national and international trends. A positive industry policy should include national economic planning, a coherent science policy, and invigorated research and development efforts to nurture and enhance our existing comparative advantages within and between industrial sectors vis-à-vis other nations. Such efforts should acknowledge that much can be learned from certain individual firms that may be in the most challenged industrial sectors but which are able to compete successfully in international and domestic markets. Increased productivity and employment growth, together with diminished inflation, will do more to benefit people in this nation, regardless of where they may live, than efforts to resist the local and regional impacts of a changing international economic order.

People-oriented national social policies that aim to aid people directly wherever they may live should be accorded priority over place-oriented national urban policies that attempt to aid people indirectly by aiding places directly. If the ultimate goal of federal policies and programs is to aid people in their adjustment to or migration from transforming local circumstances, the most direct and effective ways to do that should be chosen. *A national social policy should be based on key cornerstones, including a guaranteed job program for those who can work and a guaranteed cash assistance plan for both the "working poor" and those who cannot work.* Federal job creation, subsidies to private employers, and manpower training and retraining programs can significantly reduce minority, youth, and displaced worker unemployment. Where public employment programs are used, they should be considered a temporary supplement for and provide a transition into private sector employment. A federal guaranteed-income plan, implemented through either a negative income tax or a direct cash transfer program, would effectively and properly shift the welfare burden to the federal government, which can administer it more efficiently and with a greater capacity for responding to equity considerations than subnational governments.

Where the problems faced by people exist in such concentrations that the impacts of people-oriented social policies and programs are negated, or where communities bear the brunt of special circumstances (such as massive foreign immigration), federal funds should be carefully targeted to local governments and to the private sector to assist them in meeting collective needs. Nonetheless, the federal government should develop the will and capability to assist local governments in identifying both places that are unlikely to realize any significant improvement through targeted urban aid and appropriate strategies to disinvest public resources and to channel public and private resources to locations that retain the capacity to absorb and benefit from federal assistance.

These major social policy initiatives and realignments should largely substitute for, rather than add to, existing federal policies. Prime candidates among the federal urban (and rural) development assistance program efforts that should be scrutinized for eventual reduction or elimination are in the place-oriented policy domains, including economic development, community development and public facilities investment, housing, transportation, and development planning. Instrumentalities such as community development block grants, urban development action grants, general and countercyclical revenue sharing, CETA grants, and water and sewer construction grants can be useful tools for an adjustment process. However, their use can be justified only during localities' major transitions in size and function. In addition, such mechanisms should be tilted toward the goal of assisting localities to adjust to changing circumstances and should be used to supplement marginally, but not substitute for, efforts that aid people directly. Because guidelines for establishing timeframes for ending interim transitional efforts in favor of a more spatially neutral federal presence will be exceedingly difficult to adopt, efforts should begin now.

It is important to realize that identifying tradeoffs among policies and programs with explicit urban foci is not sufficient. Tradeoffs among nominally nonurban federal policies and programs also should be considered, because they often have major, if inadvertent, urban impacts. Among the explicitly nonurban policies and programs that should be scrutinized for major restructuring or elimination are the panoply of in-kind benefits for the poor (such as legal aid services and Medicaid), the growing inventory of subsidies that indiscriminately aid the nonpoor as well as the poor (for example, veterans' benefits), protectionist measures for industry (for example, trade barriers for manufacturers and price supports for farmers), and minimum wage legislation.

Although the original goals of each policy and program may be laudable in isolation, once set into place alongside all others, their aggregate result has been policy incoherence, inconsistency, internal contradictions, and inertia. Solutions regarded as permanent or sacrosanct tend to outlive and become poorly articulated with the characteristics of the problems that they were intended to address. The thrust of this extended proposal is that the problems of people and the places where they live can be handled in better ways than by continuing to tinker with hundreds of different programs that assist individuals, households, neighborhoods, businesses, and subnational governments. Although a "people-place" distinction may often be more apparent than real, the aim should be a reorientation of emphasis, which involves avoiding the temptation to use place-oriented assistance to prop up localities rather than allowing them to transform. People are best assisted directly, and policies that best insulate people from or compensate them for painful transitional consequences should be emphasized.

Federal urban policy efforts should not necessarily be used to discourage the deconcentration and dispersal of industry and households from central urban locations. Interregional and intrametropolitan shifts of households and industry are essential to the efficient functioning of the national economic system on a scale that supercedes local and regional economies. Each emerging deconcentration trend is nothing more than an aggregate of countless choices by and actions of individuals, families, and firms influenced by social, cultural, and economic considerations; our public policy tools are least useful when attempting to alter in a predictable way what the individual household or firm will do. Yet, an inability to alter these developments should be appreciated apart from the fact that their net impact is probably positive and beneficial. The ongoing deconcentration processes that leave very undesirable local consequences in their wake justify a federal policy role that principally attends to these consequences, rather than flails against the change processes that generate them.

The relocation of population and economic vitality to nonmetropolitan and previously rural areas also should not be discouraged. The current revitalization of traditionally rural areas should neither obscure the fact that much of the traditional basis for urban-rural distinctions no longer exists, nor veil the fact that much of formerly rural America remains unaffected by expanding and diversified economic bases. Although the poor of this nation are largely city-bound, the incidence of poverty in rural areas still exceeds that in urban areas.

The energy and environmental implications of the continuing trends toward relatively low-density development in new growth areas and the thinning out of existing high density areas do not unequivocally justify the need for a national effort to encourage reconcentration in historically central locations. The emergence of decentralized social and economic systems, which encompass increasing scope and territory and dictate that new, more specialized functions be performed by cities, should generally be encouraged. Although energy and environmental considerations will and should assert themselves in important policy debates in the coming decade and beyond, as yet little compelling and unambiguous empirical evidence exists to justify explicit public policy designed to alter the way in which our nation's communities grow and contract. Conservation of existing energy and environmental resources is not necessarily inconsistent with, and may even be enhanced by, the shift to lower density development, small-scale reconcentration in new growth areas, and the thinning out of large-scale, centrally located concentrations of people and activities. Nonetheless, the federal government should not abdicate its responsibility to assist localities and states in anticipating and countering the negative consequences that low-density development may have in some locations, including those instances where prime agricultural land is invaded indiscriminately by urban uses.

Federal policies should not be revamped, without careful consideration given to their primary functions and net effects, simply because unintended or inadvertent "anti-urban" consequences are discovered. Bending federal policies that do not have an explicit urban focus to serve locational or spatial outcomes may be undesirable. Although countless federal policies initiate a barrage of unintended anti-urban effects, these policy thrusts most often have simply reinforced larger demographic and economic trends or have marginally increased the pace with which they have unfolded.

In the end, the federal government does not have that much control over what happens to localities and regions. There is little justification for using explicit urban policies to do more than assist people primarily and places secondarily to anticipate and adjust to the emergence of a continually transforming national economy and society. Federal policies, including investment tax credits and environmental regulations, have important narrow sectoral goals that may be unwisely sacrificed if they are manipulated to secure specific urban outcomes.

In close partnership with the private sector, the federal government should develop strategies to assist localities in adjusting to economic-base transformation and population change. In a federal policy lexicon, "development policy" should be expanded to imply policy-guided local contraction and not simply local revitalization and expansion. Policy-guided contraction and disinvestment can help to ease the impact of decline on individuals and local institutions and to position communities for regaining their health at new lower levels of population and industrial activity.

The federal government should acknowledge that the problems of population and economic growth can be as troublesome and painful as those of shrinkage. Shifts in population and economic activity, which current policy instrumentalities probably cannot reverse, pose specific adjustment problems for metropolitan and nonmetropolitan communities in all regions. Both growth and decline present opportunities to local governments to become better articulated with their populations and economic bases through carefully planned expansion or contraction. *The federal government should assist communities during their transition and adjustment to new levels of population and economic activity.*

Federal policies aimed at achieving beneficial urban outcomes should be consistent with efforts to ensure a strong national economy and to implement national programs in health, welfare, housing, transportation, energy, environmental protection, and local governmental assistance that are consistent with dominant trends. These policy domains should not use allocational strategies for federal efforts that attempt to counter larger social and economic transformations or to maintain specific local or regional advantages that are slowly being eroded in the course of metropolitan and regional development. Nonetheless, the federal government should be fully sensitive to the fact that even though certain large-scale transformations bode well for the nation, they do imply serious transitional distress for some localities.

Accordingly, *the federal government should continue to assist localities in providing basic services to local residents.* Meeting the collective needs of citizens wherever they live will continue to require close federal-local cooperation. *The federal government should refrain wherever possible from assigning new responsibilities to localities unless they also provide the resources that localities need to meet those obligations.* This intergovernmental relationship recognizes both the well developed capacity of the federal tax system to collect and disperse revenues efficiently and the developing capacity of localities to provide the necessary services in the most efficient manner. Although much place-oriented federal assistance to localities is ill advised to the extent that it is expended to reverse the largely inevitable shrinkage of larger and older communities, some short-term federal transitional assistance to localities is justified to assist them in meeting the expanding range of their responsibilities. As localities experience difficulty in funding basic services or in meeting the financial obligations incurred through federal orders and mandates, the principle of federal adjustment assistance to localities should be inviolate.

Improved access to jobs involves helping people relocate to take advantage of economic opportunities in other places, as well as retraining them to take advantage of economic opportunity in their own communities. Enhancing the mobility of Americans to enable them to relocate to areas where economic opportunity exists should receive greater attention. Accordingly, *a people-to-jobs strategy should be crafted with priority over, but in concert with, the jobs-to-people strategy that serves as a major theme in current federal urban policy.* Greater emphasis on developing a policy of assisted migration would help underemployed and displaced workers who wish to migrate to locations of long-term economic growth. This option is especially necessary for residents of severely distressed, older industrial cities facing relatively permanent contraction of their economic and population bases.

THE STATE GOVERNMENT ROLE

States should be encouraged and aided in their efforts to assist local governments, as well as their individual and corporate residents, to adjust to changing social and economic circumstances. The nation's cities are national assets that will continue to perform vital, although changing, functions for the United States. Although transforming socially and economically, cities remain the legal creations of the states. In past decades, many subnational governments have improved substantially their capacities to implement economic, community, and manpower development policies. Intergovernmental relationships in the coming decade should preserve the spirit of the federal-local government ties without undermining the emergence of state governments as key urban policy partners.

THE LOCAL GOVERNMENT ROLE

Localities should be encouraged to reexamine their municipal service packages and their funding and delivery arrangements. Much local fiscal distress can be traced to an inability to adjust public service infrastructures to changing population size and composition. Municipal service arrangements should either expand in growing communities or contract in shrinking communities in ways that give localities the flexibility to adjust to future changes. Growing localities should be encouraged to consider carefully the breadth of functions and depth of responsibilities that they wish to assume, thereby avoiding a ritualistic imitation of those local governments that assumed their responsibilities in an earlier historical era. Greater reliance on private sector delivery of public services and the transfer of fiscal/administrative responsibility for selected functions to other levels of government should be carefully considered.

IMPLEMENTING FEDERAL URBAN POLICY: PARTNERS AND PARTNERSHIPS

The patterns of relationships between localities, counties, states, and the federal government have grown increasingly complex. Responsibilities for funding and administration have become hopelessly intergovernmentalized. The unfortunate and inescapable consequence of our broader, bigger, and deeper federal aid system is intergovernmental overload. This report endorses the general recommendations made by the Advisory Commission on Intergovernmental Relations aimed at the decongestion of the federal system [2].

The federal role in urban policy should allow for the sorting out of roles and responsibilities among levels of government and between the public and private sectors. Once those reassignments are made, policy and program activity should seek to abide by and to maintain those assignments. In addition to seeking to reintroduce distinctions between federal and subnational responsibilities, efforts should proceed to decide under what conditions and to what extent state and local budgets should become dependent on federal revenues.

Any policies targeted at the nation's communities should engage the federal government as a policy partner with other levels of government and with the private sector to assist people (primarily), places, business, and political jurisdictions (secondarily) to cope with changing circumstances. The resulting policy division of labor should continue to emphasize the decentralization of federal power and the assignment to each partner of the tasks that it can best undertake.

The federal level of government is relatively efficient at enunciating broad policy goals and raising revenues for distribution to subnational levels of government which, in turn, can best define specific program features. Over time many subnational governments have expanded their capacitites to initiate and to implement localized community and economic development efforts without complex federal controls. Local general purpose governments should continue to be the principal policy implementers at the local level, and policy instruments that encourage local initiative consistent with national purpose should be emphasized. *Despite problems associated with granting wider discretion to local governments, on balance accepting local judgments is wiser than implementing federal policies that are relatively unable to be articulated with local circumstances.*

The federal government should retain responsibility for ensuring that local initiatives, while reflecting local circumstances, are consistent with national goals—particularly in the area of civil rights. The nation needs to develop ways of accomplishing this valid purpose without requiring duplication of the federal government's organizational complexity at the local level. The public sector should endeavor to enhance and encourage private sector vitality and, where necessary, to alleviate its undesirable consequences without hampering that vitality.

Although place-oriented federal urban and rural development policies and programs eventually should be reduced in significance in favor of more people-oriented national economic and social policies, during the transition between emphases, the former should become more coordinated and coherent, with greater emphasis on policy consistency than on level of program funding. While housing, transportation, and urban economic, community, and manpower development programs marshal relatively meager resources in efforts to ameliorate the impacts of unfolding demographic and economic trends, their potency can be enhanced through better organization and consolidation. General fiscal and monetary policies, transfer payments to individuals, and development assistance to the public and private sectors have their collective impact diluted by indefinite lines of responsibility, divergent delivery systems, and program procedures (including idiosyncratic funding cycles, planning requirements, and eligibility criteria) that often differ and even conflict. Consequently, the efforts of subnational governments and the decisions of private sector actors are unnecessarily hampered by gaps, overlaps, and shifting goals at the federal level.

REFERENCES

1. R. B. Miller, "The Federal Role in Cities: The New Deal Years," *Commentary*, Washington, D.C.: National Council for Urban Economic Development (July 1979), p. 110.
2. Advisory Commission on Intergovernmental Relations, *An Agenda for American Federalism: Restoring Confidence and Competence*, Washington, D.C.: U.S. Government Printing Office, 1982.

Part I

Redistribution in Urban Society: Myths and Realities of Crisis, Decline, and Renaissance

Chapter II

THE IMPLICATIONS OF CONTEMPORARY REDISTRIBUTION TRENDS FOR NATIONAL URBAN POLICY

John D. Kasarda

Fueled by an intense interaction of technological, economic, and social forces, the demographic and industrial landscape of the United States changed apace during the 1970s. On an interregional scale, we witnessed the continuing redistribution of population and economic activity away from the traditional northern urban-industrial heartland to the more recently developing southern and western regions. On an intraregional scale, the locus of residential, commercial, and industrial growth increasingly shifted away from metropolitan central cities to their suburbs and exurbs and even on into relatively remote nonmetropolitan sectors of each region. Indeed, for the bulk of this nation's metropolitan core cities, the absolute declines in middle-income population and employment opportunities have been so substantial that some scholars have begun to question whether they can, or even should, maintain the dominant residential and commercial positions they once held [5, 37].

In the wake of accelerating dispersion of population and jobs, a number of federal policies have been implemented to mitigate the social and economic problems that redistribution trends have engendered for many core cities and their inhibitants. These policies, which were consolidated under the Carter Administration's National Urban Policy, appear to have been, at best, marginally successful and, in some instances, counterproductive, inadvertently generating side effects that have further weakened city economies. The reason for this lack of success rests with the failure of many urban policies to give adequate recognition and weight to contemporary technological, economic, and social dynamics underlying the locational decisions of people and firms, and the corresponding changing functional roles large cities most effectively perform in our own advanced service economy.

The aim of this article is to examine contemporary inter- and intraregional redistribution trends with an eye toward drawing implications for revised national urban policies. Assessment is restricted to the more general trends and, therefore, some highly diverse experiences occurring within these broader trends are not addressed. An overview of interregional demographic and economic growth patterns and their determinants is followed by a treatment of metropolitan-nonmetropolitan shifts, and by an assessment of central city-suburban redistribution patterns. The working thesis is that these three basic redistribution patterns are interwoven and commonly rooted in changes in transportation and communication technology, interacting with a rapidly changing structure of national and international economic organization. Guided by this thesis and the resulting analysis, the chapter concludes with recommendations for our national urban policymakers to contemplate.

INTERREGIONAL REDISTRIBUTION TRENDS

The most striking interregional population redistribution trend during the 1970s was the heavy net population gains the South experienced via net migration exchanges with the Northeast, the North Central region, and the West. This is in direct contrast to the net migration outflows the South experienced to all major regions for every census decade between 1900–60. As shown in Table II.1 during the 1960s the South ceased as a net exporter of people to the Northeast and North Central regions but continued to have negative net migration exchanges with the West. However, in the first half of the 1970s, 75,000 more people migrated to the South from the West than vice versa. Between March 1975 and March 1978, the net migration flow from the West to the South ac-

Table II.1. Net Interregional Migration Between 1965–70, 1970–75, and 1975–78

Regional Migration Exchanges	Net Migration (in Thousands)		
	1965–70	*1970–75*	*1975–78*
South net exchange with:			
Northeast	+438	+964	+456
North Central	+275	+790	+429
West	− 56	+ 75	+125
Total Other Regions	+657	+1829	+1010
West net exchange with:			
Northeast	+224	+311	+212
North Central	+415	+472	+290
South	+ 56	− 75	−125
Total Other Regions	+695	+708	+377
North Central net exchange with:			
Northeast	+ 53	+ 67	+ 31
South	−275	−472	−290
West	−415	−790	−429
Total Other Regions	−637	−1195	−688
Northeast net exchange with:			
North Central	− 53	− 67	− 31
South	−438	−964	−456
West	−224	−311	−212
Total Other Regions	−715	−1342	−699

Sources: U.S. Bureau of the Census, *U.S. Census of Population: 1970,* Washington, D.C.: U.S. Department of Commerce, 1972; *Mobility of the Population of the United States: March 1970 to March 1975,* Series P-20, No. 285, in *Current Population Reports,* Washington, D.C.: U.S. Department of Commerce, 1975; *Geographical Mobility: March 1975 to March 1978,* Series P-20, No. 331, in *Current Population Reports,* Washington, D.C.: U.S. Department of Commerce, 1978.

counted for an additional 125,000 migrants. Net migration to the South from both the Northeast and North Central regions increased dramatically during the 1970s. These migration flows, together with the net inflow of migrants from the West, accounted for a total net migration gain for the South of 1,829,000 people between 1970–75 and a further net migration gain of 1,010,000 people between 1975–78.

As the next fastest growing region during the 1970s, the West continued its historic trend of importing many more people from the remainder of the nation than it exported. Despite becoming a net exporter of people to the South during the 1970s, the West has continued to attract substantial numbers of migrants from the nation's Northeast and North Central regions. Thus, between 1970 and 1975, the West experienced a total net inmigration of 708,000 people and between 1975–78, a total net inmigration of 377,000 people from other regions of the nation.

Of the two net people-exporting regions of the nation, the North Central region has fared slightly better than the Northeast region during the 1970s. The small difference between the two regions in total net migration can be accounted for by net migration gains of the North Central region at the expense of the Northeast. Between 1970–75, the North Central region registered a net inflow of 67,000 migrants from the Northeast; between 1975–78, it expanded by another 31,000 net migrants from the Northeast. The large migration losses of residents of the North Central region to the South and West during the 1970s led to overall net interregional migration losses for the North Central region of 1,195,000 people between 1970–75 and 688,000 people between March 1975 and March 1978.

During the 1970s, the Northeast suffered consistent net migration losses to all regions of the nation, with particularly heavy migration streams to the South. On the whole, between 1970–75, the Northeast exported 1,342,000 more people to other regions of the nation than it imported. Of that total net outmigration, 964,000 can be attributed to net losses to the South. Between March 1975 and March 1978, the Northeast experienced an additional net migration loss of 699,000 people, of which 456,000 were net losses to the South.

What accounts for such large interregional net migration shifts, especially the dramatic turnaround of the South from a net exporter of people as late as 1960 to the powerful magnet of the 1970s? Net migration, of course, can be accounted for not only in terms of attracting residents from other regions of the nation, but also by retaining those born in the region.

In terms of attracting migrants, a number of both noneconomic and economic reasons arise:

1. A growing footloose retirement population whose private pensions, Social Security payments, and other sources of income are not tied to specific locations and who have sought the milder winter climates that the South, in particular, provides.
2. The introduction and spread of central air conditioning systems that allow far more comfortable summertime living and working conditions.
3. Lifestyle changes oriented to more recreation and year-around outdoor activities.
4. Changing racial attitudes permitting blacks new opportunities to participate in the mainstream economic and social institutions.

5. More progressive political orientation and an increasingly cosmopolitan southern metropolitan atmosphere that has put to rest much of the antiquated rural, red-neck imagery many northerners and westerners had of the South.
6. Generally lower land, living, and amenity costs.
7. A dramatic improvement in the quantity and quality of consumer services brought about largely by rising personal income levels.

Although all of the above are certainly contributory, these factors are clearly secondary in importance to or dependent on the emergence first of the West and now the South as the major industrial growth pole of the U.S. economy. Before World War II, the Northeast and North Central regions contained the bulk of this nation's industrial locational advantages, including excellent deep-water ports, extensive railroad and inland waterway systems, well developed inter- and intrametropolitan highways, proximity to rich coal deposits, ubiquitous public utilities, a diverse and relatively better educated labor force, and strong local markets. These externalities and agglomeration economies provided firms locating in the Northeast and North Central region with competitive cost and market advantages that allowed them to develop and expand much faster than in the relatively less developed, more agriculturally oriented western and southern regions. The industrial dominance of the Northeast and North Central regions, in fact, continued until as late as 1960, at which time these regions still contained more than two-thirds of the nation's manufacturing jobs, most concentrated in and around the core cities of the largest metropolitan areas.

Blue-collar job expansion between 1940–60 in the northern industrial belt—stretching across the Middle Atlantic and East North Central census divisions (from New York and New Jersey to Illinois)—continued to draw large numbers of southern migrants in search of improved economic opportunities. During the same period, the rapid growth of the aerospace, defense, solid-state electronics, and other advanced technology industries not tied to deep-water sites, together with the expansion of large-scale commercialized agriculture and western oil field development, spurred the economies of the far West, especially California. These newer growth industries were instrumental in attracting a net of nearly 6 million migrants to California alone between 1940–60. This net migration represents more than the combined total of net migration of all other states (excluding Florida) that exhibited net inmigration between 1940–60 [54].

The major locus of new post-World War II national employment growth had been toward the West until 1960, but shifted to the South during the 1960s and has become entrenched there. Between 1960–80, total nonagricultural employment increased in the South by nearly 15 million jobs—well above the combined total job increase of the Northeast and North Central region [57]. This job expansion took place not only in rapid growth areas (service sector industries), but also in the older so-called slower growth manufacturing industries.

The South's attractiveness as an industrial growth pole is a function, in large part, of dramatically improved accessibility to national markets via new interstate highway systems, of shifting energy sources and costs, and of lower manufacturing wage rates interacting with a changing structure of the national economy and growing negative externalities of the concentrated northern industrial metropolis (e.g., congestion, powerful unions, high land costs, high taxes). To these technological and materialistic conditions are added healthy doses of progrowth attitudes and industrial boosterism on the part of the southern communities and their government officials. These determinants are briefly elaborated.

Accessibility and corresponding transportation costs have always been the paramount factors in locational decisions of industrial firms. The development of major four-lane highway systems in the South, together with the steady reduction in the bulk of raw materials used in manufacturing processes and a major shift from rail to truck transport following World War II, reduced substantially the previous accessibility problems of southern industrial locations. At the same time, as the accessibility of the South to the national markets was improving, rising labor costs in a number of older northern industries and a nonunionized blue-collar labor surplus in the South served to filter many low-wage, labor-intensive industries to the South. (Indeed, as the United States became increasingly interwoven into the world economic order, large numbers of routinized labor-intensive jobs—such as electrical component assembly, processing of leather goods and apparel—filtered entirely out of the country to such low-wage, labor-surplus sites as Korea, Taiwan, Singapore, Malaysia, Hong Kong, and the Philippines.)

Changing energy requirements and costs also reduced and, in some cases, reversed the previous locational advantages held by northern industries. Encouraged, in part, by federal environmental policies, which were implemented in earnest during the 1960s, there was a major conversion of older northern industrial plants from coal to oil and natural gas as primary energy sources for production processes and plant heating. (Many electrical utilities in the North simultaneously converted from coal to oil or natural gas to generate electricity.) Since southern locations were closer to domestic sources of oil and natural gas, many were able to obtain them at lower rates, especially compared with the Northeast.

The regional energy price differences were rather small, however, throughout the 1960s as the price controls on oil and natural gas and a surplus of these fuels permitted northern manufacturing industries to be highly competitive in a national and international market, despite paying much higher wages. (Cheap energy in the North thus served to keep its industrial output internationally competitive.)

Price decontrol of oil and intermittent shortages—together with accelerating union-generated wages—removed many older northern manufacturing industries, such as fabricated metals and nonelectrical machinery, from competing effectively in the international market and, in some cases, national market. Rising heating and maintenance costs of outdated physical plants placed the North at a further competitive disadvantage for industrial growth.

Conversely, lower energy costs, lower blue-collar wages, relatively more modern physical plants, and material product shifts away from heavy metals (iron and steel) to lighter material (aluminum and plastic) have provided the South with distinct locational advantages to compete for what national growth is occurring in the manufacturing sector. Thus, between 1970–80, manufacturing jobs in the South increased by 926,000, whereas the Northeast lost 585,400 manufacturing jobs and the North Central region lost 116,300 jobs in manufacturing [57].

It would be a mistake to assume that manufacturing growth was the chief factor creating job expansion in the South. Led by remarkable growth in tertiary and quaternary industries (e.g., recreation, administration, finance, research and development), more than 7.5 million nonagricultural, nonmanufacturing jobs were added to the southern economy between 1970 and 1980, far outpacing any other region of the nation in job growth in these sectors [57].

Business Climate in the South

Driving the remarkable job expansion in the South has been what most entrepreneurs consider to be the best overall business climate in the nation. During the past two decades, there has been a substantial upgrading of mass education levels and technical training in the South; readily available and relatively inexpensive land for firm locations and plant expansions; lower costs of living, which make real wages higher than other regions; better employer-employee relationships; fewer costly shutdowns and slowdowns due to strikes, weather conditions, or energy shortages; and public and government attitudes toward business that are highly favorable. These attitudes are manifested in lower business taxes, right to work laws, fewer regulations, and a peerless form of industrial boosterism that congratulates new business developments and plant expansions rather than computing their costs [8, 40].

Most southern states have explicit policies promoting private sector development, including vigorously pursued industrial solicitation and state-sponsored training programs for prospective employees of new firms. Alabama, for instance, has fully equipped mobile units for technical and vocational training that move about the state as the needs of particular industries dictate. The State of South Carolina offers free technical training to all prospective workers in communities, tailored to the specific needs of the industry locating within commuting distance of the community. Southern governors, state officials, and local chambers of commerce travel throughout the nation and the world attempting to lure industry to their states and communities, and when representatives from these companies arrive, the states and cities roll out the red carpet [4, 8, 9, 20, 40].

Of course, officials in a number of northern states have also begun campaigns to solicit new industry. However, the inducements they offer to prospective businesses have not matched the enticements southern states and cities have often provided. Consider, for example, the Jacksonville, Fla., solicitation of a Westinghouse Corporation subsidiary that announced it planned to locate a production facility that would build large offshore power generating systems. To ensure that Jacksonville was selected, city officials initially offered the company:

1. A substantial discount on 850 acres of prime industrial land where the production facility could be located;
2. A promise to build and maintain a $137 million special access bridge to the location;
3. An offer to buy, through its municipal power company, two of the power systems produced by the company at an estimated cost of nearly $2.2 billion;
4. An offer to sell $180 million worth of low-interest bonds to provide working capital for the company; and
5. A commitment to construct an $11 million vocational-technical education center to train the 10,000 employees expected to work at the production facility [59].

With modern transportation and communication markedly expanding the range of locational choices for private investment, state and local government attitudes toward business (as reflected by regulations, taxes, and political support) clearly have assumed key importance in determining an area's prospects for employment growth or decline [25, 37]. Whereas in the South, attitudes toward business are positive, upbeat, and encouraging, in much of the North, entrepreneurial initiatives are still confronted with public reservation and government disincentives.

In the Northeast, for example, the acquisition of new business sites or additional land for plant expansion is frequently inhibited by a plethora of community restrictions, labyrinthine regulations, and public reviews, which often lead to costly delays, and, sometimes, preclude new development entirely [26]. Public policies that back strong unions, including public employee unions, contribute to periodic strikes and public work stoppages that impose heavy costs on many northern firms. States and cities in the North also are more likely to levy personal income and local payroll taxes, as well as impose special business taxes and regulatory instruments, which entrepreneurs find objectionable and substantially reduce the attractiveness of the area for private enterprise. Indeed, in many northern communities, business and industry seem to be viewed less as job generators and more as either exploiters or as captive geese who should be squeezed, by taxes and other means, to lay additional golden eggs for the remainder of the community [32]. It should not be surprising, then, that despite the many other business amenities that northern locations provide, the bulk of new business formations and expansions of existing firms are taking place elsewhere.

METROPOLITAN-NONMETROPOLITAN REDISTRIBUTION TRENDS

Until the mid-1960s, most nonmetropolitan counties were viewed as the areas left behind. For nearly 100 years, the industrialization of the U.S. economy had generated concentrative migration to metropolitan areas. So large was the migration of nonmetropolitan residents to the metropolitan centers through the 1950s, that despite higher rural birth rates, national population increases became largely synonymous with metropolitan growth.

However, by the early 1970s the net migration to metropolitan areas had reversed, and reversed significantly. Between 1970–78, more than 2.7 million more people moved out of metropolitan areas than moved into them. Whereas one-sixth of all metropolitan areas lost population, three-fourths of all nonmetropolitan counties gained population. What makes this turnaround all the more striking is that it has been apparent in all major census regions and in relatively remote counties nonadjacent to metropolitan areas as well as those adjacent. Moreover, among the nonmetropolitan counties, there is an inverse association between the size of the largest urban places within the county and its net migration. Fuguitt and Voss [18] have shown that those nonmetropolitan counties with no incorporated places larger than 2,500 experienced the largest annual net migration between 1970–75. The next largest net migration was found for those nonmetropolitan counties whose largest urban place was between 2,500 and 10,000; and net migration gains were the least in those nonmetropolitan counties containing an incorporated place greater than 10,000. Furthermore, in all these counties, the rural unincorporated areas grew much faster than the incorporated towns, and the incorporated towns themselves exhibited an inverse growth rate with their size. One must wonder, then, that if extensive public services are deemed so necessary or desirable by government officials, why the American population continues to move to areas where they are not available. This policy issue will be addressed in the recommendations.

The reasons for the unanticipated turnaround in net migration to those counties relatively removed from metropolitan areas appear to be multifaceted and complex. They include, among others:

1. The extension of the interstate highway system through many remote areas and the expanded all-weather surfacing of rural roads;
2. The expansion and linkage of locally owned telephone companies into the Bell system;
3. The extension of power lines and other public utilities and services, such as new centralized rural water systems, throughout most nonmetropolitan counties;
4. Telecommunication advances, including cable television;
5. The proliferation of nationally standardized consumer goods and service establishments in nonmetropolitan counties;
6. Dual residences associated with rising real incomes and increased leisure time;
7. A growing footloose retirement population; and
8. Lifestyle changes oriented to more bucolic, less densely settled environments [22].

One thing that is not happening, however, is a rediscovery of the joys of working the land or any new "return to the soil" ethic [2]. During the 1970s, the farm population continued its precipitous decline, dropping by over 1.7 million between 1970–78 [56]. Today, less than 10 percent of the nonmetropolitan labor force is engaged in agricultural occupations. This would imply that, with the exception of the retirement population (which accounts for only a small portion of overall nonmetropolitan migrants), economic opportunities have substantially expanded in the nonmetropolitan counties. Indeed, this is the case. While the 225 largest Standard Metropolitan Statistical Areas (SMSA) suffered a net loss of 513,000 jobs in manufacturing between 1970–78, nonmetropolitan counties experienced an increase of 619,000 manufacturing jobs. But, as is the case with the South, manufacturing growth accounts for only a small portion of the nonmetropolitan job growth. An additional 3,452,000 service sector jobs emerged in the nonmetropolitan counties between 1970–78 [21]. By 1980, nearly two-thirds of all nonmetropolitan workers were employed in the expanding service-performing sector and the trend shows no signs of abating.

Other economic forces that have provided increased employment opportunities in nonmetropolitan areas include the revival and expansion of highly localized energy-related industries in the Rocky Mountain states, Appalachia, and upper Midwest; the growth of nonmetropolitan university and college towns; a dramatic increase in construction jobs created by nonmetropolitan residential and economic growth; and an increase in local government employment administering to growing nonmetropolitan political units.

Underlying much of the growth in nonmetropolitan America are changes in transportation and communication technology that broke the traditional locational ties many economic activities had to metropolitan areas. These technological advances enabled industries to become more footloose so that substantially more weight could be given to social, political, and environmental factors in locational decisions. Simultaneously, as previous urban-industrial agglomeration economies were transformed into agglomeration diseconomies (e.g., congestion, higher costs of land and labor), business sites in nonmetropolitan areas become more profitable.

Again, as was the case with migration turnaround in the South, new business formations and business expansion in nonmetropolitan areas served not only to reduce substantially the number of rural residents who migrate to metropolitan areas in search of employment, but also to attract millions of additional people from metropolitan areas. The trends appear secular and mutually reinforcing because more migrants means larger nonmetropolitan population to serve and sustain, which in turn generates more local employment opportunities, which further acts to attract additional migrants. Moreover, most recent data indicate that the majority of nonmetropolitan migrants are married couples whose heads are better educated, more likely to hold white-collar occupations, and, consequently, have higher incomes than either those who migrated from nonmetro to metro or the nonmetropilitan residents in general [14, 18]. In fact, Williams and Sofranko [61] show that approximately 75 percent of metropolitan-to-nonmetropolitan migrants exhibit either rising or steady wages and salaries, which means the migrants have even higher real wages and salaries, since costs of living are typically less in nonmetropolitan areas.

Finally, the research on residential preferences over the years has shown that Americans perfer smaller, more rural, and less densely settled areas [17, 62]. Changing technology and nonmetropolitan employment opportunities are now apparently allowing more and more Americans to achieve their residential preferences. In the meantime, the net movement of better educated population with more disposable income who have experienced urban lifestyles is dramatically changing the texture of nonmetropolitan America. This change is a "rural renaissance" only in the strict demographic sense. From an economic and sociological standpoint, the transformation is more of an urbanization of nonmetropolitan territory, as traditionally urban occupations and consumption patterns have diffused to more remote areas.

With improved highways, telecommunications advances, and the nonmetropolitan increase of specialized consumer goods and services heretofore restricted to large urban areas, the nonmetropolitan population can enjoy the cultural, informational, and material fruits of a metropolitan lifestyle without suffering many negative externalities often associated with metropolitan residence (high taxes, noise, congestion, pollution, social turmoil). In short, the cultural isolation as well as the physical isolation of many rural communities from metropolitan activity patterns and lifestyles have been substantially reduced. This sociological factor is, in all likelihood, the sufficient condition that sparked many metropolitan residents to migrate to more remote nonmetropolitan communities after the necessary condition of economic opportunities developed there.

INTRAMETROPOLITAN REDISTRIBUTION PATTERNS

Whether or not the metro-to-nonmetro migration turnaround just discussed represents what some have called a "clean break" from previous trends depends on the vantage point of the rural-urban continuum from which one is observing the phenomenon. From the point of metropolitan core cities, this new migration trend merely represents a continuation of urban deconcentration that began more than a half-century ago [7, 22, 30].

With some exceptions, the deconcentration of population from central cities to suburbs historically has been selective by income level. The automobile and commuter train—along with rising real incomes, state and federally funded radial and suburban highway systems, and federally insured home mortgages—encouraged and facilitated the mass suburbanization of the middle and upper class in metropolitan America. However, almost as quickly as these groups moved beyond central city boundaries, they were replaced by lower income groups in the classic Burgess city growth pattern [12]. The outcome, of course, has been growing numbers of metropolitan poor concentrated in the central cities, as the suburban rings have become the residential locus of the upwardly mobile urban social groups [29].

Now, some social scientists and journalists are claiming that the Burgess-type growth pattern is being reversed; that a "back to the city" movement of the suburban middle class is leading to urban "regentrification" (an interesting, but totally inappropriate term), and that the nation is on the threshold of an urban residential renaissance. While it is encouraging to observe selective neighborhood upgrading in most cities, current demographic surveys and quantitative analyses show that for central cities as a whole, their residential conditions and aggregate personal income levels are continuing to deteriorate. Before presenting this sobering evidence, however, let us examine what has been happening to employment opportunities in the central cities and suburban rings, which are instrumental to the vitality of any larger area.

First, consider changes in the number of jobs within those industries where employment conditions typically do not require substantial education: manufacturing, retail, and wholesale trade. When one examines changes in central city and suburban ring employment levels within these industries in terms of the size of the SMSA, age of the SMSA, and region, extremely sharp gradients and distinctions appear [28]. For example, the central cities of the 33 SMSAs over one million population in 1970 lost more than 880,000 manufacturing jobs between 1947–72, while manufacturing jobs in their suburbs grew by over 2,522,000. These same 33 central cities lost more than 565,000 retail jobs and 302,000 wholesale jobs between 1947–72, while retail and wholesale jobs in their suburban rings grew by 2,360,000 and 798,000, respectively. On the other hand, central cities as well as suburbs of SMSAs under 250,000 population showed substantial net gains in manufacturing, retail, and wholesale employment.

The 49 central cities that had attained 50,000 or more population before 1900 showed losses of 1,370,000 in manufacturing, 750,000 in retail, and 366,000 wholesale jobs between 1947–72. The suburban rings of these same 49 central cities showed job gains of 2,300,000 in manufacturing, 2,200,000 in retail, and 805,000 in wholesale trade. When employment changes within central cities and within suburban rings are summed, respectively, across the three industrial categories, the total job losses in central cities and job gains in suburbs are mind-boggling.

Examining central city-suburban job changes in the Northeast and North Central regions, the same massive central city job losses and suburban ring gains are observed. On the other hand, younger SMSA central cities and central cities in the South and West show aggregate increases in manufacturing, retail, and wholesale employment in both their central cities and suburban rings between 1947–72, even after adjusting for annexation [28].

When one analyzes changes in occupation data by place of work between 1960–70, it is found that large, old, Northeast and North Central region central cities suffered huge losses in blue-collar occupations (craftsmen, laborers, and operatives) but experienced substantial gains in professional, technical, managerial, and clerical occupations. Assessment of migration data during the same period shows that the same set of cities (large, old, northern cities) experienced the largest absolute inflows of population with education levels ill suited to the requirements of the expanding white-collar jobs. The result is a growing mismatch between the employment opportunities in these cities and the skill composition of their residential population. The outcome of this mismatch is increased reverse commuting of central city blue-collar workers to suburban jobs and increased suburban to central city commuting of white-collar workers, as well as growing structural unemployment among those lower skilled persons residentially confined to cities where blue-collar jobs are declining [28].

The selective redistribution of population and jobs between central cities and their suburbs has been well documented through 1972. What has happened since 1972? Although definitive statements must await the release of the 1980 population census results, Current Population Surveys conducted by the U.S. Bureau of the Census during the latter half of the 1970s, together with various U.S. Department of Commerce surveys of urban employment trends, suggest that the residence-job mismatch and corresponding structural unemployment problems have become worse in most large citites. Despite incentives contained in present urban policies, most industries providing blue-collar jobs are continuing to eschew a central city location. The most frequent reasons cited by industrialists for not choosing an inner city location include expensive and difficult to assemble tracts of land, congested streets and highways, high taxes, local government regulations and restrictions, shortages of manpower with the right skills, and problems of employee absenteeism and discipline [15, 25, 45, 51]. Directed by their sixth sense of profit, entrepreneurs of blue-collar industries have sought alternative, more cost-effective sites in the suburbs, exurbs, and nonmetropolitan areas that are far better suited to today's advanced transportation and production technologies, avoiding what has become some serious negative externalities of an inner city location.

The Advantages of Decentralized Locations

To escape the costs and headaches of a central city location, yet to maintain important agglomeration and scale economies, many manufacturers and wholesalers have banded together in modern industrial parks along major suburban and exurban expressways. These peripheral industrial parks (over 2,000 of which have formed since 1960) not only are particularly well adapted to advanced production and transportation-distribution technologies, but also generate their own self-contained agglomeration and mutual-scale economies [35]. More specifically, they offer ample, relatively inexpensive space for employee parking, freight transfer, and automated single-story production and distribution facilities, as well as excellent accessibility to regional and national markets via interconnecting expressways, beltways, and interstate highways. Information, material, and personnel can be quickly and conveniently transferred between and among proximate plants, and by pooling the costs of security, public utilities, insurance, and taxes, mutual-scale economies are obtained that lower the expenses of the individual firms and improve their competitive positions. The decentralized industrial parks provide explicit testimony that agglomeration and mutual-scale economies, themselves, have become footloose, allowing firms to locate almost anywhere in the metropolitan region and beyond.

Further testimony that agglomeration and mutual-scale economies are no longer tied to central locations can be found in the remarkable growth of suburban shopping centers and regional malls during the past 25 years. Between 1954–78, more than 15,000 shopping centers and malls were constructed to serve the expanding middle and upper income suburban and exurban populations. By 1975, these shopping centers and malls produced over one-half of the annual retail sales in the United States [35].

For most suburban Americans, the enclosed regional malls have become their Main Street, Fifth Avenue, and the community social and entertainment center, all wrapped into one. The malls not only include retail establishments of every size, price range, and variety, but also contain professional offices, elegant restaurants, fast food shops, movie theaters, public service outlets, community meeting rooms, and common space used for a plethora of inexpensive patron attractions such as concerts; dances; stage and fashion shows; boat shows; auto shows; scout jamborees; antique fairs; science fairs; stamp, coin, and art exhibits; skating rinks; and even petting zoos. The broad spectrum of goods and service offerings, along with special customer amenities that malls provide—controlled temperature and humidity; pedestrian arcades insulated from automobile traffic, noise, and air pollution; excellent security for safe and relaxed nighttime shopping; convenient, free customer parking—and their accessibility to the automobile-oriented suburban population, have combined to give the regional malls a distinct competitive edge in capturing the metropolitan retail dollar. Indeed, regional malls have become so successful that many larger central cities are now trying to simulate them in their downtowns in an attempt to recoup some of their lost shares of metropolitan retail sales and employment.

Advances in transportation and communication technologies not only have reduced the economies of centrality for older, slower growth manufacturing, wholesale, and retail industries, but also have impacted on economies of location in the newer, rapid growth administrative office and research and development sectors. The quintessential feature of our emerging footloose economy, in fact, may be observed in the substantial development during the past two decades of expansive, style-setting administrative office and research parks in deconcentrated surburban and exurban settings. The telecommunications revolution, in particular, has almost entirely wiped out the advantages of concentrated centrality for many administrative office and research and development functions. For those firms that must maintain regular contact with other persons or units located either in the central cities or outlying areas, conference picture phones, two-way cable television, rapid facsimile teleletters, and computerized information transmission networks allow a substitution of efficient, high-speed electronic interaction for often time-consuming personal gatherings [23, 35].

Like many ultramodern industrial parks, quite a few of the decentralized office and research parks are located in bucolic, campus-like settings complete with executive clubs, restaurants, swimming pools, tennis courts, jogging tracks, and other amenities attractive to contemporary, more leisure-oriented, lifestyles. Moreover, since most executives, middle managers, and professionals currently reside in the suburbs and exurbs (by preference, recall), the decentralized office and research complexes permit an actual reduction in much residence-workplace commuting time, energy use, and expense. Organizational cost-effectiveness is enhanced by the large, relatively well-educated suburban clerical pool who are eager to work in nearby office complexes at lower wages than would be required if they had to commute to offices in the central cities. Further cost-effectiveness is provided by lower land costs, office rents, and taxes and by substantially reduced rates of employee turnover and absenteeism compared with counterpart firms located in the central cities [35]. The interaction of these social, demographic, and economic forces would seem to assure that the suburbs and exurbs will far outpace the central cities in white-collar job growth during the 1980s.

Realities and Myths of the Urban Renaissance

This is not to say, however, that there will not be significant central city job growth in white-collar office and professional functions, particularly in those financial, managerial, professional, and "knowledge class" occupations that require a substantial amount of quick, nonroutine, face-to-face interaction. Central city employment growth may also be expected in administrative headquarter offices that continuously use diverse sets of externalized support services such as advertising and public relations, job printing and publishing, legal, accounting, and management consulting services. There are still important economies of proximity for many of these activities, and most who perform them can be stacked one upon another, layer after layer, in downtown office buildings, with no loss of productivity [42].

There is another extremely high-growth industry in older, larger central cities that has received little scholarly inquiry: the dramatic rise in convention and tourism business fostered by the growing number of professional and trade associations and rising incomes of a sizable and geographically fluid segment of the population. This rich potential for cities will be commented on shortly.

First, however, let us take a hard quantitative look at the "back to the city" movement and the purported urban residential renaissance. A number of publications—mostly impressionistic and journalistic in nature, but supported by few actual facts—have suggested that white middle-class residents are streaming back to inner city neighborhoods and that cities are showing remarkable new signs of residential and economic health. Unfortunately, carefully conducted demographic surveys and research on recent residential and commercial changes in the central cities point predominantly to the opposite conclusion. The main findings of these surveys and research are:

1. The overwhelming flow of middle-class households during the 1970s has been out of, not into, the central cities. For every household with income levels of $15,000 or more who entered central cities between March 1975 and March 1978, three left the cities [55]. During this period, four out of five family heads who left the central cities had incomes over $15,000 per annum. As a result, aggregate personal income of central city residents continues to drop precipitously. The aggregate income difference between movers out of the central city and movers into the central cities between 1970–75 resulted in a loss of $29.6 billion in disposable personal income for the cities. The aggregate income differences between movers out of the central cities and movers into the cen-

tral cities between 1975–78 led to another $18 million loss for cities. Sternlieb [49] computed the cumulative effect of central city migration between 1970–78 on the aggregate personal incomes of central city residents. He found that during this period, the central cities experienced a net loss of $64.8 billion (in constant 1976 dollars) due to the differential income levels between inmigrants and outmigrants and the greater number of outmigrants than inmigrants. Analyzing changes in the central city-suburban income gap during the 1970s, Long and Dahmann show that the gap widened in terms of both family income levels and per capita income [33].

2. Revitalization has occurred in only a tiny fraction of any city's neighborhoods and has affected only a small portion of their housing stock. Between 1968–79, only one-half of 1 percent of the nearly 20 million housing units in cities have been affected by revitalization or restoration efforts [58].
3. The vast majority (more than 70 percent) of households residing in revitalized central city residential units were intracity movers and not suburbanites or nonmetropolitan residents who moved back to the city [19, 24].
4. Displacement of minorities and lower income groups by neighborhood upgrading or gentrification is quite small compared with displacement caused by neighborhood deterioration.
5. The concentration of minorities and poverty level population in central cities is continuing to increase, both in absolute and proportional terms. Between 1970–80 central cities lost approximately 4 million white residents while the central city black population increased by 1.6 million. Despite a net national decline of 2.2 million persons below the poverty level between 1970–78, the total number of central city residents below the poverty level continued to grow, with dramatic increases in those dependent on welfare.
6. Substantial residential and commercial disinvestment continues to be active in almost all older, larger, central cities, and far exceeds reinvestment. During the 1970s, expanding blighted neighborhoods and increased residential abandonment that characterized so many central cities were matched with accelerated deterioration and abandonment of commercial and industrial subareas of cities [50].
7. The growth of central business district office employment during the 1970s has not nearly compensated for central city losses of manufacturing jobs and employment declines in the retail and wholesale sectors. As a result, the overall employment base of

> most large cities is continuing to deteriorate. In New York City, for example, while white-collar professional, clerical, and managerial jobs were expanding in Manhattan during the 1970s, New York City as a whole lost 600,000 jobs. It has been estimated that this net job loss alone resulted in a tax loss to the city of almost $500 million annually [16].

In sum, many major U.S. cities are still in deep trouble as their residential, employment, and fiscal bases continue to weaken. This is especially the case for most large, older central cities in the Northeast and North Central regions of the country. In these regions, the forces of counterurbanization are so strong that it is unlikely that any National Urban Policy that would be economically and politically feasible at this time could reverse them, or even substantially slow them down. Nevertheless, based on what can be learned from contemporary interregional, metropolitan-nonmetropolitan, and central city-suburban redistribution trends, a number of implications for revised national urban policies can be drawn.

POLICY IMPLICATIONS OF REDISTRIBUTION TRENDS

1. *From the push-and-pull factors involved in the remarkable job growth in the South.* An urban policy apropos northern cities should be well informed by the favorable business climate that has fostered so much recent economic development in the South. To help improve the business climate in northern cities and suburbs, the U.S. Department of Housing and Urban Development and state officials may wish to work vigorously with local officials to reduce building permit delays and other bureaucratic red tape and to modify certain regulatory policies and community restrictions that unnecessarily inhibit new business development and plant expansions. Such a policy might even include an educational campaign to help create a generally more favorable attitude toward business on the part of local officials and their residents. It might also involve forming a close working relationship with private and public employee unions to prevent work stoppages and public employee strikes that tarnish the image of central cities and act as a disincentive to businessmen who are considering locating plants and other employment units in the cities.

2. *From the metropolitan to nonmetropolitan population shifts, particularly the increasing migration of urban Americans to smaller nonmetropolitan towns*

and to unincorporated rural areas where many public services are unavailable. Our policymakers should ask themselves why growing numbers of urban residents are *choosing* to move from areas of extensive public service delivery to areas where public service delivery is minimal. Is it because the positive externalities and halo effects of deconcentrated residence overshadow apparent public service deficiencies? Are the migrants, in fact, misinformed, expecting much higher levels of public service delivery than actually exist? Or may it be that growing numbers of urban residents do not view many public services and government programs as nearly so important or desirable as the articulate lobbyists promoting their funding and implementation often lead government officials to believe? Put somewhat differently, to what extent are urban outmigrants "voting with their feet" and consciously trading what they deem nonessential public services and counterproductive government programs for lower taxes and reduced government activity?

A National Urban Policy should begin with a systematic and objective appraisal of the short-run necessity and longer term consequences of retaining the full range of public services and government programs currently in effect in our larger cities. Such appraisal may well reveal superfluous services and nonproductive programs whose prudent trimming or elimination could help reduce the fiscal strain that many cities are experiencing, while simultaneously permitting increased allocations of government expenditures to services and programs that would improve the competitive position of the cities, such as upgrading the public schools or refurbishing and maintaining the urban public infrastructure (e.g., streets, bridges, water and sewer systems).

3. *From continuing residential dispersion and suburban sprawl.* No longer necessarily assume that dispersion is bad and concentration is good in terms of relative social, economic, and environmental costs and benefits. By dispersing from the central cities, tens of millions of Americans have been able to improve their housing, employment conditions, and living environments.

Sprawl, in fact, is a loaded term, full of pejorative connotations. Despite the conventional wisdom found among many city planners and academics who continue to label suburban and exurban growth as haphazard, inefficient, and undesirable, it is now becoming apparent that peripheral growth is not nearly as random or inefficient as was once believed. Without the guidance of any conscious master design, the suburbs and exurbs are evolving their own relatively self-sufficient hierarchy of activity centers, ranging from higher order regional commercial and employment centers to lower order convenience goods and residential centers.

The evolution of this multifunctional nested hierarchy of activity centers has given rise to a new form of spatial organization—the polycentric ecological field—which has replaced the technologically antiquated primate structure of the monocentered industrial metropolis. Within this new, more diffuse form of spatial organization, the traditional metropolitan central business district has become just one specialized node in a multinodal, multiconnective ecological field of interdependent activity centers, extending outward as far as 100 miles from the metropolitan core. The fact that the cost-effectiveness and productivity of many modern economic activities are enhanced in outlying nodes has made them valuable job generators for the U.S. economy. Moreover, as outlying activity centers have grown, they have begun to develop their own nearby labor sheds, permitting reduced employee commuting distances and thus daily travel expenses. Polycentric nodes also reduce problems of convergence, congestion, air pollution, and wear and tear on core infrastructure (i.e., streets, highways, bridges) associated with extensive journey-to-work commutation and truck shipments into and out of the traditional monocentered metropolis [46].

In terms of residential energy consumption, large concentrations of high-density housing preclude widespread use of steady-state energy sources (e.g., solar collectors and windmills). Likewise, potential greater reliance on replaceable fuels to supplement home heating (such as the use of woodburning stoves) would create unbearable air quality conditions in larger concentrations. Dispersed, low-density settlements, on the other hand, are able to tap more pragmatically the energy of natural systems as partial replacement of expensive fossil fuels [60]. They are also able to obtain benefits directly from the natural environment in the form of green belts, waste absorption, noise buffers, microclimate, and water quality control that must be compensated for in large population concentrations by purchased services that raise costs and taxes [38].

Large, dense population concentrations, in general, require and/or demand more expensive packages of public services and programs than do smaller, more dispersed communities. Increased demand for (and dependence on) public services in large population concentrations, in turn, not only substantially raises government costs both directly and indirectly, but also makes residents and businesses located in these concentrations more vulnerable to the organized actions of public employees [3]. Numerous factors such as these were omitted from analysis in the highly publicized, government-sponsored report, *The Costs of Sprawl* [44], which purportedly offers a baseline comparison of the relative cost-effectiveness of high-density urban concentrations versus lower density, more widely spaced communities.

Since that report, whose conclusions add up to a powerful indictment of the American penchant for low-density living, was given considerable exposure by the architects of our current urban policy in developing their case against deconcentration, three important caveats merit emphasis. First, *The Costs of Sprawl* represents an analysis of prototype development patterns, not actual developments; therefore, it contains no real data at all. Second, the results of the prototype analysis were not calibrated against the experience of actual communities. Third, research and quantitative analyses based on the experience of actual communities point predominantly to the opposite conclusions of *The Costs of Sprawl* [3, 60].

Finally, preservationists' arguments that urban sprawl and residential dispersion are gobbling up prime agricultural land and diminishing available wildlife and recreation areas (while having some local empirical basis) appear to be overly alarmist. U.S. Department of Agriculture surveys document that the nation has more than sufficient productive cropland that advanced agriculture technology continues to increase [10, 13, 27, 31, 41]. In point of fact, all the land covered by urban areas plus roadways in the United States totals less than 3 percent of the land area.

Since 1920 (the conventional date given for when suburban rings began growing faster than the central cities), urban and roadway expansion combined have absorbed only 0.0025 percent of total land annually [47]. The bulk of U.S. cropland that goes out of production yearly has nothing to do with residential dispersion or urban sprawl, but results from its poor soil quality or terrain that is not suitable to the efficiencies of modern agricultural machinery [6]. Apropos the approximately 900,000 acres of productive farmland that are converted annually to urban and transportation use, recent land-use surveys document that these losses have been more than compensated for by new additions annually to the productive cropland base [27]. More importantly, the newly added cropland has been of high quality and not marginally productive as one might have guessed [10].

According to extensive hearings conducted in the latter half of the 1970s by theU.S. Senate Agricultural Committee, the primary concern for future American agriculture is *not* a potential shortage of productive cropland. Because of continuing biological, chemical, and technological advances in food and natural fiber production, the primary concern is potential oversupplies of crops which depress farm prices [43]. For this reason, acreage allotments, price supports, and set-aside programs have been authorized by Congress to keep cropland idle and to maintain farm price levels when agricultural supplies are deemed excessive.

Regarding available wilderness recreation and wildlife areas, an average of one million acres are added to our reserves each year [47]. Between 1920–74, wildlife refuges and state and national parks increased from 8 million acres to 73 million acres, and they are still expanding [6,

47]. In short, before future policies apropos residential dispersion are shaped, the opinions of preservationists that population deconcentration and urban sprawl are resulting in *critical* reductions in our nation's productive agricultural base and available wildlife and recreation areas should be weighed against evidence that suggest otherwise.

4. *From the pervasive deconcentration of industry and most other forms of economic activity away from more densely settled central cities to the suburbs, exurbs, and remote rural areas.* A National Urban Policy must clearly recognize that the era of massive centralized industrialization is over and that large dense concentrations of people and firms, for the most part, have become technologically obsolete. Urban policies based on the assumption that productivity is enhanced in large urban areas are outdated and wrong, as evidenced by the consistent location decisionmaking of industrial leaders [34]. No policy will overcome prudent entrepreneurial decisions to locate where costs are minimized and returns maximized.

A National Urban Policy should work *with* the forces of redistribution rather than fruitlessly attempting to reverse them. In this regard, if policymakers are really serious about revitalizing our urban cores and avoiding future central city economic stagnation, they should cease attempting to entice older production industries back to the central cities, and implement programs to help develop the competitive strengths of urban cores. Here, technological changes during the past three decades have transformed major cities from centers of material goods production to centers of service consumption. Thus, along with continuing to foster the development of administrative and professional office jobs in the central business districts (CBDs), the cores of our major cities should be revitalized as culturally rich, architecturally exciting magnets for conventions, tourism, and leisure-time pursuits of regional, national, and even international populations.

All structural indicators point to the office and cultural-leisure service industries as providing the greatest potential for central city economic expansion and job generation over the next two decades [39]. Special efforts should be made to enhance central city cores as pedestrian-safe complexes of restaurants, hotels, nightclubs, museums, theaters, sport arenas, and other cultural, recreation, and entertainment facilities that would attract round-the-clock, growth-industry resources to the core, as well as economically and aesthetically complement the increasing number of nine-to-five, high-rise office buildings that are now beginning to dominate most CBDs. These efforts should include concurrent support for the revitalization and restoration of close-in historic neighborhoods, which would both contribute to the cultural appeal of the urban core and provide convenient residences for a portion of those employed in the CBDs.

5. *From the growing mismatch of the skills of the residential labor force of cities and the types of job opportunities expanding in the city.* A National Urban Policy must work to break down the restrictive covenants, zoning regulations, and barriers of racial or income housing discrimination that exist near many expanding suburban, exurban, and nonmetropolitan blue-collar job bases. Building more public housing in the inner city will likely exacerbate the problems of residence-job opportunity mismatch and ensure that a large portion of their inhabitants remain dependent on the state. Indeed, it is becoming increasingly apparent that some urban-targeted welfare programs may be inadvertently anchoring the disadvantaged in areas of economic distress and, thereby, damaging their long-term employment prospects. Dependent on public housing and place-oriented income and inkind transfer payments, the disadvantaged cannot follow low-skilled jobs that have dispersed from the cities. Discrimination and lack of low-cost housing in many areas of employment growth compound the problem. As a result, a growing urban underclass finds itself increasingly isolated in segregated economic wastelands where there are few prospects for permanent or meaningful employment.

New urban policies are required that will help dissolve bonds that well-intentioned prior policies unintentionally forged between cities and the dependent poor; that help structurally unemployed urban residents acquire the skills necessary to participate in their transforming local economies, as well as assist (rather than hinder) those who desire to migrate to places where jobs appropriate to their skills are still expanding. A thinner central city population composed largely of those who actually desire to live in the city and who have appropriate job opportunities nearby would create a far more vibrant central city than results from present policies that unintentionally warehouse millions of disadvantaged in U.S. cities, to the benefit of neither.

Moreover, it must be recognized that large concentrations of the poor around the CBDs pose serious negative externalities for the cities by discouraging shoppers and tourists from using core facilities at night and by substantially increasing the risk of new capital investment on CBD peripheries. Stifled central city business expansion, in turn, feeds back to the detriment of the urban poor by reducing potential city tax revenues that could be used, in part, to provide better services to those in need.

6. *From the incipient inner city neighborhood revitalization movement.* Our National Urban Policy should be informed that this movement got started without any government involvement and there is a possibility that future government involvement may only lessen the likelihood of its success. Already cries are beginning to be heard about "displacement,"

which, like sprawl, is a loaded term. From the standpoint of the city, the movement represents neighborhood upgrading and urban reinvestment. Indeed, it is curious that some who not long ago were deploring the growing homogeneity of lower income minority neighborhoods in and around the core areas of our cities are now so upset about the arrival of relatively small numbers of middle and upper income white residents into a portion of the neighborhoods. These apostates see revitalization not as an ecological process of inner city neighborhood rejuvenation that can improve the urban revenue base and return some of the cherished social and income residential heterogeneity that our central cities once possessed, but as an uprooting phenomenon that is occurring at the expense of the poor.

Accordingly, these observers argue that strong federal policies and programs must be implemented to monitor and control urban reinvestment so as to guard against possible displacement (see, for example, Congressional testimony by Brown [11]). The potentially chilling effect that such a policy would have on private reinvestment initiatives in our core cities should be obvious even to the casual urban observer. This is not to suggest that our urban policies be insensitive to those displaced by neighborhood upgrading and other forms of urban reinvestment. It does mean that extreme caution should be undertaken in formulating such policies to ensure that they do not in any way jeopardize the one fledgling movement that is providing our larger cities with some hope that their core residential areas can serve as more than the dumping grounds for the nation's disadvantaged.

CONCLUDING REMARKS

Much has been written over the years about the role that federal domestic policies have played in shaping the territorial redistribution of population and economic activity in the United States. In this chapter, these roles were reversed to discuss how contemporary redistribution trends might inform a more fruitful National Urban Policy. The broadest conclusion is that for our National Urban Policy to be successful it must: first, give greater recognition and weight to current technological, economic, and social forces underlying the locational decisions of people and firms; and second, be grounded in a better understanding of the functions our metropolitan core cities are best equipped to perform in a changing national and international economic order.

Regarding the former, modern transportation and communication technologies have made compactness unnecessary for conducting most of today's economic and social exchanges. In fact, in many situations, compactness hinders them. Given the overwhelming preference of most Americans for low-density living, the growing evidence that large concentrations are more costly, and the greater productivity of many modern industries in deconcentrated settings, the architects of our National Urban Policy should be careful not to allow their own apparent *opinions* favoring compactness to obstruct rational locational decisionmaking of our citizens and industrial leaders.

Regarding the second condition, the economic metamorphosis of our large cities from centers of material goods production to centers of service consumption calls for urban policies that foster the cities' new, rapid growth, service sector activities. It would be an expensive mistake to attempt to draw (by tax incentives or other means) larger production facilities back to the metropolitan cores or continuously to prop up declining urban industries that are no longer nationally or internationally competitive. On the contrary, national economic prosperity (on which the health of our cities is inextricably dependent) and increasing worldwide economic competition dictate policies that (a) encourage the location of our industrial facilities where their overall productivity and cost-effectiveness are maximized, and (b) reinforce those sectors of central city economies that have the greatest comparative advantage in the national and world economic order. Instrumental to the latter would be policies that help our major cities exploit their unique position as international market and cultural-service nodes to capture increased capital investment and revenue from abroad (e.g., via multinational corporate office development, international finance complexes, foreign tourism).

To ease structural unemployment, a revised urban policy should simultaneously facilitate the development of lower and moderate-income housing near expanding suburban, exurban, and nonmetropolitan job bases and support intensive, up-to-date technical training programs that provide all those desiring employment with appropriate skills. Proposals by some government officials to subsidize massive numbers of jobs in traditional and marginal employment sectors of central cities and "reindustrialize" older, declining urban industries will do little either to strengthen the competitive economic position of cities or to improve long-run employment opportunities for their residents. As implied above, economic advancement of the cities and maximum job creation can best be accomplished through policies that promote urban growth industries whose functions are consistent with the roles computer-age cities most effectively perform. Expeditious development of these industries not only would directly add substantial numbers of new jobs in the cities, but also would have local revenue spin-off and employment multiplier effects that would likely create far more jobs in the traditional and marginal sectors of central city economies than could federal subsidies to these sectors. Moreover, the jobs generated through this form of private sector expansion would be relatively self-sustaining and, hence, less vulnerable to the political vicissitudes of public funding.

A successful National Urban Policy, then, must take an entirely new view of the functions of cities and of the triadic relationship among deconcentration, private-sector development, and urban economic welfare. It will require programs that are consistent with the redistributional forces of economic development and that address the roots of urban structural unemployment rather than programs that attempt to reverse the paths of development and to ameliorate symptoms of underlying problems through antimarket intervention. In this regard, even the most socially sensitive and humane seem to be increasingly concurring that the patchwork of government programs implemented in prior national urban policies have poorly served the long-term economic health of the central cities and the bulk of their disadvantaged residents. Although well intentioned, urban public housing subsidies, social welfare assistance, and CETA and federal manpower job programs have continued to attract and residentially bond larger numbers of disadvantaged in our urban cores while offering them little hope for meaningful or permanent employment. Similarly, income transfer payments, designed to help the least fortunate, have also had the perverse effects of creating a sense of permanent dependence among many potentially productive workers, stifling their initiative and mobility, and contributing to damaging social frictions and prejudices between the advantaged and disadvantaged [1]. Rent controls have resulted in accelerated deterioration of central city apartment complexes and discouraged private developers from investing in the construction of needed moderate-income rental units, while federal minimum wage laws thwart private sector job generation for the unskilled in the cities and prevent millions of marginal workers (especially teenagers) from participating in the urban economy.

The nation must have a National Urban Policy that provides for the welfare of those incapable of economic self-sufficiency. Yet our policymakers also must recognize that the long-term economic health of our central cities and their inhabitants will be served only through increased private sector investment and through the relocation and/or appropriate retraining of the structurally unemployed. This implies a fundamental reorientation of our National Urban Policy from emphasizing expensive stopgap programs to counter market and job redistribution trends to emphasizing economic development programs that stimulate private-sector investment and job expansion and facilitate the relocation and/or retraining of those able to fill the newly generated jobs. As long as our National Urban Policy is dominated by programs that work against, rather than with, the modern forces of change discussed, the policy will fail. In the meantime, it will continue to waste an immense amount of human and fiscal resources and further impede prospects for improved national industrial productivity.

ACKNOWLEDGMENT

Paper prepared for the President's Commission for a National Agenda for the Eighties panel on Policies and Prospects for Metropolitan and Non-metropolitan America, June 1980. A modestly abridged version of this paper appeared in *Social Science Quarterly,* Vol. 61, No. 3 and 4, December 1980, pp. 373–400. Reprinted with permission.

REFERENCES

1. Alexis, Marcus, "The Economically Disadvantaged in the Mature Metropolis," in C. Leven, ed., *The Mature Metropolis,* Lexington, Mass: D. C. Health and Company, 1978.
2. Alonso, William, "The Current Halt in the Metropolitan Phenomenon," in C. Leven, ed., *The Mature Metropolis,* Lexington, Mass: D. C. Heath and Company, 1978.
3. Altshuler, A., "Review of the Costs of Sprawl," *Journal of the American Institute of Planners,* 43, April 1977, pp. 207–209.
4. Angel, William D., "Zenith Revised: Urban Entrepreneurship and the Sunbelt Frontier," *Social Science Quarterly,* 61, December 1980.
5. Baer, William C., "On the Death of Cities," *The Public Interest,* 45, Fall 1976, 3–11.
6. Barlowe, Raleigh, *Land Resource Economics: The Economics of Real Property,* 3rd Ed., Englewood Cliffs, N.J.: Prentice-Hall, 1978.
7. Berry, Brian J. L. and John D. Kasarda, *Contemporary Urban Ecology,* New York, N.Y.: MacMillan, 1977.
8. Biggar, Jeanne C., "The Sunning of America: Migration to the Sunbelt." *Population Bulletin,* 34, No. 1, March 1979.
9. Breckenfeld, Gurney, "Business Loves the Sunbelt (and Vice Versa)," *Fortune,* June 1977, pp. 132–146.
10. Brown, David L., "Agricultural Land Use: A Population Distribution Perspective," in Max Schnepf, ed., *Farmland, Food and the Future,* Ankeny, Iowa: Soil Conservation Society of America, 1980.
11. Brown, Ronald H., Statement prepared for the Subcommittee on Fiscal and Intergovernmental Policy of the Joint Economic Committee of the Congress of the United States, March 20, 1979, Washington, D.C.: U.S. Government Printing Office.
12. Burgess, Ernest W., "The Growth of the City: An Introduction to a Research Project," in Robert Park, Ernest Burgess, and R. D. McKenzie, eds., *The City,* Chicago, Ill.: University of Chicago Press, 1925.
13. Cotner, M.L., M.D. Skold, and O. Krause, *Farmland: Will There Be Enough?,* Washington, D.C.: U.S.D.A. Economic Research Service, ERS 584, 1975.
14. DeJong, Gordon F. and Kenneth G. Keppel, *Urban Migrants to the Countryside,* Bulletin 825, University Park, Pa.: The Pennsylvania State University College of Agriculture, Agriculture Experiment Station, 1979.

15. Economic Development Administration, *Survey of Industrial Location,* Washington, D.C.: U.S. Department of Commerce, 1971.
16. Embry, Hon. Robert C., Jr., statement prepared for the Subcommittee on Fiscal and Intergovernmental Policy of the Joint Economic Committee of the Congress of the United States, March 20, 1979, Washington, D.C.: U.S. Government Printing Office.
17. Fuguitt, Glenn V. and James J. Zuiches, "Residential Preferences and Population Distribution," *Demography,* 12, August 1975, pp. 491–504.
18. Fuguitt, Glenn V. and Paul R. Voss, *Growth and Change in Rural America,* Washington, D.C.: The Urban Land Institute, 1979.
19. Goodman, John, *Urban Residential Mobility,* Washington, D.C.: The Urban Institute, 1978.
20. Goodman, Robert, *The Last Entrepreneurs,* New York: Simon and Schuster, 1979.
21. Haren, Claude C. and Ronald W. Hollins, "Industrial Development in Nonmetropolitan America: A Locational Perspective," in Richard E. Lonsdale and H. L. Seyler, eds., *Nonmetropolitan Industrialization,* New York: Wiley, 1979.
22. Hawley, Amos H. and Sara M. Mazie, "Structural Changes in Nonmetropolitan America: An Overview," prepared in the Future of Rural America Advisory Group, 1980.
23. Hiltz, Starr Roxanne and Murray Turoff, *The Network Nation,* Reading, Mass.: Addison-Wesley Publishing Company, Inc., 1978.
24. James, Franklin J., "The Revitalization of Older Housing and Neighborhoods," in Arthur P. Soloman, ed., *The Prospective City,* Cambridge, Mass.: MIT Press, 1980, pp. 130–160.
25. Joint Economic Committee, Congress of the United States, *Central City Businesses—Plans and Problems,* Washington, D.C.: U.S. Government Printing Office, 1979.
26. Kasarda, John D., "To Revitalize the Cities: In Search of an Urban Policy," *American Demographics,* January 1981, pp. 13–19, 44–48.
27. ———, "Spatial Redistribution Trends and Public Policy: Descriptions and Proscriptions," Review symposium *Journal of the American Planning Association,* Vol. 47, No. 3, July 1981, pp. 340–345.
28. ———, "Urbanization, Community, and the Metropolitan Problem," in David Street and Associates, *Handbook of Contemporary Urban Life,* San Francisco, Calif.: Jossey-Bass, 1978.
29. Kasarda, John D. and Robert L. Lineberry, "People, Production and Power: Converging Issues in Urban Studies," *American Behavioral Scientist,* Vol. 24, No. 2, November/December 1980, pp. 157–76.
30. Kasarda, John D. and George Redfearn, "Differential Patterns of Urban and Suburban Growth in the United States," *Journal of Urban History,* 2, November 1975, pp. 43–66.
31. Lee, Linda K., *A Perspective on Cropland Availability,* Agricultural Economic Report No. 406, Washington, D.C.: U.S. Department of Agriculture, 1979.
32. Leven, Charles L., "The Emergence of Maturity in Metropolis," in C. Leven, ed., *The Mature Metropolis,* Lexington, Mass.: D.C. Heath and Company, 1978.
33. Long, Larry H. and Donald C. Dahmann, *The City-Suburb Income Gap,* Washington, D.C.: U.S. Bureau of the Census, 1980.
34. McCarthy, Kevin F. and Peter A. Morrison, *The Changing Demographic and Economic Structure of Nonmetropolitan Areas in the United States,* Santa Monica, Calif.: Rand Corporation, 1979.
35. Muller, Peter O., *The Outer City,* Resource Paper No. 75–2, Washington, D.C.: Association of American Geographers, 1976.

36. ______, "Suburbia, Geography, and the Prospect of a Nation Without Important Cities," *Geographical Survey,* 7, April 1978, pp. 3–8.
37. Muller, Thomas, "Central City Business Retention: Jobs, Taxes, and Investment Trends," presented at the U.S. Department of Commerce 2nd Urban Roundtable, March, 1978.
38. Odum, H. *et al.*, "Net Energy Analysis of Alternatives for the United States," in *Middle- and Long-Term Energy Policies and Alternatives: Volume I, Appendix,* hearings before the Subcommittee on Energy and Power of the Committee on Interstate and Foreign Commerce, House of Representatives, Washington, D.C.: U.S. Government Printing Office, 1976.
39. Perloff, Harvey S., "The Central City in the Postindustrial Age," in C. Leven, ed., *The Mature Metropolis,* Lexington, Mass.: D.C. Heath and Company, 1978.
40. Perry, David C. and Alfred J. Watkins, eds., *The Rise of the Sunbelt Cities,* Beverly Hills, Calif: Sage, 1977.
41. Phillips, Ronald E. *et al.,* "No-Tillage Agriculture," *Science,* 208, June 1980, 1108–1113.
42. Porter, Paul R., *The Recovery of American Cities,* New York, N.Y.: Two Continents Publishing Group, Ltd., 1976.
43. Rasmussen, Wayne D. and Gladys L. Baker, *Price-Support and Adjustment Programs from 1933 through 1978: A Short History,* Washington, D.C.: U.S. Department of Agriculture, 1979.
44. Real Estate Research Corporation, *The Costs of Sprawl,* Vol. 1: *Executive Summary;* Vol. 2: *Detailed Cost Analysis;* Vol. 3: *Literature, Review and Bibliography,* Washington, D.C.: U.S. Government Printing Office, 1975.
45. Schmenner, Roger W., *The Manufacturing Location Decision: Evidence from Cincinnati and New England,* Cambridge, Mass.: Harvard-MIT Joint Center for Urban Studies, 1978.
46. Schnieder, Jerry and Tomoki Noguchi, "The Role of Advanced Transit in the Implementation of the Polycentric City Concept," *High Speed Ground Transportation,* 12, 1, 1978, pp. 1–22.
47. Simon, Julian, "Resources, Population, Environment: An Oversupply of False Bad News," *Science,* 208, June 27, 1980, pp. 1431–1437.
48. Soil Conservation Service, *Potential Cropland Survey,* Statistical Bulletin 578, Washington, D.C.: U.S. Department of Agriculture, 1977.
49. Sternlieb, George, statement before the Subcommittee on Fiscal and Intergovernmental Policy of the Joint Economic Committee, Congress of the United States, March 20, 1979, Washington, D.C.: U.S. Government Printing Office.
50. Sternlieb, George and James W. Hughes, "New Dimensions of the Urban Crisis," presented before the Subcommittee on Fiscal and Intergovernmental Policy of the Joint Economic Committee, Congress of the United States, March 20, 1979, Washington, D.C.: U.S. Government Printing Office.
51. Struyk, Raymond J. and Franklin J. James, *Intra-Metropolitan Industrial Location: The Patterns and Processes of Change,* Lexington, Mass.: Lexington Books, 1975.
52. U.S. Bureau of the Census, *U.S. Census of Population: 1970,* Washington, D.C.: U.S. Department of Commerce, 1972.
53. ______, *Mobility of the Population in the United States: March 1970 to March 1975,* Series P-20, No. 285, in *Current Population Reports,* Washington, D.C.: U.S. Department of Commerce, 1975.
54. ______, *Historical Statistics of the United States: Colonial Times to 1970,* Washington, D.C.: U.S. Department of Commerce, 1975.

55. ———, *Geographical Mobility: March 1975 to March 1978,* Series P-20, No. 331, in *Current Population Reports,* Washington, D.C.: U.S. Department of Commerce, 1978.
56. ———, *Farm Population of the United States: 1978,* Washington, D.C.: U.S. Department of Commerce, 1979.
57. U.S. Bureau of Labor Statistics, *Employment and Earnings, Monthly Reports,* Washington, D.C.: U.S. Department of Commerce, 1960, 1970, 1980.
58. U.S. Department of Housing and Urban Development, "Whither or Whether Urban Distress," working paper presented before the Joint Economic Committee, Congress of the United States, March 20, 1979, Washington, D.C.: U.S. Government Printing Office.
59. *U.S. News and World Report,* September 1, 1975, pp. 30–33.
60. Vining, Daniel R., Jr., "The President's National Urban Policy Report: Issues Skirted and Statistics Omitted," *Journal of Regional Science,* 19, 1979, pp. 69–77.
61. Williams, James D. and Andrew J. Sofranko, "Motivations for the Immigration Component of Population Turnaround in Nonmetropolitan Areas," *Demography,* 16, May 1979, pp. 239–255.
62. Zuiches, James J., "Residential Preferences and Rural Population Growth," prepared for the Future of Rural America Advisory Group, Farmers Home Administration, U.S.D.A., Washington, D.C., 1980.

Chapter III

REVITALIZATION OF RURAL AMERICA:

PATTERNS AND CONSEQUENCES OF NONMETROPOLITAN AND RURAL GROWTH

John M. Wardwell

INTRODUCTION AND OVERVIEW

During the middle decades of the 20th century, a subtle but total transformation swept across rural America. Rural areas lost the social isolation that historically had been the single most striking attribute of the hinterland. They lost the economic homogeneity characteristic of dependence on agricultural-extractive industries and small-scale manufacturing and processing. They lost what degree of autonomy they had possessed as they became more fully integrated in the national economic system. They began to lose the peculiar age structure that had evolved through decades of high fertility and heavy outmigration of young adults. They lost much of the distinctiveness in lifestyle that had once sharply defined the point at which urban ended and rural began.

Among the classic components of the definition of rural areas, they retained only small size and low-settlement density.

In the process of losing all of this, they began regaining population and economic activity—and at a more rapid rate than that in metropolitan areas. In the 1970s, nonmetropolitan counties more than made up the population losses they experienced in the 1960s. This reversal in the relative growth rates of metropolitan and nonmetropolitan territory came about both through a reduction in the rate at which people were leaving rural areas and through an increase in the rate at which people moved from metropolitan to nonmetropolitan areas. The combination of these two changes has come to be called the "migration turnaround."

Both nonmetropolitan counties adjacent to and remote from Standard Metropolitan Statistical Areas (SMSAs) experienced the reversal from population loss to gain and from net outmigration to net inmigration. The size of this reversal was greatest for the most remote and entirely rural counties. By the middle of the 1970s, the reversal had become evident in virtually all of the subregions of the United States, in fully four-fifths of the nonmetropolitan counties. Only those counties that remained most like the traditional concept of rural areas failed to participate in this renewal of economic and population growth: those that remained most dependent on an agricultural base for employment, those that remained most isolated from national and regional transportation and economic systems, those that offered the least to an expanding and unifying national urban system.

The causes of the two changes in migration patterns—increased rural retention of population and increased metropolitan outmigration—that together produced the reversal in growth patterns are both simple and complex: simple to identify and list, but difficult to incorporate in a cohesive whole that offers a general explanation of the phenomenon. After reviewing a virtual laundry list of causes that joined to generate new and unexpected directions in urban-rural migration, this chapter offers one attempt to organize the interrelationships of these changes. That effort takes a set of consumption values as given, and explains the migration turnaround primarily in terms of changes in national income levels, transportation systems, and the scale effects of changes in the infrastructures of smaller sized places.

Changes in the character of rural America are both causes and consequences of the migration turnaround. Increasing diversity is evident in the varied reasons for new economic growth in different regions of the country; in the more complex occupational structures of rural and nonmetropolitan counties; in the demographic and other differences between new migrants and prior residents; and in the lifestyles and activity patterns of rural Americans in the latter decades of this century. If one word could capture the nature of contemporary rural society, it is "diversity." Freed from both the dependence-induced homogeneity of earlier decades and the crushing size and density of large metropolitan systems, growing smaller sized cities and open countryside have the flexibility to develop in a wider variety of ways than could have been imagined even so short a time as two decades ago. Diversity in all spheres of activity is the result of that flexibility, and it is the one fact of contemporary rural character that must serve as the starting point for further inquiry.

Energy may be called the hidden dimension of structural changes in rural societies in the past four decades. So long as the friction of space appeared in the forms of higher costs, longer travel times, and greater inconvenience of access, rural territory would remain largely remote and isolated. The transportation developments that have done much to reduce this isolation took place in the context of low and declining real costs of most forms of energy. Because of the primacy given the development of modern transportation and telecommunication systems in the view of social change taken in this chapter, it is essential to look carefully at the consequences of the abrupt changes in the cost and availability of petroleum in the past few years. Increasing costs and potentially erratic supplies assume further importance when they occur in the context of stable or declining real income, as was the case at the end of the 1970s and the beginning of the 1980s.

The new population and economic growth has been called many things, ranging from rural renaissance to rebirth. The notion of revitalization is strong throughout the literature, with the implication that growth is in itself an indication that the growing community is healthy. But still it must be asked, revitalization for whom? Who benefits from renewed growth? How are prior residents affected by unanticipated waves of new migrants? Which groups are left largely untouched by the phenomenon, and which groups are actually disadvantaged by the new growth patterns?

The fact that the reversal in net metropolitan-nonmetropolitan migration was unanticipated is in part due to an accelerating rate of change in the 1970s on most of the dimensions that are most influential in determining patterns of population movement. The early 1980s have witnessed a further acceleration in the rate of change on several determinants and other largely unanticipated patterns of change with other migration determinants. As mentioned, real income growth has slowed or reversed, and the energy context of population distribution has changed radically. Two-career households are increasing rapidly, with unknown effects on the volume and patterns of migration.

Many argue that much of the migration of the past decade was motivated by a search for a more satisfying quality of life. To the extent that this view is accurate, and to the extent that migrants of the past decade were successful in finding that better quality of life, this would suggest that we should expect less mobility on their part, as they experience reluctance to leave high quality of life residences and workplaces. The continuation of exceptionally high home mortgage rates and the consequent difficulties in selling and buying homes must also be expected to depress somewhat the mobility rates that would otherwise be occurring in the 1980s. It is essential that some speculative attempt to place these changes in the context of metropolitan-nonmetropolitan population exchange inform any forecast of the movement patterns that might be anticipated in the coming decade.

Finally, the consideration of these many aspects of changing society is essential to the shaping of a set of policies designed to provide for an enduring rural lifestyle in America. In the past, policies for the rural segments of the society were designed to alleviate depressed economic conditions in local areas, to ease the transition accompanying the mechanization and enlarged scale of agriculture, to provide the basic material amenities that were readily available in urban locations, to reduce the isolation of rural peoples, and to address chronic problems of poverty, malnutrition, education, and health care. Such long-standing problems do remain in particular rural areas, but they are no longer as characteristic of these areas as they once were. A new set of policies is needed—policies that take account of greatly increased ease of access, affluence, flexibility, and diversity in rural America.

CAUSES OF NEW NONMETROPOLITAN GROWTH

Changes in population behavior never take place in a socioeconomic vacuum. Population change is never a prime mover, and often is more usefully analyzed as an effect than as a cause. When migration between places is viewed in this manner, it may be seen as an equilibrating mechanism, reducing the differentials between places on the primary determinants of migration. The net direction of movement tends to be from areas of low or declining employment opportunities to areas of higher or growing opportunities; from areas of lower incomes to areas of higher incomes; from areas that are judged unpleasant by migrants toward areas that are thought to be more desirable.

Migration functions to equilibrate the system because it becomes causally active in determining subsequent levels of differentials at both origin and destination. Wage and employment differentials diminish as they decline in destinations relative to the origins. Similarly, in terms of amenities related to the size of places, as growing areas expand through inmigration, their attractiveness diminishes relative to the characteristics of the places people left.

The net urban-to-rural movement of the past decade does not easily fit this traditional model of migration. This should not be surprising because that traditional model did not forecast any reversal of the historical patterns of population exchange between metropolitan and nonmetropolitan places. The search for explanations—both of the new patterns and of the inability of traditional models to anticipate those new patterns—could not be confined to factors peculiar to the United States, because new and unexpected population and economic growth in rural areas was characteristic of most, if not all, of the more developed, highly urbanized, postindustrial societies of the world.

Data from opinion surveys on residential preferences are scanty and fragmentary prior to the 1970s. What little information exists, however, indicates that as early as 1950, a substantial number of residents of large urban centers preferred residence in smaller places. But throughout that decade, the net direction of population movement was counter to these expressed preferences, and in the direction of net economic benefits. In the past decade, net movement has been in the direction of residential preferences, but counter to the net of economic benefits. This has led many to conclude that the major explanation of migration turnaround is found in the area of value changes—away from pecuniary values and toward a broader array of quality-of-life considerations. In this view, contemporary migrants are willing to sacrifice potential income gains in exchange for desired nonmonetary characteristics of residence in small cities, towns and villages, and open countryside.

While undoubtedly an important part of the explanation, this view is weakened by at least three considerations. First, it begs the question of why and how such a change in values could take place simultaneously in nearly two dozen developed societies. Second, it lacks the empirical base to demonstrate conclusively that a change of sufficient magnitude has taken place to account for the reversal of migration patterns. Finally, it does not address the question of why the change did not take place earlier, when what little opinion data could be obtained indicated that people were not moving in the direction of their preferences. What was holding them back?

They were held back by the lack of opportunity and the high cost of implementing their residential preferences. Urban-rural employment and income differentials were much greater in the 1950s than in the 1970s. Those differentials had to diminish before potential migrants who desired residence in smaller sized places had the employment opportunities necessary to make a choice. Income differentials had to diminish before those potential migrants could afford the cost, in terms of reduced income, of moving from large metropolitan to nonmetropolitan areas.

Those differentials have demonstrably diminished. Employment growth in nonmetropolitan counties during the 1970s has been significantly more rapid in virtually all industries than in metropolitan counties; in manufacturing, nonmetropolitan expansion has stood in marked contrast to absolute declines in metropolitan areas. The diversification of nonmetropolitan employment is evident by comparing the employment industries of new migrants with those of longer term residents. Construction, trade, professional services, finance, insurance, and real estate are more characteristic of recent migrants, while manufacturing and agriculture are more characteristic of longer term residents [3].

Kasarda argues that reduction of the cultural and physical isolation of rural communities from nonmetropolitan activity patterns and lifestyles is the "sufficient condition that sparked many metropolitan residents to migrate to more remote nonmetropolitan communities after the necessary condition of economic opportunities developed there" [21: 383]. In this view, it is not necessary to bring residential preferences and values changes into the discussion at all. The fact of reduced isolation is sufficient, given the necessary condition of employment opportunities. But that view understates the relationship between the reduction of isolation and the growth of employment opportunities, and neglects the relationship between income growth and the ways in which values have been implemented.

Socioeconomic changes in national systems over the past three decades have reduced the competitive advantage of large urban centers for population and economic growth in several ways.

Transportation and Communication Technologies

Improvements and changes in transportation and communication technologies have been the primary means by which the cultural and physical isolation of remote rural communities has been reduced. Expansion of improved, divided national highway systems and upgrading of regional systems have lowered the time and dollar cost to move goods and people. Expansion of flexible personal and commercial automotive transport using these highway systems may well be the single most important factor underlying the decentralization of population and activities [15: 358]. The friction of space has been further eased by the development of telecommunications systems that increasingly substitute communication for movement, that enhance the quality of transmission, and that expand the array of metropolitan-originating transmissions in nonmetropolitan space.

As access to formerly remote rural locations has increased, the cost of residence in these locations has diminished and the opportunities for employment have increased. The consequent expansion of the cost-effective radius for virtually all transportation-dependent activities has made it easier for smaller communities to "borrow scale" from nearby larger communities and from each other [1]. Smaller sized places now offer many of the production and consumption capacities formerly available only in large cities. As the need for location in large urban centers has diminished, the combination of relative diseconomies and disamenities have come to weigh more heavily in the location decisions of households and firms.

Growth in Personal Affluence

Growth in real income during the 1960s and early 1970s in the United States and in other countries experiencing migration turnaround favored the expansion of employment and other activities in nonmetropolitan areas. Convergent income elasticities of demand guided the disposition of this income growth into activities that placed little premium on centrality, such as housing, personal transportation and leisure, and outdoor recreation. As the real cost of activities in distant rural areas was declining, the availability of resources for these activities was growing, both in terms of disposable income and of leisure time. The resulting shifts in the composition of consumer demand gave further impetus to the relative growth of rural economies. As these two complementary changes interacted, the drift in consumer expenditures outward from the metropolitan core to the nonmetropolitan periphery accelerated rapidly.

Expansion of Urban Social Organization

Urbanization is often viewed less as the demographic measurement of the proportion of a population located in places defined as urban and more as the expansion of urban forms of social organization [18]. Changes in transportation and communications systems provided the media through which urban forms could more rapidly diffuse to what had formerly been rural hinterlands. Growth in affluence and reduced need for residential and employment location in the physical urban form—the city—provided the engine that drove urbanization outward. Transformation of national economies from primarily goods-producing to primarily services-providing offered the attracting force that drew those urban forms of organization into the hinterland. In terms of such traditional urban-rural differentials as demographic characteristics, personal lifestyles, employment patterns, and values, recent urban-to-rural migrants were both attracted by and contributed further to the ongoing urban transformation of the countryside. The consequence of this pervasive convergence between metropolitan and nonmetropolitan areas was to reduce simultaneously the gains of movement from rural to urban areas (thus diminishing that component of the population exchange between the two areas) and the costs of movement from urban to rural areas (thus increasing the other component). Convergence between urban and rural areas in employment opportunities, in real incomes, in access to what would once have been classified as urban lifestyles, and in activity patterns gave households and firms the ability to take advantage of these trends by expanding their range of locational choices.

Contributing Factors

These changes are in themselves sufficient to account for the turnaround in net migration patterns that has been witnessed in the United States and several other countries. These changes are common to all of the turnaround nations [34]. But they have not been solely responsible for the dimensions of the turnaround in the United States. As in other nations, a number of idiosyncratic factors have contributed to the growth of rural America.

Perhaps first among these in volume is the expansion of governmental activities located in nonmetropolitan counties. These include the growth of state and local government, enrollment growth in four-year colleges and universities, and some defense-related expansion during this period [2, 26]. Two of these three factors are either unique to or assume far greater proportions in the United States than in other developed turnaround countries. Growth of enrollment in nonmetropolitan colleges and universities is a short-term phenomenon largely restricted to the past decade as a result of the aging of postwar baby-boom cohorts that were proportionally larger in this country than elsewhere. The expansion of station strengths during the Vietnam-era military build-up was of course entirely confined to the United States, and also to the 1970s (although such a mobilization could of course occur again). One of the implications of these factors is that as enrollments diminish in the 1980s, as military-induced migration diminishes, and as state and local governments constrict through federal and state budget reductions, the patterns of urban-rural population exchange in the United States are likely to approach much more nearly the patterns of other more developed nations. (See Vining and Kontuly [32] for information on the extent to which the United States departed from these patterns in the 1970s.)

A second factor, perhaps not unique to the United States, but again taking on a more important role in nonmetropolitan growth in this country, is the growth and increasing mobility of retirement-aged populations [16]. These populations have grown both through the high birth rates of the early decades of this century and through trends toward earlier retirement. Their mobility has increased through the growth and expansion of Social Security and other pension programs during the middle decades of this century, as these cohorts were moving through their prime employment ages. With increased freedom to move, these populations show marked preferences for retirement residence in smaller sized places.

Finally, a continuing preference on the part of many residents of large urban centers for relocation to smaller sized places has impelled an increase in such movement, as it was made possible by expanding employment opportunities and increasing real incomes. Again, the patterns that have been observed might be adequately explained by the increasing ability to implement pre-existing preferences [33]. But there is also evidence of some value change entering the picture and accelerating the decentralization trend [41]. Long and DeAre [25] find indications that the trend has itself accelerated through the 1980s, including the period in which higher energy (and hence transportation) costs might have been expected to exert a recentralizing influence [36]. Long and DeAre also find that noneconomic motivations rank higher among migrants from metropolitan areas than they do among migrants to metropolitan areas, a finding that supports Stevens' [29] argument that nonmetropolitan-bound migrants are increasingly willing to forego income gains in exchange for nonmarket attributes found disproportionately in smaller towns and nonmetropolitan counties. Williams and McMillen [38] have documented the extent to which reasons for destination selection may differ from reasons for leaving the place of origin, and demonstrate that noneconomic motivations may predominate in the former even when economic considerations are prominent in the decision to leave. Finally, Zuiches and Rieger [42] have some evidence to suggest that the desire of rural youth to remain in rural areas may be increasing over time.

It seems clear that increasing flexibility with respect to location has allowed residential preferences to play a larger role in guiding migration streams than in earlier decades. This is not to suggest that the economic and other structural determinants of migration have weakened over time [40], but rather that the differentials between urban and rural places on these traditional determinants have diminished. This diminishing of differentials on the stronger determinants of migration has allowed the more proximate, more value-oriented determinants to enter the picture with greater impact than they have hitherto exercised.

This implies two interesting facets of the complex of causes that are thought to be responsible for the migration turnaround. First, the change in migration patterns is due more to the increasing similarities between urban and rural areas than to their residual differences, in that the former has changed and thus better accounts for the change in the migration patterns. Second, if firms and households have in fact been more motivated by the search for a satisfying quality of life in new locations in the past decade, we should expect a dampening of further migration in the 1980s to the extent that these searches have been successful. If regional and scale shifts in industries in the next decade permit continued competitive employment in smaller sized places, there would seem to be little reason to anticipate further movement on the part of prior migrants to these areas. That would of course counter the typical relationship between prior movement and probably of additional future movement [27].

RURAL SOCIETY IN POST-INDUSTRIAL AMERICA

In earlier decades, knowledge of where a person lived provided a reliable indication of "what he did for a living, the pattern of his values, and his normal interactions situations" [4: 256]. Now, "being highly rural in regard to one component does not imply a high degree of 'rurality' in regard to other components," so that "the use of various meanings of 'rurality' no longer necessarily leads to the designation of the same person" [39: 10]. or even of the same geographic areas or places [18]. While nonmetropolitan areas do remain significantly less diverse on such indicators as occupational differentiation, availability of a variety of goods and services, and measures of deviant behavior, the gaps between urban and rural have been narrowing dramatically in the past few decades, so that differences between rural now and rural then are greater than the residual differences between urban and rural as we enter the 1980s.

This increasing diversity is readily apparent in that the array of reasons for the migration turnaround do not apply to all types of nonmetropolitan areas, nor do similar reasons necessarily result in similar kinds of growth in different areas. Nonmetropolitan counties adjacent to metropolitan centers seem to manifest increased commuting and metropolitan employment deconcentration, location of retirement communities, and expansion of recreation activities. More remote and entirely rural counties have experienced recreation and retirement growth also, and have been more impacted by transportation changes, as completion of the interstate highway system has made them more readily accessible.

Diversity in the population and the mix of economic activities is also increasing. Migrants on the whole tend to be younger, more highly educated, more affluent and have smaller households than do the prior residents of nonmetropolitan areas, but these same migrants tend on the whole to be older, less well-educated, and less affluent than the people who continue to move from nonmetropolitan to metropolitan areas.

Even the very wide variations in rates of growth within the nonmetropolitan category defy gross generalization or the temptation to overlook the extreme diversity that exists within this category. Approximately 400 nonmetropolitan counties are still experiencing net outmigration or stability. These counties tend chiefly to be located in the Great Plains, Corn Belt, and Mississippi Delta. At the other extreme, another group of 350 counties are experiencing net inmigration at rates of 2.5 percent per year and greater—growth rates that are more usually associated with the high fertility of rapidly growing developing nations [35].

This diversity in population composition, in types and rates of change, in industrial and employment mix, in reasons for renewed population and economic growth, and in changing community structure and function is the single most noteworthy characteristic of the changing nature of rural society in the United States. The temptation to continue to equate rural or nonmetropolitan interests with agricultural-extractive interests completely misses this diversity and fails to address the needs of the more than 50 million residents of nonmetropolitan America who are *not* employed in these industries. In 1975, less than 10 percent of the nonmetropolitan labor force was employed in agriculture, and approximately 2 percent in mining. Less than 4 percent of the nonmetropolitan population lives in counties where 30 percent or more of the labor force is engaged in agriculture. Whatever else it may represent, the new nonmetropolitan growth of the past decade is *not* a "back to the land" embracement of agricultural life on the part of disenchanted urbanities. It would be more accurate to suggest that it represents the extension of urban lifestyles and forms of social organization into the countryside, in an urban transformation of rural society.

The terms "urban" and "rural" are usually used as though their meanings were distinct and agreed on by all. In most contexts, there is usually an explicit statement to the effect that these terms are used interchangeably with "metropolitan" and "nonmetropolitan" or the settlement-size referent of the terms is understood. But when the terms are used in such contexts as "urban organizational forms" or the "urban transformation of rural society," the conceptual ambiguity becomes more problematic.

One of the conceptual difficulties with the urban transformation of the total society is that one remains certain that something is different in the countryside, but one is not so certain of how to find it or what to call it. The problem is kept in the forefront by the fact that either in the form of size-of-place or in the form of metropolitan-nonmetropolitan classifications of counties, use of rural as a spatial concept continues to work effectively when studying relative rates of growth and migration. It discriminates rates of growth in manufacturing and other industries and it imperfectly but reliably indicates distinctions in patterns that are at the very heart of the study of urbanization and migration.

Some have argued that the reversal of net migration patterns leading to pervasive decentralization should be called "counter-urbanization" [6, 8]. But that phrase, directed specifically at the demographic characterization of residential and economic dispersion, connotes an organizational change that is not what is really happening. Urban-originating social organizational forms are occurring now in rural space. In terms of its activities, rural growth is as much the manifestation of continued urbanization as it may be of a new, counter-urbanization trend. "Urbanity" in terms of type of employment, level of income, and ability to select lifestyles has become ubiquitous through the organizational processes of urbanization themselves. And because of that very ubiquity of these characteristics that were once appropriately and distinctively labeled "urban," the concept of "rural" must acquire an important shift in meaning. Apart from size, density, and residual homogeneity, it may increasingly be defined in terms of the relative absence of the negative externalities of large cities—less crime, less noise, less pollution, less congestion.

That in turn raises the question of whether the positive externalities of large cities are now less size-density dependent than are the negative. What other implication can be drawn from the fact that many positive urban characteristics have grown much more rapidly in rural space than have the negative? If these positive externalities are now more nearly ubiquitous than are the negative, why?

This possibility suggests caution in speaking less glibly in phrases like the "urban transformation" of the total society. Rural areas have indeed been transformed so that they are much more like urban places *in some ways,* and that is conceptually confusing. But at the same time, they have remained very unlike large urban areas in other ways. Only together can these twin facts of rural change and rural persistence adequately account for the phenomenon of rural growth. Only through identifying the linkages between rural persistence and the ecological conditions of rural space can we find our way to a concept of rural that is as clear as it is useful.

ENERGY, THE HIDDEN DIMENSION

The treatment of energy in urbanization and migration theories prior to the early 1970s was clear, even though it was usually implicit. These theories were predicated on energy that was cheap, abundant, versatile, and yet directive. The forecasts of these theories rested on the assumption that the circumstances determining the costs and availabilities of energy would continue indefinitely, except perhaps for change in the direction of even greater abundance, lower costs, and in more forms. It is difficult to think of any other single characteristic of the ways in which we conceived of human-environment relations in the 1950s and 1960s that was as pervasive as was the assumption that energy constraints on the expansion and distribution of social systems in space would continually be relaxed.

Those circumstances have indeed changed in the 1970s—in a direction other than that which had been anticipated. The direction of change is now toward greater constraint. For the remainder of this century, emergent distribution patterns cannot be realistically discussed without taking into account this renewal of constraint.

And we don't really know yet how to do so; that is why the word "hidden" becomes appropriate to describe the energy base of the distribution of activities and the migration of households and individuals [20, 24, 36]. We do know well the ways in which the friction of space (and the consequent isolation of remote rural regions) has been alleviated by transportation development predicated on the continuance of cheap and abundant energy for the movement of goods, and for the production and consumption commuting of households. We know well how the declining real costs of energy in the context of rising incomes fed the proliferation of consumption activities with high income elasticities. And we know how that proliferation both contributed directly to the growth of employment and incomes in those now-more-accessible rural regions and further reduced their isolation through increased contacts with residents of urban regions pursuing urban activities in rural space. And we know that declining energy costs contributed directly to the ubiquity of more goods and services both through declining production costs and declining distribution costs.

However, we know very little about the ways in which higher energy costs in the context of stable or declining real incomes will constrain future expansion, given that the infrastructure developed in response to a different energy cost-availability context remains in place. We can more readily forecast the consequences of energy changes for the continued development and maintenance of that infrastructure (indeed, we are seeing those consequences this winter in the form of the higher costs of snow removal and roadway maintenance), but not the future uses of the existing infrastructure. It is difficult to identify reductions in use of the freeways in place, and most difficult of all to allocate reductions in total use across types of use, and then to identify the impact of the mix of use-changes on the economic base and social integration of the rural regions affected by the changes.

We do not know, for example, the factors that will differentiate between countries in determining the tradeoffs between increasing energy efficiency and decreasing energy use that are being made at the household level. And if that tradeoff is not being chosen in some societies, we must then know the tradeoff between energy uses and other consumption expenditures that is being made. So long as energy costs rise more rapidly than real income, one of the following three responses (or some combination of them) is necessary: increased efficiency to maintain level of use while managing costs; decreased use; or, sacrifice of some other area of expenditure to accomodate rising costs while maintaining level of use.

Each of these trade-offs implies constraints on continued expansion on the paths established in the past decade: they imply yet more new directions in urban-rural migration. Increased efficiency bought at the expense of diverting capital from other uses may, for example, permit leisure travel at lower or stable unit costs for the energy consumed, but at the same time it may reduce the amount of money available for all other travel expenditures. Decreased use of the movement infrastructure implies a geographic concentration of consumption expenditures that may significantly undercut the retail and service base of employment growth in outlying areas [7]; it may also to some measure restore the isolation from social interaction that was long characteristic of remote rural regions. Sacrificing expenditures in other areas to accomodate energy costs may also undercut the consumption base of the dispersal of economic activities, depending on the preference schedules according to which those sacrifices are made.

But to argue that any combination of these responses restores to some degree the friction of space is not to argue that they will restore the movement patterns of the 1950s. The freeing of urban organizational forms and activity patterns from urban space was dependent on the energy context of prior decades, but it also created an infrastructure for movement that had not previously existed and that will not go away as the energy context changes. It is that fact that makes it difficult to forecast the forms in which renewed constraints on the spatial expansion of social systems will manifest themselves [23]. Do they imply a tendency toward reconcentration of population and activities? If so, at what settlement size and regional levels? How will reconcentration tendencies differ within and between societies? How will the transportation systems created in past decades shape the adaptation to higher movement costs in the next decade?

Increasing real costs of energy seem necessarily to imply some curtailment of lifestyles, particularly when the very high cost of capital makes it more difficult to preserve choices by increasing energy efficiency. Rural areas do possess some advantages over large urban areas in adaptation to new energy constraints, and may possess more flexibility in developing social organizational forms to accomplish that adaptation. At least for the relatively well off, rural areas provide a wider range of alternatives for meeting nontransportation uses of energy. That wider range derives in part from the smaller scale of rural settlement and the lower degree of dependence on large, centralized grid systems. While large regional variations make generalization by size of place risky at best, residents of smaller communities often have readier access to alternative fuels, use of passive solar supplements, and informal transportation pooling arrangements.

Two myths of small-community living may become increasingly significant in regards to uses of energy and the perceived differential benefits of large and small places. The first is the myth of self-reliance and the association of that myth with small town and open country living; the second is the myth of easier personal relationships with neighbors and other residents of the community. These beliefs may be seen to offer a large measure of relief from anxiety in these energy-scarce, inflationary, and constraining opening years of the 1980s—both for the nonmetropolitan resident contemplating a move to a large place and for the large metropolitan resident considering a rural destination.

REVITALIZATION FOR WHOM?

What does the new growth mean to those affected by it? A term like "revitalization" implies the bringing of renewed health to an ailing sector of society. Which sectors are benefitting? Are these benefits a mixed impact, advantaging some groups and disadvantaging others?

The New Migrants

Certainly the new migrants themselves would seem to either experience or at least anticipate some measure of revitalization of their lives with their movement from large urban centers to smaller cities, rural towns, and open countryside. This revitalization is implicit in their greater freedom to implement their residential preferences, to enjoy the special qualities of life they are seeking without as great a sacrifice of employment and income as would have been necessary even two decades ago. But it is also evident in community satisfaction and residential preference surveys, in which residents and recent migrants consistently express high degrees of satisfaction with and preference to continue residing in their communities ([13, 17]; for an overview of this research, see Zuiches [41]).

This enhancement of quality of life is particularly true for the mobile aged, who frequently need maintain only a mailbox to receive their income. To pervert a phrase that has enjoyed some popularity in recent years, these new "urban villagers" are almost certainly enjoying increased benefits in ways important to them. Dailey and Campbell [11:254] note that they are not so much seeking to escape urbanity as to find the best of both worlds: country living with urban services. Conflicts do ensue, as new residents find communities less than their expectations on some dimensions, or as their values clash with those of longer term residents [11, 28, 30]. Many of these conflicts, however, would be attendant on any change of residence and should not be considered as unique consequences of the recent growth of rural areas of the past decade.

Prior Residents

The migrants themselves constitute only a small minority of the total population resident in nonmetropolitan and rural areas. What of the growth impacts on these prior residents? In his acceptance of the Nobel Peace Prize for his work in improving cereal productivity, Norman Borlaug noted that he "would rather be struggling with the problems of abundance than with the problems of scarcity." Implicit in that preference is the assumption that problems will be recognized and solutions sought. There is a danger in the new nonmetropolitan growth that the growth itself will be taken as a sufficient indicator of good health, and that a climate of benign neglect for the nonagricultural sectors of rural society will dominate the formulation of a national agenda for the present decade [12].

Owners of housing and other forms of fixed capital are likely to benefit from growth, at least monetarily, as are providers of retail goods and services. Renters and other purchasers of those goods and services are more likely to experience cost increases without direct offsetting monetary benefits. Household incomes may rise with labor force participation rates, as some new employment forms provide additional opportunities to unemployed or underemployed workers and to those members of the household not formerly active in the labor force.

All residents experience an enrichment of human resources, as new migrants bring skills and experiences not widely available in many rural areas [28]. That may be a mixed blessing, however, for different value systems and preference schedules for community activities and services often accompany those new skills and experiences. Traditional community leaders may find their roles usurped by newcomers or, alternatively, resentful toward those same newcomers for not sharing more widely their skills and special expertise.

Communities

New growth does bring problems in its wake, particularly when growth is rapid and unanticipated. Because new residents often differ in behavior and expectations from prior residents, the level and mix of demand for community services changes with new growth. Many hundreds of these impacted communities had adjusted their level of services to a stable or declining population base, and to the peculiar age composition that results from relatively high fertility combined with high rates of outmigration of young adults. For the most part these communities had no reason to anticipate change. The resulting problems were compounded by the historically low institutional capacity to adapt to change, and by the often very rapid rate of change that has taken place [12].

The resources needed to provide more and different services typically lag behind the growth in demand for those services. The results may include long lines, traffic congestion, overcrowded facilities, competition between newcomers and older residents for scarce facilities, overburdened water and sanitation systems—in short, some of the very conditions that were instrumental in the migrants' decision to leave their prior, larger places of residence! While an expanded revenue base might eventually provide the resources necessary to create new and to expand existing infrastructure, a great deal of dissatisfaction on the part of both newcomers and older residents may arise in the short term.

Two complicating factors coincident with the migration turnaround exacerbate these problems and make acceptable solutions less likely. The first of these is the reduction in state and local fiscal authority that is pervasive throughout the nation and particularly prevalent in more sparsely settled nonmetropolitan areas. Often this reduced taxing ability is enthusiastically supported by the most recent migrants, who have moved in part to get away from higher taxes in metropolitan centers but who still demand a higher level of urban services than had been provided in their destination communities prior to their arrival. The problems are made more severe by the proportionally very high front-end costs of new infrastructure creation in the context of rapid inflation and high interest rates.

The second factor that makes addressing these problems of new growth more difficult for community leaders is the uncertainty they feel regarding the duration and rate of growth. New growth for the most part came unexpectedly. Too little is known of the interaction of scores of changes at the national level that eventuated in the outcome of net urban-to-rural migration to offer specific communities reliable guidance as to how long that growth will continue, what dimensions it will assume, or what degree of turnover is buried beneath the gross growth statistics. Without this information, planning for new classrooms, community parks, traffic signals, street widths, and a host of other community services is most difficult.

Traditionally Rural Problems

Another impact of the new population and economic growth is found in the danger that a wide range of traditionally rural problems will go unnoticed as these areas of "the people left behind" become the most rapid growth areas of the nation. Rural poverty, inadequate education, malnutrition, and poor health remain significant problems in our society [12]. There is no necessary connection between new population and economic growth in nonmetropolitan counties and the amelioration of these problems.

These problems may in fact worsen under conditions of growth in some cases. Poverty in the midst of poverty is one thing. Poverty in the midst of a community transformed by the arrival of more affluent peoples from the cities may be quite another. Relative deprivation may be increasing, and absolute deprivation may be increasing also, as the poorer residents are bid out of competition for higher priced goods and services, and as consolidated facilities are burdened by the increased level and changed mix of demands brought by new arrivals.

Traditionally Urban Problems

Finally, the new nonmetropolitan growth hardly suggests revitalization of the large metropolitan centers that have been left behind by the migrants. There is some danger of exaggeration of effects, however. Metropolitan-to-nonmetropolitan migrants represent a very small fraction of the total metropolitan population, and those mythical "net migrants" an even smaller fraction. There is no danger of the depopulation of the large metropolitan areas of the nation. The numerical impact on large cities is miniscule in the aggregate, although it may be significant in individual cities. Impacts in terms of the composition of changes are probably more significant than are the impacts of the sheer numbers of people leaving these cities. Attention is better focussed on which types of people are leaving and on the reasons why these migrants are increasingly leaving the large cities than on the gross number of people and households that are leaving.

CONSTRAINTS OF THE 1980s

Net migration between places is both influenced by and, to some degree, independent of the total volume of movement within a social system. To speculate on the migration patterns between urban and rural places in the 1980s, it is necessary not only to forecast the future of the determinants of the general level of mobility in the society, but also to try to identify whether anticipated changes will differentially affect conditions of working and living in urban and rural places. It would be one thing, for example, to forecast how the growth of two-career households would influence the levels of movement of affected households. But before any forecast of the effect of this phenomenon on continued nonmetropolitan growth, it would also be necessary to understand whether this factor differentially influenced metropolitan and nonmetropolitan households.

It would also be necessary to place this factor in the context of all other foreseeable migration-influencing factors. The impact of the growth of two-career households on migration might well differ, for example, in an expanding economy and in a stable or contracting economy. Similarly, its effects may differ during inflationary periods, under the influence of high home mortgage rates, or in the context of reduced levels of expenditure at all levels of government.

That is the goal of the present section: to identify insofar as possible the principle changes evident at the outset of this decade that are known to be closely related to migration, to put these changes in the context of the total pattern of change in the society, and to attempt to forecast the ways in which the total context may affect continued population and economic exchange between metropolitan and nonmetropolitan areas of the United States.

Economic Factors

Explanations of the migration turnaround of the 1970s place heavy emphasis on the economic conditions of the decade, even while they may be asserting the primacy of noneconomic quality of life values in guiding location decisions. The climate of personal affluence and increasing real incomes, employment expansion, low-cost and abundant energy, and inflation that was low by contemporary standards formed a context without which the deconcentration of population and economic activities would not likely have taken place.

All of these factors have changed radically in the late 1970s and early 1980s. Real incomes have been stable or recorded actual declines in this latter period. As measured by real increase in Gross National Product (GNP), economic expansion has slowed markedly. Inflation has been dramatically higher throughout the second half of the 1970s as compared with the 1965–75 period, and energy costs have quadrupled as supplies became more uncertain. That these changes will affect the patterns of societal growth and expansion is unarguable. What differential effects they will have on nonmetropolitan and metropolitan expansion is less clear.

There are reasons to believe that the net of these effects will disadvantage metropolitan areas more than nonmetropolitan. First, it would appear that these trends exacerbate diseconomies and disamenities in large urban centers and in doing so may well move the "tip-over point" at which metropolitan residents decide to relocate to smaller sized places. The rate at which living conditions worsen in large cities may accelerate, while the rate at which living conditions in nonmetropolitan places improve may decelerate. While the slope of both curves would be changing, they would remain on a convergent course, and it is even possible that the rate of convergence would accelerate. Metropolitan outmigration represents in part the desire to get away from dense aggregations of crime and poverty, while nonmetropolitan inmigration has taken place in spite of the persistence of proportionally greater poverty. Were the general welfare to worsen in both sectors, the differential impact on present migration trends is likely to maintain or accelerate the direction of those trends, because a causally significant factor in large cities is increasing in intensity, while a causally passive factor in nonmetropolitan areas increased no more than proportionally.

Secondly, constraints on expansion of the total economy might well accelerate present reasons for employment relocation away from large urban centers. This could come about through the relative concentration of some industries that are hit the hardest by inflation and high interest rates, by a reduction in the rate of new industry formation (which tends disproportionately to be a large urban activity), and by the acceleration of resource extraction activities located in rural areas. As increasingly scarce capital shifts from those activities that tend more to be metropolitan-concentrated toward activities that are widely dispersed throughout the nation or that are nonmetropolitan-concentrated, the shortage of capital may become a more severe constraint in large cities than in nonmetropolitan areas. This shift of capital will not be proportionally matched by a shift of labor, because these industries greatly tend to be capital intensive and technology dependent. But what labor effects do exist are likely to net in favor of nonmetropolitan areas, as labor markets follow patterns of economic expansion and move away from areas that are more severely constrained.

The high capital costs of increasing energy efficiency will place further demands on increasingly expensive capital for both households and production and thus is likely to continue to contribute to conservation in use. However, the direct effects of change and expansion of high interest rates is probably a much greater factor. High home mortgage rates indubitably are reducing overall mobility, particularly for homeowners, as it becomes more difficult both to sell at origin and finance at destination. But existing metropolitan-nonmetropolitan differentials in the costs of homeownership suggest a third reason why this constraint will disadvantage rural areas less than large metropolitan areas. The median cost of both new and older homes is substantially lower in lower density settlements, enabling movers to acquire more easily a new home in nonmetropolitan areas. Differential costs of home ownership and profits realized from selling appreciated urban homes are in fact cited by migrants as reasons for their move to rural areas. Thus, while this factor is constraining the general volume of mobility within society, it may actually be increasing urban-to-rural movement, at least proportionally, while it exerts a disproportionally depressing influence on rural-to-urban migration.

Social and Demographic Factors

Female labor force participation rates continue to rise, as do female enrollments in higher education. Career patterns are becoming more characteristic of females, while marriage rates remain relatively constant. As a consequence, the number of dual-career households is rising rapidly, and is likely to continue to do so for the remainder of the century. Such households must reside in areas that provide suitable employment opportunities within a commuting radius governed in part by increasing energy costs.

There are two reasons why change in this factor is likely to increase, not decrease, the overall level of mobility, and both reasons suggest that metropolitan areas will be the preferred destination of the majority of dual-career families. First, a disproportionate number of these families are now located in places that were chosen on the basis of employment opportunities and income levels for only one of the now two-career orientations. Another high proportion of these families are now located not in places of career employment, but in places of higher education institutions that provide necessary training for career entry. Both situations are more likely than not to require mobility to achieve satisfactory employment for both adult members of the household, if career aspirations are to be met. These places are more likely to be metropolitan than nonmetropolitan.

The second reason is that the size of the demographic pool from which dual-career families are drawn is continuing to increase as a result of the postwar baby boom. The size of the entry-level and mid-career populations will not stabilize and begin to decline until the exits from these populations exceed the entries. For decades, the exits will be drawn from the relatively low-birth cohorts of the 1930–45 period, while the entries are drawn from the 1945–65 period. Continuation of depressed economic conditions with high inflation will also contribute to the growth of dual-income households, as families find ways to insure that median family income at least keeps pace with inflation to maintain learned and preferred expenditure patterns.

It may also well be the case, however, that after an initial impetus to high rates of mobility in the aggregate, this factor could depress repeat migration and thereby depress later aggregate mobility. As households settle in locations where both members have secured employment that satisfies their career aspirations, maintenance of both careers could function to inhibit severely future movement in response to career opportunities for either (but not both) of the members of the household.

Career-oriented mobility is likely to increase apart from the questions of dual careers, again as the entry- and mid-level ranks swell with the increasing size of the baby boom cohorts. At the same time, this demographic effect will be dampened by the reduction in education-related mobility. Many have noted that a portion of the growth of nonmetropolitan counties in the past decade is due to enrollment growth at colleges and universities located in these counties. These enrollments have peaked and will decline nationally, as the comparatively very low birth cohorts of the late 1960s and particularly the 1970s reach college age. Regional effects of past migration patterns will dominate and to some extent obscure this effect, as enrollments continue to increase well into the decade in those regions that grew dramatically through migration in the 1960s and 1970s, while past outmigration will exacerbate the effects of fertility-induced enrollment declines in other regions.

Similarly, the rate of growth of early retirement populations will decline, both as an effect of the lower birth rates in the 1930s, and as a result of the emergent trend toward later retirements. This latter trend is influenced by worsening economic conditions, high inflation that makes it more difficult to make a decision to accept and subsist on a fixed retirement income, and increasing uncertainty over the maintenance of national Social Security and other pension programs, producing forces that discourage early retirement and encourage continued labor force participation.

These demographic effects interact intimately with economic conditions. Considered apart from these conditions, it would seem that the removal or lessening of forces known to have been instrumental in nonmetropolitan growth in the past decade would suggest a reduction in these growth rates in the 1980s and perhaps throughout the remainder of the century. Declining educational enrollments in nonmetropolitan colleges and universities, partially offset by increasing female enrollment ratios, are the most obvious and most certain factor. A gradual lessening of retirement-aged mobility is equally certain demographically, although less certain as a result of economic conditions. Continuation of depressed economic conditions may retard the metropolitan-bound migration of emerging dual-career families, because the rapid growth of professional and other service industries in nonmetropolitan areas may provide more entry-level opportunities for the delayed-entry member of these couples than the more stagnant economies of metropolitan areas may provide more entry-level opportunities for the delayed-entry member of these couples than the more stagnant economies of metropolitan centers, where competition for those positions is more severe in any event.

Patterns of regional redistribution provide part of the context and part of the force underlying metropolitan-nonmetropolitan deconcentration, and consequently provide a fourth consideration suggesting that rural and nonmetropolitan places will fare less badly than larger urban centers in the decade. In order to argue at the national level that the constraints of the 1980s would favor metropolitan centers, it would also be necessary to argue that present patterns of regional redistribution would be significantly affected by these constraints. Much of the westward and southward movement of the past decade has been to states and regions characterized by exceptionally low population densities. Rural counties that had for decades experienced outmigration became the destinations of inter- as well as intraregional migrants. Several of the largest western and southern metropolitan centers that accounted for virtually all of the growth of these regions in the 1950s and 1960s became net exporters of population in the 1970s. The deconcentration trend at the national level is intimately bound up with the regional redistribution trends. Those latter trends are likely to accelerate in the 1980s: toward climates less demanding of increasing home heating costs; toward regions in closer proximity to outdoor recreation opportunities;

toward places less vulnerable to the increasingly noxious disamenities of the older industrial parts of the country; toward what economic expansion is taking place; and away from centers of stagnation and decline.

Finally, the role of values and of changing residential perferences will remain active, although again conditioned by the economic context of employment and mobility. The innovators and early adopters in the diffusion of the idea of relocation to smaller sized places have already moved there, in the past decade. They will remain, to the extent that continued employment permits them to do so. The bulk of the population that constitutes the pool from which urban-to-rural migrants may be drawn has yet to make this move. Their reluctance to do so seems predicated more on the availability of incomes competitive with their present metropolitan incomes than any other factor [8], and secondarily on their ability to locate proximate to medium-sized metropolitan centers [17]. If the constraints of the early 1980s disadvantage nonmetropolitan locations less than metropolitan centers, the values factor must be expected to accelerate the present deconcentration trends. But just as rural retention of recent migrants is conditioned by the continued availability of employment [9], so too is future movement of employed metropolitan residents to nonmetropolitan areas dependent on the continued employment expansion of these areas [36].

POLICIES FOR AN ENDURING RURAL LIFE

The structural impediments to migration from metropolitan to nonmetropolitan areas were removed gradually over a period of several decades. Rural development programs, broadly conceived, have played a significant role in these processes of structural change, although it is probably impossible to separate quantitatively the role of that factor from the roles played by the other two major actors in the process—cooperatives and commercial enterprises [22]. To argue that the turnaround has taken place in large part because of structural convergence between urban and rural areas is the same as saying that differentials in social overhead have diminished over the decades [31]. One must go back at least to 1892 to find the beginnings of that convergence, with the studies in road construction and maintenance conducted by the U.S. Department of Agriculture, and to 1896, with the provision of free rural mail delivery. Around the same time, government joined with cooperatives and private enterprises to provide rural telephone services, and in 1908, President Theodore Roosevelt convened the Country Life Commission to secure "the necessary knowledge of the actual conditions of life in the open country" (quoted in Knapp [22:111]).

Over the next several decades, these and other legislation led to the creation and development of rural infrastructure: electrification, water and sewage systems, telephone service, improved all-weather roads, mail delivery, and, more recently, four-lane divided highways, community antenna and cable television systems, and decentralized retail and service facilities. The period from 1961–72 witnessed an acceleration of nonagricultural rural development legislation that was in many cases explicitly designed to stem the flow of migrants from rural to urban areas and to provide for a more rewarding quality of life in rural areas. Many of the necessary changes to achieve these results had, of course, come about and were just coming to fruition during this same period, so that this recent flurry of rural legislation can be credited with no more than a facilitating role in the migration turnaround.

If rural areas were in the process of converging on the infrastructure levels of large urban areas throughout the early and middle decades of this century, why was there such a long time lag while rural outmigration continued and even accelerated? Three reasons suggest the explanation for this lag.

1. The release of labor from agriculture with mechanization and consolidation dwarfed any countervailing processes that were going on in the countryside for decades. Although agricultural employment has continued to decline, it has ceased to be a statistically significant component of total rural-urban population movements.
2. A threshold effect was in operation, demanding that a certain level of equivalence between urban and rural areas be reached before large-scale transferences of population and economic activities could occur. Failure to achieve this threshold is held to be the reason why other developed countries, such as Spain, Greece, Finland and Poland, have not yet experienced the migration turnaround.
3. Nonmetropolitan inmigration and retention of prior residents could not become the dominant trends until changes had taken place in the total economy and in the large urban centers that would permit pervasive deconcentration of economic activities.

Copp suggests that "one of the objectives of rural development should be to widen people's range of choices" [10:520]. Rural development and other policies have achieved exactly this over the long term. That widened range of choices of rural residents is seen in the decreased nonmetropolitan outmigration component of the migration turnaround, as well as in the increased nonmetropolitan inmigration.

Rural Development Programs in the 1980s

The climate of legislative opinion and policy formulation is likely to be less sympathetic toward rural development in the present and the future than in the past. This is manifest in the proposed reductions in the programs of the Farmers Home Administration and Economic Development Administration, two agencies charged with the disbursement of the bulk of federal rural development funds. But it is also manifest, and somewhat surprisingly so, in the tone and content of the debate over the farm bill, in the lessened cooperation between Senators and Congressmen from farm states in voting for compromises in commodity support programs.

It is likely to become increasingly evident as micropolitan places (that is, smaller metropolitan centers as well as all nonmetropolitan territory) continue to gain population and employment at the expense of large metropolitan centers. There may be a great and interminable debate over whether growth is in fact developmental, but there is general recognition that growth is better than decline. This outlook is implicit in the use of such phrases as "revitalization," "rebirth," and "rural renaissance." The biological metaphor identifying growth and health has always been strong, and the cancer metaphor has somehow never really caught on. Consequently, an argument such as that recently advanced by the Democratic Study Group of the U.S. House of Representatives to the effect that the Reagen Administration's cuts in rural programs are coming "at precisely the time that rural areas most need these programs—when they are growing" is quite likely to fall on unsympathetic ears [14, p. 3].

Pleas for continued infrastructure development will receive the least sympathetic hearing. Past programs have been strongly oriented toward infrastructure, and it must be recognized that they have been largely successful, perhaps now embarrassingly so. Roads have been built, paved, widened, and divided. Telecommunications systems are in place and functioning. Many a modern small town water and sewer system will be flowing for decades as overburdened and technologically obsolete systems in larger cities drip away. Access to community services in small towns and cities is frequently easier and less intimidating than in large metropolitan areas. Nothing in cutbacks implemented and proposed by the current Administration would direct that this social overhead be dismantled, ripped up, or thrown out. What was gained in the past is not being lost, although maintenance of the infrastructure will become increasingly burdensome in the context of federal, state, and local budget reductions.

Where scale and density effects are significant for maintenance costs, rural lobbyists might well profit by identifying these areas and presenting their case for representation. But it may be more effective in the long run to attempt to move away from the argument for infrastructure entirely, and toward the development of arguments based in equity and impact mitigation.

Current and past equity arguments take the form of rural proportionality (either in terms of population or income) and seek to persuade that the rural poor should receive special consideration because they are rural. It is time to move away from this perspective, as it becomes increasingly difficult to demonstrate that the rural poor are somehow more deserving than the urban poor (and, indeed, as the attention to poverty itself diminishes at the federal and state levels). Arguments that focus on the distribution of the benefits of growth, on the negative externalities of growth that are often visited upon the prior residents of an area, or on the residual concentrations of poverty and associated problems that are often exacerbated by the context of growth, will be less attended to at a time of systemwide stagnation than they might have been in times of systemic expansion.

Equity arguments that are predicated first on a recognition of the dependence on the national economy that Hobbs wrote of in the context of rural development [19:12, 16–17] and that Bender has documented in the Northern Great Plains [5], and second on the demonstration that some areas are more vulnerable to the new constraints of the 1980s than are others, are likely to be more effective. High interest rates impact some subregions of the nation more heavily than others. The benefits of higher energy prices accrue to a few resource-rich states while the costs are disproportionally visited upon the many resource-poor states. Areas that developed in response to the boom in long-distance automobile travel for recreation suffer as recreational areas closer to large metropolitan centers prosper.

With the full integration of rural areas into the national system, terms like rural, nonmetropolitan, and even micropolitan, have become inappropriate tools with which to approach policy formulation and legislative debates. To the extent that the areas designated by these terms seem to be prospering relative to large SMSAs, they may even become counterproductive tools. By redirecting the debate from place labels to activity patterns, and by seeking to identify differentials on the bases of the activity patterns that do in fact serve to distribute impacts of national changes to both places and peoples, the debate may become more persuasive, and the resultant policy may well more nearly correspond to the realities of our emerging postindustrial society.

In the current context of constraints, it is difficult to argue that the impacts of unanticipated growth merit more of a claim on the federal and state dollar than do the equally unanticipated impacts of decline. It is consequently difficult to demonstrate that the micropolitan impacts of contemporary patterns of population and economic redistribution are more severe than are the metropolitan impacts. Corresponding to the suggested emphasis away from infrastructure-oriented policy, the debate should move away from place-oriented policy altogether. The focus should be on human resources as they are impacted by the patterns of the new decade, quite apart from where those human resources reside. A period of benign neglect lies ahead for the nonagricultural portion of past rural development programs. It is doubtful that that tendency can be effectively combatted by a renewed lobbying for a strict proportionality for the residents of rural areas merely because they are rural and consequently are entitled to "their share."

Old political coalitions based on the geographic distribution of constituencies have persisted, as our social system organized itself anew on the basis of activities rather than on the basis of places. These old area coalitions led to emphases on place and infrastructure that were mutually reinforcing in the formation of rural development policy, and now may become mutually counterproductive. A new emphasis on human resources, oriented not by place but by activity patterns, can become the basis for the formation of new coalitions to combat the ways in which the current Administration is turning away from the historic role of the federal government in providing a buffer against the vicissitudes of time, fortune, and social location. The beneficiaries of such a change in strategy would be the people, neither rural nor urban, nonmetropolitan nor metropolitan, who are now in the process of losing their representation in the debate. Mere reminders of their type of residential location are unlikely to restore that representation.

ACKNOWLEDGMENTS

This is a revised combination of testimony presented before the President's Commission for a National Agenda for the Eighties, Washington, D.C., June 3, 1980, and of papers presented at the Population Association of America Annual Meetings, Washington, D.C., March 26–28, 1981, and the Southern Regional Demographic Group Annual Meetings, Little Rock, Arkansas, October 14–16, 1981. Support for preparation of the paper was provided by Project 0354, College of Agriculture Research Center, Washington State University, a contributing project to Western Regional Project W-118R. This is Scientific Paper No. 6111.

I wish to thank the following colleagues, critics, and discussants who have read and commented on various sections of this paper: Calvin

Beale, William R. Catton, Jr., Don A. Dillman, Sally Findley, Richard Forstall, William Lassey, and David Sly. I am particularly indebted to my colleague, Annabel Kirschner Cook, for insights provided during our frequent conversations on the issues and trends governing future nonmetropolitan growth.

REFERENCES

1. Alonso, William, "Urban Zero Population Growth," *Daedalus,* 102, Fall 1973, pp. 191–206.
2. Beale, Calvin L., "The Revival of Population Growth in Nonmetropolitan America," Economic Research Service Publication ERS-605, Washington, D.C.: U.S. Department of Agriculture, 1975.
3. ______, "The Changing Nature of Rural Employment," in David L. Brown and John M. Wardwell, eds., *New Directions in Urban-Rural Migration,* New York: Academic Press, 1980, pp. 37–49.
4. Bealer, Robert C., Fern K. Willits, and William P. Kuvlesky, "The Meaning of Rurality in American Society," *Rural Sociology,* 30, September 1980, pp. 255–266.
5. Bender, Lloyd D., "The Effect of Trends in Economic Structures on Population Change in Rural Areas," in David L. Brown and John M. Wardwell, eds., *New Directions in Urban-Rural Migration,* New York: Academic Press, 1980, pp. 137–162.
6. Berry, Brian J. L. and Donald C. Dahmann, "Population Redistribution in the United States in the 1970s," in Brian J. L. Berry and Lester P. Silverman, eds., *Population Redistribution and Public Policy,* Washington, D.C.: National Academy of Sciences, 1980, pp. 8–49.
7. Berry, Brian J. L. and John D. Kasarda, *Contemporary Urban Ecology,* New York: Macmillan, 1977.
8. Carpenter, Edwin H., "The Potential for Population Dispersal: A Closer Look at Residential Preferences," *Rural Sociology,* 31, March 1977, pp. 64–73.
9. Carpenter, Edwin H., "Retention of Metropolitan-to-Nonmetropolitan Labor-Force Migrants," in David L. Brown and John M. Wardwell, eds., *New Directions in Urban-Rural Migration,* New York: Academic Press, 1980, pp. 213–227.
10. Copp, James H., "Rural Sociology and Rural Development," *Rural Sociology,* 37, December 1972, pp. 515–533.
11. Dailey, George H. Jr. and Rex R. Campbell, "The Ozark-Ouachita Uplands: Growth and Consequences," in David L. Brown and John M. Wardwell, eds., *New Directions in Urban-Rural Migration,* New York: Academic Press, 1980, pp. 233–265.
12. Deavers, Kenneth L. and David L. Brown, "The Rural Population Turnaround: Research and National Public Policy," in David L. Brown and John M. Wardwell, eds., *New Directions in Urban-Rural Migration,* New York: Academic Press, 1980, pp. 51–66.
13. DeJong, Gordon F., "Residential Preferences and Migration," *Demography,* 14, May 1977, pp. 169–178.
14. Democratic Study Group, "Impact of the Reagan Budget on Rural and Small Town America," Washington, D.C.: U.S. House of Representatives, No. 97–20, 1981.
15. Downs, Anthony, "The Automotive Population Explosion," *Traffic Quarterly,* 33, July 1979, pp. 347–362.
16. Fuguitt, Glenn V. and Stephen J. Tordella, "Elderly Net Migration," *Research on Aging,* 2, June 1980, pp. 191–204.
17. Fuguitt, Glenn V. and James J. Zuiches, "Residential Preferences and Population Distribution," *Demography,* 12, August 1975, pp. 491–504.

18. Hawley, Amos H., *Urban Society: An Ecological Approach,* New York: Ronald Press, 1971.
19. Hobbs, Daryl J., "Rural Development: Intentions and Consequences," *Rural Sociology,* 45, Spring 1980, pp. 7–25.
20. Hoch, Irving, "Energy and Location," in Amos H. Hawley and Sara Mills Maize, eds., *Nonmetropolitan America in Transition,* Chapel Hill, N.C.: University of North Carolina Press, 1981.
21. Kasarda, John D., "The Implications of Contemporary Distribution Trends for National Urban Policy," *Social Science Quarterly,* 61, December 1980, pp. 373–400.
22. Knapp, Joseph G., *The Rise of American Cooperative Enterprise, 1620–1920,* Danville, Ill.: Interstate Printers and Publishers, Inc., 1969.
23. Lichter, Daniel T. and Glenn V. Fuguitt, "Demographic Response to Transportation Innovation: The Case of The Interstate Highway," *Social Forces,* 59, December 1980, pp. 492–512.
24. Long, John F., *Population Deconcentration in the United States,* Washington, D.C.: U.S. Bureau of the Census, 1982.
25. Long, Larry H. and Diana DeAre, "Migration to Nonmetropolitan Areas: Appraising the Trend and Reasons for Moving," *Special Demographic Analyses,* 80–2, November 1980, Washington, D.C.: U.S. Bureau of the Census.
26. McCarthy, Kevin F. and Peter A. Morrison, "The Changing Demographic and Economic Structure of Nonmetropolitan Areas in the United States," Santa Monica, Calif.: Rand Corp., 1979.
27. Morrison, Peter A., "Chronic Movers and the Future Redistribution of Population," *Demography,* 8, May 1971, pp. 171–184.
28. Ploch, Louis A., "Effects of Turnaround Migration on Community Structure in Maine," in David L. Brown and John M. Wardwell, eds., *New Directions in Urban-Rural Migration,* New York: Academic Press, 1980, pp. 291–311.
29. Stevens, Joe B., "The Demand for Public Goods as a Factor in the Nonmetropolitan Migration Turnaround," in David L. Brown and John M. Wardwell, eds., *New Directions in Urban-Rural Migration,* New York: Academic Press, 1980, pp. 115–135.
30. Stinner, William F. and Michael B. Toney, "Migrant-Native Differences in Social Background and Community Satisfaction in Nonmetropolitan Utah Communities," in David L. Brown and John M. Wardwell, eds., *New Directions in Urban-Rural Migration,* New York: Academic Press, 1980, pp. 313–331.
31. Tweeten, Luther and George L. Brinkman, *Micropolitan Development,* Ames, Iowa: Iowa State University Press, 1976.
32. Vining, Daniel R. Jr. and Thomas Kontuly, "Population Dispersal from Major Metropolitan Regions: An International Comparison," *International Regional Science Review,* 3, January 1978, pp. 49–73.
33. Wardwell, John M. "Equilibrium and Change in Nonmetropolitan Growth," *Rural Sociology,* 42, Summer 1977, pp. 156–179.
34. ———, "Toward a Theory of Urban-Rural Migration in the Developed World," in David L. Brown and John M. Wardwell, eds., *New Directions in Urban-Rural Migration,* New York: Academic Press, 1980, pp. 71–114.
35. Wardwell, John M. and David L. Brown, "Population Redistribution in the United States During the 1970s," in David L. Brown and John M. Wardwell, eds., *New Directions in Urban-Rural Migration,* New York: Academic Press, 1980, pp. 5–35.
36. Wardwell, John M. and C. Jack Gilchrist, "The Distribution of Population and Energy in Nonmetropolitan Areas," *Social Science Quarterly,* 61, December 1980, pp. 567–580.

37. ______, "Employment Deconcentration in the Nonmetropolitan Migration Turnaround," *Demography,* 17, May 1980, pp. 145–158.
38. Williams, James D. and David Byron McMillen, "Migration Decisionmaking Among Nonmetropolitan-Bound Migrants," in David L. Brown and John M. Wardwell, eds., *New Directions in Urban-Rural Migration,* New York: Academic Press, 1980, pp. 189–211.
39. Willets, Fern K. and Robert C. Bealer, "An Evaluation of a Composite Definition of 'Rurality'," *Rural Sociology,* 32, June 1967, pp. 165–177.
40. Zelinsky, Wilbur, "Is Nonmetropolitan America Being Repopulated?" *Demography,* 15, February 1978, pp. 12–39.
41. Zuiches, James J., "Residential Preferences in Migration Theory," in David L. Brown and John M. Wardwell, eds., *New Directions in Urban-Rural Migration,* New York: Academic Press, 1980, pp. 163–188.
42. Zuiches, James J. and Jon H. Rieger, "Size of Place Preferences and Life Cycle Migration: A Cohort Comparison," *Rural Sociology,* 43, Winter 1978, pp. 618–633.

Chapter IV

POPULATION DISPERSAL FROM CORE REGIONS:

A DESCRIPTION AND TENTATIVE EXPLANATION OF THE PATTERNS IN TWENTY-ONE COUNTRIES

Daniel R. Vining, Jr., Robert L. Pallone,
Han Lin Li and Chung Hsin Yang

ABSTRACT

Our thesis is that, in the developed world at least, the century-long migration toward the high-density core regions is over. To establish this thesis, internal migration statistics for 21 countries are examined, covering the period 1950–78. Of these 21 countries, five categories are distinguished:

1. The countries of Northwest Europe—Belgium, Denmark, France, the Netherlands, West Germany—in which there is moderate net outmigration from the core regions.
2. The countries of North America—Canada, the United States—in which there is quite substantial net outmigration from the core regions.

3. Countries on the periphery of West Europe—Finland, Iceland, Italy, Norway, Spain, Sweden, the United Kingdom, and including Japan—in which there was an increase in net migration toward the core regions between the 1950s and the 1960s, with the largest net flows occurring at the beginning and end of this last decade, followed by a sharp decline in the 1970s, though not to the point where a sustained net flow of population away from these regions has been observed.
4. The countries of East Europe—Czechoslovakia, East Germany, Hungary, Poland—in which net migration toward the core regions, though moderate, has yet to show a systematic decline.
5. Two advanced developing countries in East Asia—Taiwan, South Korea—in which net migration toward the core regions is both very large and possibly still increasing.

The countries of the first three categories belong to the developed world, in which economies of further agglomeration in the core regions no longer exist, according to the hypothesis put forward in the second half of this chapter. The distinguishing feature of the countries in the first two categories is that their less urbanized, peripheral regions offer sites for urban and industrial development that are competitive with those of the core regions. Population losses from these peripheral regions in the past, it is conjectured, were due to the agglomeration advantages of the more densely populated core regions—advantages that now appear to be much weaker, if not absent altogether.

In contrast, the peripheral regions of the third category countries, according to the tentative hypothesis outlined here, do not offer competitive sites for industrial and urban development because of fundamental deficiencies in physical geography. Thus, despite the disappearance of the agglomeration advantages of the core regions, a sustained net flow of population away from these regions has yet to be observed.

Finally, the countries of the fourth and fifth categories, according to our hypothesis, are those in which diseconomies of further agglomeration in the core regions have yet to appear, due to a lower level of economic development. What distinguishes these last two categories is the strong state policies of decentralization in the former (East Europe), which seem to have successfully avoided the very large and growing net flow of population toward the core regions observed for the latter (South Korea and Taiwan), where such policies, though existent, are still subservient to national economic growth policies and are consequently much weaker.

INTRODUCTION

[U]rban growth is essentially a great-city growth. [34:448]

[O]nce a city is larger than any other in its country, this mere fact gives it an impetus to grow that cannot affect any other city, and it draws away from all of them in character as well as in size. [15:227]

> The evident tendency of people to congregate in larger and larger cities represents an attraction of people for people that turns out to have a mathematical as well as a merely verbal resemblance to Newton's law of gravitation. [29:471]

> The macro-locational tendency throughout the world is for industrial regions already large and powerful to attract still more population, and thus the industrial population of the world has become concentrated in a few regions. [7:195]

> The historical evidence in both the developing and the developed economies indicates that the concentration of population in the big cities is a strong and pervasive trend. [3:24]

> Steady urbanization *in situ,* equal in rate from region to region, and without large-scale accelerating internal migrations, would create few serious problems, if any. But the reality in nearly all countries seems to be the polarized growth pattern of the urban system with the background of an increasing regional imbalance. Rapid urbanization has distorted the traditional network and hierarchy of settlement. Unco-ordinated, often excessive, expansion of the largest cities and leading urban agglomerations is accompanied by stagnation of most of the old regional centres and medium-sized and smaller towns. By rapid out-migration, peripheral and less developed rural areas are losing their main potential, a young and active labour force. [27:39]

> The demographic history of most countries in this century suggests a strong tendency for population to cluster. This has been especially true in the period since the advent of industrialization and the decline of the agricultural sector. . . . Generally, not only have urban populations grown substantially more rapidly than populations as a whole, but the most rapid urban growth has been in the largest cities. [9:258]

> Different parts of the world are shrinking at different rates, . . . mainly to the advantage of large settlements, which are benefiting from the cumulative advantages of early growth. . . the main consequence of these trends is centralization—the growth of big cities . . . [8:238]

These passages express *the* dominant paradigm in spatial demography—we shall call it (after Alexandersson and Falk [1]) the "concentration paradigm." There is growing evidence, however, that the "macro-locational tendency" toward an ever-increasing concentration of population in the core regions of the developed world, at least, is near exhaustion. The objective of this chapter is to document that fact. We defer to other scholars the task of explanation, though we do advance a tentative explanation to explain the variations observed. The important business now, however, is to establish that the concentration paradigm no longer provides an accurate model of the developed world's population geography.

The data used to demonstrate this thesis are internal migration statistics showing the number of persons moving between the major administrative subdivisions of 21 countries: Belgium, Canada, Czechoslovakia, Denmark, East Germany, Finland, France, Hungary, Iceland, Italy, Japan, the Netherlands, Norway, Poland, South Korea, Spain, Sweden, Taiwan, the United Kingdom, the United States, and West Germany. (Data sources are given with the Figures that follow.)

The core regions of a country are those regions that are economically and politically dominant; they contain the principal cities of the country and have traditionally experienced high rates of net inmigration from the other, less urbanized, peripheral regions. The identification of these regions poses little difficulty. Their areal extent, however, is subject to considerable controversy and disagreement. The regionalization problem, of course, remains unsolved in our field, and we do not intend to solve it here. To establish our thesis, however, it suffices to overbound the core regions to such an extent that no scholar would argue that the core regions are not fully contained within the overbounded regions. If the overbounded region shows declining net inmigration, then the "true" core region contained within it must also, unless there is net migration from the remainder of the overbounded region to the core's portion—a doubtful proposition in light of the strong decentralization tendencies within highly urbanized regions. We have therefore drawn very wide boundaries around the core regions in anticipation of the objection that the net flows away from them recorded here are simply an overspill of population beyond their conventionally defined boundaries. Moreover, to allay fears that the results are sensitive to the ways in which these regions are defined, we also show, wherever it is feasible to do so, net migration into the core regions for alternative definitions of these regions. These definitions—i.e., the constituent administrative subdivisions of the regions, and their principal cities—are given in Table IV.1.

It is a fact that the trends in immigration and in natural increase sometimes run counter to those in internal migration. This subject is taken up at several points in the chapter. Here, however, we wish to stress the fact that *within* the countries of the developed world, migration is no longer, on balance, toward the core regions.

A DESCRIPTION OF THE TRENDS

Among the countries of this study, it is useful to distinguish five categories:

1. The countries of Northwest Europe, whose core regions by and large have experienced a long-term decline in net inmigration since the 1950s and are now experiencing net outmigration to the peripheral regions.
2. The countries of North America (Canada and the United States), where the decline in net inmigration to the core regions has been more abrupt but has come recently to amount to very substantial net losses.

Table IV.1. Major Cities and Constituent Administrative Subdivisions of Core Regions as Shown in Figures IV.1, IV.2, IV.3, IV.4, IV.5

Country	*Core Region(s)*	*Major Cities*	*Constituent Administrative Subdivisions*
Belgium	Greater Brussels	Brussels	Brabant *province*
	North (Flanders Region and Brussels)	Brussels, Antwerp, Ghent	Greater Brussels *plus* Oost-Vlaanderen, West-Vlaanderen, Antwerpen, Limburg *provinces*
Canada	Central Region	Toronto, Montreal	Ontario, Quebec *provinces*
Czechoslovakia	Czech Republic Capital	Prague	Praha *city*
Denmark	Eastern Islands	Copenhagen	København og Frederiksberg, Københavns, Frederiksborg, Roskilde, Vestjaellands, Storstrøms, Bornholms *counties*
East Germany	Center	Berlin	Berlin, Cottbus, Frankfurt, Potsdam *districts*
	Southeast	Dresden, Leipzig	Karl-Marx-Stadt, Leipzig, Dresden, Halle *districts*
Finland	South	Helsinki, Tampere, Turku	Uudenmaan, Turun-Porin, Ahvenanmaa, Hämeen, Kymen *provinces*
France	Paris Region and Basin	Paris	Région Parisiènne, Picardie, Haute-Normandie, Champagne-Ardenne, Centre, Basse-Normandie, Bourgogne *regions*
Hungary	Central Industrial	Budapest	Budapest, Pest *counties*
Iceland	Southwest	Reykjavik	Reykjavíkursvæði, Reykjanessvæði *regions*

(continued)

Table IV.1. (Continued)

Country	*Core Region(s)*	*Major Cities*	*Constituent Administrative Subdivisions*
Italy	Northwest	Milan, Genoa, Turin	Piemonte, Valle d'Aosta, Liguria, Lombardia *regions*
	Lazio	Rome	Lazio *region*
Japan	Kanto	Tokyo, Yokohama	Ibaraki, Tochigi, Gumma, Saitama, Nagano, Yamanashi, Chiba, Tokyo, Kanagawa *prefectures*
	Tokai	Nagoya	Shizuoka, Aichi, Gifu, Mie *prefectures*
	Kinki	Osaka, Kobe, Kyoto	Shiga, Kyoto, Nara, Wakayama, Osaka, Hyogo *prefectures*
The Netherlands	Randstad	The Hague, Rotterdam, Utrecht, Amsterdam	Utrecht, Noord-Holland, Zuid-Holland *provinces*
	Total South	The Hague, Rotterdam, Utrecht, Amsterdam	Randstad region *plus* Zeeland, Noord-Brabant, Limburg, Gelderland, Overijssel *provinces*
Norway	Oslo	Oslo	Oslo, Akershus, Østfold, Vestfold *counties*
	Østlandet (East)	Oslo	Oslo Region *plus* Hedmark, Oppland, Buskerud, Telemark *counties*
Poland	Industrial	Katawice, Kraków	M. Krakow, Katowickie, Krakowskie, Opolskie *voivodships* (after 1975 reclassification: Nowy Sącz, Tarnów, Kraków, Bielsko-Biala, Katowice, Częstochowa, Opole *voivodships*)
	Warsaw	Warsaw	M. st. Warszawa, Warszawskie *voivodships* (after 1975 reclassification: Warszawa, Siedlce, Ostrolęka, Ciechanów, Plock *voivodships*)
	Gdańsk	Gdańsk	Gdańskie *voivodship* (after 1975 reclassification: Elblag, Gdańsk *voivodships*)

South Korea	North	Seoul	Seoul *city*, Gyeongi, Kangwon *provinces*
Spain	Cataluña	Barcelona	Barcelona, Gerona, Lèrida, Tarragone *provinces*
	Valencia	Valencia	Alicante, Castellón, Valencia *provinces*
	Madrid	Madrid	Madrid *province*
	Vascongados y Navarra	Bilbao, San Sebastián	Viscaya, Navarra, Guipúzcoa, Alava *provinces*
Sweden	Stockholm and Central Regions	Stockholm, Uppsala, Västerås	Stockholm, Uppsala, Södermanlands, Östergötlands, Örebro, Västmanlands *counties*
	Western Metropolitan Region	Göteborg	Hallands, Göteborgs O Bohus, Älvsborgs, Skaraborgs *counties*
	Southern Metropolitan Region	Malmö	Blekinge, Kristianstads, Malmöhus *counties*
Taiwan	Capital	Taipei	Taipei *city*, Taipei *county*
	Kaohsiung	Kaohsiung	Kaohsiung *city*, Kaohsiung *county*
United States	Industrial Heartland	New York, Chicago, Philadelphia, Detroit, Boston, Cleveland	Maine, Vermont, New Hampshire, Massachusetts, Connecticut, Rhode Island, New York, New Jersey, Pennsylvania, Ohio, Indiana, Illinois, Michigan, and Wisconsin *states*.
West Germany	Ruhr	Essen, Duisburg, Dortmund, Düsseldorf, Wuppertal, Cologne	Nordrhein Westfalen *state*
	Rhine Valley	cities of Rhur *plus* Frankfurt, Mannheim, Stuttgart	Ruhr Region *plus* Hessen, Rheinland-Pfalz, Baden Württemberg, Saarland *states*

3. The countries on the periphery of West Europe, including Japan, whose core regions experienced a sharp drop in net inmigration beginning around 1970, after stable or rising net inmigration between the 1950s and 1960s, although not to the point where a sustained net outmigration has been observed.
4. The countries of East Europe, in which net inmigration to the core regions, though moderate, has yet to exhibit a sustained decline.
5. Two rapidly developing countries of East Asia (South Korea and Taiwan), where net inmigration is both very large and showing no signs of abatement.

Northwest Europe

In the first category are the countries of Europe's most densely populated and heavily industrialized region—the Northwest, the core itself of Europe: Belgium, Denmark, France, the Netherlands, and West Germany. Figure IV.1 shows a gradual decline in net migration toward the core regions of these countries since the 1950s, and, with the exception of West Germany, where this net outmigration occurred much earlier, migration, on balance, away from these regions over much of the 1970s. In the case of the Netherlands, this net outmigration is more than just an extension of the Randstad region into the southeastern part of the Netherlands, which lies on the periphery of Europe's strongest urban field (the Rhine-Ruhr area), contrary to a claim by Blumenfeld [5:562]. Figure IV.1 shows the south as a whole to be losing population to the relatively isolated and rural north.

The Rhine-Ruhr itself, after decades of gaining population from the more rural states of West Germany in the north and southeast, is now losing population to these states. However, despite the Rhine-Ruhr's being the dominant urban field in Europe, it is, of all the core regions of Europe, paradoxically the least dominant within its own country. West Germany's peripheral regions to the north and southeast contain two of Germany's largest cities: Hamburg and Munich. This rather even distribution of cities across West Germany may explain the early flow of population away from its largest agglomeration in the Ruhr, though, of course, the distribution of cities itself must eventually be explained.

The core regions of the remaining three countries shown in Figure IV.1—those surrounding the capitals of Denmark (Copenhagen), Belgium (Brussels), and France (Paris)—are uncontroversial. They are clearly dominant and primate in character and are just as clearly overbounded. To the Brussels region we have added the entirety of the

Flanders region, which contains the other large city in Belgium: Antwerp. Migration is clearly away from this region and toward the less densely populated Wallonia—a reversal of the long-standing drift of the Belgian population toward the more densely populated northern half of the country [32]. In Denmark and France, the migration away from the capital regions toward Jutland and southern and western France, respectively, seems to have become an enduring trend.

North America

In the second category are the countries of North America: Canada and the United States. Of all the countries of the developed world, they present the most impressive case of deconcentration and core decline. In the United States, where there was roughly a balance in the migration of persons to and from its traditional heartland in the Northeast and Midwest during the 1960s, the 1970s witnessed net losses amounting to nearly 400,000 a year (Figure IV.2). The data used here include, unavoidably, net immigration from abroad; if data were available for internal migration alone (as they will be from the 1980 census sometime in 1983 or 1984), the net losses from the core to the West and South would almost certainly turn out to be much larger than the total net loss of population from the core shown in Figure IV.2, since one can reasonably assume net foreign immigration into the U.S. core to be positive and probably growing over the 1970s. In fact, the U.S. heartland, or core region, alone among the economic cores of the developed world, has experienced a significant and continuous net loss of population through internal migration to the rest of the country since at least World War II (Table IV.2). The 1970s, however, saw a severe acceleration in this erosion of population, to judge from the rapid fall in total net migration to this region.

Canada's core area has likewise experienced an impressive and wholly unanticipated decline in its attractive power over the rest of the national population. Ontario and Quebec, which together contain Canada's two major cities (Montreal and Toronto) and its capital (Ottawa), consistently drew population away from the rest of Canada throughout the 1960s. The beginning of the 1970s witnessed a precipitous decline in the rate of net inmigration to this region—a decline that persisted throughout the remainder of this decade and showed no signs of bottoming out (Figure IV.2). A large proportion of these net outflows are directed toward the West, as they are from the U.S. core, but even the Maritime provinces—Canada's most peripheral and traditional "lagging" region—are now gaining population at the expense of the core area.

Figure IV.1. Annual Net Internal Migration to Core Regions of West Germany, Belgium, the Netherlands, France, and Denmark

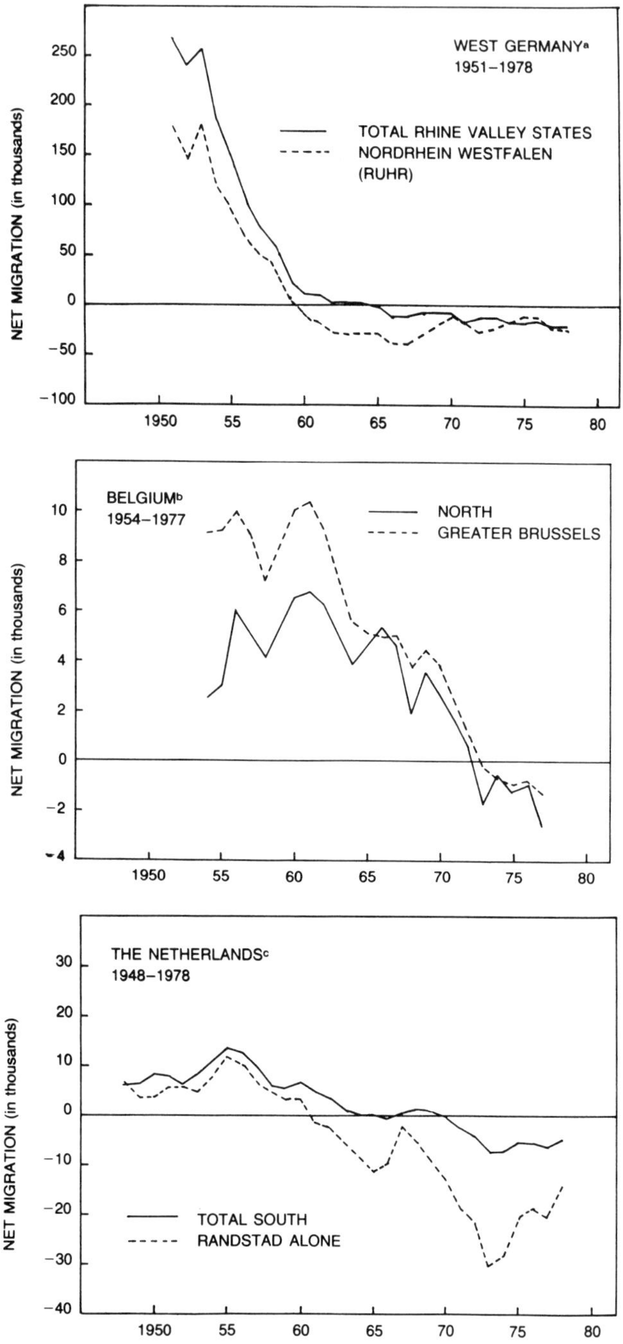

Fig IV.1. (Continued)

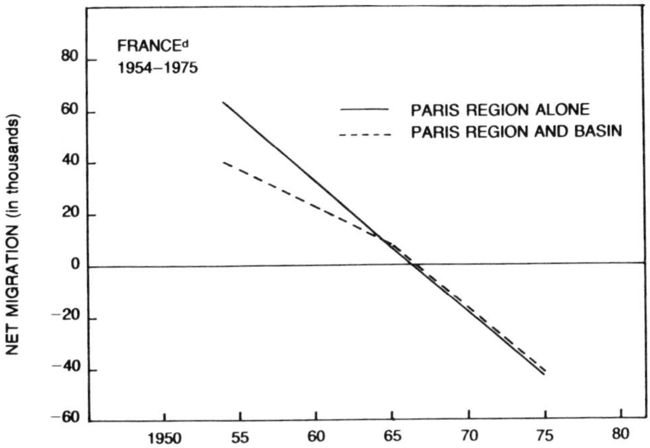

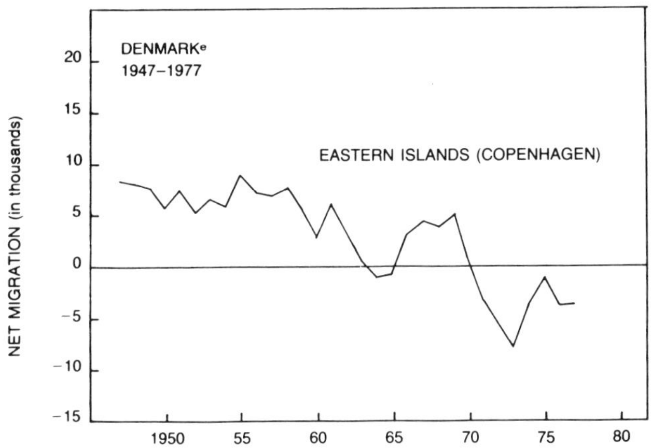

[a]Excludes net migration from West Berlin.
[b]1963 data not available.
[c]Net migration from Z. I. J. Polders and moves of unknown destination and origin omitted.
[d]Annual average net internal migration for 1954–62, 1962–68, and 1968–75, shown at midpoints of these periods.
[e]Excludes net migration from Greenland and the Faroe Islands

Sources: Belgium: "Annuaire Statistique de la Belgique," annual issues; Denmark: "Befolkningens Bevaegelser," annual issues; France: "Annuaire Statistique de la France," various issues; the Netherlands: "Statistiek van de Binnenlandse Migratie," biannual issues; West Germany: "Statistisches Jahrbuch," annual issues.

Figure IV.2. Annual Net Migration to the Core Region of the United States, 1959–78, and Annual Net Internal Migration to the Core Region of Canada, 1961–79

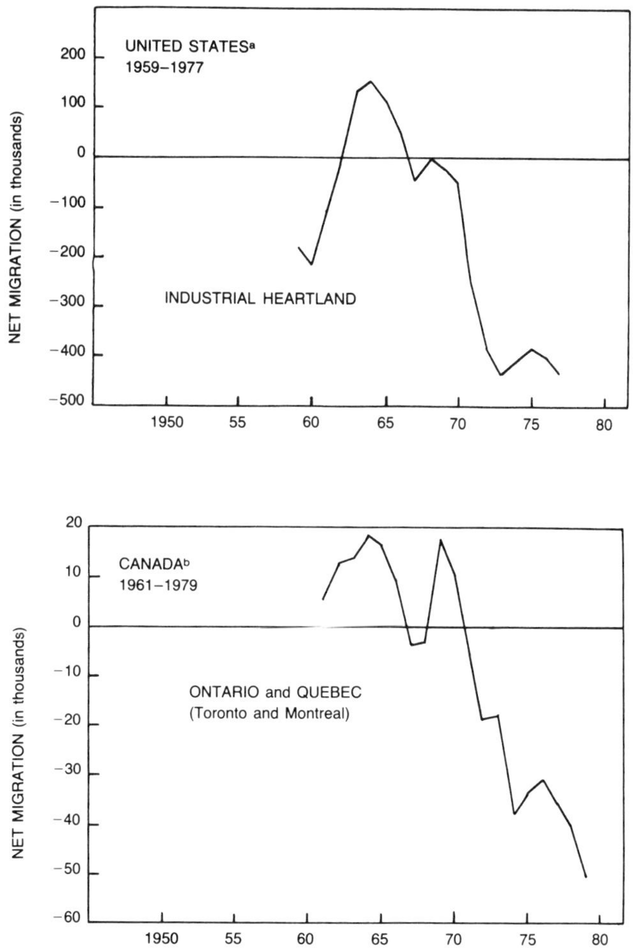

[a]Three-year moving averages, includes net movements of Armed Forces personnel from abroad.
[b]Fiscal years.
Sources: United States: unpublished data, U.S. Bureau of the Census; Canada: "International and Interprovincial Migration in Canada," various issues.

Table IV.2. Average Annual Net Migration to the U.S. Core Region from the Rest of the U.S., 1935–40, 1949–50, 1955–60, and 1965–70[a]

Period	*Eastern Part*[b]	*Western Part*[c]	*Total*
1935–40	– 29,326	8,341	– 20,985
1949–50	–135,295	–34,100	–169,395
1955–60	–109,479	–78,555	–188,034
1965–70	–144,456	–69,031	–213,487

[a]Based on persons one year old and over reporting on 1949 state of residence in the 1950 census and on persons five years old and over reporting on 1935, 1955, and 1965 state of residence in the 1940, 1960, and 1970 censuses.

[b]New England and Middle Atlantic Census Divisions.

[c]East North Central Census Division.

Sources: U.S. Bureau of the Census, *U.S. Census of Population: 1940,* Internal Migration 1935–1940, Color and Sex of Migrants, Washington, D.C.: U.S. Printing Office, 1943, p. 17; *U.S. Census of Population: 1950,* Vol. 4, *Special Reports,* Part 4, Chapter B, Population Mobility—States and Economic Areas, Washington, D.C.: U.S. Government Printing Office, 1956, pp. 4B–32—4B–33; *U.S. Census of Population: 1960, Subject Reports, Lifetime and Recent Migration,* Final Report PC(2)-2D, Washington, D.C.: U.S. Government Printing Office, 1963, p. 15; *U.S. Census of Population: 1970, Subject Reports, Mobility for States and the Nation,* Final Report PC(2)-2B, Washington, D.C.: U.S. Government Printing Office, 1973, p. 354.

Peripheral West Europe

The third category contains countries on the periphery of western Europe—Finland, Iceland, Italy, Norway, Spain, Sweden, and the United Kingdom—and one country outside of Europe itself—Japan. In these countries, a significant decline in net migration toward the core regions occurred after 1970, following very large net in-flows during the 1960s. However, this decline has not proceeded to the point where a sustained net out-flow is observed (Figure IV.3). Japan's Tokaido region, Italy's Northwest, Finland's South, Norway's Southeast, and Iceland's Southwest all experienced very rapid declines in net inmigration from the peripheral regions of these countries in the 1970s, to the extent that there is now in all a rough balance in migration between core and periphery. In none of these countries, however, has this decline turned into an actual net flow of any magnitude away from the core. Only Sweden's core shows a consistent net out-flow, and even here it is rather small.

Annual statistics showing net internal migration toward Great Britian's principal attractor region—the southern half of England—are unfortunately unavailable. What is available, however, are data showing net

Figure IV.3. Annual Net Internal Migration to the Core Regions of Japan, Italy, Sweden, Norway, the United Kingdom, Finland, Spain, and Iceland

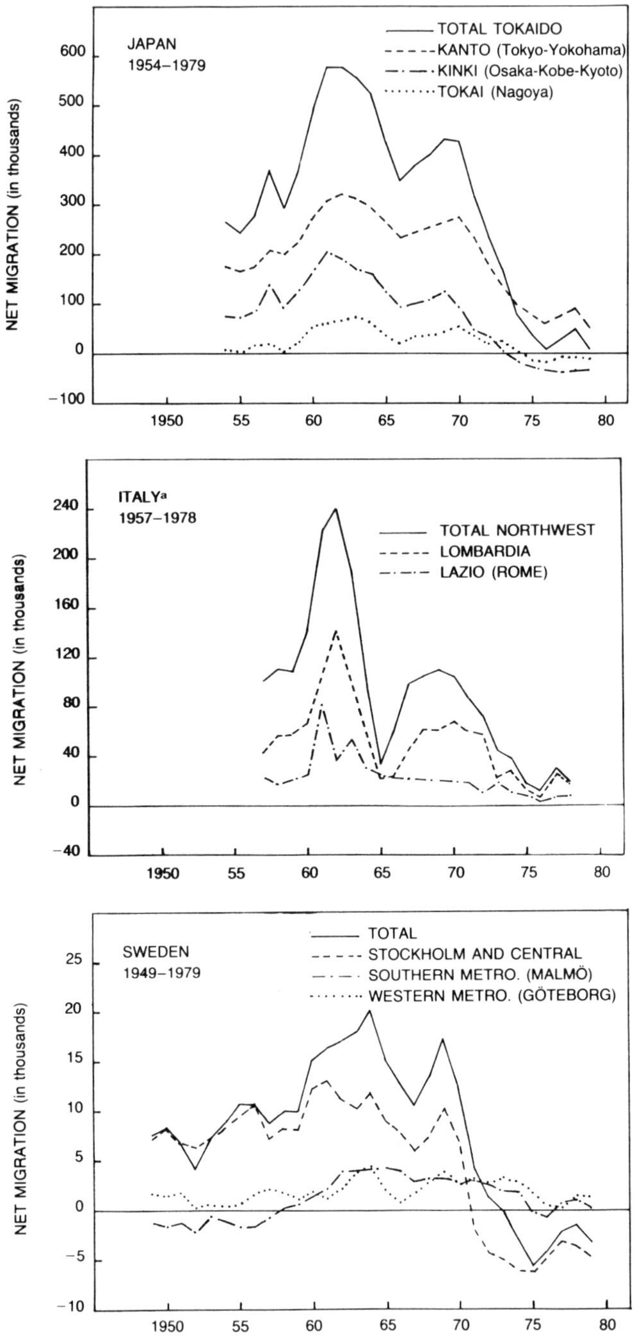

Fig. IV.3 (Continued)

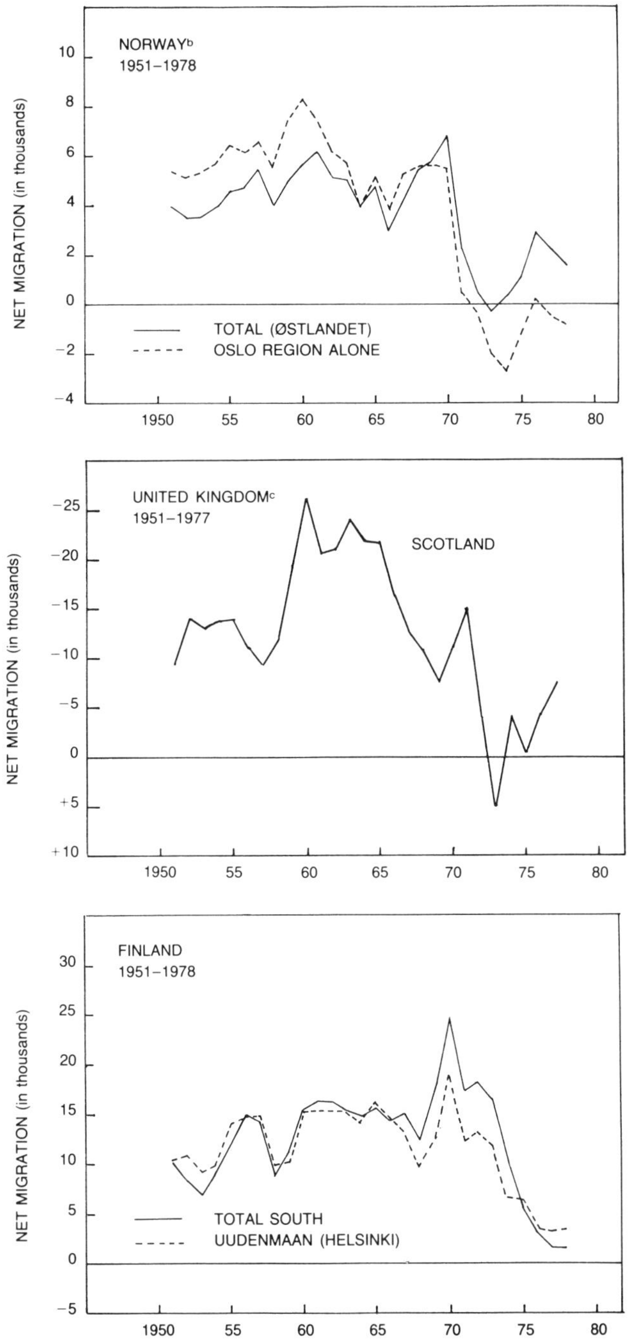

FIG. IV.3 (Continued)

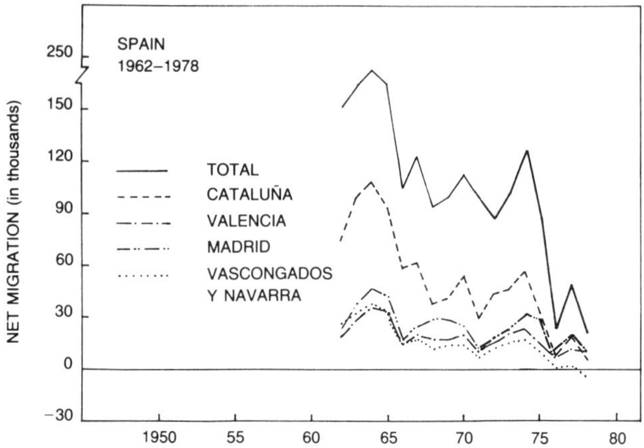

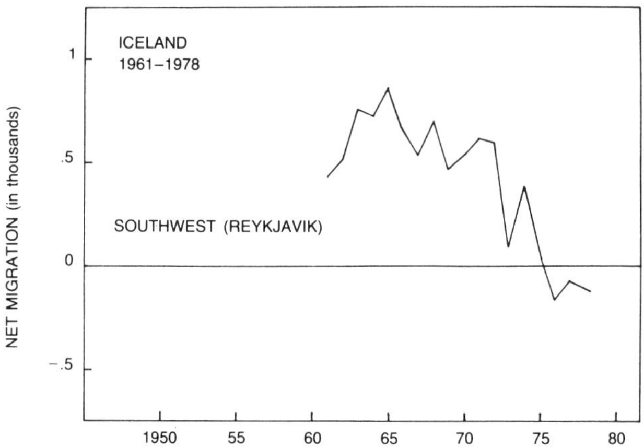

[a]"1961–1962 migration figures are inflated as a result of the abolishment in February 1961 of the 1939 law regulating internal migration. . . overreporting for these years . . . may be on the order of 20 percent" [25:398]. The 1978 data are provisional.

[b]Data for 1970 include migration occurring in previous years but not reported until the population census of 1970.

[c]Fiscal years.

Sources: Finland: "Suomen Tilastollinen Vuosikirja," annual issues; Iceland: unpublished data, Statistical Bureau of Iceland; Italy: "Annuario Statistico Italiano," annual issues; Japan: "Internal Migration in Japan," annual issues; Norway: "Flyttestatistikk," annual issues; Spain: "Anuario Estadístico de España," annual issues; Sweden: "Statistisk Årsbok för Sverige," "Befolkningsförändringar," and "Statistiska Meddelanden," various issues; United Kingdom: "Annual Report, Part 2—Population and Vital Statistics," Registrar General Scotland, various issues.

movements between Scotland and the rest of the United Kingdom, which should provide an approximate mirror image to net movements into the South, as net movements into marginal regions of other countries (e.g., northern Norway and Sweden, or Italy's Mezzogiorno) provide a mirror image for net movements into these countries' core regions (e.g., eastern Norway, southern Sweden, and northwestern Italy). Our figure for the United Kingdom therefore shows net migration into Scotland from the rest of the United Kingdom going from negative to positive along the vertical axis. The picture is of sharp decline in net outmigration from Scotland after 1970, the mirror image of which should be a decline in net inmigration to Great Britain's core region of southern England.

Spain is a difficult country to classify. Beginning around 1974, its principal attractor region—roughly the northeastern quadrant of the country—experienced a rapid drop in net inmigration. But it is difficult to call this a long-term trend, given the recession that struck the country around this time. The level of interregional migration as a whole has dropped very substantially in Spain, and this explains a large part of the decline in net migration toward its core regions. By contrast, the decline in net migration toward the core regions of the other countries of categories 1, 2, and 3 preceded the great economic contraction of 1974–75 and cannot be attributed to large declines in overall levels of interregional migration, which have remained steady or declined slightly. Moreover, net migration into northeastern Spain has fallen nowhere near zero. By the mid-1970s, however, all countries of category 3 except Spain had a rough balance in population flows between core and periphery, although there are reasons, discussed in the next section, for believing that sustained net flows away from the core regions of these countries will never be observed, in contrast to the countries of categories 1 and 2.

East Europe, Taiwan, and South Korea

The fourth and fifth categories contain countries that do not yet fully belong to the developed world, but are rapidly industrializing and possess living standards not far below those of West Europe, North America, and Japan. None of these countries—Czechoslovakia, East Germany, Hungary, Poland, South Korea, and Taiwan—show systematic and sustained declines in net inmigration toward their major cities and surrounding regions. In the countries of East Europe, net migration to the core regions is approximately stable. East Germany's Saxony region, which contains all of its major cities except Berlin and is the country's principal industrial district, has lost population to the rest of East Ger-

Figure IV.4. Annual Net Internal Migration to Core Regions of Poland, Hungary, East Germany, and Czechoslovakia

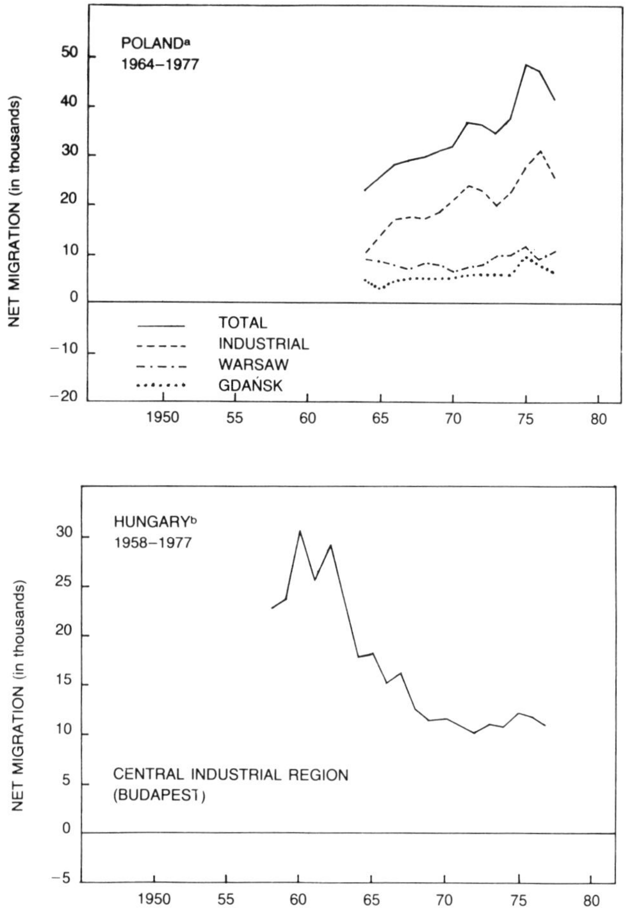

many since the early 1960s. As such the Saxony region resembles West Germany's own great industrial district, the Ruhr, where a similar depopulation has taken place over the past 20 years. But in contrast to the countries of West Europe, internal migration in East Germany remains focussed on the capital city, Berlin. In fact, net migration toward Berlin has actually drifted upward over the 1970s, as it has toward the large cities of Poland (Figure IV.4). Net flows into the capital of Czechoslovakia, Prague, have been approximately constant over the last decade and a half. Although net flows toward Hungary's capital, Budapest, fell

Fig. IV.4 (Continued)

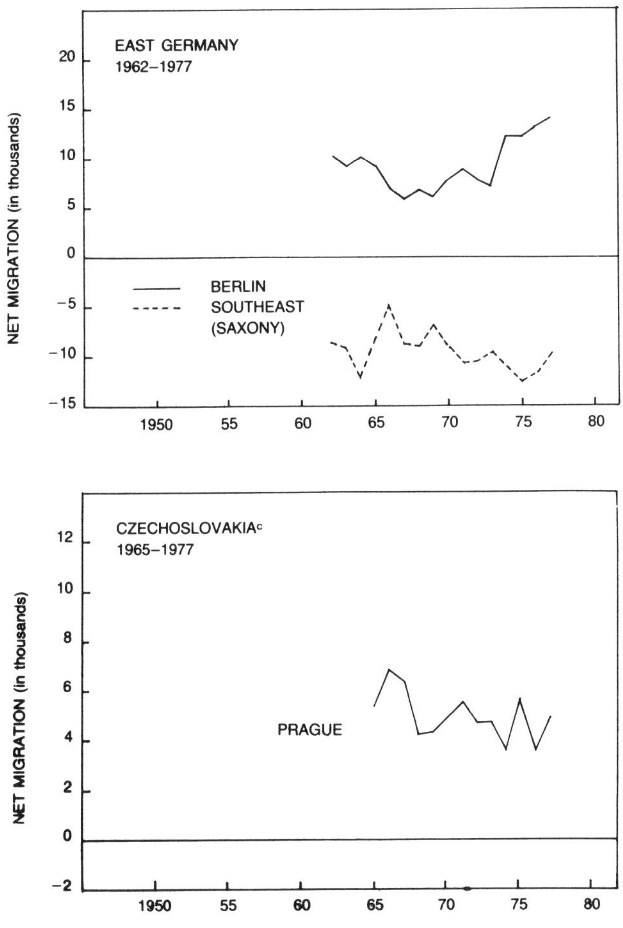

[a]Definitions of core regions changed slightly from 1975 onwards due to changes in administrative subdivisions.
[b]Temporary migrants excluded.
[c]Net foreign immigration included.
Sources: Czechoslovakia: "Statistická Ročenka Československé Socialistické Republiky," annual issues; East Germany: "Statistisches Jahrbuch," annual issues; Hungary: "Magyarorsźag Népesedése" and "Demográfiai Évkönyv," various issues; Poland: "Rocznik Demograficzny," annual issues.

over the 1960s, they fell nowhere near zero, and the 1970s have shown no continuation of that trend of decline (Figure IV.4).[1]

Finally, in our fifth category are two examples of countries in which net migration toward the core remains both very large and possibly even growing: Taiwan and South Korea (Figure IV.5).

Figure IV.5. Annual Net Internal Migration to Core Regions of Taiwan and South Korea

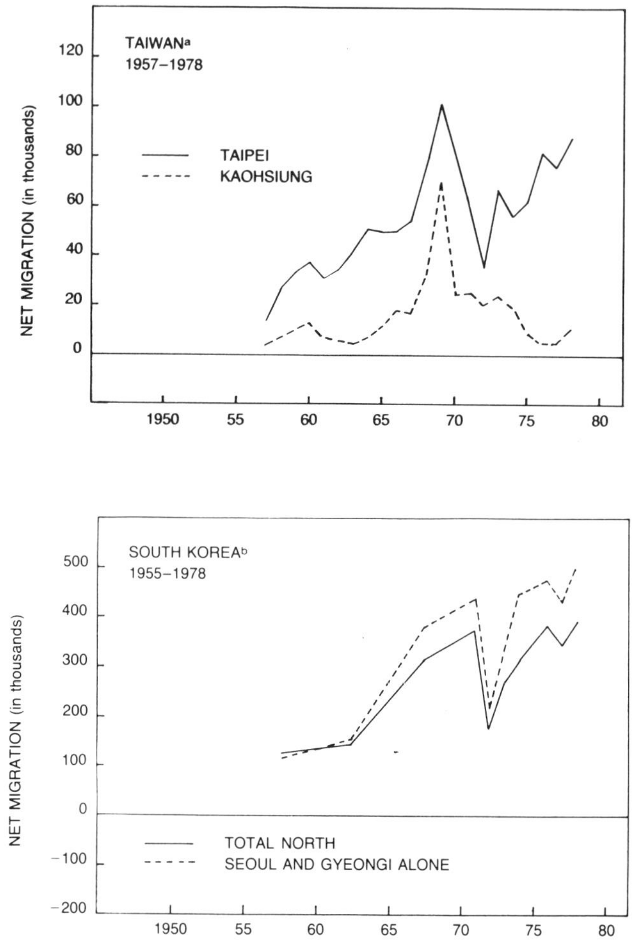

[a]Net foreign immigration included; very large net migration into the Taipei and Kaohsiung regions in 1969 is due to change in registration system to include moves of armed forces personnel.

[b]Net migration for 1975 unavailable; annual average net migration for 1955–60, 1961–65, and 1966–70, shown at midpoints of these periods.

Sources: South Korea: "Korea Statistical Yearbook," annual issues; Taiwan: private communication, Ministry of Interior, Taipei.

A TENTATIVE EXPLANATION OF THE PATTERNS OBSERVED

How can we explain the patterns observed in Figures IV.1–IV.5? We submit the following tentative "model" of these patterns.

During the phase of rapid industrialization, there is a universal tendency for a country's population to agglomerate in those regions containing the largest cities, for a movement to take place from the sparsely populated peripheral regions to the densely populated core regions. This movement is, in Weber's words, "mainly in obedience to economic causes. . . . Production increases with increasing density, and more particularly with increasing concentration" [34:417]. (For more modern statements of the economic theory of population concentration, see Alonso [2] and Mera [20].) With the exception of the United States, all countries in the sample were in this phase during the 1950s, and six countries (perhaps seven if we include Spain) continued to be in it in the 1970s. In the United States, there has been a significant net movement away from the core region over the entire post-World War II period, although the 1970s marked a severe acceleration in the rate of net loss.

As economic growth proceeds, however, the net returns to agglomerating ever more population and capital in the high-density core regions fall, eventually choking off the economic advantages of further agglomeration in the core (see the essays in Leven [17]). The point at which returns to location in core and periphery are equalized will come sooner, however, in countries whose peripheries offer competitive sites for urban and industrial development (that is, competitive in the absence of agglomeration economies) than in countries where these sites are inherently inferior. In fact, in some countries' peripheries, the deficiencies of physical geography may be so great as to virtually preclude urban and industrial development in any region but the core. What distinguishes the countries of categories 1 and 2 from those of category 3 is precisely the absence of physical barriers to urban and industrial development in the peripheries of the former and the existence of these barriers in the peripheries of the latter.

The countries of Northwest Europe have peripheries well endowed with sites for urban and industrial development. The climates, soils, and topographies of southwest France, Denmark's Jutland, northern Netherlands, or Germany's Bavaria—all predominantly rural areas that have previously experienced net outflows of population toward large cities in other regions—are all perfectly suitable for large-scale urban and industrial development.[2] As long as there were productivity advantages to agglomerating population and production in the core regions, these areas stagnated and in some cases actually suffered depopulation.

But once these agglomeration economies began to disappear and even to become diseconomies, there was a strong tendency to locate new productive facilities in the peripheral regions, because the sites for production in these regions were equal to those of the core regions, except perhaps for their location—a disadvantage largely neutralized through modern transportation and communication systems.[3] According to this theory, therefore, the gradual decline in migration toward the core regions of the countries of Northwest Europe (shown in Figure IV.1) merely reflects the concurrent gradual decline in the productivity advantages of agglomerating still more population and industry in the core regions, given the competitive sites that exist in the peripheries of these countries.

The peripheries of the North American countries not only do not possess site disadvantages vis-à-vis the core regions for urban and industrial location, but also, in many respects, have positive advantages of site, which perhaps explains the larger net losses from the cores of these countries to their peripheries than is observed from the cores of the category 1 countries. The provinces to the west of Ontario and Quebec do not suffer from any deficiencies of site but rather of location vis-à-vis the population centers of the United States and Canada. Indeed, the physical resources of these provinces (e.g., oil, wheat, timber) give them absolute site advantages over the eastern provinces, and the rapidly increasing value of these site-specific resources perhaps now exceed the agglomeration and locational advantages of the more densely populated eastern provinces. The fact that the rise in this site-specific value was largely concentrated during the 1970s may explain the abrupt change in the balance of net flows between Canada's core and the remainder of Canada, particularly the West.

The most striking case of a periphery having site-specific assets superior to those of the core is, of course, the United States. As Kirkpatrick Sale observes,

> . . . it is no accident that . . . the region that has grown the fastest, is that broad arc of states across the bottom of the country, from Southern California through Texas and the Deep South and down to Florida, that has been called the "Southern Rim." This is the area that has the most perfect climate in the nation—especially so since the advent of air-conditioning. . . . It has the most extensive coastline, the most developed inland waterways, four of the five largest ports, and the most efficient railroad and highway systems. . . . It has the most available space, . . . open areas for homeowners to build on, suburbs to sprawl to, factories to expand to, freeways to extend on, and empty areas for such industries as agriculture, defense manufacturing and movie production to spread out in. It has the oil and gas resources that have become so vital for all of modern industry, the long growing seasons and extensive water-reclamation projects so crucial for modern agribusiness. . . . [24:15]

None of the peripheral regions of the countries of northwest Europe can claim this combination of relatively unexploited environmental assets. As a consequence, none of the core areas of these countries exhibit rates of net outmigration to their peripheral regions even approaching the magnitude found for the U.S. core region.

In contrast to the countries of northwest Europe and North America, the peripheries of Nordic and Mediterranean Europe as well as Japan are at a clear natural disadvantage relative to the core regions. In the Scandinavian countries, apart from Denmark, the regions outside of the major urban regions all possess difficult topographies and/or climates—Northern Norway, for example, possesses little flat land, and what there is is broken up into small patches by mountains and fjords. In the northern areas of both Sweden and Norway, the winters are long and dark and the summers cool and damp. Mountainous terrain makes industrial development difficult and unprofitable. Flat plains are necessary for the building of cities, the laying down of roads, the construction of factories, etc. An oppressive climate makes it difficult to attract and keep labor. Northern Norway is particularly cursed in both respects.

In Italy, the physical limitations of the Mezzogiorno are well known and count among them a difficult topography and an uncertain water supply [26:35, 39]. Its Mediterranean climate, however, seems to be optimal for humans and may work ultimately to its advantage, if its other deficiencies in physical geography can be overcome.

In Japan, the singular lack is flat land for building outside of the Tokaido area. The plains of central Pacific Honshu, where Japan's largest population concentrations are located, are by far the most extensive in Japan [16:14]. Hokkaido—the northernmost island of the Japanese archipelago and still relatively underpopulated—has ample flat land but a difficult and oppressive continental climate. Kyushu, the southernmost island, has a warm and relatively benign climate but a serious deficiency of plain land. The rest of the central island of Honshu outside of the Tokaido area is likewise deficient in plain land. Iceland's southwest and southern regions and the southern half of England are also clearly much the favoured regions environmentally in those countries [19:253–255; 22:356–357].

In light of the greatly inferior natural endowments of these countries' peripheries, the near balance in migration flows between core and periphery in these countries is remarkable. But it is only a balance and a precarious one at that. As illustrated in Figure IV.3, a positive net migration into the core regions of Norway, Japan, and Italy from their peripheral regions is still occurring, and Scotland continues to lose population to the remainder of the United Kingdom, although in all cases, net

Table IV.3. Average Annual Net Internal Migration and Net Foreign Immigration to the Stockholm Region[a], 1961–78

Years	*Net Internal Migration*	*Net Foreign Immigration*	*Total Net Migration*
1961–65	9,161	4,648	13,809
1966–70	6,582	6,120	12,702
1971–75	−3,907	138	−3,769
1976	−4,942	8,426	3,484
1977	−2,922	10,695	7,773
1978	−4,048	8,009	3,961

[a]Stockholm, Uppsala, Södermanlands *counties*.
Sources: "Statistisk Årsbok för Sverige," "Befolkningsförändringar," and "Statistiska Meddelanden," various issues.

migration to the core is significantly lower than its 1960s levels. In Sweden, the decline seems to have bottomed out at a very moderate rate of net loss from the core. None of the countries of Nordic and Mediterranean Europe have strong migration away from the core toward the periphery such as we find in Northwest Europe, Canada, and most prominently, the United States. Furthermore, in Sweden and Norway, there continues to be a strong migration from abroad into the core regions, which has more than compensated for the losses due to internal migration (Tables IV.3 and IV.4). (There is virtually no recorded immigration into either Japan or Iceland, and immigration into Italy now consists in the main of former emigrants returning to their homes in the Mezzogiorno.)

By contrast, in France and West Germany, foreign net migration has been substantially slowed, and net total migration to their core regions was negative for several periods in the 1970s [28:100; 33:62]. Likewise in

Table IV.4. Average Annual Net Internal Migration and Net Foreign Immigration to the Oslo Region[a], 1961–78

Years	*Net Internal Migration*	*Net Foreign Immigration*	*Total Net Migration*
1961–65	5,701	−87	5,614
1966–70	5,135	545	5,680
1971–75	−1,216	2,091	875
1976	50	1,738	1,788
1977	−546	2,168	1,622
1978	−985	1,806	821

[a]Oslo, Akershus, Østfold, Vestfold *counties*.
Sources: "Flyttestatistikk," annual issues.

Table IV.5. Average Annual Total Net Migration to the U.S. Core Region, 1950–60, 1960–70, and 1970–79

Period	*Eastern Part*[a]	*Western Part*[b]	*Total*
1950–60	33,558	69,913	103,471
1960–70	33,653	−16,705	16,948
1970–79	−196,865	−162,811	−359,676

[a]Maine, Vermont, New Hampshire, Massachusetts, Connecticut, Rhode Island, New York, New Jersey, Pennsylvania.
[b]Ohio, Indiana, Illinois, Michigan, and Wisconsin.
Sources: G. Fuguitt, *Reference Tables: Population Trends and Net Migration for the States and Regions of the United States, 1950–1974*, Population Series 70-8, Applied Population Laboratory, Department of Rural Sociology, University of Wisconsin, Madison, Wisconsin, 1977, pp. 9,22; U.S. Bureau of the Census, *Annual Estimates of the Population of States: July 1, 1970 to 1979*, Series P-25, No. 876, *Current Population Reports, Population Estimates and Projections*, Washington, D.C.: U.S. Government Printing Office, February 1980, p. 6.

the United States, where the core region is currently losing 400,000 persons per year through both internal and external migration (Table IV.5). In Canada, although net foreign immigration is both positive and disproportionately concentrated in the core region, in recent years it too has failed to compensate for the net losses from this region due to net internal migration (Table IV.6).

Finally, in a number of the countries of peripheral West Europe, recent upturns have been recorded in the net migration of persons toward the core regions. All of these facts makes us doubt that a strong movement away from the core regions of these countries will be observed. The prospects are, at best, for a net balance between core and

Table IV.6. Average Annual Net Internal Migration and Net Foreign Immigration to the Central Region of Canada[a], 1961–1979

Fiscal Years	*Net Internal Migration*	*Net Foreign Immigration*	*Total Net Migration*
1961–65	13,102	27,436	40,538
1966–70	5,595	63,572	69,167
1971–75	−23,234	66,694	43,460
1976	−31,012	49,517	18,505
1977	−36,813	21,429	−15,384
1978	−40,179	−2,507	−42,686
1979	−50,870	27,429	−23,441

[a]Ontario and Quebec *provinces.*
Sources: "International and Interprovincial Migration in Canada," various issues.

periphery rather than an actual migration away from the core toward the periphery. This is in contrast to the countries of Northwest Europe, Canada, and, most dramatically, the United States, where the net movement away from the traditional industrial heartland of the Northeast and Midwest has become quite significant.

It is not clear why a net balance should occur at all in countries where physical geography so overwhelmingly favors the core regions and where the returns to further investment remain higher in the core than in the periphery, even in the absence of agglomeration economies. It is possible that at a certain level of economic development there is an economic surplus sufficient to maintain population levels in the peripheral areas, despite the inefficiencies borne in doing so. Such policies appear to be in response to a widespread, perhaps even universal, preference on the part of human populations to live in low-density settlements and particularly in the highly valued one-family house (for discussion of this preference, see Brox [6], Alexandersson and Falk [1], Blackwood and Carpenter [4], Golini [12], Zuiches and Rieger [35]).

Dispersal policies are nearly universal [31], and it is at least arguable that the universality of the policy is related to the universality of the preference [11]. That is, deconcentration policies may be an expression of and a response to a fundamental drive on the part of human populations to live in low-density and natural surroundings, and not an independent cause of this drive, as urbanists have habitually argued. The drive, however, has been traditionally frustrated by the lack of modern services and facilities (the demand for which may be said to take preference over the demand for space and natural surroundings) in precisely the areas where space and natural surroundings are cheapest and most abundant, i.e., in the sparsely populated peripheral areas. Only a wealthy nation is able to accomodate this drive by extending modern urban infrastructure and services into virtually all parts of its territory. In countries where the economic returns to maintaining such settlement systems are low, because, for example, the topography requires that the settlements be extremely dispersed (as in Norway), the costs to doing so are at least partially borne by the importation of foreign workers into the core regions. Such workers take the place of natives who are no longer forced by economic necessity to move to the core (as has been argued, in the case of Norway, by Hansen [13])—the only region where modern industrial economic activity is profitable or even possible. These costs, however, are also reflected in a continued erosion of population from the peripheries of many of the category 3 countries, although this erosion is dramatically lower now than in the past because of subsidies and transfer payments to the periphery [30].

The countries of East Europe, according to this hypothesis, are those in which (like the category 3 countries) the state has adopted strong deconcentration policies [10, 21], but in which, due to the relatively low level of economic development, there is not sufficient economic surplus to raise living standards in the rural periphery to that of the large cities. In addition, in these countries there are still strong agglomeration economies to be enjoyed through the concentration of population in a few large centers. Thus, a continued, though moderate, net flow of population toward the large centers of East Europe is observed, as if to balance these opposing forces.

Taiwan and South Korea, by contrast, are characterized by much weaker deconcentration policies and much stronger commitments to high rates of overall economic growth and rapid industrialization. For this reason, the very large net flows toward their major cities have yet to show any signs of slackening.[4]

CONCLUSION AND SUMMARY

One of the most stable regularities in the data of population geography is the tendency in industrial nations for the most densely populated regions to attract population from those less densely populated—in a word, for population to concentrate. Colin Clark calls this tendency the law of "macro-location," whereby regions already large and powerful attract still more population [7]. The law of "micro-location" refers to the opposing tendency *within* regions—namely, for populations to spread out—for density to repel density at the intraregional scale. The purpose of this paper was to show that the macro-locational tendency toward concentration is, in the developed world at least, near exhaustion and is beginning to resemble that of micro-location.

Although the overall tendency is clear for the entire developed world, there are variations from country to country that lend themselves to the following classification. First, in some countries, the decline in net migration toward the core regions has proceeded to the point where there is now an actual sustained net movement of population away from these regions and a corresponding net movement into the traditional lagging and peripheral regions. The countries of this group are located in Northwest Europe and North America. The second group consists of those countries in which the decline in net inmigration to the core regions has not proceeded to the point where there is a significant net migration out of these regions and therefore not to the point where there is a significant net flow of population into their peripheral and low-density regions. The countries belonging to this group are on the periphery of West Europe as well as Japan.

What distinguishes these two groups of countries, according to the tentative hypothesis put forward in this paper, is the potential for economic development in their respective peripheries. Where the physical geography of the periphery is favorable to modern economic development, economic growth will eventually bring a country to the point where productive capacity (including urban infrastructure) is added faster in the periphery than in the core, with a corresponding flow of population from core to periphery. Where the physical geography is less favorable to or actually precludes modern economic development in the periphery, there is a tendency as economic development proceeds for net flows from periphery to core to decline but not to reverse in direction.

Finally, a third group of countries acted as a kind of control group. These are countries where economic development is less advanced. The sample of such nations is of necessity small because the required data is only available for a few countries outside North America, Japan, and West Europe. The countries belonging to this last group are located in East Europe (East Germany, Czechoslovakia, Hungary, and Poland) and in East Asia (Taiwan and South Korea). All show either rising (Taiwan and South Korea) or stable but low (the East European countries) rates of net inflow to their core regions.

In sum, our thesis, based inductively on the data collected from a sample of 21 countries, is as follows. As economic growth and the accumulation of capital proceeds, a population concentrates first in a few regions in response to the higher economic returns to population agglomeration, followed eventually either by an exhaustion of these higher returns and a concomitant exhaustion of the tendency toward concentration or by the attainment of a level of national wealth sufficient to subsidize population maintenance in the periphery. The level of economic development required to reach this stage is obviously rather high. Countries as highly industrialized as South Korea and Poland have yet to show significant declines in the rate of net inmigration to their largest cities and surrounding regions. But the important point to be noted here is that the concentration of population in a few core regions does have limits and that these limits are reached rather quickly, once a certain, albeit high, level of economic development is attained.

NOTES

1. While the level of net migration into the principal cities of eastern Europe has not declined over the 1970s, and actually gives all signs of growing, this level itself, when expressed as a rate, is significantly lower than in many countries of western Europe and in Japan during their period of rising population concentration. Furthermore, the rates of

natural increase in the principal core regions of eastern Europe tend to be low relative to the regions outside of the core regions, a fact which has reduced the growth differentials between core and periphery significantly [33:55].

2. Southwest France, for example, has been characterized as the greatest expanse of developable land left in West Europe and is regarded as a substantial national asset as such by the French government. "'A kind of French Texas,' is how President Valery Giscard d'Estaing described France's huge, backward southwest region last year when he launched a 10-year plan to develop it" [18:6E].

3. An exception here would be Austria, where the "peripheral" areas of the west, though possessed of a much less ideal terrain for modern settlements than the Vienna region, are situated in a much superior location, particularly with respect to traffic and trade with West Europe. There has accordingly been a long-term westward drift of the population centroid in Austria, which has gone on since the breakup of the Austro-Hungarian empire. (See [23:9].)

4. Higgins [14:611] writes, ". . . the enormous problems of regional disparities and urban agglomeration generated by the rapid industrialization of Korea . . . have led to a concentrated effort to plan the entire urban structure in relation to the pattern of regional development, and a strategy of decentralization, that holds much interest for other countries facing similar problems." Whatever the interest this effort to plan South Korea's urban structure may hold, there is no evidence of its having any effect on the net flow of persons towards South Korea's largest city and surrounding territory. The 1976–78 net flows toward the Seoul region were among the highest in recorded history.

REFERENCES

1. Alexandersson, G., and T. Falk, "Changes in the Urban Pattern of Sweden 1960–1970: The Beginning of a Return to Small Urban Places?," *Geoforum,* 18, 1974, pp. 87–92.
2. Alonso, W., "The Economics of City Size," *Papers of the Regional Science Association,* 26, 1971, pp. 67–83.
3. Beier, G., A. Churchill, M. Cohen, and B. Renaud, "The Task Ahead for the Cities of the Developing Countries," International Bank for Reconstruction and Development Staff Working Paper No. 209, 1975.
4. Blackwood, L., and E. Carpenter, "The Importance of Anti-Urbanism in Determining Residential Preferences and Migration Patterns," *Rural Sociology,* 43, 1978, pp. 31–47.
5. Blumenfeld, H., "The Effects of Public Policy on the Future Urban System," in Larry Bourne and James Simmons, eds., *Systems of Cities—Readings on Structure, Growth, and Policy,* Oxford: Oxford University Press, 1978, pp. 562–565.
6. Brox, O., "Local and Political Conditions for the Maintenance of Marginal Communities," in E. Bylund, H. Linderholm, and O. Rune, eds., *Ecological Problems of the Circumpolar Area: Papers from the International Symposium at Luleå, Sweden, June 28–30, 1971,* Luleå: Norrbottens Museum, 1974, pp. 245–255.
7. Clark, C., "The Location of Industries and Population," *Town Planning Review,* 35, 1964–65, pp. 195–218.
8. Coates, B., R. Johnston, and P. Knox, *Geography and Inequality,* Oxford: Oxford University Press, 1977.
9. Crowley, R. "Population Distribution: Perspectives and Policies," in A. Brown and E. Neuberger, eds., *Internal Migration—A Comparative Perspective,* New York: Academic Press, 1977, pp. 255–274.

10. Fuchs, R., and G. Demko, "Geographic Inequality under Socialism," *Annals, Association of American Geographers,* 69, 1979, pp. 304–318.
11. Glazer, N., "The Urban Dilemma: New York," *Ekistics,* 46, 1979, pp. 72–76.
12. Golini, A., "Present Interrelations Between Migration and Urbanization: The Italian Case," paper prepared for a seminar on "New Conceptual Approaches to Migration in the Context of Urbanization," International Union for the Scientific Study of Population, Committee on Urbanization and Population Redistribution, Bellagio, Italy, June 30–July 5, 1978.
13. Hansen, J., "Settlement Pattern and Population Distribution as Fundamental Issues in Norway's Regional Policy," paper presented to IGU Commission on Population Geography, Symposium on Population Redistribution Policies, Oulu, Finland, Aug. 22–27, 1978.
14. Higgins, B., "Review of *Economic Growth and Structure in the Republic of Korea,* by P. Kuznets," *Journal of Economic Literature,* 16, 1978, pp. 609–611.
15. Jefferson, M., "The Law of the Primate City," *Geographical Review,* 29, 1939, pp. 226–232.
16. Kornhauser, D., *Urban Japan: Its Foundations and Growth,* London: Longman, 1976.
17. Leven, C., ed., *The Mature Metropolis,* Lexington, Mass.: Lexington Books, D. C. Heath, 1978.
18. Lewis, P., "The Eyes of France are on 'A Kind of Texas'," *The New York Times,* Oct. 19, 1980, p. 6E.
19. Malmström, V., *A Regional Geography of Iceland,* Publication 584, Washington, D.C.: National Academy of Sciences-National Research Council, 1958.
20. Mera, K., "On the Urban Agglomeration and Economic Efficiency," *Economic Development and Cultural Change,* 21, 1973, pp. 309–324.
21. Ofer, G., "Industrial Structure, Urbanization, and the Growth Strategy of Socialist Countries," *Quarterly Journal of Economics,* 90, 1976, pp. 219–244.
22. Osborne, R., "Population," in J. Watson and J. Sissons, eds., *The British Isles: A Systematic Geography,* London: Thomas Nelson, 1964, pp. 351–357.
23. Österreichischen Statistischen Zentralamt, *Statistisches Handbuch für die Republik Österreich 1978,* Vienna, 1978.
24. Sale, K., "The Rising 'Southern Rim'," *The New York Times,* Nov. 2, 1975, Section 4, p. 15.
25. Salvatore, D., "An Econometric Analysis of Internal Migration in Italy," *Journal of Regional Science,* 17, 1977, pp. 395–408.
26. Schachter, G., *The Italian South,* New York: Random House, 1965.
27. Schöller, P., "The Problems and Consequences of Urbanization," in R. Jones, ed., *Essays on World Urbanization,* Commission on the Processes and Patterns of Urbanization, The International Geographical Union, London: George Philip and Sons, 1975, pp. 37–46.
28. Statistical Office of the European Communities, "Regional Statistics—Main Regional Indicators—1970–1977," Luxembourg, 1979.
29. Stewart, J., "Empirical Mathematical Rules Concerning the Distribution and Equilibrium of Population," *Geographical Review,* 37, 1947, pp. 461–485.
30. Sundquist, J., *Dispersing Population,* Washington, D.C.: The Brookings Institute, 1975.
31. United Nations, "Selected World Demographic and Population Policy Indicators," New York: Population Division, Department of International Economic and Social Affairs, The United Nations Secretariat, 1979.
32. van Praag, P., "Belgium: Population Policies and Demographic Evolution in Retrospect," *Zeitschrift für Bevölkerungswissenschaft,* 4, 1978, pp. 365–382.

33. Vining, D., and T. Kontuly, "Population Dispersal from Major Metropolitan Regions: An International Comparison," *International Regional Science Review,* 3, 1978, pp. 49–73.
34. Weber, A., *The Growth of Cities in the Nineteenth Century—A Study in Statistics,* Vol. 11 of *Studies in History, Economics and Public Law, Columbia University,* New York: The Macmillan Co., 1899. (Reprinted in *Cornell Reprints in Urban Studies,* Ithaca, N.Y.: Cornell University Press, 1963.)
35. Zuiches, J., and J. Rieger, "Size of Place Preferences and Life Cycle Migration: A Cohort Comparison," *Rural Sociology,* 43, 1978, pp. 618–633.

Chapter V

THE CITY, CRISIS, AND CHANGE IN AMERICAN CULTURE:
PERCEPTIONS AND PERSPECTIVES

Harvey J. Graff

If repeated claims and evidence are believed, the nation is in a time of crisis. Sometimes termed a crisis of late capitalism, of early postmodernism, of confidence, of lack or distrust of authority, of liberalism, the dimensions and dynamics of the present problems are remarkably little understood. Nevertheless, it is certain that the sayers of doom find their greatest fears represented by the condition of our cities. How common are the assertions of social dynamite in the inner cities, of desertion of the municipalities by those with a propertied and professional stake in them, or of declines in the indicators of the quantity and the quality of urban life. The evidence of eroding tax bases, depopulation, institutional failure, shifting class and racial balances, declining services and infrastructural supports, aging human and capital stocks, fiscal crises, and the like is undeniably true, posing a serious challenge to those who embrace the importance of an urban way of life and its significance for culture and civilization in terms that transcend the cities themselves. The "discovery" of urban problems in the 1960s has returned with a vengeance in the late 1970s and 1980s.

The prophets of urban doom have more than ample empirical grist for their rhetorical mills. Their assertions of urban crises and decline must be addressed whether their prognostications prove correct or exaggerated. There is a powerful consensus in the perception of urban decline and failure in our times; this has powerful implications for society and culture, just as it does for polity and economy. Its meaning and comprehension—and the steps required to deal with it—remain far from clear.

Neglected in most discussions are the historical and human dimensions of perceived "crises" of advanced urbanity. In the first place, these aspects of the larger picture are less immediately accessible, certainly less amenable to simple statistical unravelling, than the fiscal or demographic dimensions. Second, they are precisely the parts of the problem that are often slighted, in some ways a result of our legacies of positivistic, political-bureaucratic, policy research and decisionmaking. They are, finally, the most difficult to discuss facilely yet coherently, regardless of their centrality to the problems at hand. The consequences are sometimes major; the failure to consider the human issues often signifies a neglect of the variations among populations at risk, be they demographic, racial, class, or ethnic. The roles of tradition, culture, differential perceptions, and the like are precluded from analysis; incomplete solutions are the best possible ends. The potential impact of change or policy options on the "human environment" can only be "guesstimated" without a fuller humanistic perspective.

The humanistic perspective is not the only one slighted by normative approaches. So is the historical dimension. As is well known, North American social and policy science, including that which centers on the city, developed professionally and institutionally in large measure by shedding its historical heritage. Consequently, an understanding of development over time has been lost. An appreciation of context, the major contribution of the historical viewpoint, has been ignored. As with humanistic understanding, the neglect of the historical leaves us with a social and policy science that wears thick blinders. The liberating perspectives that these approaches may provide have not become part of a "normal science" of policy and the city. An incomplete, internally contradictory, and shackled set of paradigms and models results.

This admittedly speculative essay seeks to overcome those limitations by sketching a historical and humanistic perspective on the cultural roots of the contemporary urban crisis. Its primary purposes are several. Rather than survey the literature or data as a first step toward problem definition, an original orientation toward the relevant issues is adopted. Current urban thought is put in a framework shaped by historical analysis. On one hand, this requires a longer term conceptualization of issues and problems than is usually taken; on the other, it stresses the variation in human perceptions, experience, and actions to the impact of social and economic change. This viewpoint allows a new way of constructing the problems under discussion, permitting us to expose and confront several impressively resilient myths relating to urban development, urban culture, and thought about the nature of the city in American history. Breaking the hold of the contradictory myths is the first step toward a more flexible understanding of urban culture and the problems facing it.

CULTURE AND THE CITY: MYTHS

The state is set with the following quotation:

> Since the era of the American Revolution, it has been a national sport to ridicule or despise the city. From Jefferson through Frank Lloyd Wright prominent Americans have argued that great cities were to a national community like sores to a healthy body. Corruption, crime, poverty, and congestion were nourished by the anonymous urban masses; better by far a nation of yeomen than a people of city-dwellers.
>
> But despite the national mythology, the religious suspicions, and the patriotic warnings, our cities grew at an unprecedented pace. Up through the Great Depression of the twentieth century, millions of people flocked to urban centers, and their pressure of numbers helped produce the complex networks of goods and services that characterize the modern city. Why did they move? Some, obviously, had no alternatives; boats and trains deposited them in cities and they could never find the money or energy to leave. Others came principally for economic reasons, to find better jobs or to abandon demeaning ones. But for many the city was a magnet because it offered experiences and opportunities impossible anywhere else, a cure for loneliness and isolation, a source of variety, amusement, education, and information.
>
> We now live at a time when cities are undergoing unprecedented crises. Pollution, social tension, and congestion have driven millions into the suburbs. Instead of being a place of hope, the city for many has become a symbol of despair and a demonstration of failure. It is hard to recall the bright promises once held out; we remember the warnings instead.
>
> Crises, however, if they do little else, usually stimulate historians [and others] to action. When going arrangements are challenged or break down, the commonplace acquires a new relevance, and scholars re-examine old assumptions.[1]

With this statement, historian Neil Harris reveals much about Americans, their cities, and the culture of urban places. First, he reiterates the distorted interpretation, widely popularized by Morton and Lucia White in *The Intellectual Versus the City,* that from the early national period henceforth, many influential Americans feared and distrusted cities and the nature of the communal life that grew up in them. The Whites' book has been influential as cultural analysis; it is, however, a poor substitute for historical understanding and background for contemporary perceptions. The discussion is superficial, weakened by a lack of rigor in defining either intellectuals or the city, the selectivity of the leading actors, and the unbased conclusions. Thomas Bender, in *Toward an Urban Vision* and *Community and Social Change in America,* points to the fallacies in the Whites' argument and begins the reconstruction of an intellectual and cultural history that is both closer to the past and more representative of serious inquiry. America's urban cultural heritage is both richer and more complex than the Whites would lead most readers to believe.[2]

Harris joins other observers, past and present, in recognizing the lure, the magnetism, of the metropolis. Regardless of what a handful of intellectuals have been thought to believe, towns and cities grew like topsy throughout the 19th and first half of the 20th century. An astonishing variety of push-and-pull motivations underlay the mass migrations of the native and foreign born to the burgeoning cities. The romanticism and rich national lore attached to the concurrent march westward obscure the magnitude of urban development—a development that preceded the advent of industrialism and onset of large-scale transatlantic migration.[3]

Implicit in this recognition is the importance of "an urban frontier," in the apt phrase of Richard Wade. Towns were the beachheads of settled life in the colonies; urban places and market centers from the very first years of colonization have been the spearheads of economic, political, social, and cultural life, even before the achievement of nationhood.[4] Numerous Americans and immigrants saw the roles that these centers played in development. The boosterism and competitiveness that marked urban rivalries and growth throughout the 19th century (and which we see again today) strikingly attest to the contributions that cities made to development and the popular expectations associated with them.

It will not do, therefore, to consider cities and their cultural interactions from the perspective of a long-term intellectual, or, even more popular, obsession with their evils. The fact of urban attraction and attractiveness is at least as pervasive as a cultural current in the American past. Yet, to center attention only on the hopes for and promotions of cities would be a distortion.

In Harris' statement and this commentary, another point is implicit, with a meaning for the present and future. Two themes are identified; ideas that have in their insistent repetition and reification attained the status of transcendent cultural myths relating to the development of cities and cognitive responses to them in American history. One is the "myth" of the evil, corrupting, dangerous city, a place that must be feared and avoided at best, or otherwise humanized, policed, or artificially natured as an arcadian garden. A close corollary of this notion is a myth of urban decline. If such students as the Whites and their echoers are heeded, from an early acceptance of the cities as places that were needed for functional, administrative, and commercial reasons but that could also be contained (a familiar concept or strategy in urban *and* military analysis), there developed a fear that urbanization was a destructive force that must be avoided and censured whenever possible. With growth and expansion came a regular perception and assertion of decline in the vitality of life in densely settled places. As with the family, literacy, and religion, to take three examples, the cities have also been the scenes of imputed constant decline. Population increase, economic and industrial concentration, and the inmigration of non-natives only hastened the process and increased the scale of danger and destruction. "Schools" of sociology and social psychology have grown up around these pervasive cultural assumptions and metaphors. This idea should be familiar to anyone acquainted with scholarly, journalistic, or even literary writing on the urban experience. It underlies a tremendous amount of contemporary commentary and analysis and is rising in popularity once again.

A second but contradictory theme has coexisted with the first. This set of ideas also comprises a social or cultural myth and has also had sufficient grounding to insure its acceptance and propagation. I refer to the "myth" of the city as a place of opportunity, uplift, social mobility, new beginnings and increased options for destinations, or "streets paved with gold." Here we must remember that millions of native-born sons and daughters fueled the streams of migration that peopled the cities, joining the foreign born who have received a disproportionate share of attention. The cultural attractions and possibilities of the cities constitute one key element. While some have seen the urban world as perpetually in distress and decline, others—more numerous if judged by number of statements and by "voting with their feet"—have brought to the cities incredibly high expectations that in a sense are particularly American and that were destined to result in some frustration and disappointment. That an optimism, a myth of rising cities and persons rising in them, often has been punctuated by a frustration of hopes and desire for the solution of social problems is not surprising. (Analogously, "long cycles" of the "discovery" of urban social problems, in the 1830s, 1890s, and 1960s, for example, have been followed by periods of optimistic environmentalist reform, but then by times of pessimistic hereditarian despair: 1850s, 1910s and 1920s, 1970s.[5])

Recognizing two dominant, conceptual "myths" is a major step. These pervasive, long-term threads of cultural thought, assumption, and understanding focus much thinking about cities and the quality of urban life. They also inform policy considerations. Another step must be taken. This is suggested in the preceding paragraph. Whereas it is not difficult to note how such ideas influence theories, studies, and interpretations of urbanization, urbanism, and urban life, or how the two contradict each other, that alone is insufficient to escape the implicit paradox. It is somewhat more difficult, however, to embrace the simultaneity of the existence of both myths and their interaction in determining ways of perceiving the nature of urban culture. Acceptance of the contradictions emanating from the coexistence and interplay of these conflicting orientations toward the city, and the implications for their contribution to its life, is the principal requirement for developing another perspective, one no longer blinded by linear prospects of rising or declining. This is the point of origin for a fresh discussion.[6]

There is another set of obstructions to understanding the cultural dimensions of urban life; a series of dichotomies also results in obfuscating contradictions. Consider how commonly, from the time of the Tönnies and before, the development of large-scale urban societies has been construed in simple categories that signify passage from one state of civilization and nature to another. Typical phrases include gemeineschaft and gesselleschaft, community and society, public and private, primary and secondary, active and passive, integrated and segregated, informal and formal, noninstitutional and institutional. As a part of progressive, linear, and evolutionary social thought and theory, such an orientation has been a major conceptual one.[7]

The work of the Chicago School of Urban Sociology is the best example. Implicit within a dichotomized viewpoint is a limiting epistemology, linked to change or radical shifts, and related to the two myths. Usually, the myth of decline, at least over the short term, is the expectation. Taken together, not only is the rich adaptability of human culture and tradition slighted, but also the flexibility of conceptualizations that allow for other behaviors is lost. Given these dominant modes and models of understanding and discourse, the frequency of linear conclusions about the condition of culture in cities is not surprising. They must be eclipsed; the demands of the present crisis require no less.

Before continuing, several key terms and concepts demand attention. First is "culture." The word:

> . . . has had a complex history and is the subject of continuing debate. Until the nineteenth century changed its meaning, culture was more an activity than a state of being; it represented growth or nourishment and could be applied to almost anything. Some years ago Raymond Williams showed how Victorians made culture into a noun signifying the highest and most valued human activities, connected particularly with the high arts. People were defined as cultured according to their interest in certain traditional areas: music, painting, architecture, belles lettres. In the twen-

> tieth century the word culture has been transformed again, made more comprehensive and catholic. We assume that every people, every civilization, and even every subgroup possesses a culture of some kind, that is, a pattern of value structures, mores, and institutions. It may be a nonliterate, or a violent, or a pre-industrial culture, but a culture it is, nonetheless.[8]

This point is of the utmost significance. Culture as a concept or a fact must be conceptualized in flexible terms. The contribution of anthropology is obvious here. Harris reminds us, first, that the semantics of "culture" have changed radically during the course of the past three centuries, and, second, that any understanding needs to be flexible and relative. No one definition will suffice.No universal standard will hold; past definitions are too exclusive and biased to encompass the cultural variations and divergences within any complex society. For example, the 18th- and 19th-century definitions would, if used analytically, lead to the neglect of the majority of populations! A "more comprehensive and catholic," if not all-inclusive and reductionist, definition must be employed.

In the case of the American city, past or present, any notion of culture must be sensitive to the widest range of class, ethnic, gender, or racial variation. A focus on formal institutions, public or private, as has been common among cultural historians or sociologists—museums, theatres, libraries, pleasure gardens, associations, or organizations—neglects the rich and variegated patterns of neighborhood communal life, street life, work cultures, pub or tavern sociability, church-related voluntary activity, or even the important 19th-century fire companies. The high, middle, and low must be included. Thus, notions like those represented by the primary meanings that the *Oxford English Dictionary*, for example, provides—from worship to cultivated condition, training of the body, cultivating or developing of mind or manner, improvement or refinement by education and training, the intellectual side of civilization—need to be taken as specific historical forms of culture, rather than as operational definitions for analytic or policy purposes.

Anthropological meanings are much more useful. The roles of tradition and change as well as social organization and institutions must be included, and culture must be seen as differentiated, variegated, patterned, and dynamic. There must be a sense of pluralism, but also of power relations among and between different cultures within a larger, complex society or social whole. Such a general perspective is required to deal with local and regional cultures, ethnic patterns, working-class activities, or black culture, and grant them the attention they deserve. The study of culture need not be radically relativist or reductionist, but it must be inclusive without assuming universality or unity. Knowledge and appreciation of the habits, customs, values, and norms of different groups and their relationship both to other groups and the larger society is a prerequisite to any understanding of "urban culture," its changes over time, relations with demographic, economic, or political trends, and the parameters for policy and allocation of always scarce resources.[9]

About definitions of the city or urban places, little need be said by way of introduction. The conflicting definitions of urbanization, urbanism, or urbanity need not detain us here. Some comment, finally, on the special role of cities for culture is useful, however. Any notion about the city pivots on the demographic and geographic; questions of population size, population concentration, and density of settlement are primary. These simple facts have implications for culture. First, the aggregation of human lives within a relatively compact place with a usually accompanying concentration of (surplus) wealth and resources gives a special intensity to places called urban. This leads to relatively greater opportunity, on one hand, and the relatively greater necessity, on the other, for cultural expression and activities, regardless of differentiation or variation among classes or other social divisions. Second, urban places tend to attract a more varied, divided, and heterogeneous body of inhabitants than do nonurban places. This also stimulates cultural activity and expression on a larger, more visible, and often more organized scale, as well as cultural conflict.

Within urban places, differing social groups are brought into closer contact, giving rise to incomprehension, intolerance, hostility, and efforts to socially control. This is an important point, for with the modern history of cities, in the United States as elsewhere, there arises social reform and welfare. Not infrequently this has involved, as a part of benevolent motives, the attempt to establish cultural and social hegemony, remold one class or group in the habits and values of another, and reproduce the social structure while improving the stock of "human capital" within it. Efforts to reform, periodically sweeping through American urban society, have not always been marked by greater concern to understand the "foreigners" or "aliens" on their own terms, to accept other cultures as different, rather than deficient. American social science and social policy continue to struggle with this issue.[10]

From the study of the past does not come any *one* special understanding of urban culture. Rather, history provides us not only with a set of negative lessions, but also with a firmer grounding in the roots of contemporary perceptions and problems.

AN URBAN PAST

Our next task lies in the past. We require (1) a general understanding of the processes behind contemporary configurations, and (2) a baseline from which to assess the state of urban culture. This section offers a sketch of urban cultural development. It is, I caution, the synthesis of one historian, for there are no accounts to turn to for guidance.

Numerous complications block the path. There are special problems of conceptualization, evidence, and interpretation. Most accounts and source materials are limited for a reinterpretation of urban culture in the American past. Much of the expression and activities that belong within our scope has not been so defined, and not recorded, by the makers of the "official" record. This involves especially the behavior and values of groups outside the "establishment" of white, middle-class, Protestant (and often male) members of society: blacks, the working class, immigrants (European or American), Asian-Americans, and so on. Developments outside socially approved or normative activities are seldom documented. When they appear, it is usually in the context of censure, criticism, or the need for reform. The cultural expressions of most persons, in other words, are often "anonymous" and unarticulated, making them difficult to discover. Historians recently have begun to sketch out that history. "New" histories, of blacks, the working class, ethnic groups, women and the family, mass or popular culture, are just beginning to revise historical comprehension.

The orienting "myths" of American urban studies are further complications. Linear, evolutionary, or devolutionary metaphors have dominated interpretations, oversimplifying issues, distorting evidence, and narrowing the range of human experience and adaptation. Recent research weighs against interpretations of linearity and simple progression, be it declining or rising.[11] Shedding the search for either simple rises or declines within the culture of urban places is mandatory. Our questions must seek understanding of change and adaptation in close relationship with the processes of economic, demographic, social, and political development. An acceptance of the contradictory forces working for new balances and syntheses regularly and an awareness of culture's lags and partial independence from other forces are required. Let us turn to the urban past anew.

Colonial America

Within the colonial period, before the Revolution and the establishment of nationhood, social and economic growth brought cultural change and heterogeneity. Massive Irish, southern and eastern European, or southern black migrations were not required for the onset of cultural complexity or heterogeneity. A harmonious past of "cities upon the hill" in New England was confined to a relatively short period, if Boston, for example, is examined. In the early days of settlement, towns were small, compact, and homogeneous units of persons more English than American in their cultural ways and institutional arrangements.

Relative uniformity in belief and background, however, did not insure a lack of conflict, stability, or consensus. One base of American cultural patterns is found in the early years of settlement; with the largely English colonists came a transplantation of Old World, "traditional" values, habits, and institutions. With time, by the early eighteenth century, population growth and social development had interacted with the "cultural baggage" to provide a basis for a distinct, if not unique, set of cultural configurations and patterns. These would of course be redefined in the interaction with the forces of change and the "baggage" carried by new immigrants throughout the course of the next 250 years.[12]

A sensitive look reveals the complexity of even early developments and the difficulty in framing simple generalizations about culture. Class differences and ethnic diversity and sectarianism were beginning to emerge, as was inequality, especially in the cities and larger towns. Different patterns divided the new English from the middle-Atlantic and southern colonies by the 18th century. Despite the dominance of the frontier in American historiography, towns and cities were present from the first years of colonization, in all regions. Colonists founded towns on first encounter with the Atlantic coasts. Although they held a very small portion of the population (less than 5 percent by the Revolutionary era), the urban contribution was enormously important. As markets, entrepôts, centers of administration, legislation, and judiciaries, the towns played a role that far exceeded their number or population. Gary Nash's recent major study assigns them (especially Boston, New York, and Philadelphia) a large weight in the social changes that culminated in a colonial war for independence by the 1770s.[13]

Not yet so distinct from nonurban culture, foundations were laid:

> . . . They remained islands in an agricultural sea, and few worried about their drawing power. Dominated by the needs and interests of the propertied, urban institutions fulfilled their special requirements at work and at play. Schools and churches were located not only in towns but in villages as well . . . but mercantile exchanges, where information was transmitted and commercial transactions concluded, coffee houses, dancing assemblies, debating societies, library companies, racing associations, fishing and hunting clubs, these could not be duplicated without the patronage of concentrated wealth and gentility. . . . The ambitions of urban aristocracies [sic], both North and South, centered about the recreation of an environment recalling the Old World at its most sophisticated. . . . Their style of life was meant to be cosmopolitan and international, not tied to geography or nationality.[14]

Still, the cosmopolitanism ascribed to the urban elite was equally true of the landed gentry. Presumptions of urban-rural distinctions are dangerous; more precision is needed in such comparisons. More important, however, is that this view neglects the cultural lives of the greater number of urban residents, in this or any other period inAmerican history. International or interregional trade and conspicuous cosmopolitan consumption were the activities of a distinct minority, just as they were not solely an urban phenomenon. A broader net of institutional and associational activities is needed to capture the cultural lives of most urban residents.

In the 17th and especially the 18th centuries, urban society was gradually growing more complex and stratified. In comparison with the next two centuries, however, these cities were still relatively small and homogeneous. Class was just beginning to encroach on status and rank in the internal differentiation of the population, and with the exception of the most wealthy among the elites, urban cultures may in fact be viewed cautiously as somewhat unified. For comparative purposes this is true. Institutions were only beginning their development, and while growing in importance, they did not dominate the urban cultural landscape. Social and cultural life was based mainly in more informal association and sociability: the church and meeting houses; the street, tavern, and coffee house; the market place, counting house, and exchange. As with political participation and property ownership, cultural participation was broad. Close physical proximity was reinforcing. A laboring or working class of landless and tradeless was only beginning to form, stimulating the first organized and institutional poor relief actions, hospitals, orphanages, and the like. Informality and lack of institutionalization, outside the church and legislative bodies, were the cultural norm, although the seeds of change were already growing. There was little distinction between the public and private. Widespread schooling and high levels of literacy also helped to insure a mass, if low level, of cultural participation. A popular press was the principal press; the theatre of the streets, the major stage.

Cities if important were not yet distinct sociocultural entities:

> Cities were physical entities not obviously different in character from the rest of society. . . . [T]he transit from country to city could be made naturally, for business or pleasure, by those whose needs took them that way. Urban laborers and mechanics, of course, did not enjoy the luxury of several residences, but the presumption ran that many urban artisans would end up owning their own land and go into farming as soon as they could afford it . . . Urban culture in this period, then, acted neither as a lure to ruralities, nor existed as a distinctive entity.[15]

Urban culture was in most respects not yet class specific. Nor was it especially ethnic in origin. Pluralism did exist, in the middle colonies for example, but it was a limited heterogeneity by the 18th century. Culture was relatively "popular" in most respects, but that is not to suggest that it was well developed in an institutional sense or comparable with the great cities of Europe. It was not. Provincialism, imitation, and a blend of the traditional with the beginnings of the indigenous were the major elements for both the elite and the commonality.

Illustrating the difference between this age and the one that followed is the fact of persisting, if diminishing, deference and patriarchalism as dominant elements of cultural cohesion. These were the primary agents of the relative unity or homogeneity in the face of increasing differentiation which spread with the growth of wage labor and commerical capitalism. The habits, values, norms, beliefs, or customs that dictated cultural assumptions and behavior were more holistic than exclusive, although the degree of cultural activity and the extent of cultural consumption (in terms of direct costs) differed among patricians, middling persons, and the incipient working class. Despite the degree of deferential hegemony within the urban culture, middling persons and many among the laboring ranks were able to act for themselves and by themselves politically, ideologically and culturally when the need arose. This may be seen in their associational patterns and their responses to economic and political events, especially during the time of the Revolution.[16] Foreshadowing the future, this pattern of time-, place- or event-specific independence allowed the urban culture to cohere in ways in which it would no longer two or three generations later.

The Antebellum Era

An integrated culture persisted for several decades after the Revolution's end trumpeted the onset of a new era. In traditional historiographic terms:

> Self-consciousness about the role of the city in a young republic develops, and alongside it appears criticism of traditional urban amenities and amusements. Some of this is owing to the revivals of evangelical religion at the turn of the century, some to lingering Puritan suspicions, but even more is caused by the new political ideology which rejects many English and Continental social traditions. The city becomes suspicious from two different points of view—as a stronghold of the idle rich who pose a threat to republican security, and as a haven for the mob, who endanger the future from an opposite direction. . . . These two elements were supplemented by other things such as devastating epidemics of yellow fever and later cholera that decimated our urban areas. As a threat to health, sanity, simplicity, and honest government, the city becomes the subject of such fictional analysts as Charles Brockden Brown, Poe, Hawthorn, as well as of the more sober writings of ministers and political leaders.[17]

This perspective is partial. The degree of dis-ease, and perhaps disease too, about urban places is often exaggerated. Ambivalence and concern there were, especially in light of contemporary actions by middling and laboring Americans during the 1760s and 1770s. A desire to avoid the industrialism, overcrowding, and fetidness of burgeoning English factory towns was expressed during the early national period.

A consciousness of the role of cities in economy, polity, society, and culture firmly took hold during these years. To classify this new awareness, and the responses to urbanization that advanced ever more rapidly in the antebellum era, as pro- or antiurban is distorting. Despite the efforts of some intellectuals and critics to underplay, or even ignore, the expanding influence and scale of cities, urban places soon assumed a prominence in the national mind—and political economy—that they would never relinquish. From less than 5 percent of the total population in 1790,

> The number of people living in places of over 5,000 inhabitants jumped from 597,000 in 1820 to over 5,600,000 in 1860. Nineteen cities had a population of over 125,000 in 1860, nine counted a population of over 100,000 persons, and New York (including Brooklyn) reached the one million mark. Moreover, while the urban population was increasing by nearly tenfold between 1820 and 1860, the total population of the nation only tripled.[18]

The rate of urban growth before the Civil War was the most rapid in the nation's history. This expansion was underway before the famine Irish immigration in the late 1840s and early 1850s; mass urbanization also preceded the onset of urban industrialization. Commercial capitalism was the driving force, as industrialization emerged outside the cities at first.

Tremendous inmigration, native and foreign born, joined with rapid economic growth and ideological change, had a special significance for culture. The commercial cities, mercantile entrepôts, and places of light manufacture and exchange were distinctive spatial and social forms. Relatively small and compact, most remained "walking cities" as spatial and social differentiation and segregation slowly reshaped their physical forms and the patterns of their inhabitants. But they no longer contained the relatively holistic and relatively homogeneous cultures that marked their colonial predecessors. The 19th-century, urban cultural world was distinguished by several new trends. First is the emergence of well-developed *and* distinct *class* cultures. We know much about elite and middle-class culture, their ideals, institutions, values, and activities. Working-class culture, divided by ethnicity, also emerged during these decades, although it has been less studied and less appreciated as definite cultural patterns. Second, conflict among and between cultures, classes, and ethnic groups (the sexes as well) became more frequent and took a variety of significant forms. Third, this was a great age of institution building, from the development of municipal services, to asylums for reform, to schools of all types, and to self-conscious palaces of culture, high, low, and middling. These institutions were central to the cultural landscape of the emergent metropolis.

Americans, rather than either loving or hating the city, tended to grasp at and confront the challenge that urbanization and urbanism represented. Many men and women sought to reestablish and maintain balances between the city and the country, nature and the city, the machine and the garden. Periods of optimism and periods of despair alternated throughout the century. Today's presumed uniqueness must be placed in this context.

Neil Harris captures some of this development:

> Self-consciousness also developed as the economic needs of the city and countryside began to diverge in the older states. As cities grew, their services—water, sanitation, policing, fire fighting, street repair—grew also, and within state legislatures expensive choices had to be made. The city also attracted notice because of the increasing number of immigrants who began to crowd it—Irish and German—whose religions, languages, or living standards differed significantly from native citizens. Warnings increased in the early nineteenth century about the snares and corruptions of an urban proletariat, and so did fears of public disorder.
>
> But, despite changes and challenges, the city was not abandoned in this early time of troubles. . . . elites did not desert their communities. . . . they remained committed to the cause of cosmopolitanism which eighteenth-century urban life had symbolized, and they now had powerful patriotic considerations as well. For it seemed clear that whatever inspiration romatic writers and artists might find in the countryside, the creation of a national art, the fulfillment of the genius of democracy, required communities of writers and artists, living in cities, nourishing one another's ambitions, supported by generous civic patrons. . . .
>
> . . . in the first half of the nineteenth century, an extraordinary range of institutions [were] created, having as their goal some form of art popularization or patronage. Libraries, historical societies, art unions, art academies, lyceums, theaters, and opera companies appear, not only in eastern cities but in the newer western towns such as Lexington, Cincinnati, Pittsburgh, Buffalo, Indianapolis. . . . the factor bringing all these institutions under one heading in this period was the zeal of residents in publicizing their home cities as places deserving outside respect (and patronage) because of their cultural amenities. Literary societies and academies were advantageous alongside convenient railroad lines and fine harbors.[19]

The elite and the middle class had dreams of a cultural institutional world of schools from the most primary to the highest levels, museums, artistic public monuments, fitting architecture, societies and voluntary associations for the good life among the best company and for uplifting those who were deemed deficient and required help. Yet, the two classes did not share completely the same ideals, values, or lifestyles. The gap separating them was small when compared with that distingushing them from the urban working class and poor; this gap only grew during the course of the 19th century. This was a period not only of tremendous social and economic change which remade the nation and laid the ground for urban-industrial modernity, but also of intense cultural and class formation. Institution building, on the one hand, and emergence of spatial differentiation, on the other, were impressive signs of the process of transformation. The cultural consciousness of nationality and search for distinctive achievements should be seen as marked by the formation of classes blurred by ethnocultural political and party culture. These aspects contributed to the formation of urban cultures in the antebellum era.[20]

Twin, but contradictory forces shaped this period of cultural formation. The urge for integration stood at one pole and underlay many formal cultural and institutional reform activities. At the other pole were processes of decentralization and separation—among social classes, ethnic groups, races, the sexes, and even age groups. Contemporary commentary reveals the strains and tensions. Participants and observers, foreign and domestic, were well aware of the massive transformations that surrounded them. How could they not be? They showed signs of hope but also fear and deep concern about the state of culture and society and the consequences of change and heterogeneity. Above all there was confusion; this is seen in mixed motivations to control socially the urban population and to dispense benevolent, uplifting Christian charity. The diversity and variety of cultural expression and activities stemmed from this complex of concerns.

It is misleading to claim, for example, that "The genius of democracy and local pride required institutions that were patronized by the whole community, that succeeded in integrating the population, bringing together representatives from all social grades in the pursuit of intellectual, aesthetic, and moral improvement"[21] when different classes defined the composition of the "community" differently; different institutions and activities were aimed at different clienteles; and cultural developments had tendencies within them that were not so cohesive or consistent. To comprehend the scale and scope of activities in a formative period requires considering efforts aimed at integration, distinct class cultural forms, and the balance of contradictory forces and consequences.

The conception of the integrative must be subtle, for at least two major cultural forms were initiated. On one hand, there were those to serve all classes within the urban population (in theory but seldom in fact), regardless of wealth, occupation, religion, race, or ethnicity. The urban garden is perhaps the best example, but the common school also serves well. The garden existed as fact and metaphor; it took a number of forms, from parks like Olmsted's renowned Central Park in New York City to the urban cemetery like Boston's Mt. Auburn. In such carefully crafted environments, all the residents of the city were to take pleasure, relax from the toils of their labor, take nurture from nature's civilizing force, and return renewed for their struggles. Romanticism, aracadianism, and naturalism were key strands in the thought underlying such ideals. Gardens were for all people, but their promoters and designers never suggested that the classes might freely intermingle, get to know one another, or break through barriers that separated their lives from each other. The evidence suggests that by their hours of availability, in terms of the working class' limited free leisure time, a large share of the urban population was unable to benefit. The garden metaphor proved more appropriate and accessible for the middle and upper classes, who not only had the opportunity to stroll or ride through these beautiful places, but who also could embrace the reality of such metaphoric imagery in their new residential enclaves outside the central business districts and later in suburbs.[22] The separation of workplace from residence, which occurred first for the working class, leading to a unique separation for others, contributed to a level of residential segregation unparallelled with the past and destructive to attempts at cultural integration.

School reform and expansion is an analogous subject. Of all the institution building in the struggle to realize the dream of the Enlightenment and Revolution, schools had a special prominence. Schooling must be seen as cultural "capital" as well as social or economic stock. Underlying many of the school reformers' activities and giving rise to the term "common school" was the ideal that this institution would not only embrace and socialize all the children of the community, but also provide a common experience: common, that is, in shared experiences among the youth of different classes and nationalities and in a shared set of (largely middle-class) values, habits, and norms. A common experience of schooling was never meant to end in a social, or cultural, levelling of social hierarchies, but rather to guarantee social order through the instillation of morality and discipline and to provide some minimal opportunity and skills.[23]

Students, past and present, debate the outcomes of public schooling; nevertheless, several conclusions are merited. First, the shared cultural experience pervading reformers' rhetoric was seldom found in the urban reality: common schools were never quite common to youths of different backgrounds and origins. Elites chose to support the development of private, class-based schools.[24] Ambivalent about the common schools, the middle class soon grasped that their children could benefit from regular attendance and achievement in a way others might not. For the children of the working class, the poor, and recent immigrants, a number of factors militated against the schools' success. The clash of culture between Anglo-American Protestant values that permeated the curriculum and non-Protestant immigrants was severe, but poverty, lack of relevance, familial need for children's aid, parental illness and death, and transiency took their toll. Residential segregation also obstructed commonalty.

The integration that took place was painful to many. National culture building was not a simple, swift, or easy process. Schools undoubtedly assisted, as did the culture of urban institutions, press, workplace, church, community, among other agencies. Integration to a degree sufficient for the society to "hang together," in the words of John Higham, was achieved, but it was (and is) an integration that had to accept cultural and social differences. The role of American cultural efforts was a partial one in this process of incomplete integration usually termed Americanization or assimilation. Many students of culture and cities have been misled by contemporary comments that apparently implied a far greater degree of integration than likely occurred.[25] A popular culture, as distinct and distinguished from the high or elite culture, was indeed forming. The formation of one was related to the other.

However incomplete in comparison with middle- or upper-class cultural ideals, popular culture was undoubtedly significant. As with culture at other levels of society, one must be wary of overgeneralization or abstraction, but class and ethnic, as well as age, gender, and racial, cultures were present. Anthropological insight contributes to an understanding. For decades, historians and other social scientists have demonstrated remarkably little understanding or appreciation of the strength, resilience, or depth of customs or traditions. Human adaptability and cultural malleability were not considered either sufficiently "cultural" or worthy of attention; rather, they were obstacles to assimilation and acceptance of new, (presumably) better ways. Today, a new, more complex and richer understanding of the strong multiple roles of human culture is developing.

This perspective is needed for analysis of the urban landscape as it evolved from the inmigrations of native-born rural folk, to the coming of the Germans, Irish, Scandinavians, Italians, Poles, Russians, other southern and eastern Europeans, and southern blacks, Puerto Ricans, and Mexican-Americans. Each group brought a culture of its own: norms, habits, customs, traditions, expectations, and institutions. Each used this as a mediating basis for negotiating its association with an alien land and a foreign dominant culture. Each drew upon its roots, and each group changed with time. Inevitably, the degree to which adaptation with urban America was successful—in their own eyes or those of the host culture's bearers—varied greatly.

The process is as complex as it is multifaceted. A description for any is impossible here.[26] An example helps to clarify the issues. Consider that a great many Irish immigrants to the United States at the end of the 1840s and 1850s were poor, with orientations more rural than urban. Their values and goals were survival oriented, based on the achievement of property ownership, full use of familial labor (the domestic economy), appreciation of the uses of drink, adherence to Catholicism, maintenance of customs, and hopes for the present generation as well as the next. Given these customs, language, and cultural background it is hardly surprising that the native-born middle class responded to their settlement with alarm, incomprehension, and sometimes overt hostility. But, could not the immigrants' strategies, based on their cultural roots and concerned with reestablishing cultural symbols and institutions, be more rationally and sensibly adaptive? Mounting evidence suggests that they were. Immigrants' cultural orientations differed from those of the native-born middle class; that difference need not cloud understanding of the use of cultural resources. Strategies of adaptation and adjustment rooted in the use of the family, sustenance within the Church, the search for security through homeownership (a goal typically higher ranking than the school attendance of older children, for example), and the use of fellow immigrants and kin for meeting a wide range of needs took precedence over imitative or "melting" behavior. Italians, Greeks, Jews, Blacks, and others, within the context of cultural differences, acted similarly.

The adaptive use of culture led to the establishment of working-class and ethnically based institutions, organizations, and cultural lives. These have not been accorded the attention given to the activities of the native middle class. The native working class was also forging its culture in this period. These activities were, for many years, more localized and community-based than the kinds of institutions promoted by upper and middle classes in the very same cities. The kind of nationalistic and competitive striving that marked the founding of schools and colleges, museums and libraries, theaters and clubs, and presses and periodicals was absent from ethnic and working-class expression—at least until the time at which communities were sufficiently well entrenched to achieve their own schools, periodicals, or formal institutions.

Other activities began more quickly. Churches, not surprisingly, were among the first cultural arenas that immigrant communities sacrificed and struggled to erect; the parish church stood not only as a symbol of their arrival, but also as a sign of God's shepherdship over their toils and a place to congregate socially as well as religiously. The cultural role and influence of places of worship was, and remains, immense.[27] Local taverns and places of business, developing with and as part of neighborhoods and communities, were also sites for association, sociability, and mutuality—crucial elements of culture. A vast variety of voluntary associations formed rapidly among immigrants, as there were corollaries among the native born of all classes. The American urge to join and participate flowered in the 19th-century city. Voluntary societies existed for any purpose imaginable; a glance at contemporary newspapers illustrates this well.

Patterns of associational life were also diverging in this period. In response to cultural and social change, the middle and upper classes were adopting a more private form of family life with their new residential patterns, while the working class, native and foreign born lived much more out-of-doors, collectively, and actively. Their homes and neighborhoods, as well as customs and traditions, encouraged this kind of cultural life. Life, on street corners, door stoops, or fields was central, stimulating rivalries in sports or among fire companies with members of other ethnic groups and with natives (sometimes nativists), and mockery or censure by other classes. Conflicts—sometimes bitter, violent, and bloody—erupted periodically, for example, during the 1840s, when members of the middle class also took to public "rioting" in support of their causes and interests (against abolition of slavery and abolitionists, in one prominent instance).

Different but not wholly separate forms of sociability and cultural expression were forming among the classes and native groups. Some immigrants' concern with events in their homelands, and efforts to import and/or support music, theater, and literature of their languages and countries, exacerbated tendencies that ran counter to integration or complete assimilation. In this regard, it is important to know that most immigrants were not illiterate, socially disorganized dregs of their places of origins. To the contrary, while often poor and sometimes destitute, they were much more often literate than those who stayed behind and seldom came from the bottom levels of society. Culture they had, and they participated in its movement and expression.

During the 19th century, countervailing forces propelled the emergence of distinct and divided patterns of urban culture. There were overlaps: in upper and middle class participation in formal "elite" cultural institutions, such as museums, libraries, colleges and high schools or academies, concerts and theaters, and in middle class and some working class sharing in public education, self-improvement programs, circuses and shows, sports, music halls, and musical-theatrical performances. The differences remain important.[28] Within the upper classes, and to a fair extent among the middle, privatistic residential and familial cultures became dominant, as specific, often long-lasting, formal "high" cultural institutions were erected and endowed.

This was the formation of class-specific cultural activities and expressions, which had parallels in journalistic and literary outlets. As several scholars have argued, the goals were sometimes more inclusive than exclusive; enculturating, reforming, and integrating ideals were present. But some institutions, whether libraries, museums, or clubs, were expressively elitist and exclusive. Helen Horowitz, for example, notes,

> In the pre-Civil War period American patricians were responsible for important efforts to create institutions of culture in their cities. They established or encouraged museums, libraries, cemeteries, and parks. While contemporaries lumped these institutions together as part of a single effort, there were important distinctions between even the most closely related of these. . . . There was one basic difference, however, between the American Academy [of Fine Arts in New York] and a museum. With the exception of an annual exhibition, the academy was essentially closed to the public. Rather than being, as it seemed, an institution to uplift the public—to mold its manners and to disseminate the revelation—it was designed to provide the older New York businesses and professional elite with aesthetic pleasure and to confirm their status by identifying them with the cultivated life. . . . the Pennsylvania Academy in Philadelphia and the Boston Athenuem seemed to have served similar functions for the patricians in their communities.[29]

Regardless of hopes for the cultivating and settling effects of art, libraries, music, or parks on the urban masses, intentions and physical realities joined to insure that such integration did not occur in this manner. As Horowitz's history of cultural institution building in late 19th- and early 20th-century Chicago illustrates, most other attempts achieved little more.

The Later-Nineteenth Century

During the century, class and ethnic cultures grew more distinct. Even the ideals expressed for cultural achievement narrowed. Harris comments,

> But at some point in the nineteenth century emphasis shifts away from participation and more to what I would call certification, certification of either the experiences or objects the institution protected, or the good taste and social standing of its supporters. From being devices which brought the population of cities together, self-conscious cultural institutions now started to segment portions of the citizenry, and their managements became preoccupied with different problems, and defensive about their own social status.[30]

This period—from about 1870 to the eve of the First World War—was, ironically, the most impressive and intensive era of cultural institution building in American history. Consider how many of our greatest symphonies, libraries, museums, operas, schools, and universities, with their magnificent but foreboding edifices, date from this period: for example, the Boston Museum of Fine Arts; the Metropolitan Museum of Arts; the Boston, Chicago, and Philadelphia symphony orchestras; Chicago's Art Institute; the Metropolitan Opera; and Chicago's Newberry Library. This was also, not accidentally, the greatest age of capital accumulation in American history.

> These were the years when great temples and palaces were built to house the new orchestras, libraries, and museums; they often were grouped together in great plazas or squares near the city's center. These enterprises were noncommercial in their objectives, but they continued to be popular in objective: their goal was public enlightenment, the same goal proclaimed by earlier founders of cultural institutions. But the circumstances had changed. Efficiency combined with class bias to dictate that the new cultural institutions be organized more with an eye to protecting the standard of the arts than with the theatricality and mingling of tastes which might have drawn mass audiences. The new interest in achievement and cosmopolitan excellence was not solely a product of snobbishness, as many critics of the Gilded Age have charged. . . . Professionalization began to overtake the ranks of museum directors and opera managers, as it was coming to dominate the worlds of higher education and business management. . . .[31]

The character of audiences also narrowed. The previously limited but still heterogeneous mingling was replaced with more homogeneous, genteel, middling to wealthy groups. Urban spatial changes, transportation costs, and ticket-pricing policy, as well as the lack of leisure for many groups, combined to prevent mass participation. The power of urban geographic and social transformation—from commerical cities to modern manufacturing metropolises—had a powerful impact on culture. With the poor, the working class, and immigrants more spatially segregated than before, not only was there less contact between classes and groups, but also there was less physical and material opportunity for common cultural participation. The facts of their lives joined with institutional policies (often in contrast with institutional ideals) to insure this end. While not unprecedented,

> . . . one of the things the new institutions were doing in this period: separating audiences out, by class, wealth, or ethnic background, dividing up what had become for many participants an impossibly heterogeneous gathering. No longer meant to gather profits, the institution's function was one of accreditation, and its major interest the perpetuation of a world of older objects and experiences. Museums, libraries, and orchestras were meant to be asylums—the word is used frequently—refuges for the best that world culture had produced. Unlike the antebellum institutions, the new temples were not expected to fit into the pattern of national life; they were consciously expected to move across these patterns, to improve, oppose, protect, and conserve. Although museum promoters argued that their enterprises relaxed and softened the rigors of urban life, they did not constitute a means for adapting to it.[32]

This is important. This urban elite tendency found numerous parallels in other cultural forms—from endowments of schools and colleges to club life. Not accidentally, this was also the greatest age of private preparatory school founding in American history. The seeds of present-day cultural problems were planted in this time: fiscal, popular, and participatory. More recent urban economic crises brought them to the fore, but the narrowing of audience and clientele and the lack of commercial support brought many cultural institutions to financial uncertainty and instability. From one ample and munificent private endowment, the great cultural institutions have become dependent on massive public contributions, state and federal assistance, and campaigns to popularize and promote their offerings.

The cultural division must not be overstated. At the same time, cultural institutions continued to appeal, if not always successfully, to a wider public. Patrons and promoters still held ideals of the civilizing and reforming power of "high" culture. They offered classes, lectures, improved labelling, free or low admission charges, and physical accessibility. These incorporated a fair degree of middle-class participation (especially among those seeking culture as identification of their respectability) and some few among the working classes. The hope, of course, lay in "the notion that by bringing together masterpieces and arranging them attractively and intelligently an uplifting effect would be had, not only on the crowds of spectators but on the ranks of American artists as well."[33] Children and the young were prime target audiences; many programs were devised to secure their participation, through schools and other organizations. But the extent to which such efforts penetrated very far into working-class and immigrant culture was not very deep. Moreover,

> . . . even the museums, which were far more oriented to public service than the other cultural institutions, represented a freezing of older notions of patronage. Instead of money going to living artists, it went to dealers and other collectors. . . . Membership on museum boards, despite the rhetoric, remained largely confined for many years to representatives of old and established families . . . . despite the high attendance figures and the active lecture programs, museums cut themselves off from much of the life of their cities. Visits to museums were for many like visits to sacred services, and in place of comprehension there was frequently simple awe.[34]

This was not calculated to make the working class, native or immigrant, among others, feel at home.

Another divisive element splintered the relatively homogeneous "higher" culture of the urban upper and middle classes. This was the emergence of professionalization and specialization in the second half of the century. As Thomas Bender has described the process, *a* culture of intellectual life and *a* community of discourse among intellectuals in the leading cities was replaced by distinct, professional communities, more national than local in orientation. "Before the rise of modern professionalism, there were identifiable audiences that judged and affected the work of American thinkers. Until the middle of the nineteenth century, in fact, the city provided the primary context for the life of the mind."[35] Civic professionalism gave way to disciplinary or subgroup professionalism, as the community orientation of early American professionals eroded. Civic culture and civic leadership, previously, did not depend on extralocal qualifications, professional credentials, or accreditation. But concomitant with other socioeconomic transformations of the cities and the nation, this changed relatively rapidly after the Civil War:

> . . . neither city nor metropolis shaped intellectual life. The collapse of intellectual vitality in American towns and cities coupled, perhaps, with an anti-urban resentment of the metropolis, opened the way for the rise of a multicentered and nonlocal system of professionalism stressing individual membership and the fragmentation of elites. That an urban-based metropolitanism failed to develop cannot, however, be blamed entirely upon provincial antipathy to the metropolis. Urban culture itself was in crisis.[36]

A culture of professionalism emerged as an alternative to the less organized urban cultures. If earlier elite patterns were centripetal, then the new ones were centrifugal. The professions were no longer paths converging on the same end; they now diverged, and they looked beyond the city. New goals, orientations, career lines, educational programs, and conceptual bases encouraged the crisis and remolding of culture on an extralocal model.

> Intellect's clear association with general urban elites had achieved for it a certain legitimacy and hegemony within society in the eithteenth and early nineteenth centuries. The social fragmentation, isolation, and anonymity that characterized the chaotic mid-nineteenth century eroded these customary sources of intellectual authority. Neither personal knowledge nor clear social categories were available to organize and discipline intellectual life. Intellectual distinctions were blurred, and the identity of audiences became rather diffuse. . . . With traditional rituals of accreditation abandoned, producers and consumers of intellectual work found it increasingly difficult to fix on the cues that made coherent intellectual discourse possible. Lacking a solid personal basis for establishing a relationship with their audience, urban intellectuals relied on their personalities and the appearance of intimate disclosure to establish the trust and authority essential for the intellectual community. But personality was a poor substitute for the shared intellectual framework and clear social categories that had earlier given shape to local intellectual life. In such a situation, the eighteenth-century penchant for argument gave way to the quest for "influence."[37]

Professionalism arose in part to meet the challenge of urban cultural disorganization, to reform, to stabilize, and to control it. Many who sought an active and rigorous intellectualism withdrew from the general urban culture and embraced the new model of professionalism. Their purposes could be clarified while they were simplified. Conventional formulas, specialized training, and career lines followed, as discourse and expression were restricted. Security came with withdrawal and professional protection. Withdrawal was also taking place in residential and political terms. The new power of specialized professions for solving problems, the rise of the expert, was underway.[38] Cultural expertise exacerbated divisive tendencies; "expertise" proved no answer.

Working-class cultural development continued, perhaps more firmly, rapidly, and, in this period, independently, but also with efforts of the middle and upper classes to reform and acculturate them.

> . . . if the wealthy urban classes encouraged the construction of these great institutions, the city supported contemporaneously other institutions which nourished other cultures—cultures with class, ethnic, or generational ties. What one sees in the late nineteenth century is the creation of many spheres within city populations, rarely touching except in moments of crisis, each supplied with its own forms of expression and means of recreation. Each duplicated the other's institutions—newspapers, clubs, fraternal societies—but none of these institutions was inclusive enough to comprehend more than one group. . . . these institutions merely mirrored the increasingly sharp divisions which made up the metropolis. . . .[39]

These cultural forms were diverse. Many centered on communities and neighborhoods and they developed their own cultural "infrastructures." Through churches, parks, clubs, taverns, meeting halls, work groups, street life, fraternal and benevolent groups, and more, intense and active cultural participation was maintained. Music, theater, religious observance, male and female and youth sodalities, sports, journalism, and much more were encouraged and expressed. Although often underendowed or scantily funded, working-class and ethnic cultural affairs were rich and enriching. They also tended to blend, sometimes subtly and semiconsciously, the forces of tradition and change, such as Americanization.

Large cultural institutions, rooted in class and ethnicity, grew up too. Transcending neighborhoods or residential enclaves within the cities were newspapers, ethnic and popular theatres, music halls, amusement parks, and recreational grounds. Some ethnic groups, particularly Jews and Italians, founded their own theatres; many supported newspapers. Music halls and popular theatre, including vaudeville and light dramas or comedies, brought somewhat diverse audiences together. With experiences based more in observation than active participation, they did not integrate or bind them together. Even "in spectator sports, long presumed to be among the most integrating areas of urban culture, onlookers began to divide themselves according to class, with polo, cricket, and college football at one end, boxing on the other end, and baseball somewhere in between. Private athletic clubs made it possible, of course, for exercise and spectatorship to be pursued in still more sanitized surroundings."[40] The possibility, nevertheless, of a rich and diverse, if divided, set of cultural institutions and experiences was achieved; that possibility was sometimes realized.

Another element of possible integration existed. These were the great urban fairs and expositions of the late 19th and early 20th centuries.

> . . . These festivals celebrated historical events, commercial and trade routes, and investment opportunities, but what many were striving for was some visible unity to the social, economic, and artistic lives of their divided communities. . . . Attracting huge and heterogeneous crowds, the fair managers sought to legitimize, by sheer numbers, the principles of historical community and moral gentility which official urban culture enshrined. The many foreign exhibits, each housed in its own pavilion, symbolized for some the variety of America's own population. The acres of painted allegory and the sculptured figures of Patriotism and Fame stood in miniature though not minute fair cities, demonstrating that it was possible to objectify the spiritual values which a community might hold in common.[41]

Their integrating impact proved to be limited in effect.

> The fairs, however, although they influenced a generation of urban planners, were evanescent glimpses of an imaginary world, a realm of concord guided by the ideals of art, as the middle classes conceived them. Behind and beyond the White City was the Black City, and temporary festivals were inadequate solutions to the problems of division. The civic squares, the courthouses with their Latin mottoes and patriotic statuary, the war memorials, and great public libraries were tributes to an ideal, not an actuality.[42]

Ideals did not disappear; culture as fantasy, imaginary, and escapist, however, was probably reinforced. This looked perhaps more to the future than to the past. From the age of urbanism of the 19th century came a powerful legacy. The foundations and the material world of 20th-century cities were created. The divisions between cultures based on class, ethnicity, race, gender, and age was part of that process. Distinctions between the formal institutions and the commercial and recreational activities of different social groups were formed; they have continued well into the present century.

One further development needs comment. This is the "Progressive" period of cultural reform, the activities of educators, settlement house workers, and "Americanizers" to reform the social and cultural orientations of the working class and the immigrants. "Schooling" of all sorts and for all ages was a renewed rage. Progressive reformers came in all stripes and shapes, defying generalizations. For every rigid, conservative Americanizer who sought to "melt" the aliens into white, middle-class, Protestant American molds, there were sensitive, if sometimes manipulative, philanthropists and social workers who struggled to tolerate, understand, and respect immigrants' and working class' ways and to blend more pluralistically the native and ethnic cultures. Among the latter group, some persons, such as Jane Addams, criticized the ideals of urban elites who hoped that huge culture palaces would socialize the masses properly. Helen Horowitz writes,

> . . . Initially she and her coworkers had seen that the existing civic institutions were not meeting the immigrant community's needs. They established a homelike environment in the neighborhood to make possible a close contact with the population. Their cultural programs were designed to encourage people to go to existing institutions or to place in a more accessible location the same collections or programs as the city-wide museums, libraries, university, or orchestra. In time Hull-House residents came to place value in the settlement house experience for its selective reconstruction of life. And broader experience, contact with their clients, and the stimulation of new modes of thought led them to question whether or not the cultural standards they had shared with the major cultural institutions of the city any longer had meaning.[43]

Less highbrow academic programs were instituted; more was based on the culture, lives, and work of the immigrants themselves. Although adjustment, acculturation, and assimilation to the host society remained the goal, a partial redefinition of culture occurred.[44] Education in tune with the daily lives and the everyday needs and welfare of the ethnic groups replaced, in part, socialization by exposure to classical art and other elements of "high" culture. The latter was not ignored, nor was it derogated; rather, its role was diminished. Industrial education, to Addams and Dewey among others, was deemed more appropriate: to integrate the worlds of home and work, to teach people about the society in which they now resided, to ease the tensions between the generations. Cultural relativism replaced, to some extent, cultural idealism. The present was more important than the classical past; culture may be seen as social and economic.

Culture in the city was redefined, music and art newly appreciated for their usefulness in this context. They must be brought closer to those who needed the soothing, enriching influence. Despite the successes that social workers and settlement house people achieved, neither the philanthropists nor the keepers of the major cultural institutions were willing to accept or to modify their approach in this way. Public libraries did decentralize, some historical museums did adopt such an approach, and some philanthropic groups took interest; schools also made some efforts. A partial reorientation, an attempted meeting of cultures, occurred in the period immediately before the First World War. Its success was not complete.

The Twentieth Century

The more recent past may be considered more briefly than the formative decades of the 19th and early 20th centuries. The story is one of strong continuities and important changes, which together gave rise to even more contradictions. Many of the seeds of the past germinated in the period from the 1920s into the 1970s; the fruits were often bitter. On one hand, the divisive tendencies of the 19th century were exacerbated; on the other, electronic media introduced new elements into the cultural arena. Social and economic trends continued to take their toll. American urban culture has suffered, in this century, the contradictory effects of increasing homogenization at a relatively low or "mass" level, while also incurring the impact of persisting divisions deepened by urban crises on a broad, if not unprecedented scale.[45]

First, consider the usually stressed novelty of the period, which is taken to demonstrate the undermining and replacing of traditional urban cultural forms. The myth of decline has returned forcefully. It is said, for example, that:

> . . . two important trends have helped undermine the meaning of urban culture in its traditional forms. The first was the growth of mass media—motion pictures, radio, picture magazines, and television. . . . they constituted . . . a challenge to the carefully gathered treasures of the older cultural institutions. The ability to popularize on a huge scale objects of art, images, and living styles helped thrust urban culture into a new stage. . . . the media pioneers . . . were successful because they knew how to exploit public taste and manipulate the new possibilities. . . . They were not responsible to conservative boards of trustees, but to bankers or stockholders who demanded profit, not aesthestic accomplishment. In some way their motives resembled those of the urban impresarios of the middle nineteenth century; movie makers integrated enormous audiences and sought inclusiveness and comprehensibility. . . .
>
> From one point of view, radio and film might seem to signal the urban take-over of American culture . . . urban mobility and moral relativism replacing the older fixed standards, agrarian and small town. . . . The glitter and glamour of city life beckoned from the urban settings that the radio and films projected.
>
> But from another point of view, the mass media challenged and erased the city's older cultural advantages and replaced urban culture with a new amalgam of its own. For the media now permitted Americans everywhere to duplicate the possibilities which only physical concentration had previously permitted. . . . Smaller groups of people could replicate the advantages of cities. Radio, film, and later television replaced older urban entertainments; motels and shopping centers competed with central hotels and department stores. . . . The media, in this sense,

> represented not the triumph of urban values but a menace to urban existence, a destruction of once exclusive privileges. . . . The homogeneous world of the mass media, moreover, contradicted the values of separated heterogeneity that had constituted urban culture in the previous period. . . .
>
> The media indirectly undercut both levels of urban culture—the upper middle-class facade of formal institutions and the competing heterogeneity of various classes and ethnic groups. . . . Various groups within the community are no longer willing to permit their own identities and achievements to be ignored by public spokesmen.[46]

It is undeniable that the growth of electronic media distinguishes the recent period from the past. It is equally true that their impact has been exaggerated out of context and proportion. There is little evidence, for example, that television or the cinema have the power to change or radically shift one's values or norms. Analogously, one similarly cannot generalize about the impact of radio and television, as largely privatized and domestic cultural activities, and the collective experience of the movies. To the extent that the recent period has marked the end of a great urban age, it has also witnessed the triumph of urbanism as a way of life, to borrow a phrase. Its roots we now see in the past; novelty is reduced. Myths do remain, however.

The simultaneous existence of these countervailing states must be grasped to understand the present. Despite the homogenizing tendencies of the mass media, in the direction of a diffuse middle-class culture, crucial cultural differences between classes, races, ethnic groups, and age groups remain, despite the pronouncements of many sociologists and psychologists to the contrary. The "popularization" of "high" culture via the airwaves has not been successful in gaining support for museums, symphonies, opera companies, or the like, especially if the history of the Public Broadcasting System is examined. In a world so thoroughly urban and urbanized as that of the late 20th century, to speak simply of the cities' cultural advantages as being either increased or diminished is absurd.

THE PAST *AND* THE PRESENT

In this section, two related tasks are undertaken. The first is to sketch broadly a historically based understanding of contemporary urban culture. The second is to draw some "lessons" from the past. It is not difficult to understand how much of the legacy of urban cultural development has come to "roost" in the past 15 years. Deep divisions of class, race, and ethnicity, in their spatial, demographic, and economic dimensions, underlay many of the urban crises that have shaken our cities and been seen to threaten their cultural configurations.

From this perspective, several conclusions can be offered. First, from the discussion above, it can now be seen that there was *no* truly rosy past to look back on romantically. We must guard against the myth of decline, as stated at the onset. From a divided past has come a divided present. Standards of living, access to transportation, opportunities for schooling, possibilities for cultural participation, quality of diet and nutrition, access to health care, and the like are for most persons *greater than ever before,* within the cities, as elsewhere, despite the insufficiency of all these aspects of life. That basic fact must be accepted beside the long list of urban crisis points. The urban past of the United States, second, from the early nineteenth century, may be read and written as a *history of crises.* If contemporary sources are consulted, it is difficult to find a period of any reasonable length in which the major cities are *not* perceived to be suffering crises of one kind or another: population growth, sanitation, pollution, leadership, fiscal policy, transit, education, culture, and on and on.

This argument must *not* be misunderstood as radically relativistic: that *ca plus change, c'est la même chose,* nothing changes, regardless. That is not my point. Rather, I seek to avoid the gross oversimplification and fallacies of the linear rising-declining perspectives, while establishing the essentially *historical* and *precedented* nature of the contemporary malaise. This does not, I stress, reduce the significance of the problems the nation faces today and in the coming decade. It establishes a context that may well prove to be liberating.

Two observations follow. The first is historical. From the foregoing account of urban cultural history and urban development, it is clear that current circumstances are outcomes of a long-term historical process of development. The movement of the wealthy and then the middle class from the inner cities began before the Civil War; the end of urban expansion in the older cities was foreshadowed by municipal incorporation and expansion activities by the late 19th century; the role of federal aid dependency by the New Deal and state aid a century earlier, and so on. The differentiated, segregated, and divided nature—socially, spatially, demographically, economically, *and* culturally—of the cities has developed over a period longer than one and one-half centuries. The historical development of the present was not, I caution, an inevitable one; it was the result of many human choices within the context of the physical and ecological environment and the logic of an emergent capitalist economy.[47] The timing was not inevitable, although the culmination in crises was more than likely, given the nature and the facts of development. Larger economic problems, especially the end of growth and political ideologies of hope and optimism, in the national and world systems by the early 1970s forced the breaking point. That, however, is not the issue; rather, we seek to place the present in a general context, a historical and developmental one.

The second conclusion is sociocultural. It must be stressed that the urban crises have serious impact on the quality of life within urban places, the nature and quality of social relationships, and the condition of culture: institutional and organization, formal and informal, public and private, observational and participational, exclusive and inclusive. The state of the public school systems is one well-known example. The insecurity of the greater cultural institutions—museums, libraries, symphonies, even botanical gradens, parks, and zoos—is equally well known. Private philanthropy, endowments, combinations of public and private funding, vandalism, safety of neighborhoods in which many reside, are all points of special concern. In the past decade, most institutions have gone "public" to maintain themselves, sometimes in reduced ways: mounting exhibits on the scale of spectacles to attract huge throngs of paying visitors; establishing commercial ventures and lines of products with their imprimatur stamped on them; becoming dependent on state and federal humanities and arts councils for subsidies in addition to other fund-raising schemes. Their collective futures are far from certain; but it is indicative that relatively few have failed.

To this is added the relative lack of educational and public broadcasting to date in the United States. A decline in funding for cultural activities on all levels has become a special problem in the past few years, a shift from the relative munificence of federal, state, and city grants a decade ago. The political nature of these programs, moreover, has resulted in manipulation, patronage, power contests, and waste of scarce resources. The private foundations, which liberally assisted cultural organizations and institutions in the 1960s and early 1970s, have withdrawn, due to political criticism, lack of measurable results, and, especially, the severe impact of inflation on reducing endowment values.

Noteworthy and equally worrisome are the facts of increasing unwillingness of many to return to the inner city locations of major cultural institutions: the result of fear of transit through declining and sometimes dangerous areas of cities, rapidly climbing (although still cheap by international standards) fuel and energy costs, and rising admission fees that result in very high expenditures for a day or afternoon venture to museums, concerts, amusement parks, or even sporting events by a family of four or five. The many persons whose spending power has been reduced sharply by inflation and by wages that do not keep up with rising costs, and the unemployed (especially the young and minorities), are most restricted. Many of the latter groups, regardless of efforts by cultural institutions to "democratize" or "popularize," have yet to be attracted by exhibitions or other lures. On one hand, it is true that real efforts have been made to celebrate the histories and traditions of all segments of the population:

> Temples of course continue to rise, such as the Kennedy Center in Washington, and attendance is enormous at our great galleries. But along with the criticisms, the entertainments and exhibitions have grown more various. Ethnic culture can be presented inside the buildings once preserved for traditional masterpieces, and jazz and rock can share the orchestra halls with Mozart and Beethoven.[48]

On the other hand, it should be asked how broadly have these changes affected urban culture. Audiences perhaps have broadened, but probably not very far down the social scale or across the racial spectrum. Similarly, many are not yet attracted to, comprehending of, or able to afford the great institutions or the concerts. Analogously, while the recent "rediscovery" and celebration of ethnicity has been a positive and impressive cultural sign and has attracted funding and support for ethnic institutions and museums as well as inclusion within "national" galleries and halls, it does not seem that many persons outside the individual groups or the curious, educated classes have participated in or observed them closely. Much remains to be done in these directions.

Despite the apparent pessimism of recent circumstances and the present moment, another set of trends seems under way, if current economic tendencies of inflation, recession, and perhaps even depression do not stop them in their tracks. While granting the significance of the "crisis," a movement to rebuild the central cities is also under way. The ethnic revival, in some ways, is one sign of this, but more important are those activities that fall under the heading of revitalization, rehabilitation, and preservation. Massive urban renewal programs are in progress in a number of cities; all of them have important cultural implications as well as direct significance. One can point to the recent and continuing work in such diverse centers as Chicago, Detroit, Philadelphia, Pittsburgh, Boston, Atlanta, and Dallas.

Urban revitalization programs, despite the commonality of federal and corporate support, are a diverse and sometimes contradictory set of actions. They are thus far also incomplete. Such plans and their beginnings typically include: community development; center city building; gentrification; public housing; improved transportation; preservation of noteworthy historical and recyclable structures; park and recreational facilities; new or redeveloped cultural institutions; "urban homesteading"; urban renewal; support, funding, and planning by combinations of national corporate leaders, politicians, governmental agencies, and community groups; and dis- and sometimes relocation of the poorer residents. This list reveals the complexity of the issues, involvements, and possible outcomes. Such efforts, about which any knowledgeable person (including this author) cannot but have mixed, if mildly optimistic sentiments, mark a developing *sense of urban vision:* a growing awareness, on one hand, that all is not well with central cities, but, on the other, that a need for activism by a variety of interests is required.

A tour through "revitalized" areas of a number of cities shows many beginnings. Despite the hope of such programs, barely the surface has been scratched. Comparing the results of such programs with any roster of urban problem areas shows how much farther the nation must go. Real progress has been made; a look at many cities is revealing.

History has not been, and cannot be, reversed. The costs of revitalization and renovation are high. Whole neighborhoods of the poor, nonwhite and white groups, and others have been destroyed; many are threatened by renewal or redevelopment. Although often in poor condition, a great deal of needed housing has been lost. The benefactors of such programs have not come equally from all class, ethnic, and racial groups. Renovation and preservation, as the suggestive term "gentrification" indicates, have rarely had the lower income groups who densely populate the central cities as the target of their improvement. These persons are most likely to suffer from unemployment, restrictive welfare policies, inflation, and higher transportation costs. Conversely, they are least likely to share in new or renewed cultural attractions, whether by choice or lack of choice. Financial resources often are not available for their rehabilitation; redlining is one of many obstacles. Their future has not always been made in part of the emerging urban vision of our day.

The benefits are not without complication, contradiction, or irony. If present trends continue—about which one cannot be certain—the nation may well in the next decade or two find itself with renewed, somewhat rebuilt central cities. They will house different classes of residents than they had previously. Dominated by the wealthy and well-to-do, central city housing will be filled with young to middle-aged professionals, often married and often childless. A homogeneous population, with a narrow demographic and socioeconomic profile, will have replaced another homogeneous population with the latter more displaced than before and probably more angry and alienated.

Some may find the results of this hypothetical but not implausible scenario to be a better state of affairs than the present or immediate past. The need to choose between either extreme is not a choice we should easily make. The former would not mark a return to the form of preindustrial or early commerical cities in which richer groups tended to live more in town centers than the poorer (but were more mixed than segregated). These visions are neither historical, complete, nor satisfactory. The implications for cultural life are restricted, unless we wish to return to stultifying "high" cultural ideals, which proved their own limitations over a century ago.

AN URBAN VISION

What is required today is a larger but still realistic *urban vision*. This need not be utopian or "visionary." The nation may have achieved part of that vision already, but that is not enough. To go farther, we need to learn from the past, to regain some of the past's own urban vision. Historian Thomas Bender has attempted this in his important book, *Toward an Urban Vision: Ideas and Institutions in Nineteenth-Century America*. Bender found that many persons, including economic, social, and cultural leaders, in the past century were not all opposed to the burgeoning cities, regardless of the assertions of previous students. To the contrary, he realized that there were important hopes, ideas, and plans to humanize and civilize the "wilds" of the urban environment, cultivate the residents of all classes, and harmonize their interests. Class conflicts and motives to control socially one group by another were clearly part of this "urban vision." The creative and flexible manipulation of the environment and creation of malleable institutions constituted another element. Bender writes,

> . . . The interpretation offered challenges the notion that American thinkers of that period were simply anti-urban. In most areas of thought, it turns out, many Americans gradually but definitely abandoned agrarianism in favor of the more complex environmental vision. By mid-century they were seeking a new understanding of city and country, art and nature, that would allow them to hold key values identified with each.[49]

This urban vision, Bender asserts, was lost by the last decades of the 19th century. Bender perhaps exaggerates the positive aspects of the urban vision he seeks to rediscover and promote, but he is surely correct in claiming that "If the study of history can sensitize us to the burden of the past, it can also release us from the myths of historical inevitability. The commitment of Brace, Olmsted, and many of their contemporaries to art *and* nature, spontaneity *and* structure, community *and* organization, science *and* sentiment, deserves the serious consideration of historians"[50] and other urbanologists today. It is revealing and ironic that

> This mid-century urban vision represents a lost heritage. When American intellectuals were confident that the fundamental problems facing the United States required centralization, professional expertise, "science," and federal planning, the romantic impulse in mid-century social thought evoked little sympathy. The continued presence of these social problems, in an era of unprecedented centralization, bureaucratization, and scientism, however, has shaken the confidence of many.[51]

The previous vision was neither complete nor unbiased, nor were its successors. It is not a blueprint to resurrect and follow. But it is *one* lesson to be learned.

There are other lessons: conceptualization, perspective, evidence, and interpretation. For example, not only need we escape the twin but distinct blinders of linear, rising or falling interpretations, but also we must gain some understanding of the historical roots and processes that shaped the present urban crises. Deep divisions within urban space, decay, reforms, and the like are neither new, nor have we succeeded in escaping a kind of failure that is repeated regularly. The past, to be sure, contains no guidelines for action, but it does give us perspectives, a sense of alternatives and options, and some understanding of what fails and what may succeed. It also teaches us how efforts before our own have fared and that we are not quite the pioneers of the unknown that we sometimes think we are.

The point is that we need to broaden the emerging urban vision of reclaiming and renewing the central cities. There are a number of avenues that lead to such a *re-vision-ing*. First, we may look at the experience elsewhere, especially in Europe, where in many places the cities were not left to crumble or die and where they have remained populated and popular among a wide variety of classes, races, and age groups. Second, we may see the city as more than a physical space or environment. Rather, we need to see and also plan the central cities as flexible areas: not only as spaces, but also as resources and education. In this regard, anyone concerned with these issues will profit from such superb works as Paul and Percival Goodman's *Communitas* or Colin Ward's *The Child in the City*.

Ward, for example, in a book that should become a contemporary classic, asks how and in what ways children use and learn in and from the city. With words and pictures, he shows the riches to be found in the urban environment, the creative experiences possible, and the tremendous learning that can take place with freedom to explore and the smallest of additional resources and guidance. He also sees, incidentally, the death and destructiveness in the inner city. Ward concludes

> . . . we have to explore every way of making the city more accessible, more negotiable and more useful to the child. We have seen that some children develop the habit of exploiting everything that their environment can provide. They unfold as individuals through creatively manipulating their surroundings. But there are many others who never get a foot on that ladder, who are isolated and alienated from their city. Often they take revenge on it. . . .
>
> The faces of contemporary city children don't have that haunted look which we read into those of the long-dead nineteenth-century children. We are touched by the way in which they seize what fun they can from an environment which others have shaped without their needs in mind. . . . Most people's recollections of childhood include some moment in some context when their pride and self-esteem were lifted by the fact that they were being treated as though they were not children. They rose to the occasion. Rather than throw in a few playthings, shouldn't we help them climb out of the sandbox and into the city?[52]

What better place to begin a new vision in and of the cities than with the young? Rather than presuming and self-fulfillingly prophesying their problems, as we have for over a century, one might rethink their relationship with the city. That would be a start: educational, cultural, and recreational programs, designed to reintroduce the young to the city—the young of all classes and races, sharing and learning together. Why not have them work, too, as they are older, as they are able, and as they learn. Innumerable ways are possible.

One cannot stop with the young. There are also the old—one of the most segregated and growing groups within our cities, and those in the middle. If there is one point to add to Colin Ward's (whose words do not apply only to the young), it would be to put people of all kinds in the city, to learn, play, work, and live. Policies or plans must have that as their central goal.

But stop. If we have learned anything from the past, recent or distant, it is foolhardy to wish for any major integration, of any large but separated elements within our societies, *without* structural social and economic change. One must admit and respect the limits to urban vision and policy that follow this recognition. Still, the blending of the lives and the sociocultural experiences of the diverse parts of our urban populations may be furthered without utopian notions of eradicating divisions and differences, rooted typically in historical patterns of development. That is, one must at once respect the differences, learn from them, and encourage others to do so, without seeking to eradicate them. Policy only then can follow.

NOTES AND REFERENCES

1. Neil Harris, "Four Stages of Cultural Growth: The American City," in Arthur Mann *et al., History and the Role of the City in American Life,* Indianapolis, Ind.: Indiana Historical Society, 1972, p. 25.
2. Morton and Lucia White, *The Intellectual Versus the City,* New York: Oxford University Press, 1978; Thomas Bender, *Toward an Urban Vision: Ideas and Institutions in Nineteenth-Century America,* Lexington, KY.: University Press of Kentucky, 1975; Bender, *Community and Social Change in America,* New Brunswick, N.J.: Rutgers University Press, 1978. See also Gunther Barth, *City People,* New York: Oxford University Press, 1980.
3. See, for example, David Ward, *Immigrants and Cities,* New York: Oxford University Press, 1971; Stephan Therstrom, *Poverty and Progress,* Cambridge, Mass.: Harvard University Press, 1964; Thernstrom and Knights, "Men in Motion: Some Data and Speculations about Urban Population Mobility," *Journal of Interdisciplinary History,* 1, 1970, pp. 7–36; Michael B. Katz, *The People of Hamilton,* Cambridge, Mass.: Harvard University Press, 1975; Katz, Michael Doucet and Mark Stern, "Migration and the Social Order in Erie County, New York, 1855," *Journal of Interdisciplinary History,* 8, 1978, pp. 669–701; Katz, Doucet and Stern, "Population Persistence and Early Industrialization," *Social Science History,* 2, 1978, pp. 208–229.

4. Richard Wade, *The Urban Frontier,* Cambridge, Mass.: Harvard University Press, 1959; Carl Bridenbaugh, *Cities in the Wilderness,* New York: Oxford University Press, 1938; Bridenbaugh, *Cities in Revolt,* New York: Oxford University Press, 1955; Darret Rutman, *Winthrop's Boston,* New York: W. W. Norton, 1972; Carville Earle and Ronald Hoffman, "Urban Development in the Eighteenth-Century South," *Perspectives in American History,* 10, 1976, pp. 7–79.
5. See, for example, Michael B. Katz, *Class, Bureaucracy and Schools,* New York: Praeger, 1975; Katz, *The Irony of Early School Reform,* Cambridge, Mass.: Harvard University Press, 1968; Katz, *School Reform Past and Present,* Boston: Little, Brown, 1971; Katz, "The Origins of Public Schooling: A Reassessment," *History of Education Quarterly,* 16, 1976, pp. 381–408; Katz, "Origins of the Institutional State," *Marxist Perspectives,* 1, 1978, pp. 6–23; Charles Rosenburg, *No Other Gods,* Baltimore: Johns Hopkins University Press, 1976; David J. Rothman, *The Discovery of the Asylum,* Boston: Little, Brown, 1971; Rotham, *Conscience and Convenience,* Boston: Little, Brown, 1980; Arthur Mann, "The City as a Melting Pot," in Mann, *et al., op. cit.,* pp. 2–23; Helen Horowitz, *Culture and the City: Cultural Philanthropy in Chicago from the 1880s to 1917,* Lexington, KY.: University Press of Kentucky, 1976; Raymond Williams, *The Country and the City,* New York: Oxford University Press, 1973; Daniel Calhoun, "The City as Teacher," *History of Education Quarterly,* 9, 1969; Calhoun, *The Intelligence of a People,* Princeton: Princeton University Press, 1973.
6. In this and related respects, see Williams, *op. cit.;* David Harvey, *Social Justice and the City,* Baltimore: Johns Hopkins University Press, 1975 and his more recent articles; Manuel Castells, *The Urban Question,* Cambridge, Mass.: MIT Press, 1977, and Castells, *City, Class and Power,* New York: Oxford University Press, 1979.
7. Robert Nisbet, *Social Change and History,* New York: Oxford University Press, 1969; Bender, *Community, op. cit.;* Charles Tilly, *An Urban World,* Boston: Little, Brown, 1974.
8. Harris, *op. cit.,* pp. 26–27. See also Raymond Williams, *Keywords,* New York: Oxford University Press, 1976; Williams, *Culture and Society,* New York: Oxford University Press, 1958.
9. See, for example, Milton Singer, "Culture as a Concept," *International Encyclopedia of the Social Sciences,* New York: Macmillan and Free Press, 1968; Alfred Kroeber and Clyde Kluckholm, *Culture,* New York: Vintage, 1963; Clifford Geertz, *The Interpretation of Cultures,* New York: Basic Books, 1973. See also note 26. Gender-based culture is only one of the significant elements this essay must neglect.
10. See, in general, the literature cited in note 5, above, and Carroll Smith Rosenberg, *Religion and the Rise of the American City,* Ithaca: Cornell University Press, 1971; Paul Boyer, *Urban Masses and Moral Order,* Cambridge, Mass.: Harvard University Press, 1978; Bender, *Urban Vision* and *Community, op. cit.;* Herbert Gutman, *Work, Culture and Society in Industrializing America,* New York: A. A. Knopf, 1976; Richard Fox, *So Disordered in Mind,* Berkeley: University of California Press, 1978; Carl Kaestle, *The Evolution of an Urban School System,* Cambridge, Mass.: Harvard University Press, 1973; Stanley Schultz, *The Culture Factory,* New York: Oxford University Press, 1973; Samuel Bowles and Herbert Gintis, *Schooling in Capitalist America,* New York: Basic Books, 1975; David Tyack, *The One Best System,* Cambridge, Mass.: Harvard University Press, 1974; Harvey J. Graff, *The Literacy Myth: Literacy and Social Structure in the Nineteenth-Century City,* New York and London: Academic Press, 1979; John Schneider, *Detroit and the Problem of Order,* Lincoln: University of Nebraska Press, 1980, among a larger literature; see also the parallel contemporary studies.
11. See, for example, Gutman, *Work, op. cit.,* and Gutman, *The Black Family in Slavery and Freedom,* New York: A. A. Knopf, 1976; Josef Barton, *Peasants and Strangers,*

Cambridge, Mass.: Harvard University Press, 1975; Virginia Yans McLaughlin, *Family and Community,* Ithaca: Cornell University Press, 1977; John Briggs, *An Italian Passage,* New Haven: Yale University Press, 1978; Thomas Dublin, *Women at Work,* New York: Columbia University Press, 1979; Daniel Walkowitz, *Worker City, Company Town,* Urbana: University of Illinois Press, 1978; Alan Dawley, *Class and Community,* Cambridge, Mass.: Harvard University Press, 1976; Brue Laurie, *The Working People of Philadelphia,* Philadelphia: Temple University Press, 1980; Tamara K. Hareven, "The Dynamics of Kin in an Industrial Community," in John Demos and Sarane Boocock, eds., *Turning Points,* Chicago: University of Chicago Press, 1978, pp. 151–182; Susan Hirsch, *Roots of the American Working Class,* Philadelphia: University of Pennsylvania Press, 1978; Milton Cantor, ed., *American Workingclass Culture,* Westport, Ct.: Greenwood Press, 1979; *Journal of Urban History,* Special Issue, 4, May 1978; Oliver Zunz, "The Organization of the American City," *Journal of Urban History,* 3, 1977, pp. 443–466; Kenneth Kusmer, *The Ghetto Takes Shape,* Urbana: University of Illinois Press, 1976; David Katzman, *Before the Ghetto,* Urbana: University of Illinois Press, 1973; Elizabeth Pleck, *Black Migration and Poverty,* New York: Academic Press, 1979; Alan Spear, *Black Chicago,* Chicago: University of Chicago Press, 1967; James Borchert, *Alley Life in Washington, D.C.,* Urbana: University of Illinois Press, 1980; Nancy Cott, *Bonds of Womanhood,* New Haven: Yale University Press, 1978; Michael Gordon, ed., *The American Family,* New York: St. Martin's Press, 1979; among a growing body of important works. See also below.

12. See, for example, T. H. Breen, "Persistent Localism," *William and Mary Quarterly,* 32, 1975, pp. 3–28; Breen, "Transfer of Culture," *New England Historical and Genealogical Register,* 132, 1978, pp. 3–17; Phillip Greven, *Four Generations,* Ithaca: Cornell University Press, 1970; S. C. Powell, *Puritan Village,* Garden City: Doubleday, 1965; Kenneth Lockridge, *A New England Town,* New York: W. W. Norton, 1970; Lockridge, *Literacy in Colonial New England,* New York: W. W. Norton, 1974; Lockridge, "Land, Population, and the Evolution of New England Society," *Past and Present,* 21, 1966; Darrett Rutman, *op. cit.;* James Henretta, *The Evolution of American Society,* Lexington, Mass.: D.C. Heath, 1973; Douglas Greenberg, *Crime and Law Enforcement,* Ithaca: Cornell University Press, 1976; Thomas Archdeacon, *New York City,* Ithaca: Cornell University Press, 1976; Alan Tully, *William Penn's Legacy,* Baltimore: Johns Hopkins University Press, 1978; T. Tate and D. Ammerman, eds., *The Chesapeake in the Seventeenth Century,* New York: W. W. Norton, 1979; A. C. Land *et al.,* eds., *Law, Society, and Politics in Early Maryland,* Baltimore; Johns Hopkins University Press, 1977; and note 4 above.
13. See the literature cited above, and Gary Nash, *The Urban Crucible,* Cambridge, Mass.: Harvard University Press, 1979; Frederick Tolles, *Meeting House and Counting House,* New York: W. W. Norton, 1973; Sam Bass Warner, *The Private City,* Philadelphia: University of Pennsylvania Press, 1968; Warner, *The Urban Wilderness,* New York: Harper and Row, 1972; Alfred Young, ed., *The American Revolution,* DeKalb, Ill.: Northern Illinois University Press, 1975; Lawrence Cremin, *American Education: The Colonial Experience,* New York: Harper and Row, 1970; Kaestle, *op. cit.;* Stanley Katz, ed., *Society and Politics in Colonial America,* Boston: Little, Brown, 1976; Rothman, *Discovery, op. cit.*
14. Harris, *op. cit.,* pp. 27–28.
15. *Ibid.,* pp. 28–29.
16. Nash, *op. cit.;* Warner, *Private, op. cit.;* Young, ed., *op. cit.*
17. Harris, *op. cit.,* pp. 29–30. Compare White, *Intellectual, op. cit.,* with Bender, *Urban Vision, op. cit.*
18. Bender, *Urban Vision, op. cit.,* pp. 7–8; Ward, *op. cit.;* Alan Pred, *Urban Growth and the Circulation of Information,* Cambridge, Mass.: Harvard University Press, 1973.

19. Harris, *op. cit.*, pp. 30–31; Harris, *The Artist in American Society*, New York: 1966; see also, Bender, *Urban Vision* and *Community, op. cit.;* Horowitz, *City, op. cit.;* note 20 below; but compare with Paul Faler, "Cultural Aspects of the Industrial Revolution," *Labor History*, 15, 1974, pp. 367–394; Bruce Laurie, *op. cit.*, and "Nothing on Compulsion," *Labor History*, 15, 1974, pp. 337–366; Dawley, *op. cit.;* Walkowitz, *op. cit.*
20. Harris, "Four Stages" and *Artist, op. cit.;* Bender, *op. cit.;* Ronald Story, *The Forging of An Aristocracy*, Middletown, Ct.: Wesleyen University Press, 1980; Edward Pessen, *Riches, Class, and Power*, Lexington, Mass.: D.C. Heath, 1973; Frederick Jaher, ed., *The Age of Industrialism*, New York: Free Press, 1966; Jaher, ed., *The Rich and the Well-Born, and The Powerful*, Urbana: University of Illinois Press, 1973; E. Digby Baltzell, *Puritan Boston and Quaker Philadelphia*, New York: Free Press, 1980; and Baltzell, *Philadelphia Gentlemen*, New York: Free Press, 1958.
21. Harris, "Four Stages," *op. cit.*, p. 31.
22. Bender, *Urban Vision, op. cit.;* Warner, *Streetcar Suburbs*, Cambridge, Mass.: Harvard University Press, 1962; Kenneth Jackson, "Urban Deconcentration," in Leo Schnore, ed., *The New Urban History*, Princeton: Princeton University Press, 1975, pp. 110–142; Joel Tarr, "From City to Suburb," in A. Callow, ed., *American Urban History*, New York: Oxford University Press, 1973, pp. 202–212.
23. Katz, *Class, Irony*, "The Origins," "Origins," *op. cit.;* Graff, *op. cit.;* Katz and Paul Mattingly, eds., *Education and Social Change*, New York: New York University Press, 1975; Kaestle, *op. cit.;* Tyack, *op. cit.;* are among the most suggestive studies.
24. See James McLaughlan, *American Boarding Schools*, New York: Scribners, 1970; Story, *op. cit.*
25. *See, for example, Milton Gordon, Assimilation in America*, New York: Oxford University Press, 1964; The studies of immigrants cited elsewhere; Harris, "Four Stages," *op. cit.*, pp. 31–32.
26. Geertz, *op. cit.;* Mary Douglas, *Natural Symbols*, Hammondsworth: Penguin, 1973; Douglas, *Implicit Meaning*, London: Routledge and Kegan Paul, 1975, among her writings; Victor Turner, *The Ritual Process*, Hammondsworth: Penguin, 1969, among his writings; Charles Valentine, *Culture and Poverty*, Chicago: University of Chicago Press, 1969; McLaughlin, *op. cit.;* Kathleen Conzen, *Immigrant Milwaukee*, Cambridge, Mass.: Harvard University Press, 1976; Katz, *People, op. cit.;* Thomas Kessner, *The Golden Door*, New York: Oxford University Press, 1977; John Bodnar, *Immigration and Industrialization*, Pittsburgh: University of Pittsburgh Press, 1977; Thernstrom, *Poverty, op. cit.;* David Montgomery, *Worker's Control in America*, New York: Cambridge University Press, 1979; Clyde Griffen and Sally Griffen, *Natives and Newcomers*, Cambridge, Mass.: Harvard University Press, 1978; Gutman, *Work, op. cit.;* Graff, *op. cit.;* Barton, *op. cit.;* Oscar Handlin, *Boston's Immigrants*, Cambridge, Mass.: Harvard University Press, 1940; Rudolph Vecoli's many articles; Charlotte Erickson, *Invisible Immigrants*, Coral Gables: University of Miami press, 1972; Borchert, *op. cit.;* among an important, growing literature.
27. See, for example, Jay P. Dolan, *The Immigrant Church*, Baltimore: Johns Hopkins University Press, 1975; Conzen, *op. cit.*, among other studies.
28. Montgomery, *op. cit.;* Laurie, *Working People, op. cit.;* Leonard Richards, *Gentlemen of Property and Standing*, New York: Oxford University Press, 1971; Michael Feldberg, *The Philadelphia Riots*, Westport, Ct.: Greenwood Press, 1975; Feldberg, *The Turbulent Era*, New York: Oxford University Press, 1980; Benjamin Rader, "The Quest for Subcommunities and The Rise of American Sports," *American Quarterly*, 29, 1977, pp. 335–369; Barth, *City People, op. cit.*
29. Horowitz, *City, op. cit.*, pp. 7–8; Harris, "Four Stages" and *Aritst, op. cit.;* Bender, *Vision, op. cit.*

30. Harris, "Four Stages," *op. cit.*, pp. 34–35.
31. *Ibid.*, p. 35.
32. *Ibid.*, pp. 37–38.
33. *Ibid.*, p. 38.
34. *Ibid.*, pp. 38–39.
35. Bender, "The Cultures of Intellectural Life: The City and the Professions," in John Higham and Paul Conkin, eds., *New Directions in American Intellectual History*, Baltimore: Johns Hopkins University Press, 1979, p. 181.
36. *Ibid.*, p. 183.
37. *Ibid.*, pp. 186–187.
38. *Ibid.*, p. 189; Thomas Haskell, *The Emergence of Professional Social Science*, Urbana: University of Illinois Press, 1977; Burton Bledstein, *The Culture of Professionalism*, New York: W. W. Norton, 1977; Robert Wiebe, *The Search for Order*, New York: Hill and Wang, 1967; Calhoun, *Professional Lives in America*, Cambridge, Mass.: Harvard University Press, 1965, and *Intelligence, op. cit.*
39. Harris, "Four Stages," *op. cit.*, p. 40; Hareven, ed., *Family and Kin in Urban Communities*, New York: New Viewpoints, 1977; John Crumbler, *Working Class Community*, Westport, Ct.: Greenwood Press, 1979; Cantor, ed., *op. cit.*
40. Harris, "Four Stages," *op. cit.*, p. 41; John Kasson, *Amusing The Million*, New York: Hill and Wang, 1978; Rader, *op. cit.; Barth, City People, op. cit.;* Lewis Erenberg, *Steppin' Out: New York Nightlife and the Transformation of American Culture*, Westport, Ct.; Greenwood Press, 1981.
41. Harris, "Four Stages," *op. cit.*, p. 41.
42. *Ibid.*, p. 42; Horowitz, *Culture, op. cit.*, Kasson, *op. cit.;* Lary May, *Screening Out the Past*, New York: Oxford University Press, 1980; Gutman, *Work, op. cit.;* for another interpretation, see Gabriel Kolko, *Main Currents of American History*, New York: Harper and Row, 1974.
43. Horowitz, *City, op. cit.*, p. 133; Joel Spring, *Education and the Rise of the Corporate State*, Boston: Beacon Press, 1972; Clarence Karier *et al.*, *Roots of Crisis*, Chicago: Rand McNally, 1973; Karier, *Shaping the American Educational State*, New York: Free Press, 1975; Marvin Lazerson, *Origins of the Urban School*, Cambridge, Mass.: Harvard University Press, 1971; Paul Violas, *The Training of the Urban Working Class*, Chicago: Rand McNally, 1978; Allen Davis, *Jane Addams: American Heroine*, New York: Oxford University Press, 1975; Davis, *Spearheads for Reform*, New York: Oxford University Press, 1967; Roy Lubove, *The Professional Altruist*, New York: Atheneum, 1969; and Lubove, *The Progressives and the Slums*, Pittsburgh: University of Pittsburgh Press, 1962; Gutman, *Work, op. cit.;* Gerd Korman, *Industrialization, Immigrants and Americanizers*, Madison: State Historical Society of Wisconsin, 1967; Calhoun, *The Educating of Americans*, Boston: Houghton, Mifflin, 1969.
44. Horowitz, *City, op. cit.*, Chapter 6.
45. See among a huge literature, for example, Richard Sennett and Johathen Cobb, *The Hidden Injuries of Class*, New York: A. A. Knopf, 1972; Kolko, *op. cit.;* Herbert Gans, *The Urban Villagers*, New York: Free Press, 1962; Gerald Suttles, *The Social Order of the Slum*, Chicago: University of Chicago Press, 1968; Valentine, *Culture and Poverty, op. cit.*
46. Harris, "Four Stages," *op. cit.*, pp. 42–44; Barth, *City People, op. cit.;* compare with Graff, *op. cit.*, chapter 7; May, *op. cit.;* among other recent studies in culture.
47. Warner, *Private City* and *Urban Wilderness, op. cit.;* Robert P. Norton, *City Life-Cycles and American Urban Policy*, New York: Academic Press, 1979; the many papers by David Gordon, New School for Social Research, New York; Harvey, *Social Justice, op. cit.;* Harvey, "The Geography of Capitalism Accumulation," *Antipode* 1975, pp. 9–21;

Harvey, "The Political Economy of Urbanization," *Urban Affairs Annual*, 9, 1975, pp. 119–163; W. Tabb and L. Sawyer, *Marxism and the Metropolis*, New York: Oxford University Press, 1978; Castells, *City* and *Urban*, op. cit.

48. Harris, "Four Stages," *op. cit.*, pp. 44–45.
49. Bender, *Urban Vision*, op. cit., p. xi.
50. *Ibid.*, p. 193.
51. *Ibid.*, p. 194; see also the review by Michael Frish in *Reviews in American History*, 3, 1976, pp. 424–428; Williams, *Country, op. cit.;* Bender's analysis is, however, not unflawed.
52. Ward, *The Child in the City*, New York: Pantheon, 1978, pp. 210–211; Paul and Percival Goodman, *Communitas*, New York: Vintage, 1960.

Chapter VI

THE CHANGING POLITICAL REALITIES FOR NATIONAL URBAN POLICY IN THE EIGHTIES

Robert B. Bradley

The urban landscape of the United States will be transformed over the next decade. Although the precise character and extent of the transformation remains uncharted, its appearance is indicated in a number of well documented trends [69]. These range from the "subtle revolution" that is bringing ever more women into the workforce to changes in the size and character of American households [68]. They include shifts in the postindustrial economy and the revival of nonmetropolitan America. Overall, the trends are indicative of significant changes in the underlying demographic, economic, and technological order. They harbor forces of enormous portent for the future of American cities and suburbs.

Yet, these challenges must take their place beside the already pressing problems of metropolitan America. Despite their scope, it is unlikely that the changes will fundamentally alter the condition of our large, older central cities. The secular trends offer little hope for the deteriorating capital stock and municipal treasuries of numerous cities and suburbs across the country. Nor do the changes appear to contain solutions to the persistence of racial discrimination and of concentrations of poverty that underlie the distress in many of the country's urban areas [38].

The dilemma for urban policy is clear. As a new metropolitan America emerges, the old one reasserts itself. In the nationwide system of cities, both growth and decline are found. Perhaps more poignantly than at most times in our history, it can be noted that "cities do not all keep time to the same historical clock, and each is affected by a somewhat different configuration of internal and external forces" [47: 173]. These differences compound the difficulties of piecing together an effective policy response. Their sheer diversity and number resist easy theoretical attack and plague tidy organizational remedies. They place enormous demands on the intergovernmental system attending urban matters.

The difficulties have been made even greater by changes in the policy milieu sustaining urban initiatives. Not only is there a lack of consensus "on what cities should be like and what the federal government should do about them" [23: 171] but also the basis and tenor of the policy debate has shifted. The end of real growth in federal aid to the cities is symptomatic of these changes. Federal assistance to states and localities climbed from $24 billion in 1970 to $95 billion in 1981. But federal aid, in constant dollars, peaked in 1978 under the Carter Administration. The Reagan Administration has initiated the decline in real dollars. Now, as John Shannon of the Advisory Commission on Intergovernmental Relations (ACIR) has argued,

> We're returning to basics. Urban gardens, rat control, even school impact aid and the state of general revenue sharing—all were beautiful when we could do the federal tango. But (the aid is) just not going to be there. [60:639]

Public impatience with federal deficits, the widespread intolerance with the federal income tax, and the general concern over governmental waste are but isolated elements in the larger confluence of factors ranged against dramatic new national urban policy initiatives. The *Omnibus Reconciliation Bill of 1981* is only the most palpable rendering of these forces.

The altered circumstance of urban policymaking is not limited to the federal level. It bears on the possibilities at the state and local levels as well. After all, as the federal role is circumscribed, state and local governments might be expected to take up the slack and even assume new financial burdens. That, in fact, is one aspect of the Reagan Administration's "New Federalism." But failing the implementation of revenue turnbacks by the federal government, the chances for an enhanced state fiscal presence seem slight.

The states, by and large, are not in good financial health. State balances will decrease from $11.6 billion in fiscal year 1980 to about $2.3 billion in fiscal year 1981. In 1982, state balances are expected to fall to 1.5 percent of total expenditures—considerably below the 5 percent rule-of-thumb recommended by most state budget officers [19: 1872]. Further federal budget cuts and a sluggish national economy may continue to constrain state budgets in the short run. However, even in those states that still show a surplus, there is "good reason to expect progress on the community assistance front will be uneven and incremental . . ." [3: 8].

Aside from new constitutional and political obstacles, there is evidence the new public taste for austerity has also affected the states. Almost half the states cut taxes in 1978 and 1979. In the wake of California's Proposition 13, numerous states have moved toward restricting spending powers. Between 1970 and 1977, 14 states imposed various restraints on local property tax authorities. A similar number took action in 1979 alone. Several states have indexed their personal income taxes against inflation during the last three years.

In the face of such sweeping fiscal changes, the opportunities for state involvement in local affairs under the guise of programs such as the new Small Cities portion of the Community Development Block Grant appear small. More importantly financial considerations may force many states to curtail even those urban strategies that they initiated in the 1970s.

The situation at the local level is even more precarious. While most cities throughout the country are experiencing few of the fiscal pains troubling the well publicized cases of New York and Cleveland, neither is there evidence that they would willingly accept new financial burdens. Local dependence on federal funds grew substantially in the 1970s. Intergovernmental aid from federal and state sources now accounts for almost 45 percent of local receipts. This intergovernmental aid, however, tends to have a low sensitivity to inflation. Inflation's impact on relatively inelastic aid programs is shifted onto the localities. In addition, the real growth in local property tax collection has slowed in many regions of the country. Increasingly, user charges are being relied on as a method to allocate services and to reduce taxpayer dissatisfaction. Overall, the prospects for new urban policy initiatives at the local level, in the absence of additional funding sources, look bleak.

In some measure, the new austerity adopted by public officials merely reflects the growing displeasure of the citizenry with governmental waste and taxation. For example, in 1964, 47 percent of the public believed the government "wastes a lot of money;" 78 percent thought so in 1978. (Hebert and Bingham, 1979:146) But the attitudes of public officials and citizens alike go beyond the concern for expenditures alone. They are rooted in one important strand of contemporary life, so richly documented in Veroff, Douvan and Kulka's *The Inner American: A Self-Portrait from 1957 to 1976*—a general loss of confidence in many of our most prominent institutions [74]. More than ever before, Americans take sustenance from their personal adaptations to the world. There has been a growing focus on the private, the here and now, and the intimately interpersonal among the populace. A socially integrated paradigm has given way to a more personal paradigm.

The public persona of this change has several manifestations. In 1966, 43 percent of the public expressed "a great deal of confidence" in the major American institutions. Since 1974, the percentage has never exceeded a quarter of the public [71:112]. Public esteem for the federal government is especially low. In 1980, less than 20 percent of the public expressed a "great deal of confidence" in Congress or the executive branch. In 1979, the federal government briefly fell below local government for the first time on an ACIR poll asking "From which level of government do you get the most for your money [3:1].

This change in public attitudes is mirrored in the manner in which scores of programmatic efforts over the past two decades are now understood and interpreted. The great expectations held by many urbanists have been humbled before the experiences of the past 15 years. The sway of economic, demographic, and technological imperatives, which pervaded the analysis of Banfield in *The Unheavenly City*, have acquired a new respectability and greater prominence in the prevailing visions of the urban future [9]. T. D. Allman's controversial article, "The Urban Crisis Leaves Town," captured the mood of many observers if not the details of future urban growth patterns:

> Alas, our whole experience with trying to use big government to solve big social problems over the past few decades shows not, as the conservatives pretend, that it can't, but simply, as the liberals won't accept, that we really don't have all that much control over whether it does or not. [6:48]

Overall, there is in Allman's formulation, and in much of the contemporary discussion of the prospects for urban America, a profound sense of latter day Social Darwinism [57:300]. Economic, demographic, and technological forces beyond human agency are viewed as the governors. "Neighborhoods and cities, states as well, (are) so many locational sites at the mercy of national market forces" [46:83]. The compass of meaningful action has shifted. American's quest for closeness, the psychologization of experience, and the focus on the immediate are additional manifestations of the shrinking sphere of purposeful activity. In this view, the efforts of deliberative action are swamped in a tide of secular forces.

The biological metaphor acquires ontological status to the neglect of purposeful action.

Of course, these beliefs are not without foundation. There is ample reason to suspect the efficacy of governmental intervention. Despite rather massive amounts of federal aid and the continuing concern of national policymakers, the deterioration of large, older cities has continued. And what is worse, the deterioration is now appearing in other cities. Increased budgets for policies procuring greater professionalism, new equipment, and sophisticated technologies in law enforcement have been accompanied by growing crime rates and higher levels of urban insecurity. Dutiful increases in the budget for public education have been attended by declining test scores and rising public dissatisfaction. For many observers, such examples are reason enough to think what George Grier has had the temerity to express:

> By the time the policy makers start thinking about something, it's already happened. I wonder about government policy—how much of it is just a reflection of things that are already happening to us. [71:109]

It is in this cynicism born of policy disappointments that the suspicion about deliberative action has been nurtured. The lessons of the past 15 years have been many. Urban public policies often have been incapable of dealing with problems that refused to be confined to the logic of annual budget cycles or regular election intervals. They have run afoul of issues that cut across organizational boundaries or exceed the resources at hand. In many instances, they have been undone by problems spilling beyond the authority of the implementing political jurisdiction. As the supposed supplement and corrective to the failures of the *laissez-faire* market, urban policies at times have foundered on their own nonmarket failures.

As the number and complexity of governmental programs increased, policymakers learned to appreciate the manner in which factors exogenous to program design and implementation could frustrate national initiatives. Policymakers learned the limitations and obstacles in the intergovernmental mechanisms designed to redress urban problems. They came to understand the difficulties of technical design across a variety of urban policy sectors. In themselves, these lessons were well worth learning. They temper the policy milieu with necessary cautions. It is important to recognize them for what they are, however. At best, they offer a partial picture of the policy process and its difficulties. The danger is they will be misconstrued and misapplied in an era when budget cutbacks and the public appetite are already adversely inclined toward governmental action.

The difficulty is that the full meaning of the lessons is neither straightforward nor simple. Donald Rosenthal's description of the conflicting evaluations of the War on Poverty program provides a poignant illustration of this ambiguity.

> There is no agreement as to whether the "failures" of the program—assuming that one can even get sufficient consensus about the goal(s) of the program's performance—were due to the assumptions of the program designers about the character of poverty in American society, the design they evolved to respond to the defects of the existing policy approaches, the organizational mechanisms they employed to overcome those defects, the adequacy of resources made available to the packages of programs administered through Community Action Agencies, the nature of the local political arrangements, or ultimately to the foreign and domestic political environments of the 1960s which limited the potential effects of the program. [67:1]

If anything, the policy experiences of the past 15 years offer too many and contradictory lessons. They do not offer compelling evidence for any single position on the efficacy of governmental action. Yet this is itself a singularly disheartening ambiguity. There are social commentators who suggest that the national government "continue to limp along with programs which, at best, do a little bit of good for a few people but waste considerable societal resources in the process" [67:32]. Perhaps, it might be argued the real lesson of our urban policy experiences is that "the limit of national wisdom seems to be transfusing enough cash to keep city governments afloat, feed the destitute and care for the sick" [47:198]. But this advice, so lacking in its own right an affirmation of purpose and vision, seems hardly adequate in the changing national circumstance and the emerging mood of the 1980s. In failing to provide a palpable justification for public intervention, the policy experiences of the past decade act to galvanize sentiments predisposed against intervention. Bereft of a vision that might explain either success or failure, the serendipity of public intervention undermines prospects for further governmental action.

The changes in our economy and our position in the evolving international economic order challenge basic assumptions in our policymaking milieu and compound the difficulties of making profitable use of our urban policy experiences. They threaten the fundamental assumption of American Keynesianism—that economic growth can be maintained through manipulation of fiscal and monetary policy levers. Economic growth, central to the liberal polity, has been the basis on which the most thorny problems in the political thicket have been avoided. As long as real growth continued apace, questions about the distribution of wealth and income, along with the serious structural issues they raise, could be submerged in the secular rise in national well being. The symptoms of urban malaise could be treated if the disease remained uncured. In the national economy that long ago salvaged developmental capitalism with the principle of social demand, growth provided the basis on which the social demands of organized interests could be addressed through expanding government expenditures.

As growth slows, inflation continues, productivity slips, and unemployment rises, the grounds for deliberative action shift. It is not merely that the resources for urban policy initiatives have been curtailed and "cutback planning" infects Washington [30]. Nor is it only that the public will has been shaken. Rather it is, through a particular confluence of circumstances, that the set of *feasible* urban policy options has changed. The very ambiguity of the urban policy thrusts of the past 15 years is overlaid on the challenges offered by the new economic conditions. Not only have the resources available for urban initiatives become more scarce, but also the justification for their use has become less clear.

The political bases needed to forge urban policy are changing and have changed in response to this altered circumstance. It is this change itself that must be subsumed in the policy process and incorporated into an urban design for the 1980s. Policy alternatives must embody the emerging political configurations and recognize the contours of the new policy milieu lest they fall prey to the most elemental technocratic bias: the belief that politics is but an intervening variable in the policy process or merely an impediment to rational choice.

THE CHANGING BASES FOR A NATIONAL URBAN POLICY

Piven and Cloward's *Regulating the Poor* is perhaps the most provocative statement of the manner in which urban policies incorporate both political considerations and the impact of long-run demographic, technological, and economic change [63]. Recall, they argue, the welfare legislation of the 1960s had its origins in the problems created for the national political system and, more especially, for the National Democratic Party in the economic and demographic changes that swept through the postwar South. Agricultural modernization and the increasingly precarious economic condition of rural blacks resulted in the tremendous interregional migration that eventually generated a wave of mass political volatility, both at the polls and in the streets. This, in turn, critically destabilized the regional coalition of the National Democratic Party: partisan dealignment in the South occurred as powerful minority constituencies took shape in the northern central cities [13:480]. This created the conditions under which it became "feasible" for the National

Democratic administrations of the 1960s to promulgate measures that would restore their electoral stability and civil order [63].

The moral of this story, were it to be played out in the urban politics of the 1980s, would bode ill for the large central cities of the country. Between 1960 and 1976, the proportion of the presidential vote cast in the five largest cities dropped from 13.2 percent to 9.2 percent. Demetrios Caraley has calculated that:

> In the 95th Congress, only 103 (or 24% of the districts were predominantly urban while 138 (or 32%) were predominantly suburban, 121 (or 28%) rural, and 73 (or 16%) mixed. In terms of city size, of those 103 urban districts, only 90 included cities of 250,000 or more within their boundaries, either in whole or in part. Even among the seats held by northern Democrats, the 70 that were predominantly suburban slightly exceeded in number the 66 that were predominantly urban, and there were also 35 northern Democratic constituencies that were predominantly rural. [16:92]

While Caraley argues that in the 1977 session of Congress, support for urban legislation was greater among Democrats from all regions of the country than from Republicans, he also points out that interregional migrations during the 1970s advantaged those sections of the country (the West and the South) with the lowest levels of support for urban legislation.

The loss by the East and Midwest of 17 seats in the Congressional reapportionment of 1980, with a gain by the South and West of 17, may prejudice urban legislation throughout the 1980s. Table VI.1 lists the character of these changes. Perhaps more important for legislation affecting the nation's larger cities, "within states, the major losers are likely to be districts in St. Louis, Detroit, Pittsburgh, Philadelphia, Jersey City, Newark, and New York City [16:93].

The decentralization of population within the United States accelerated in the 1970s. It was the suburbs and the smaller metropolitan areas that experienced the greatest growth during the decade. Population shifts within individual states, even in some states neither gaining nor losing House seats, may act to the disadvantage of urban legislation. While this is true around such cities as San Diego, Atlanta, San Antonio, and Sacramento, it is especially evident in the older industrial cities. Table VI.2 portrays the scope of this shift in 11 major cities.

For many reasons, however, these spatial realignments in the representational system are unlikely to be as decisive in urban policy over the next few years as such simple arithmetic would allow. In great measure, this is due to the changing nature of our political economy and the adaptive characteristics of the federal system and its intergovernmental mechanisms.

Table VI.1. Projected Decennial Reapportionment of Congress, 1980

	1970 Population	*1980 Population*	*1970 Seats*	*1980 Seats*	*Change*
Northeast	54,289,183	54,585,989	113	104	−9
New England	11,847,245	12,348,493	25	24	−1
Maine					
New Hampshire					
Vermont					
Massachusetts					
Rhode Island					
Connecticut					
Mid-Atlantic	42,441,938	42,237,496	88	80	−8
New York					
New Jersey					
Pennsylvania					
Delaware					
Maryland					
D.C.					
Midwest	56,686,267	58,853,804	111	103	−6
Great Lakes	40,262,720	41,669,738	86	80	−6
Ohio					
Indiana					
Illinois					
Michigan					
Wisconsin					
Great Plains	16,423,547	17,184,066	35	33	−2
Minnesota					
Iowa					
Missouri					
Kansas					
Nebraska					
South Dakota					
North Dakota					
South	57,584,311	69,899,833	125	133	+8
South Atlantic	25,560,157	31,493,817	56	60	+4
Virginia					
West Virginia					
North Carolina					
South Carolina					
Georgia					
Florida					
South Central	32,134,154	38,406,016	69	73	+4
Kentucky					
Tennessee					
Alabama					

(continued)

Table VI.1. (Continued)

	1970 Population	*1980 Population*	*1970 Seats*	*1980 Seats*	*Change*
South	57,584,311	69,899,833	125	133	+8
South Central	32,134,154	38,406,016	69	73	+4
Mississippi					
Louisiana					
Arkansas					
Oklahoma					
Texas					
West	32,842,243	43,165,199	74	83	+9
Mountain	8,289,901	11,368,330	17	22	+5
Idaho					
Montana					
Wyoming					
Colorado					
Utah					
Nevada					
Arizona					
New Mexico					
Pacific	26,552,342	31,796,869	57	61	+4
California					
Oregon					
Washington					
Alaska					
Hawaii					
Total	203,302,004	226,504,825	435	435	

Source: National Journal, "The Winners and Losers in the '80 Census," January 10, 1981, p. 72.

Since American Keynesianism emerged as the alternative, functioning coordinative theory to laissez-faire capitalism, the principle of government by social demand has become fully established. "Every vested interest is impelled to seek government support" under these conditions [8:414]. Interests organize to express their demands much as individuals might in a private market, and effective demand still is key to the allocation of values. Lester Thurow has painted the suggestive ends of this process in *The Zero-Sum Society:*

> In the past, political and economic power was distributed in such a way that substantial economic losses could be imposed on parts of the population. . . . Economic losses were allocated to particular powerless groups rather than spread across the population. These groups are no longer willing to accept losses and are able to raise substantially the costs for those who wish to impose losses upon them. [72:23]

Table VI.2. Political Power Shifts from Older Cities, 1923–83

	1923		*1943*		*1963*		*1973*		*1983*[a]	
	City	*Area*	*City*	*Area*	*City*	*Area*	*City*	*Area*	*City*	*Area*
Boston	5	6	4	5	3	6	3	6	2	6
New York	24	1	24	1	19	6	17	5	14	4
Philadelphia	7	2	7	3	5	3	5	3	4	3
Baltimore	4	0	4	0	4	1	3	1	2	2
Detroit	2	3	6	2	5	3	5	6	4	6
Chicago	10	1	10	1	11	4	8	8	7	7
Miami	1	1	1	0	2	1	3	3	3	4
Houston	1	2	1	3	2	3	3	4	4	2
Dallas	1	3	1	4	1	4	3	3	4	3
Los Angeles	2	3	10	3	15	6	17	7	17	7
San Francisco	2	3	2	5	2	8	2	8	2	8

[a]With the exception of Houston and Dallas, 1983 figures are estimated.
Source: R. Cohen, "Task for Politicians: Keeping Up With Votes," *National Journal*, 1981, p. 2037.

To Caraley's portrait of the territorial interests involved in urban policy, Thurow and others would add the hundreds of functional interest groups—ranging from the American Federation of Community Credit Unions to the Women's Equity Action League—based in Washington, D.C., and around the country who now attend to urban matters very closely.

Yet, even this conception of the politics surrounding urban policy misses an important aspect of the developments within our national political economy and polity. Specifically, it neglects the rise of powerful new centers of influence on government within the government. Samuel Beer has been perhaps the most perceptive student of their rise. He argues:

> Within this public sector of the polity two types of influence have been on the rise during the past decade or so. One results from the functional specialization in the modern state. I call it the professional bureaucratic complex. The other results from territorial specialization and I call it the intergovernmental lobby. The action and interaction of the professional bureaucratic complex and the intergovernmental lobby constitute the new form taken by representational federalism. [14:17]

It is hardly necessary to document the growth of the technocratic sphere of the federal government. It manifests itself everywhere. Beer has observed that "in very great measure, (it has been) people in government service, or closely associated with it, acting on the basis of their specialized and technical knowledge who first perceived the problem, conceived the program, initially urged it on the President and Congress, went on to help lobby it through to enactment and then saw to its administration" [14:17]. In this view, the technocracy itself is fundamental to the policy process. Should Beer's analysis be correct, urban policy may suffer little from the secular trends changing our society. While in principle the technocratic infrastructure can be expected to respond to the emerging forces bearing on urban affairs, it also has a considerable stake in the problems, definitions, and issue positions formed under the previous configuration of social forces. In some measure, the technocratic infrustructure will continue to act on the symbols forged in earlier circumstances.

Still, there can be little doubt that the bureaucratic complex will respond to the changing political realities. Ultimately, its influence is anchored in its ability to gain political approval for its machinations. The enormous success of the Reagan Administration in cutting funds for state and local governments, as well as the size of the federal work force, during 1981 is dramatic testimony to the tentative claims of the bureaucratic complex.

Similarly, the intergovernmental lobby will respond to the altered political circumstance of urban policy. The lobby consists of organizations directly affected by the changes, and it is hardly monolithic. Already there have been splits among the "Big Six" over urban policy directions. Within organizations such as the International City Management Association, questions have been raised about the thrust of organizational policy stands by challenging groups. The accent of the 1978 urban policy bore testimony to the rise in influence of a whole group of organizations seldom given voice on such matters: The National Association of Towns and Townships, The American Association of Small Cities, The National Association of Smaller Communities, and the National Rural Coalition. During 1981, groups such as the Mayor's Conference and International City Management Association clashed over the response to the cities' role in Reagan's New Federalism.

The response of the intergovernmental lobby will be conditioned by its own changing character. Over the past decade, an incredibly diverse set of geographical interests have formed organizations to lobby in Washington. These include the Northeast-Midwest Institute and the Coalition of Northeast Governors. They range from the Southern Growth Policies Board to the Federation of Rocky Mountain States. Samuel Beer has interpreted this growth as the reaction of spatially organized political jurisdictions to the rise in influence of the bureaucratic complex. In another interpretation, it is the differentiated response of these jurisdictions to the increasingly fierce competition for the federal dollars.

The actions of Congressional representatives support each explanation. Between 1970 and 1978, Congressional staff increased from 11,061 to 17,374 [21:2638]. Although much of this increase has been devoted to case work and personal staff, a substantial portion of the increase can be tied arguably to the growth in Congressional ombudsman functions within the bureaucracy [25]. The expansion of the major Congressional agencies—the General Accounting Office, the Library of Congress' Congressional Research Service, the Congressional Budget Office, and the Office of Technology Assessment—can also be linked to the increasingly complex oversight function performed by Congress. The notion that these developments were, in some measure, a response to the expanding bureaucratic complex is reinforced by the observation that the period of greatest expansion in Congressional support came during the first half of the 1970s and in a period of reform animated by efforts to equip the Congress to handle the proposals of the executive branch.

More recent developments in Congress support the contention that an increasing awareness of the distributional consequences of budgetary limitations also is at work in expanding the intergovernmental lobby. Table VI.3 documents the growth in the number and range of informal groups formed by Congressmen to channel and combine their legislative energies. Numerous geographical groups, many with explicit economic concerns such as the Congressional Rural Caucus and the Congressional Suburban Caucus, have been organized over the past decade. Most of the activity has come within the past four years as members became increasingly aware of the ramifications associated with a slowing economy and widely publicized secular demographic and economic trends [55]. These caucuses have formed liaison with interests outside Congress, adding considerably to the resources that can be brought to bear on virtually any piece of important legislation. They are likely to remain important despite attempts to curtail their proliferation.

Where political parties once provided the organizational means for integrating territorial and functional interests in the legislative context, the changing character of politics in the 1970s has diminished their importance. The disappearance of local party organizations in the wake of reform-minded local governments, the broadened attacks on party patronage, the increased use of primaries as recruitment tools, and the improved techniques for organized grassroots efforts have taken their toll on the effectiveness of national political parties. With the growth of political and media advisors, polling services, and campaign management schools, "each elected official is his own party and is free to establish his own party platform" [72:27]. Members now raise their own campaign funds and rely little on party effort. Instead, they turn to special interests for funds. The number of political action committees almost

Table VI.3. Congressional Informal Groups: Period of Formation, Their Interest and Chamber[a]

Shared Individual Interest		
Personal Characteristics		*Beliefs/Ideology*
	1959–64	
		Democratic Study Group (H)
	1965–69	
		Members of Congress for Peace Through Law (B)
		Wednesday Group (H)
		The Group (H)[b]
	1970–74	
Congressional Black Caucus (H)		Democratic Research Organization (H)
Freshman Senators (S)[b]		Republican Study Committee
		Steering Committee (S)
		United Democrats of Congress (H)
		Wednesday Club (S)
	1975–80	
Blue Collar Caucus (H)		Ad Hod Committee for Irish Affairs (H)[c]
Congressional Hispanic Caucus (H)		Balanced Budget Caucus (H)
Congresswoman's Caucus (B)		Coalition for Peace Through Strength (B)
94th Congress New Member Caucus (H)		Congressional Ad Hoc Monitoring Group on South Africa (H)
95th Congress New Member Caucus (H)		Congressional Clearinghouse on Future (B)
96th Congress New Member Caucus (H)		Congressional Clearinghouse on Women's Rights (B)
95th Republican Club (H)		Environmental Study Conference (H)
96th Republican Club (H)		House Fair Employment Practices Committee (H)
		Senate Steering Committee (S)
		Solar Coalition (H)

(*continued*)

tripled between 1974 and 1978 [20:2455], and the contributions they made to members increased similarly. On the other hand, party contributions to individuals declined over this period. The new importance of special interests was dramatically evident in 1980 when several Senators demanded that the U.S. Chamber of Commerce modify its Congressional ratings to enhance their image in the business community [22:1112]. Indicative of their growing influence and attentiveness, dur-

Table VI.3. (Continued)

Shared District Interest		
Geographical[d]		*Economic*
	1970–74	
Conference of Great Lakes Congressmen (H)		Congressional Rural Caucus (H)
New England Congressional Caucus (H)		
	1975–80	
High Altitude Coalition (B)		Coal Caucus (S)
Metropolitan Area Caucus (H)		Congressional Alcohol Fuels Caucus (H)
Midwest Conference of Democratic Senators (S)		Congressional Port Caucus
Northeast-Midwest Coalition (S)		Congressional Roller and Ball Bearing Coalition (H)
Northeast-Midwest Congressional Coalition (H)		Congressional Shipyard Coalition
Congressional Sunbelt Caucus (H)		Congressional Suburban Caucus (H)
Western Coalition (S)		Congressional Textile Caucus (H)
		Congressional Tourism Caucus (H)
		Export Caucus (S)
		Export Task Force (H)
		Congressional Steel Caucus
		Mushroom Caucus (H)
		North American Trade Caucus (S)
		Senate Steel Caucus (S)
		Textile Caucus (H)

[a]Congressional groups organized during the period between a general election and the convening of the next Congress are credited as having been formed during the new Congress.
[b]Caucus has ceased functioning.
[c]A third of the members of the Ad Hoc Committee for Irish Affairs are of Irish descent. The group predominantly consists of Members appealing to the Irish constituency of their districts.
[d]State delegations have not been included in this listing, although they can be appropriately categorized as informal groups based upon shared geographical interests.
Source: D. Mulhollan and A. Stevens, "Special Interests and the Growth of Informal Groups in Congress," paper presented at Midwest Political Science Convention, Chicago, Ill., 1980, appendix.

ing the 1970s the number of groups publishing Congressional ratings rose from 19 to almost 70 [55:5].

These changes in the way Congress operates not only mirror the changes in the larger polity, but also affect the manner in which special interests, the bureaucratic complex, and the intergovernmental lobby can have an impact on urban policy. During the 1970s, both the House and the Senate increased the decentralization of their leadership and opened up the process whereby legislative leaders were chosen. "By 1979, 33.8 percent of House and 98.3 percent of Senate Democrats held a subcommittee chairmanship (not including temporary and ad hoc subcommittees)" [55:6]. Changes in the budget process, increased rates of turnover, rapid growth in multiple referral practices, and increasing importance of floor activities all increase the demands on members and work to increase the number of points in the legislative process where a bill can be affected by a relatively small number of members. They heighten the chances that the full distributional consequences of a piece of legislation will be assayed and widely known. They compound the difficulty of forming and maintaining coalitions of support. They help account for the novel use of the budget process by the Reagan Administration, which resulted in the Omnibus Reconciliation Bill of 1981.

There will be continuing support for national urban legislation by both Congress and the executive branch in the 1980s. But this support must be viewed against the backdrop of the new austerity and the new number and skill of the claimants for federal dollars. Despite the growing disaffection of the public at large with governmental intervention, the symbols that charged previous urban policy efforts—civil rights, the conditions of the disadvantaged, the decay of our cities—are still potent, if not preeminent. However, the bases of support for a national urban policy are changing. Federal aid to state and local governments is declining. Both the government and the claimants for its largesse have primed themselves to determine the distributive consequences of policy. This altered political reality will be of continuing importance in the possibilities for urban initiatives during the 1980s.

THE POLITICAL ADJUNCTS OF THE COMING URBAN POLICY

The ramifications of these changing political facts for the urban policies of the 1980s are yet to be seen. The full impact of the Reagan program will hit most areas in fiscal 1983. Over the next 10 years, changes in the emergent political realities are inevitable. Technical developments, such as the growing sophistication and range of urban impact analysis, may alter the problems of forging coalitions whose consequences are better known. The changing character of the economic and technological order may effect the possibilities as well. The presence of labor representatives on the board of Chrysler is but a harbinger of shifting political alignments that may yet ripple throughout the political economy. Then, too, there is the real possibility of further structural changes in the policy itself. It is difficult to assess how states will react to the challenges of the next decade, and reading the direction of change in the vast intergovernmental network is virtually impossible.

However, as long as the zero-sum characteristics of policy persist alongside the flagging economy and other secular trends noted above, the possibilities for national urban policy initiatives seem limited. But they do exist in several legislative situations. Several strategies are open which, at once, recognize the continuing problems of cities and the changing political adjuncts of fashioning urban policy.

There are a broad number of matters receiving legislative attention whose importance to the national well-being evoke general consent. The recent efforts to frame a national energy policy is but one example. This legislation harbored serious implications for metropolitan America, yet its consequences were seldom seen in those terms. Tax expenditures and the credit budget are other matters with serious ramifications for urban areas that have drawn little attention from urbanists. Similarly, environmental regulation has already had tremendous impacts on the character and location of housing in this country. States that have been reluctant to move against exclusionary enclaves in suburbia have been more than willing to reinforce such conditions under the umbrella of environmental protection.

Urban analysts are beginning to study and understand the complex effects of such initiatives on urban life. However, such legislation has seldom been used to consciously shepherd urban policies. More directly and with greater purpose than in previous decades, the 1980s will demand that national urban legislation be incorporated into a broad number of initiatives in other policy areas. Properly directed, perhaps through the agency of a body such as the Interagency Coordinating Council, this tack holds real possibilities for framing a flexible and differentiated response to the conflicting realities of metropolitan America.

Urban policy can be made in the secondary consequences of legislation. The inchoate science policy of this country provides a case in point. The spatial consequences of research and development expenditures, the funding of universities, and the location of research centers can have an indirect impact on the future of metropolitan areas and regions. Support for science and research has until recently not evoked concern from geographical interests nor has it prompted the active involvement of the intergovernmental lobby. In the next decade, controversies such as the one accompanying the award of fusion monies to a research center at the University of Texas in Austin may become more common as interests squabble over important developing technologies that foster the technological "seedbed" functions of a region. However, most science funding will remain noncontroversial. More intensive concern for and development of technology transfer techniques should allay most of the concerns that do develop. Federal policies on patent rights, the rebuilding of American laboratories, and the maintenance of research facilities will have an impact on regional growth patterns, but the scope of these factors is difficult to gauge in an era when communication and computer technology act to homogenize spatial characteristics. And precisely because the impacts are so difficult to assess, the possibilities for forging and maintaining coalitions on matters such as science policy are good. Selectly pursued, these policies can provide partial redress to regional imbalance and can offer some promise for the long-run economic condition of cities.

On the other hand, great difficulties may arise in addressing urban problems through legislation in areas such as industrial policy. Notions of balanced regional development have not become an integral part of the national agenda. Their obvious distributional consequences pose an enormous obstacle. Although it is possible to tackle the long-run viability of an area by improving its capacity to innovate and acquire export bases with government-sponsored research and monies, the idea of private capital subsidies through loans, loan guarantees, public infrastructure investments, and sectoral growth policies remains burdened by ideological opposition and the onerous prospect that the winners and the losers can be clearly identified [32]. Such policies are probably necessary in the coming decade, but their development as legislation will require extensive preparation and subtle maneuvering in the prevailing political climate.

It is important to recognize the possibilities for shaping urban America through legislation that does not itself have urban problems as its central concern. This is, after all, no more than an acknowledgment that many of our hopes for cities center not on their physical attributes, but on the people who live there. Still, it is unrealistic to suggest that legislative initiatives for urban America can regularly span the organizational structures of our policy generating mechanisms. Most urban legislation will be designed, nurtured, and implemented by agencies, committees, and individuals with a continuing concern for the problems of the cities and the worth of cities as storehouses of capital and amenities. Such legislation will have to deal directly with the new realities.

Of course, the legislation that affects the cities need not involve either great sums of money or even direct expenditures. Statutory and regulatory changes in procedures can have an enormous impact. These impacts, however, are often difficult to gauge. The recent regulation requiring owners of HUD-assisted housing to remove lead paint from chewable surfaces is a case in point. Still, the fight in the 96th Congress over the proposed Fair Housing legislation gives some indication of the incredible array of forces willing to battle over a major piece of urban legislation committing few federal dollars. Groups such as the Independent Insurance Agents of America, the Society of Real Estate Appraisers, and the National Association of Realtors lined up against the entire civil rights coalition in an attempt to influence the Fair Housing legislation. Scores of similar interests are poised to address any change in regulation or statute.

Within a milieu that galvanizes interests so thoroughly and embodies the new political realities, new tacts are necessary. John Kirlin has argued that several types of policy instruments are available within the existing intergovernmental framework [41]. They are classified in Table VI.4 as administrative strategies, organizational environment strategies, and learning system strategies. While all can be useful, in an era of fiscal limits where the polity is easily paralyzed through zero-sum politics, Kirlin argues that they should be envoked in the opposite order of their appearance in the table. That is, the prejudice should be toward policy instruments that encourage local initiative consistent with national purpose. The focus in this new era should be on national legislative actions that ensure local governments and organizations are assigned responsibilities for national purposes. There is strong evidence that this strategy allows local actors to pursue their own agendas and facilitates policy movement in the direction intended at the national level. It is much less clear that state governments, given responsibility in the Reagan Administration's block grants and mentioned prominently in its tax turnback alternatives, will serve urban interests as well.

Although local agencies of social repair may have difficulty coping

Table VI.4. A Typology of Policy Strategies for Intergovernmental Systems

I. Administrative Strategies:
   a. Entitlement programs (e.g., Aid for Families with Dependent Children)
   b. Categorical programs (e.g., UMTA grants)
   c. Universalistic, specific regulations (e.g., Federal Management Circular 74-7)

II. Organizational Environment Strategies:
   a. Market intervention (e.g., housing subsidies)
   b. Creation of bureaucratic markets (e.g., directly funded Community Action Programs)
   c. Changing the system of legal rights (e.g., Civil Rights Acts)

III. Learning System Strategies:
   a. Block grant programs (e.g., Community Development Block Grants)
   b. Create bargaining arenas under constraints (e.g., A-95 Review)
   c. General revenue sharing programs that enhance local government fiscal capacity
   d. Noncentrally directed by centrally facilitated activities (e.g., statutes that allow for development of alternative structures of delivery of local government services)

Source: Adapted from J. Kirlin, "Adapting the Intergovernmental Fiscal System to the Demands of an Advanced Economy," in G. Tobin, ed., *The Changing Structure of the City*, Beverly Hills, Calif.: Sage Press, 1979, Table 2, p. 87.

with the profound national dynamics that engulf their communities, their success can be facilitated if they are given the resources and flexibility to fashion their own policy responses. The message here has been succinctly stated by Norton Long: "That a local territorial area—if it can get its act together, mobilize and coordinate its own public and private sources, and do the same with federal and state programs—can make a significant difference in the performance in its local economy" [46:81]. But local governments and organizations, even in this scenario, would continue to need federal funds and programs to address problems such as capital infrastructure, service delivery, and debt management.

Yet another tact has been offered by some as the guide to our urban policy. Popularized as *The Third Wave,* it emphasizes decentralization, deinstitutionalization, and deregulation as the alternatives to growth or decline in an era of limits [73]. As seen in the work of the Center for Neighborhood Technology and (perhaps) the National Commission on Neighborhoods, it emphasizes self-help, mutual assistance, and incentives for mediating structures such as neighborhoods, voluntary organizations, church, and family. Its policies are those of decentralizing responsibility and control [50:229].

Although special problems exist in exporting policies involving neighborhoods to cities across the country, compelling reasons exist as to why some form of this policy initiative should be included in the urban agenda of the 1980s. Most urban policies in the postwar period have emphasized, with good reason, the economic and social uses of cities. This focus was aimed directly at the overwhelming ills of many urban areas—poverty, employment, housing, crime. Like the concern for growth, this orientation was the legacy of our liberal tradition. The presumption was that society with its coordinative mechanisms stood separate from politics. Yet, cities also have their political uses. They are sites not only for economic growth, but also for political integration. As long as growth continued, the political uses of cities could be ignored. With decline however, innovation, entrepreneurship, and leadership become the levers of social action [66:153]. Eliminating the alienation of the public from political action must now be a major goal of urban policy.

Although the accumulative and consumptive functions of cities cannot be ignored, exclusive concern for them to the neglect of other factors is likely to have its own brand of insidious side effects. As phrased by Norton Long:

> The idea that there is such a thing as a local economy whose performance can be managed in a way that can make an important difference in the lives of local inhabitants is still far from general acceptance and even further from being intelligently and effectively acted upon. There are fatal attractions to the doctrine of economic powerlessness since its corollary is that one is no way responsible for one's

> economic fate and self-help being out of the question transfer payments become the main objective. [46:82]

Although the OEO and Community Action Agencies have become *dépassé* in most quarters, their emphasis on organizing and political action is still worthy of note and development. In a period of urban adjustment, a number of obvious strategies are open to policymakers: The character of services can be altered, the level and mix of revenues can be modified, management can be improved, governmental organization can be reshaped, responsibilities can be transferred, functions can be shared, boundaries can be enlarged. Success, however, requires the cooperation of the public, not merely its acquiesence. Decentralization policies may prove to be one aspect of the solution to the central dilemma facing our cities: The maintenance of a structure of expenditure and taxation that can stimulate economic growth, while at the same time maintaining the popular legitimacy of government institutions, even as the potential for political conflict increases. [28].

Alone, a commitment to decentralist policies will not ensure legitimacy for governmental action, nor will it absolve the national government from its continuing role in the construction of social justice. Whether indirectly or, more likely, head-on, national urban policy will have to address the tenuous position of minorities and the disadvantaged. The importance of governmental action on these matters is illustrated by the progress and position of blacks in American society.

The substantial and real economic and social gains made by blacks since World War II cannot be denied. By virtually every measure, racial inequalities have been narrowed. Yet, the picture is clouded by the precarious nature of some gains by blacks and by the underlying processes that help to frame the character of black progress.

First, it is not clear which factors have contributed most substantially to black progress. In a study now a decade old, David Rasmussen suggested that the economic boom of the late 1960s might be responsible [65]. He echoed the argument of Batchelder that the standing of blacks was tied to high levels of aggregate economic demand [10]. More recent work by Stanley Masters suggested it was, in fact, the civil rights policies of 1964 that began the secular trend of black advances [51]. McCrone and Hardy suggest racial economic equality is driven by both anticyclical fiscal and monetary policies and civil rights policies [48:15]. This debate is of considerable import precisely because of the economic conditions facing the United States in the next decade. Sluggish growth in the economy could well reveal the tenuousness of the black middle class. Cutback budgeting will have severe implications for the relatively large proportion of the black labor force employed by government at all levels in this country. Without civil rights enforcement and a continuing commitment to black opportunity, the prosperity of many in the new black middle class will be threatened. In addition, cutback budgeting and slow economic growth will challenge the ability of governmental agencies such as the Equal Employment Opportunity Commission to win white support for aggressive affirmative action implementation. It may also prompt the countermanding of Executive Orders designed to insure affirmative action in the federal government's treatment of minorities.

Second, it is clear that the shifting demographic realities of America will have some impact on racial inequalities and the condition of blacks. The growth of black population in the suburbs, fostered by rising incomes, is still small, but the absolute numbers are impressive when placed in perspective. For example, the number of blacks moving into the metropolitan rings between 1970 and 1974 almost equaled the absolute growth of blacks in suburban areas for the entire previous decade. The migration of blacks from nonmetropolitan areas appears to have stopped as well. There is a new migration of blacks back to the South. While the figures hardly are indicative of a depopulation of central cities by blacks, they may demonstrate a greater propensity on the part of blacks to settle less densely in America's communities. They may alter the political possibilities of blacks in numerous settings across the country, and call for a stronger commitment to the concerns voiced by blacks on the part of leaders with other constituencies.

Third, a focus on the aggregate statistical gains made by black Americans may divert attention from the underlying dilemma of contemporary American race relations. While a new, young, better educated and better employed black middle class is being created and nurtured, a sizeable proportion of black America has been left behind as an underclass in our central cities. The lot of these Americans is tragic and is likely to worsen in an era of cutback budgeting and slow economic growth. Their problems will have to be addressed directly if the character of today's economic structure and market segmentation is not to work to their detriment. In the contemporary economy, it is no longer clear that "a rising tide floats all ships."

Finally, it is important to see that the problems of both poor and middle-income blacks are still linked. While middle-income blacks can hope to move to the periphery of the core city or to the suburbs, they still face considerable segregation in the housing market. They still must endure the costs that segregation exacts. Black gains are real enough, but significant racial differences exist in a number of areas. It is worth remembering that a higher proportion of white men held white-collar jobs in 1940 than did black men in 1976. The median wage and salary for black males engaged in year-round full-time work was only 77 percent that of their white counterparts in 1975. And in 1974, the purchasing power of the typical black family was equivalent to that of a white family 20 years earlier [23:206]. For all that separates blacks in 1980, there is even more that unites them. This unity must be mirrored in the country's urban policies if they are to be accepted as legitimate among the minority population.

The changing political realities of the 1980s may well challenge the possibilities for further governmental action on behalf of minorities and the disadvantaged. They will temper the response that can be mustered to the dynamics sweeping the nation's system of cities. Yet political action in these areas will be as crucial to the nation's well-being as reindustrialization because it validates the sense in which the United States can be represented to its own people as a democratic state and not just an economy. For this reason, as much as any other, the political adjuncts of national urban policy should not be underestimated.

> The most fundamental contribution of a politics is its ability to produce a commonly shared definition of the situation. Such definitions provide people with a map of the world to which they must adapt and through which they must make their way. The cognitive competence of this map is a major determinant of people's individual and collective capacity to manage their environments. [46:87]

Managing simultaneously the growth and decline of our cities while continuing the work toward social justice will call for skillful and imaginative politics. It will be a politics that must operate on many levels. It will be a politics without comprehensive solutions. It must be a politics that prizes both the diversity of forces at work in the polity and the currents in the emerging political milieu which can be forged into urban policy responses.

REFERENCES

1. Advisory Commission on Intergovernmental Relations, *The Intergovernmental Grant System as Seen by Local, State and Federal Officials,* A-54, Washington, D.C.: US. Government Printing Office, 1977.
2. ———, *Regional Growth Study,* preliminary report, Washington, D.C.: U.S. Government Printing Office, 1978.
3. ———, *Changing Public Attitudes on Goverments and Taxes,* S-8, Wahsington, D.C.: U.S. Government Printing Office, 1978.
4. ———, *State Community Assistance Initiatives: Innovations of the Late 70's,* M-116, Washington, D.C.: U.S. Government Printing Office, 1979.
5. ———, *The Federal Role in the Federal System: A Crisis of Confidence and Competence,* A-77, Washington, D.C.: U.S. Government Printing Office, 1980.
6. Allman, T. D., "The Urban Crisis Leaves Town", *Harpers,* 1978.
7. Alonso, W., "The Population Factor and Urban Structure," in A. Solomon, ed., *The Prospective City,* Cambridge, Mass.: MIT, 1980.

8. Averitt, R., "The Future of American Capitalism," in James Weaver, ed., *Modern Political Economy*, Boston, Mass.: Allyn and Bacon, 1973.
9. Banfield, E., *The Unheavenly City: The Nature and Future of the Urban Crisis*, Boston: Little, Brown, 1970.
10. Batchelder, Alan, "Decline in the Relative Income of Negro Men," *Quarterly Journal of Economics*, No. 78, November 1964, pp. 525–548.
11. Beale, L., "The Recent Shift of United States Population to Nonmetropolitan Areas, 1970–75," *International Regional Science Review*, Vol. 2, 1977.
12. Beck, P. A., "Partisan Dealignment in the Postwar South," *American Political Science Review*, 1977.
13. Beck, E. M., Horan, P. and Tolbert II, C., "Industrial Segmentation and Labor Market Discrimination," *Social Problems*, (forthcoming).
14. Beer, S., "Federalism, Nationalism and Democracy in America," *American Political Science Review*, 1978.
15. Black, J., "The Changing Economic Role of Central Cities and Suburbs," in A. Solomon, ed., *The Prospective City*, Cambridge, Mass.: MIT, 1980.
16. Caraley, D., "Carter, Congress and The Cities" in D. Marshall, ed., *Urban Policy Making*, Beverly Hills: Sage, 1979.
17. Cohen, R., "Peeking at PAC Power," *National Journal*, 1979.
18. Cohen, R., "Neighborhood Planning and Political Capacity," *Urban Affairs Quarterly*, 1979.
19. Cohen, R., "Task for Politicians: Keeping Up With Votes," *National Journal*, 1981.
20. Congressional Quarterly, "Energy PACs: Potential Power in Elections," *Weekly Reports*, 1979.
21. Congressional Quarterly, "Growing Staff System on Hill Forcing Changes in Congress," *Weekly Reports*, 1979.
22. Congressional Quarterly, "Liberal Senators Facing Tough Re-election Fights Moderated Their 1979 Votes," *Weekly Reports*, 1980.
23. Downs, Anthony, "Urban Policy," in Joseph Pechman, ed., *Setting National Priorities: The 1979 Budget*, Washington, D.C.: The Brookings Institute, 1979, pp. 161–194.
24. Farley, R., "Trends in Racial Inequalities: Have the Gains of the 1960s Disappeared in the 1970s?" *American Sociological Review*, 2, Vol. 44, 1977, pp. 189–208.
25. Featherman, D. and Hauser, R., *Opportunity and Change*, New York: Academic Press, 1978.
26. Fiorina, M., *Congress: Keystone of the Washington Establishment*, New Haven: Yale Press, 1977.
27. Freeman, R., "Black Economic Progress Since 1964," *Public Interest*, 52, Summer 1978, pp. 52–68.
28. Freidland, R., Piven, F. and Alford, R., "Political Conflict, Urban Structure and the Fiscal Crisis," in D. Ashford, ed., *Sage Yearbooks in Politics and Public Policy*, Beverley Hills: Sage, 1977.
29. Gallup, G., "Cities: Unsolved Problems, Unused Talents," *Antioch Review*, 1979.
30. Gans, H., "Planning for Declining and Poor Cities," *AIP Journal*, 1975.
31. Gintis, H., "The American Occupational Structure Eleven Years Later," *Contemporary Sociology*, 1, Vol. 9, 1980, pp. 12–16.
32. Harrison, Bennett and Susan Kanter, "The Political Economy of States' Job Creation Business Incentives," *AIP Journal*, Vol. 44, No. 4, October 1978, pp. 429–435.
33. Hebert, F. and Bingham, R., "Public Opinion, The Taxpayer's Revolt and Local Governments," in J. Blair and D. Nachmias, eds., *Fiscal Retrenchment and Urban Policy*, Urban Affairs Annual Review, Beverly Hills: Sage, 1979.
34. Houstown, L. O. Jr., "The Carter Urban Policy A Year Later," *Antioch Review*, 1979.

35. Job, B. C., "The Black Labor Force During the 1975–1978 Recovery," *Monthly Labor Review,* May, 1979, pp. 3–7.
36. Judd, D. and Collins, M., "The Case of Tourism: Political Coalitions and Redevelopment in the Central Cities," in G. Tobin, ed., *The Changing Structure of the City,* Urban Affairs Annual Review, Beverly Hills: Sage, 1979.
37. Kain, J. F., "Implications of Declining Metropolitan Population on Housing Markets," in G. Sternlieb and J. W. Hughes, ed., *Post-Industrial America: Metropolitan Decline and Inter-Regional Job Shifts,* Rutgers, N.J.: Center for Urban Policy Research, 1975.
38. Kain, J., "Race and Poverty: Keys to Central City Revitalization," in H. Bryce, ed., *Revitalizing Cities,* Lexington, Mass.: D.C. Health, 1979.
39. Kettle, D., *Managing Community Development in the New Federalism,* New York: Praeger, 1980.
40. King, N. R. and Coats, J. F., "The Future of Urban America: Possibilities and Prospects", *Urban Data Service Reports,* 1978.
41. Kirlin, J., "Adapting the Intergovernmental Fiscal System to the Demands of an Advanced Economy" in G. Tobin, ed., *The Changing Structure of the City,* Urban Affairs Annual Review, Beverly Hills, Calif.: Sage, 1979.
42. Kotler, N., *Neighborhood Economic Enterprises,* Neighborhood Policy Series, Dayton, Ohio, 1978.
43. Levine, C. and Posner, P., "The Centralizing Effects of Austerity on the Intergovernmental System," paper presented at American Political Science Association, Washington, D.C., 1979.
44. Levitan, S. and Taggart, "The Great Society Did Work," *Political Science Quarterly,* 1976.
45. Lewis, C. and Logalbo, A., "Cutback Principles and Practices: A Checklist for Managers," *Public Administration Review,* 1980.
46. Long, N., "Federalism and Perverse Incentives: What is Needed for A Workable Theory or Reorganization for Cities?" *Publius,* 1978.
47. Lowry, I., "The Dismal Future of Central Cities," in A. Solomon, ed., *The Prospective City,* Cambridge, Mass.: MIT Press, 1980.
48. McCrone, D. J. and Hardy, R. J., "Civil Rights Policies and the Achievement of Racial Economic Equality, 1948–1975," *American Journal of Political Science,* 1, Vol. 22, 1978, pp. 1–17.
49. Marrett, C. B., "The Precariousness of Social Class in Black America," *Contemporary Sociology,* 1, Vol. 9, 1980, pp. 16–19.
50. Masotti, Louis, "Toward a Viable Urban Future in A Society of Limits: Possibilities, Policies and Politics," in D. Marshall, ed., *Urban Policy Making,* Beverly Hills: Sage, 1979.
51. Masters, Stanley, *Black-White Income Differentials: Empirical Studies and Policy Implications,* New York: Academic Press, 1975.
52. Mergert, A. E., "The Era of Fiscal Restraint", *Urban Data Service Report,* ICMA, 1979.
53. Mikesell, J., "The Season of Tax Revolt," in J. Blair and D. Nachimias, eds., *Fiscal Retrenchment and Urban Policy,* Urban Affairs Annual Review, Beverly Hills, Calif.: Sage, 1979.
54. Mollenkopf, J., "Neighborhood Politics for the 1980's" *Social Policy,* 1979.
55. Mulhollan, D. and Stevens, A., "Special Interests and the Growth of Informal Groups in Congress," paper presented at Midwest Political Science Convention, Chicago, 1980.
56. The National Commission on Neighborhoods, *People, Building Neighborhoods,* Final Report to President and the Congress of the United States, Washington, D.C., 1979.
57. Perry, D. and Watkins, A., "People, Profit and the Rise of the Sunbelt Cities," in D.

Perry A. Watkins, eds., *The Rise of the Sunbelt Cities,* Urban Affairs Annual Review, Beverly Hills, Calif.: Sage, 1977.
58. Peterson, G., "Federal Tax Policy and the Shaping of Urban Development," in A. Solomon, ed., *The Prospective City,* Cambridge, Mass.: MIT, 1980.
59. Pettigrew, T., "Racial Change and the Intrametropolitan Distribution of Black Americans," in Arthur Solomon, ed., *The Prospective City,* Cambridge, Mass.: MIT Press, pp. 52–79.
60. Pierce, N. and Hagstrom, J., "The Cities, Not the States, May Bear the Brunt of Revenue Sharing Cutbacks," *National Journal,* 1980.
61. Pierce,N. and Hagstrom, J., "If It's Good Enough for the Cities, It's Good Enough for the Suburbs," *National Journal,* 1980.
62. Pierce, N. and Hagstrom, J., "New Migrants Mean Opportunities and Problems for Rural America," *National Journal,* 1980.
63. Piven, F. and Cloward, R., *Regulating the Poor: The Functions of Public Welfare,* New York: Vintage, Random House, 1971.
64. Plotnick, R. and Skidmore, F., *Progress Against Poverty: A Review of the 1964–1974 Decade,* New York: Academic Press, 1975.
65. Rasmussen, David, "A Note on the Relative Income of Non-White Men," *Quarterly Journal of Economics,* No. 84, February 1970, pp. 168–172.
66. Redburn, F. and Buss, T., "Public Policies for Communities in Economic Crisis: An Overview of the Issues," *Policy Studies Journal,* 1979.
67. Rosenthal, D., "Fielding a Federal Program: Problems in Implementing a Neighborhood Revitalization Grant," Paper presented at Midwest Political Science Association, Chicago, 1980.
68. Smith, R., ed., with N. Barrett, N. Gordon, S. Hofferth, K. Moore and C. Vickery, *The Subtle Revolution: Women at Work,* Washington, D.C.: The Urban Institute, 1979.
69. Solomon, A., ed., *The Prospective City,* Cambridge, Mass.: MIT Press, 1980.
70. Stanfield, R., "Toward an Urban Policy with a Small Town Accent," *Publius,* 1979.
71. Stanfield, R., "If You Want the Federal Dollars, You Have to Accept Federal Controls," *National Journal,* 1980.
72. Thurow, L., *The Zero-Sum Society: Distribution and the Possibilities for Economic Change,* New York: Basic Books, 1980.
73. Toffler, A., *The Third Wave,* New York: Random House, 1980.
74. Veroff, Joseph, E. Douvan, and R. Kulka, *The Inner American: A Self-Portrait from 1957 to 1976,* New York: Basic Books, 1981.
75. *The Washington Lobby,* 3rd ed., Washington, D.C.: Congressional Quarterly, 1979.
76. Wilson, W. J., *The Declining Significance of Race: Blacks and Changing American Institutions,* Chicago: University of Chicago Press, 1978.
77. Yates, D., "The Mayor's Eight-Ring Circus: The Shape of Urban Politics in Its Evolving Policy Arenas," in D. Marshall, ed., *Urban Policy Making,* Beverly Hills: Sage, 1979.

Part II

The Implications of Economic Transformation for Urban Society

Chapter VII

REINDUSTRIALIZATION AND THE URBAN UNDERCLASS

R. D. Norton

Federal urban policy has many dimensions, but its single acid test is central-city poverty. Despite the downtown revival of recent years, the poverty count for central-city blacks rose by over one million people during the 1970s. To that extent, the dominant place-oriented urban strategy of the past 15 years has failed. Accordingly, this chapter proposes a new approach to the problem.

More generally, the message is that a new strategy to combat urban poverty and underemployment can be effectively harmonized with the equally urgent goal of revitalizing the American economy. To do so, however, will require a shift in emphasis from the failing place-oriented strategy to one of more direct assistance to distressed people—including an end to both federal and local practices that now tie the underemployed to declining areas.

THE FAILURE OF THE INNER CITY STRATEGY

The unifying theme of present federal policies for the urban underclass is to aid the poor where they live through the intermediation of local governments. Indeed, a jobs-to-people approach has the imprimatur of the 1978 White House Conference on Urban Growth as the consensus choice of state and local political officials. Its high-level political support extends back to the days when ghetto-enrichment was an organizing focus in the War on Poverty:

> The prevailing strategy, now dominant at HUD and endorsed by the President's urban policy statement, was first given respectability by Robert F. Kennedy in the middle 1960s when he held that for a minority person "the keys to free movement" and "a real opportunity to choose whom he will call neighbor" would be won only after minorities had demonstrated their ability to rebuild their own communities to levels of "comparability in housing and full employment." That concept that governmental resources should be concentrated upon aiding the disadvantaged *where they live* has few critics today.[1]

A variety of motives—not all of them laudable—enter into the current consensus that favors this approach of keeping the poor where they are and aiding them there. The consensus consists of (1) white middle-class suburbanities, who for a variety of reasons want to keep the central-city poor out of their localities; (2) elected officials, who naturally prefer place aid to people aid because it enhances their political resources; and (3) the no-growth movement in the West, which both for environmental and for exclusionary reasons wants to keep any newcomers—but especially black newcomers—away.

The Older City: Service Station or Deadend?

Beyond the matter of motives, however, *the basic premise of a jobs-to-people attack on urban poverty and joblessness rests on a flawed historical analogy*. That analogy views blacks as just another round of "immigrants" entering central cities, capable over time, like immigrant groups before them, of working their way up the social scale and then out of the city. Witness the passage above: implicit in the consensus view is the notion that the minority poor must first "demonstrate their ability to rebuild their own communities," if they want equal spatial access to the amenities, jobs, and public services available in suburbia.

The historical precedent was touted in an influential 1972 essay, "An Urban Civilization Without Cities?" There Irving Kristol contended that "Americans have always *used* their cities, and more often than not in a casual and even brutal way."[2] The uses Kristol had in mind were less economic in character than social or political. Because it betrays the weakness of the inner city strategy, Kristol's argument is worth recounting briefly here.

Kristol conceived of the industrial city as a "service station" or upgrading central for the processing of rural migrants. As he wrote,

> One service, in particular, has been of the utmost importance: the absorption and integration of rural immigrants—mainly, but not only, foreign—into American life. . . . The American city is an entrepot, importing people and exporting citizens to the suburban towns and smaller suburban cities.[3]

This passage has the ring of historical truth, at least in a stylized way. Over time, the children or (more likely) grandchildren of the turn-of-the-century immigrants managed, by means of the city school system and of the jobs available to unskilled workers, to enter the economic mainstream of American life—and perhaps to leave the city for suburbia.

But the analogy runs into trouble at this point. Kristol flatly predicted that the same upgrading mechanism is built into mid-century urbanization. Hence, there should be a gradual absorption, upgrading, and integration function for blacks and Hispanics just as there was for white ethnics. Yet, one glaring difference exists between the industrial city at the turn of the century—the city as "dynamo," the city as a generator of jobs for the unskilled—and today's older city. That, of course, is the older city's job base, which is contracting over the long run and shifting in structure toward jobs not traditionally open to minority males.

Both tendencies (job declines and mixes changing away from manufacturing employment) leave a gradually diminishing number of jobs for black and Hispanic males. The result has been the transformation of the city from service station or "zone of passage" to a dead end for most minority families.[4]

The Rise in Central City Black Poverty

The inadequacy of the inner city strategy can be seen in poverty and unemployment trends during the 1970s. In practice, the data are much less reliable and comprehensive than one might wish. Nevertheless, and however fragmentary, the evidence points unambiguously in one direction. It suggests the formation of a permanent urban underclass of the minority poor.

One such indicator is what has been termed "official poverty," as monitored by the Census Bureau. It tells the number of people whose cash (but not total) incomes fall below a minimum adequate income level known as the poverty line. The flaw here is that by the late seventies, over half of all government aid targetted to the poor took the form not of cash payments but of in-kind assistance—notably food stamps, housing, and medicaid. As a result, many people are counted as poor when in fact their total incomes (in-kind as well as cash) are above the poverty line. By the standard of total income, the "right" measure, only about half as many people are poor as the official counts indicate.

Still, official poverty remains a useful indicator, if not of living standards then of *dependency*. The in-kind aid that this measure ignores is, after all, only a government transfer, not earned income. Official poverty tells us how many people fall below the poverty line before in-kind aid but after earnings from work and cash assistance from government. It thus reflects the degree to which people are able to rise out of poverty through their own work efforts.

In this light, trends in official poverty since the late sixties are instructive. After falling sharply during the sixties, the count stabilized after 1969 and held at about 25 million people through the seventies. Then, with the long recession after 1980, the count jumped sharply to 32 million by 1981. The incidence of poverty thus rose to 14 percent of the U.S. population, or as high as in the late sixties. For blacks, of course, the incidence was much higher. By 1981, more than one in three had incomes (before in-kind transfers) below the poverty line.

For an assessment of the inner city strategy, the most telling comparisons of official poverty over time are for 1969 and 1979, each a peak year in the economy's cyclical expansion. As already noted, the official count was about the same in both years, at roughly 25 million people. But this aggregate constancy masked a sharp spatial redistribution of poverty from rural America to declining central cities. In the early 1960s, a majority of the poverty population had been rural, and only about a quarter of it was in central cities. By the late seventies, the nonmetropolitan share had fallen sharply, in good part because of rural economic development, and the central city share had risen to match it, at nearly 38 percent. (Table VII.1.)

Table VIII.1. The Rise in Central City Poverty between 1969 and 1979

Persons below the Poverty Line (000)	*1979*	*1969*	*Change, 1969–79*
Total	25,345	24,147	1,198
Nonmetropolitan	9,613	11,063	−1,450
Metropolitan	15,732	13,084	2,648
Outside central city	6,232	5,091	1,141
Inside central city	9,500	7,993	1,507
Proportion (percent)			
Total	100.0%	100.0%	—
Nonmetropolitan	37.9	45.8	−7.9%
Metropolitan	62.1	54.2	7.9
Outside central city	24.6	21.1	3.5
Inside central city	37.5	33.1	4.4

Source: U.S. Bureau of the Census, *Current Population Reports*, Series P-60, *Characteristics of the Population Below the Poverty Level: 1978*, Washington, D.C.: U.S. Government Printing Office, 1981, Table 4.

Table VII.2. Changes in Central City Poverty by Race: 1969–79

Whites Below the Poverty Line (000)	*1979*	*1969*	*Change, 1969–1979*
Total	16,823	16,659	164
Nonmetropolitan	7,117	7,855	−738
Metropolitan	9,706	8,804	902
Outside central city	4,934	4,038	896
Inside central city	4,772	4,765	7
Blacks Below the Poverty Line (000)			
Total	7,838	7,095	743
Nonmetropolitan	2,277	3,089	−812
Metropolitan	5,561	4,005	1,556
Outside central city	1,142	930	212
Inside central city	4,419	3,076	1,343

Source: U.S. Bureau of the Census, *Current Population Reports,* Series P-60, *Characteristics of the Population Below the Poverty Level: 1979,* Washington, D.C.: U.S. Government Printing Office, 1981, Table 4.

The reason for this rising city share lies in the deteriorating positions of central city blacks during the 1970s. As Table VII.2 illustrates, the number of poor central city blacks was far larger in 1979 than in the late 1960s. After a rapid decrease during the sixties, the count had climbed back up to 4.4 million by 1979, for an increase of more than 40 percent over 1969. By contrast, the corresponding count for whites did not change during the period.

So whatever the process that threw an additional 1.3 million central city blacks into official poverty between 1969 and 1979, it had no comparable impact on city whites. But what was it? What led to the rise in black dependency in cities during the 1970s?

Ghetto Malaise as an Economic Outcome

A standard analysis ascribes the rise in black poverty during the 1970s to an epidemic of teenage illegitimacy and to family breakups in the northern ghetto. And without question, current Census Bureau studies read like an updated version of the Moynihan Report of the mid 1960s. Noting that "central cities had, by far, the highest proportion of poor families with female [heads]," a recent Census account predicts a hardening of central city poverty:

> The predominance of female-householder families in central cities is one sign that future progress against poverty in these areas may be slow, since the incidence

of poverty among families of this type has not declined as it has among male-householder families. In fact, the poverty rate for female-householder families residing in central cities was actually higher in 1978 (38 percent) than in 1969 (33 percent).[5]

But the more fundamental question is: Why was the ghetto family structure hit so hard in the 1970s when black progress in other places continued? In terms of the city-as-service-station model, it seems clear that the answer lies in the cumulative deterioration of the ghetto *as an economic environment.* Indeed, a variety of indicators reveal that economic opportunities for ghetto residents have gone from bad to worse, with predictable consequences for minority families.

In particular, black youth unemployment rates have doubled over the past generation. Jobless rates for black teenage males in 1979 were twice those of the mid-1950s. More strikingly, jobless rates for black men between 20 and 24 rose nationally from below 10 to 20 percent between the mid-1960s and the late 1970s. For both age categories, the figures are consistently higher for central cities. And for both, the increases are secular, not cyclical.

High and rising youth unemployment in the ghetto rudely short-circuits the scenario by which groups at the bottom of the American ladder have traditionally found a foothold. As the labor economist Eli Ginzberg observes,

> Many minority children . . . living in neighborhoods where few people who do go to work regularly have much to show for it, see little point in taking school seriously or believing it can help to get a job that will lead anywhere. If their early job history and work experience confirm their pessimistic expectations, many give up. . . .[6]

The malaise of the ghetto as a social environment is thus but a concluding tableau in an unfolding historical tapestry. In the past, the older city's social upgrading capacity was a function of the economic opportunity it offered the unskilled. Today, the cumulative erosion of the older city's industrial base, together with the shift in the city's job structure toward white-collar occupations, has brought the process to a halt.

Ginzberg's additional comments highlight the deindustrialization of older cities as a causal factor:

> . . . the steady out-migration of manufacturing jobs from the inner cities, where large minority populations are concentrated, to the suburbs and beyond has surely compounded the difficulties many young blacks (especially men) face in getting a job they could do and that pays fairly well.[7]

Not that labor economists agree as to the precise causes of the rise in black youth unemployment rates—far from it. But the wholesale elimination of entry-level jobs in older cities clearly adds to the problem. Is it only coincidence, for example, that the fragmentary evidence available shows far higher black unemployment rates in older cities in 1979, when the economy was peaking, than in Dallas or Houston? (See Table VII.3.)

What is clear is that older cities no longer perform the social upgrading function that was once uniquely theirs. A key illustration of this change is New York City, historically the gateway to American opportunity. During the 1970s—a decade in which the city lost roughly a half-million jobs—the proportion of the city's population holding jobs fell steadily behind the national average. By 1979, the share of the city's teenage (16–19) population that was gainfully employed had fallen to half the average for the United States as a whole. Once the gateway to opportunity, in other words, New York has now become the "youth unemployment capital" of the nation.

Thus the proposition. The inner city strategy is premised on historical conditions that have come to an end. The next section explores some structural factors behind this change.

Table VII.3. Minority Unemployment Rates in 10 Central Cities in 1979

	"Black and Other" Unemployment Rate[b]	
City[a]	*Men*	*Women*
Philadelphia	20.3%	17.6%
Detroit	17.2	19.0
Cleveland	15.8	11.4
Baltimore	15.2	20.6
St. Louis	14.4	12.9
New York	13.2	10.4
Chicago	11.9	10.0
Washington, D.C.	9.2	9.4
Dallas	7.9	8.7
Houston	6.3	8.1

Note: Error ranges at a 90-percent confidence level are typically 2 to 4 percentage points on either side of the estimates listed.

[a]These are the only central cities for which minority unemployment rates are reported in the Bureau of Labor Statistics compilation.

[b]Blacks constitute roughly 90 percent of the "black and other" Census category.

Source: U.S. Department of Labor, Bureau of Labor Statistics, *Geographic Profile of Employment and Unemployment, 1979*, Washington, D.C.: U.S. Government Printing Office, 1980, Table 8.

THE DEINDUSTRIALIZATION OF THE OLDER CITIES

If older cities have lost their traditional economic functions, then requiring the urban poor to "rebuild their own communities" is misguided. In the late 1970s, federal policy attempted to shore up the economic base of the older city, both for fiscal reasons and to combat poverty and unemployment. But the deindustrialization of the older city continued. This section offers an interpretation of why that happened—and suggests that the older city's decline is now a matter of economic history.

City Life Cycles: An Overview[8]

Many observers have noted the tendency for declining cities to be in some sense old, and for growing cities to be young. Our purpose here is to define the link between city age and city growth according to explicit criteria, which can shed light on the causes of decline. To this end, consider the 30 largest cities in 1970. If we ask which of their larger urban settlements were already of great size on the eve of World War I, and which were still small, the answer provides a basis for labelling one group of central cities as "old" today, and the other "young."

Table VII.4 reveals that every older city, so defined, has lost population since 1950, while every younger city has grown substantially. Such age-correlated tendencies were defined most sharply for the 1950–70 period. But even in the 1970s, when city growth rates generally plunged as a result of a sharp decline in U.S. birth rates, most younger cities held their own, even as older cities lost large numbers of residents. A similar pattern could also be shown for city job changes. For both jobs and population, in other words, the timing of urban development has been a decisive influence on city growth and decline.

Accounting for City Growth Contrasts. However clearcut, empirical patterns in themselves tell us nothing about causes. Why has the timing of urban development proved so fundamental to the rise and fall of American cities?

On the surface, at least, the age-correlated structure of city growth rates has a strikingly simple explanation. During the 1950–70 transition, when growth contrasts were especially well defined, city growth performance had two obvious determinants. One, annexation—the degree to which a city could expand its legal boundaries—was political. The other—the growth rate of the larger urbanized area (or of the SMSA)—was broadly economic in character.

Table VII.4. Population Changes in 30 Large Cities by Age Category

Age Class	*City, by 1910 Metropolitan Size*	*Percentage Changes* 1950–80	1970–80
Old	New York	−11%	−11%
	Chicago	−18	−12
	Philadelphia	−19	−14
	Boston	−30	−12
	Pitsburgh	−37	−19
	St. Louis	−47	−28
	San Francisco	−11	− 6
	Baltimore	−17	−13
	Cleveland	−37	−24
	Buffalo	−38	−23
	Detroit	−35	−21
	Cincinnati	−24	−16
Anomalous	Los Angeles	50	5
	Washington, D.C.	−21	−16
	Milwaukee	0	−12
	Kansas City	− 2	−12
	New Orleans	− 2	− 6
	Seattle	5	− 7
Young	Indianapolis	64	− 7
	Atlanta	27	−15
	Denver	18	− 5
	Columbus	49	4
	Memphis	63	3
	Nashville	152	3
	Dallas	108	7
	San Antonia	93	20
	Houston	164	26
	Jacksonville	164	7
	San Diego	162	25
	Phoenix	622	34

Source: U.S. Bureau of the Census, decennial census reports; 1980 data are preliminary.

As Table VII.5 shows, younger cities benefitted not only from consistently large-scale annexations, but also from high urban growth rates. Meantime, the boundaries of every older city were virtually immutable, and areawide (or, equivalently, urban) growth rates were far below those for the younger urban settlements. Statistically, these two explanatory variables account for roughly 90 percent of the variation in 1950–70 growth rates for both population and jobs. What is equally interesting, however, is that urban growth rates test out as a more important long-run growth determinant than annexation.

Table VII.5. Correlates of Population Growth in the 30 Largest Cities, 1950–70

Age Class	*City, by 1910 Metropolitan Size*	*City Population*	*Urbanized Area Population*	*City Territory*
Industrial	New York	0%	32%	0%
	Chicago	−7	36	7
	Philadelphia	−6	38	0
	Boston	−20	19	0
	Pittsburgh	−23	20	2
	St. Louis	−27	34	0
	San Francisco	−8	60	0
	Baltimore	−5	36	0
	Cleveland	−18	42	1
	Buffalo	−20	36	5
	Detroit	−18	49	0
	Cincinnati	−10	36	4
Anomalous	Los Angeles	43	109	3
	Washington	−6	93	0
	Milwaukee	12	51	90
	Kansas City	11	64	292
	New Orleans	4	46	0
	Seattle	14	102	18
Young	Indianapolis	74	63	587
	Atlanta	50	131	256
	Denver	24	110	42
	Columbus	44	80	242
	Memphis	58	64	108
	Nashville	157	73	2208
	Dallas	94	148	137
	San Antonio	60	72	165
	Houston	107	140	171
	Jacksonville	159	118	2436
	San Diego	108	177	219
	Phoenix	444	300	1350
EXHIBIT				
Class means:				
Industrial Cities		−14%	37%	2%
Young Cities		115	123	676
Difference		128	86	674
Significance		<.001	<.001	<.01

Source: R. D. Norton, *City Life-Cycles and American Urban Policy*, New York: Academic Press, 1979, p. 35. Original data are from U.S. Bureau of the Census, decennial reports.

The reason these two proximate influences were so important to a city's growth lies in the universal tendency toward urban decentralization. For both jobs and population, either annexation or rapid metropolitan growth helped a city counter the impact of suburbanization. The younger cities were aided by both these offsets to decentralization. But in older cities, borders remained frozen, and areawide growth rates were low. Accordingly, suburbanization took a severe toll, and the older cities (as per the stereotype) lost large numbers of middle-income white residents and manufacturing jobs.

Why Annexation Power Varies with City Age. Yet, only the surface has been scratched. Why were the younger cities able to annex new territory, and why did their SMSAs grow so rapidly? Alternatively, why are the boundaries of the older cities permanently frozen, and why has the older metropolis as a whole stagnated? Despite the complexity of these issues, it is possible to isolate the key historical processes that have brought older cities down and that work against their restoration.

First, city annexation differences reflect fairly systematic contrasts in state guidelines governing cities between the Manufacturing Belt and the rest of the nation. In other words, the older cities have been encircled and territorially sealed with the historical support of state governments. By one reading, this process can be traced back to the massive influx of non-English speaking newcomers in the decades before World War I, a flow that was channelled to the then burgeoning industrial cities of the Manufacturing Belt. The resulting political tensions in the industrial metropolis contributed to a tightening of state rules governing city annexations. Nothing of the kind happened in the South and West, where annexation laws typically remain more permissive.

In that light, it is easy to understand why proposals for metropolitan government have come to so little in the older metropolis. Central city borders there serve not only fiscal functions but also the veiled function of regulating spatial access of the central city poor, who are effectively excluded from higher income suburbs. Whether that is good or bad is not the issue at the moment. The point is only that, for deep-rooted historical reasons, *areawide or metropolitan government is out of the question for older central cities.* In that measure, the older cities will remain especially vulnerable to both further suburbanization and fiscal distress.

Urban-Industrial Realignments. As for the urban growth factor, two tendencies dominate the recent historical data. First, most older urbanized areas failed to attract net white inmigration between 1950 and 1970, even as white migrants were moving in large numbers to younger areas. (In the 1970s, of course, rising outmigration would end the population growth of the older areas altogether.) In turn, this drying up of white migration precipitated the sharp racial and income changes hitting the declining older cities, since it exposed them to the full brunt of the tendency toward white suburbanization within their metropolitan areas.

Second, *the typical older metropolis failed to generate new manufacturing employment between 1947 and 1972.* As artifacts of the American industrial revolution, these areas began the post-World War II era with distrinctively high shares of their labor forces holding manufacturing jobs (Table VII.6). But over the quarter-century before 1972 (and thus even before the energy price explosion), when manufacturing employment rose by one-third nationwide, the older metropolis was left out. Meantime, younger SMSAs (which were initially much less oriented to manufacturing) experienced sustained job growth in that sector at rates well above the U.S. average.

Such was the context for the accelelerated industrial exodus from older cities in the decade after 1967. Partly as a result of two increasingly severe recessions, the median older city lost 30 percent of its manufacturing employment between 1967 and 1977. Meantime, most young cities weathered this period fairly well. One reason was that several younger cities experienced annexations or city-county consolidations. But the SMSA data also make it clear that over the long haul, the younger cities have shared in the areawide industrial expansion that has long since ended in older areas.

Hence the proposition. The economic decline of the older city reflects deep-rooted industrial realignments within the continental system. But are such shifts irreversible? Putting it differently, why have the nation's older metropolitan areas stagnated industrially? For perspective on this question, it is essential to look at the matter from a regional standpoint.

The Vanishing Regional Division of Labor

On the eve of World War I, the then largest cities were linked together in a focussed regional grid that traced out the super-region known today as the Manufacturing Belt. For the most part, the rest of the nation was left out of America's urban-industrial transformation. Instead, the South and West functioned primarily as raw-materials suppliers and agricultural producers for the industrializing core region.

Since these economic differences were matched by regional contrasts in urbanization, the South and West remained largely rural in 1910. Most of the younger regions' urban development would thus come later, under technologies more like those of the present day. So much is reflected in the fact that 10 of our dozen younger cities lie in the South and West, while all but one of the older cities is in the Manufacturing Belt.

The regional clustering of the industrial SMSAs within the Manufacturing Belt gave it a commensurately high share of the nation's industrial activity. As recently as 1940, for example, the Belt had 69 percent of all U.S. manufacturing jobs—or nearly half again as much as its share of the national population. That meant that much of the South and West continued to rely on imports of both finished and intermediate goods

Table VII.6. 1950 Industrial Structure and Post–1950 Growth in 30 Large SMSAs

Age Class	*SMSA, by 1910 Metropolitan Size*	*Percent of Urbanized Area Workforce in Manufacturing 1950*	*Percentage Change in SMSA Manufacturing Jobs, 1947–72*	*Percent Change in City Manufacturing Employment, 1967–77*
Old	New York	30.8%	−8.6%	−32%
	Chicago	37.7	6.0	−33
	Philadelphia	35.6	−6.3	−10
	Boston	28.7	−5.1	−36
	Pittsburgh	38.0	−22.5	−35
	St. Louis	33.8	0.8	−30
	San Francisco	19.4	11.7	−18
	Baltimore	30.9	1.8	−31
	Cleveland	40.5	−2.0	−30
	Buffalo	39.7	−17.5	−30
	Detroit	46.9	−2.6	−27
	Cincinnati	33.4	9.2	−24
Anomalous	Los Angeles	25.6	121.2	2
	Washington	7.4	140.8	−20
	Milwaukee	42.9	3.4	−50
	Kansas City	24.5	50.6	−21
	New Orleans	15.6	16.9	−37
	Seattle	19.8	70.9	− 5
Young	Indianapolis	33.1	20.3	4
	Atlanta	18.3	113.1	−26
	Denver	16.8	169.5	5
	Columbus	25.0	60.6	−15
	Memphis	20.5	73.2	0
	Nashville	22.9	102.2	n.a.
	Dallas	18.4	204.5	0
	San Antonio	11.6	91.4	31
	Houston	21.4	142.0	51
	Jacksonville	13.1	95.9	n.a.
	San Diego	15.7	211.1	24
	Phoenix	10.4	871.6	38

Source: U.S. Bureau of the Census, *Census of Population: 1950*, Washington, D.C.: U.S. Government Printing Office, 1950; and *Census of Manufactures*, Washington, D.C.: U.S. Government Printing Office, 1947, 1967, 1972, 1977.

from the core region. Accordingly, they had much less manufacturing employment than that warranted by their population size.

Now all that has changed. By the late 1970s, the core region had less than half of all U.S. manufacturing employment. Moreover, the regional decentralization of manufacturing has proceeded at a much faster pace than the redistribution of population. As a result, the Belt's share of U.S. manufacturing jobs relative to its population fell from a ratio of 1.46 in 1940 to 1.19 in 1979.

Nevertheless, *the divisions of the South and West still have less manufacturing employment than their population shares warrant.* If anything, one might therefore expect a further "filling in," through import substitution, of the local manufacturing base in the younger regions. Any such continued convergence of regional employment structures also implies a further erosion of the Manufacturing Belt's industrial base. By the same token, it would all but rule out a reindustrialization of the Belt's central cities.

In any case, so much merely belabors the obvious. The interplay of suburbanization, on the one hand, and regional change, on the other, has stripped the older cities of their former industrial roles. Accordingly, and whatever the success of marginal adjustment policies geared to elite services functions, the capacity of the older city to upgrade the labor force has been unalterably weakened.

But apart from the feasibility of restoring the older city's bygone industrial prominence, what of its *desirability?* Would the nation as a whole be better off if the industrial cities were again truly "industrial"?

TENSIONS BETWEEN URBAN AND NATIONAL REVITALIZATION

In the course of the 1970s, a number of observers concluded that the United States was losing ground to its foreign economic competitors. Large and unprecedented trade deficits, vanishing productivity growth, and low investment-GNP ratios seemed to signal an historic decline in the American position within the world economy. Well before reindustrialization gained media currency, scholars debated an appropriate American response. In 1975, for example, Robert Gilpin wrote that the only viable long-term solution to the tendency by industry and economic power to migrate abroad is through domestic innovation and productivity increases.

What role should the industrial cities play in any such national revitalization strategy? This section notes some inherent conflicts between the goal of restoring the older city's industrial base and that of revitalizing the American economy. But it is useful to begin with a look at current proposals for city-focused reindustrialization—proposals identified with Felix Rohatyn and, at a more operational level, with Kemp-Garcia urban enterprise zones.

City-Focused Reindustrialization?

Rohatyn contends that older cities should serve as the focal points for a national reindustrialization effort. He argues that the nation's industrial position is inseparable from that of its declining older cities:

> The reconstruction of our older cities will have to take place alongside the restructuring of our basic industries. Like Siamese twins the disease of one inevitably infects the other. As the industrial effort needed over the next two decades begins to take hold, a deliberate effort will have to be made to funnel activity into the [older] urban areas.[9]

From different premises, Art Laffer also argues that cities must be reindustrialized if urban dependency is to be reduced. In his more laissez-faire view, "The problem is partially taxation and the disincentives inherent in the welfare system." If government reverses existing central-city tax incentives, the private sector will take care of minority joblessness:

> As an initial move, businesses that locate within the inner city should be taxed at lower rates. This removal of a direct impediment to employment would enhance business incentives to bring jobs where they are needed most. . . . Secondly, businesses that locate within the inner cities . . . should be relieved of both employer and employee payroll taxes.[10]

Laffer thus proposes that the kinds of incentives now offered via Urban Development Action Grants and federal loan programs be broadened to work through the tax system as well.

The Kemp-Garcia proposal for urban enterprise zones now before Congress is consistent with Rohatyn's framework and Laffer's tactics—and with the inner city strategy generally. While the details of the legislation are still unresolved, the aim is to use tax incentives in specially designated city poverty areas to spur private-sector job creation. In other words, a Reagan urban policy centered on enterprise zones would carry the inner city strategy to a logical extreme. Hence, it would be vulnerable to the same basic problem—the overriding momentum of a spatially decentralizing industrial system.

But the issue at hand is the approach's implications for the national economy. What are the present and potential linkages between this extreme form of the inner city strategy and the goal of national revitalization? For perspective on the question, it is worth considering the view that the U.S. economy as a whole is experiencing a diminishing capacity to adapt to change.

Place Competition and Structural Rejuvenation

The brunt of the argument is that as the world's second oldest industrial power, the United States is increasingly vulnerable to the British syndrome. The source of the first industrial revolution, Britain experienced a so-called "climacteric," or economic change of life, in the late 19th century. American industrial primacy dates back a full century to the 1880s, when the nation overtook Britain in steel production. Beyond its early industrial maturity, however, the American economy's relative age is heightened by the fact that its chief industrial rivals, Germany and Japan, were both modernized by the sweeping institutional reforms imposed on them after 1945, and by a new capital stock.

Hence, the view that the U.S. economy's structural problems signal a crisis of economic aging. As Tibor Scitovsky observes, "Capitalism works when it's flexible, but self-destructs when it's not. . . . With the passage of time [in the U.S.] . . . the joints of that once wondrously flexible structure are becoming more and more rigid."[11] Similarly, Charles Kindleberger contends that in

> . . . shoes, textiles, steel, automobiles, urban finance—*adjustment is postponed by delaying actions* rather than by getting out of deteriorating industries and into new ones. The capacity of the economy to adjust has perceptibly declined. Productivity increases have fallen, as has the formation of new business. Risk-taking is declining. . . .[12]

Kindleberger's reference to postponing inevitable adjustments points up the fundamental issue. In effect, Rohatyn advocates a turning back of the historical clock in the sense of restoring "basic" (i.e., old) industries, and thereby bolstering the economic positions of declining places as well.

By contrast, reindustrialization as rejuvenation would attempt not to retard but to adapt to change. Rather than recapturing a bygone past through governmental intervention, the goal would be to outflank industrial change within the world economy. Government's role, in this view, should be to aid the transition to activities in which the country enjoys a clearly defined comparative advantage. In a world of advanced communications and virtually unlimited supplies of low-cost labor, that means agriculture and high-technology (or science-based) manufacturing.

At the regional scale, the New England precedent shows how such a strategy can succeed. In the late 1970s, New England emerged from a half-century of stagnation with an industrial structure reorganized around its knowledge base. The region's low wages, skilled labor force, and (above all) high-technology entrepreneurship have gradually coalesced to offset the loss of older industries. New England thus illustrates Gilpin's strategy of innovation and productivity increase as the solution to the tendency for mature industries to migrate to competing, less-developed areas.

But while the New England scenario is illuminating, in practice the rise of new industries within the American economy has worked through another, more general process as well. This second process of structural rejuvenation occurs through *the eclipse of older by younger centers of activity*. In other words, geographical realignments are an integral part of industrial modernization within the U.S. industrial system.

The rise of California, and more recently of Texas, as seedbeds for new industries are widely recognized. But high-technology entrepreneurship is also evident over the entire arc from North Carolina's Research Triangle Park through Scientific Atlanta and Texas Instruments to Seattle's aircraft complex. Such younger centers are at the cutting edge of world development: their rise enhances the American economy's global competitive position.

By the same token, city-focused reindustrialization would obstruct the economy's market-based, regionally driven rejuvenation. As a case in point, a key obstacle facing a Rohatyn-style restoration is the tendency for new private investment to follow markets South and West, as part of the filling-in process mentioned previously. What is at stake is perhaps best illustrated by the current regional controversy over accelerated depreciation allowances.

Almost everyone agrees that in a time of high inflation, faster plant and equipment writeoffs are needed to spur investment. The principal opposition emanates from Congress' Northeast-Midwest Coalition. In their view, a faster rate of capital formation will hurt the older cities of the Manufacturing Belt by encouraging companies to phase out aging plants and to invest in growing regions. And they may well be right.

In a recent paper devoted in part to a similar measure—the investment tax credit (ITC)—McHugh and Puryear suggest that a faster rate of investment will indeed occur at the expense of older cities:

> . . . firms are more likely to move in order to exploit new technologies than for any other reason. The existence of ITC encourages firms to relocate to exploit new technologies without delay. . . . By stimulating such new investment, ITC accelerates the process of shutting down older factories . . . in central cities and to rebuild in the suburbs, the Sunbelt, or the Third World.[13]

Thus the basic tension. A rising tide may *not* lift all boats. In practice, new technology comes on-stream in new places. And to spur the economy's development might well reinforce the industrial exodus from older cities. Does it follow that the American capital stock should not be renewed?

The argument so far is that permanent and irreversible changes have occurred in the economic functions of older American cities. Triggered initially by (1) suburbanization and more recently by (2) the regional revolution, (3) urban-rural shifts, and (4) the rise of the newly industrializing countries, the deindustrialization of the older city makes a jobs-to-people strategy increasingly unrealistic.

But if changes in the economic roles of older cities are now a fact of life, they are also the basis for a new beginning.

ELEMENTS IN A MOBILITY STRATEGY

A people-to-jobs or mobility strategy would serve two paramount purposes. It would open new opportunities for the minority poor and for structurally displaced workers generally. In addition, it would serve the objective of greater flexibility—an increased capacity to adapt to change—in the national economy.

Definitional Issues

A few preliminary points may help place the people-to-jobs approach in perspective.

City Fiscal Relief Is a Separate Issue. Mobility assistance to individuals is fully consistent with continued or, for that matter, increased federal fiscal relief to city governments. A fundamental people versus place issue refers not to city fiscal relief but to whether "people aid" should be *place-tied,* as welfare and training programs are.

Migration as a Middle-Class Prerogative. It is sometimes said that mobility measures would be superfluous became so many Americans already move in response to job opportunities. However, there is abundant evidence that the urban poor are far less mobile than the rest of the population. In practice, the mobility option appears to be a function of income.

Government Policies Restrict the Mobility of the Poor. One reason low-income people are less mobile than the rest of the population is that both federal and local government practices restrict their mobility. Hence, even a *neutral* mobility strategy would require changes in public policies.

Choice and Community. The goal of equalizing the spatial possibilities for low-income people is not in conflict with the values of community, which can be assumed to be both strong and general. But if poor people have more to gain from leaving a community than from staying, they should have the same choices others do.

Mobility Is a Prerequisite, Not a Solution. Mobility is a means to a market-based solution to the problem of structural unemployment. Clearly a people-to-jobs strategy will take time to work, and its effectiveness will depend in part on how effectively it is coordinated with training and income measures.

Mobility's Benefits Fade in a Recession. As a means to long-term adjustment, mobility corrects people with job opportunities. But when unemployment rates are rising everywhere, as in 1981, the process breaks down. This is less a weakness of mobility measures than it is testimony to the damage wreaked by unemployment rates above 10 percent.

Removing Governmental Barriers

To repeat, both federal and local policies have the perverse effect of tying the minority poor to declining cities. At the local level, the obvious problem is suburban exclusion. Through minimum-lot-size zoning, differential housing code enforcement, and discriminatory real estate practices, the minority poor are kept out of suburban jurisdictions offering high-quality public services and access to manufacturing jobs. In the long run, such practices must be eliminated, not only for reasons related to equal opportunity, but also for the simpler reason that housing discrimination is against the law.

At the federal level, changes are just as evidently needed, and easier to accomplish. Key federal barriers to mobility are posed by the administration and structure of both public assistance (welfare) and unemployment compensation. As Table VII.7 reveals, the pattern of interstate differences in welfare levels sets up a perverse set of locational incentives—incentives that have the effect of tying the poor to areas offering them diminishing job opportunities.

Moreover, as welfare programs are now administered, a move from one state to another means loss of benefits, with no automatic resumption. The same thing goes for CETA participation, which was locally administered. In both cases, "mobilizing" program entitlements would be a step toward providing poor people with the spatial choices other Americans already have. On grounds of both structure and administration, then, welfare generates perverse locational incentives.

A negative income tax could combine the spatial advantages of na-

Table VII.7. State Contrasts in 1979 Average Monthly Payments to Families with Dependent Children

State	*Payment*	*State*	*Payment*
Hawaii	$390	Ohio	$250
California	370	Maine	240
New York	370	Delaware	230
Michigan	370	Colorado	220
Massachusetts	370	Montana	220
Wisconsin	350	Maryland	220
Washington	350	South Dakota	210
Connecticut	340	Missouri	210
Alaska	340	Virginia	210
Vermont	330	Nevada	200
Oregon	330	Indiana	190
Minnesota	330	Florida	180
Iowa	310	New Mexico	170
New Jersey	300	West Virginia	170
Utah	300	Arizona	170
Pennsylvania	280	Kentucky	170
Illinois	270	North Carolina	160
New Hampshire	270	Arkansas	150
Idaho	270	Louisiana	140
Rhode Island	270	Georgia	120
Kansas	260	Tennessee	110
District of Columbia	260	Alabama	110
Nebraska	260	Texas	110
Oklahoma	250	South Carolina	100
North Dakota	250	Mississippi	90
Wyoming	250	Puerto Rico	60

Note: Amounts have been rounded to the nearest $10.
Source: Social Security Administration, *Social Security Bulletin*, 43,6, June 1980.

tional uniformity with work incentives clearly superior to those of the present system. Here as with suburban exclusionary zoning, political crosscurrents appear to rule out a nationally administered negative income tax for the present. But for the long run, the plan's potential for (1) spatial neutrality, (2) improved work incentives, and (3) stable planning horizons for the poor themsleves, could prove decisive.

Relocation Assistance

As Niles Hansen observes, the United States, virtually alone among developed capitalist countries, has no program

> . . . to help underemployed, unemployed, and low income persons in lagging areas to move and find employment in areas with greater opportunities. European experience . . . together with labor mobility demonstration projects in the United States,

> have shown that such programs are effective. . . . *Failure to institute a permanent program of comprehensive relocation assistance is perhaps the most deficient aspect of . . . spatial resource allocation in the United States.*[14]

The European precedent suggests some basic guidelines for American policy design.

According to Organization for Economic Cooperation and Development reports, nine separate forms of relocation assistance are used in Europe:

1. Interregional job announcement and *clearing systems* list job openings in tight labor market areas.
2. *Travel assistance* is typically given to workers relocating to take specific jobs.
3. Some countries provide money for *commuting* as well, presumably in the early stages of a relocation, when housing is transitional.
4. *Starting assistance* can help tide relocating workers over to the first paycheck.
5. A few countries maintain *lodging and maintenance* for single movers, mainly trainees.
6. Less frequently, governments help finance *youth hostels* for relocated younger workers.
7. *Separation and travel allowances* are provided for married workers to return home for family visits and for the transition.
8. *Moving expenses* are typically reimbursed through government grants, normally for the full cost of the move.
9. *Installation and housing search assistance* are common in the United Kingdom, Germany, and Scandinavia.

The length of this list may seem to indicate that relocation is a complex and expensive proposition. Complex it surely is, in the sense that two-way information networks and noncash adjustment services are critical to a successful program. But relocation may be much less expensive for the public sector than the alternative, which in practice is semipermanent welfare payments. As the then director of the Swedish Labor Market Board observed in the 1960s:

> It costs less than one million kroner ($200,000) to move 1,000 persons to employment [i.e., from northern to southern Sweden]. For the same amount, these persons might have been given [unemployment] assistance for less than 2 months or employed in public relief works for not more than 5 days . . . the money is well spent. . . .[15]

But is European experience relevant to the United States, with its continental scale and decentralized administrative system? Between

1965 and 1969 the Department of Labor conducted a series of mobility demonstration projects to discover the feasibility of mobility policies in an American context. Some 14,000 unemployed or underemployed workers relocated in connection with the program, roughly two-thirds of them through state employment agencies. Of workers surveyed after the moves, the preponderant majority reported that they were satisfied with the relocations.

A majority of survey respondents also indicated that they would not have moved without relocation allowances. As Hansen points out, however, cash assistance is, if anything, less important than such *noncash* forms of support as assistance in locating housing, arrangement of pre-job trips for interviews, family counseling, and—above all—an extensive and responsive job clearing system to match workers with openings.

When such support services are combined with relocation grants in a carefully administered project, the results are clearly advantageous to the people who relocate. But the advantages of relocation would also register in public budgets. As one analyst concludes,

> . . . society benefits greatly from these relocation projects. . . . These pilot projects show that there is a sizable group of unemployed workers who are willing to relocate to obtain employment. Providing relocation assistance to these people is the least expensive governmental method of providing employment for them. For those unwilling or unable to move, unemployment insurance and welfare payments will be available. *What is important is giving the unemployed worker a choice,* rather than condemning him to unemployment. . . . [16]

The upshot is that mobility assistance for people who want the choice would help reduce structural underemployment and dependency. Bolstered by training initiatives, it would be a useful step toward the positive adjustment strategy the nation urgently needs.

ACKNOWLEDGMENTS

I am indebted to Charles Geisler and John Rapoport for valuable criticisms, and also to Sandra Olson and Barbara Helgeson for statistical assistance. Errors are my own.

NOTES AND REFERENCES

1. Ernest Erber, review of Alexander Polikoff, *Housing the Poor: The Case for Heroism,* Cambridge, Mass.: Ballinger, 1978; *Journal of the American Planning Association,* January 1980, p. 104.
2. Irving Kristol, "An Urban Civilization Without Cities?" *The Washington Post,* Dec. 3, 1972.

3. *Ibid.*
4. See Norton Long, "The City as Reservation," and George Sternlieb, "The City as Sandbox," both in *The Public Interest,* 25, Fall 1971.
5. U.S. Bureau of the Census, *Current Population Reports,* Series P-60, *Characteristics of the Population Below the Poverty Level: 1978,* Washington, D.C.: U.S. Government Printing Office, August 1980, p. 8.
6. Eli Ginzberg, "Youth Unemployment," *Scientific American,* 242, 5, May 1980, p. 47.
7. *Ibid.,* p. 48.
8. This subsection is based on R. D. Norton, *City Life-Cycles and American Urban Policy,* New York: Academic Press, 1979, which provides a more thorough treatment of the arguments sketched out here.
9. From correspondence with Congressman Richard Bolling of the Joint Economic Committee.
10. Art Laffer, prepared statement submitted to the Joint Economic Committee, July 28, 1980.
11. Tibor Scitovsky, "Can Capitalism Survive?—An Old Question in a New Setting," *American Economic Review,* 70, 2, May 1980, p. 2.
12. "The Economic Aging of America," *Challenge,* January-February 1980, emphasis added.
13. Richard McHugh and David Puryear, "Tax Credits for Urban Revitalization," in L. Kenneth Hubbell, ed., *Fiscal Crisis in American Cities,* Cambridge, Mass.: Ballinger, 1979, pp. 324–325.
14. Niles Hansen, *Location Preferences, Migration, and Regional Growth,* New York: Praeger, 1973, pp. 62–63. My treatment of mobility policies relies heavily on Hansen, chapter 2, "The Case for Assisted Migration."
15. Quoted in *ibid.,* p. 36.
16. Quoted in *ibid.,* p. 48.

Chapter VIII

INTERNATIONAL TRADE, CAPITAL MOBILITY, AND ECONOMIC GROWTH:

SOME IMPLICATIONS FOR AMERICAN CITIES AND REGIONS IN THE 1980s

Norman J. Glickman

INTRODUCTION

On April 13, 1980, *The New York Times* reported three events that at first glance might appear to be unrelated both to each other and to the future of American cities and regions. The headlines read:

- "Protectionism Raises Its Head As Free Trade Proves Costlier"
- "Wide Job Loss Seen in Plants' Closing"
- "Organized Labor's New Strength in the South"

The first article reported that the U.S. Steel Corporation, in the face of competition from Europe and Japan, was charging European steelmakers with "dumping." Cries for protection from American manufacturers of cars, golf carts, synthetic fibers, television sets, and automobiles (and some of their associated trade unions) were also noted. The report raised the spectre of trade wars and protectionism reminiscent of the 1920s and 1930s looming behind this situation, with increased international competitive pressures confronting American firms. A 1980 public opinion poll showed 70 percent of Americans in favor of protectionist measures in order to save jobs.

The second article discussed a study by two economists about problems attendant to the closing of factories and general movements of capital from place to place. The research (which is discussed in greater detail in the "Capital Mobility" section) indicated that the serious economic and social dislocation that results from plant closings is not, as is commonly believed, solely a northern problem. This phenomenon is affecting the South and West, as well as the North, as plants and financial capital move across international borders, as well as among regions. Thus, the movement of capital, with its ramifications for local communities, is a national, not only a regional, issue. The role of conglomerate and multinational corporations in this process was emphasized in the economists' report.

The third article noted the increasing strength of industrial unions in the South, a region with a history of relatively little organized labor. The increase in unionization is due, in part, to inflationary pressures on unorganized workers. "As inflation ravages the pocketbooks and clouds the futures of American workers. . . ." unionization becomes more appealing to them, the report added. The desire for increased economic security, whether because of high inflation or the threat of job loss during recession, is the motivating force in this movement toward greater unionization, according to *The New York Times.*

These articles highlight three important factors that affect urban and regional change in the United States: (1) the role of international trade; (2) the importance of capital mobility; and (3) the affects of inflation, unemployment, and long-term economic growth.

It became clear in the past decade that the nature of the American economy has changed. First, our economy has become more interdependent with the economies of the other industrialized countries and more dependent on imported supplies of many resources, especially oil. U.S. exports increased by a factor of five in real terms between 1950–52 and 1979. Foreign trade as a proportion of Gross National Product has more than doubled, rising from 3.8 percent to 7.8 percent over the same period.[1]

Some cities and regions have benefited from international trade, while others have not. For example, the banking centers of New York and San Francisco have gained from their role in the national and international system of cities; the agricultural states, especially those producing grains, have also been helped by increased international trade. On the other hand, Detroit has experienced the job loss associated with competition from foreign automakers.

Second, the movement of capital—both physical and financial—has been rapid. Multinational (and other multiplant) corporations have played an increasingly important role in this phenomenon. Changes in job locations have led to population redistribution within the country as workers are drawn to new locations by the lure of jobs. The decades-long migration from the South to the North and from rural to urban areas has been reversed during the 1970s. The economic and social dislocation from plant closings and population loss in some areas has become apparent in cities such as Youngstown, Ohio, and, as illustrated below, it is probably a more widespread and serious problem than commonly believed. "Boomtown" conditions, such as those in fast-growing western mining communities, create different kinds of problems, such as poor housing and low levels of public infrastructure. Such rapid shifts in capital leave many localities unable to cope with the attendant social disruption.

Third, the role of the business cycle and the slower growth of the U.S. economy have become even more important in public policy. The sense that the Keynesian tools of monetary and fiscal policies could guide us through recessions and booms was shattered with the recession of 1974–75, the worst since the Great Depression. Similarly, the role of demand management in spurring long-term growth has been questioned as our economy grew more slowly in recent time periods. Productivity has fallen dramatically in the late 1970s, contributing to our high inflation rates. Also, the decline in productivity growth has worsened our competitive position. The international terms of trade have changed adversely, making economic growth more difficult to maintain.

Business-cycle developments and the long-term growth of our economy have been recognized as important at the local level as well. First, recessions are felt unevenly across the country: some regions lose jobs earlier than other regions, some lose them later. Similarly, the magnitude of job change is felt differentially among regions. Second, the regional impacts of recoveries from recessions are also unevenly distributed. Third, the slower overall growth of the economy is felt differently in the various parts of the country. Depressed conditions have been more common in northeastern and midwestern cities during the 1970s than in the South and West. Fiscal crisis has accompanied "stagflation" in many of our metropolitan areas.

In looking to the decade ahead, the development of American cities and regions will be influenced by a large number of factors. Many of these influences have been felt by cities and regions (both urban and rural) in the past and are well known. The factors that have traditionally affected development include: industrial structure; wage levels and labor productivity; quality and quantity of the labor supply; availability of raw materials; public infrastructure; tax rates; energy costs and availability; environment; "business climate;" and others.

Since these factors have been widely studied,[2] this chapter focuses on those influences that have not been perceived as central to urban and regional development in the past, but may become more important in the 1980s: international trade, capital mobility, and long-term and cyclical growth of the national economy. Although the principal focus is on urban phenomena, the changing nature of nonmetropolitan areas is also discussed. The five remaining sections of this chapter review the three major factors and relate these to each other and to other elements that bear on the future of American urban and regional development; followed by some conclusions.

INTERNATIONAL TRADE

U.S. Economy in an International Setting

The role of international trade in our economy has changed dramatically over time. Part of the differing pattern occurred in relation to merchandise trade (for example, manufactured products) and part to financial and real capital flows between the United States and other countries. Some dimensions of both elements are noted in the following sections.

Increasing Importance of International Trade in the U.S. Economy. First, the growth of exports and imports, both absolutely and in relation to Gross National Product (GNP), has been substantial. Exports amounted to $17.0 billion in 1950–52 (5.3 percent of GNP), but grew to $257.4 billion (11.0 percent of GNP) by 1979. This fifteen-fold growth in exports was surpassed by increases in imports from $14.3 billion to $260.9 billion over the same period (from 4.5 percent to 11.1 percent of GNP). On a per capita basis, imports increased from $80 (1960) to $787 (1978). Therefore, the trade share of GNP more than doubled in less than 20 years. A significant proportion of this increase took place in the 1970s.[3] Importantly, our balance of trade (exports minus imports) became increasingly negative, especially in the late 1970s. By 1978, the merchandise balance of trade was about $34 billion in deficit, although there was a recovery in 1979. In addition, net foreign investment income (receipts from abroad minus payments to foreigners) increased to about $22 billion by 1978; overall, the trade balance on the current account was minus $13.5 billion. Much of this deficit can be attributed to increases in the cost of imported oil.

The increasing involvement in foreign trade is also seen in our foreign investment. U.S. net assets invested abroad increased from $4 billion to $61 billion between 1960 and 1978. At the same time, foreign investment in the United States increased from $2 billion to $64 billion.[4] In 1978, 24 percent of federal government debt was held by foreign investors. Direct foreign investment in U.S. manufacturing grew by 5.9 percent per year over the 1960–65 period and doubled to 12.3 percent per year from 1970–77.[5]

The Changing Patterns of U.S. Trade. Our trading partners and the types of commodities the country trades have also changed. Exports to developed countries, particularly those in Europe, have declined significantly—from 66.7 percent to 59.7 percent of total exports between 1965 and 1978. Our exports to developing countries (and socialist nations) increased more than proportionately during the same period. Among individual countries, the percentage of exports increased to Mexico, Brazil, and Saudi Arabia. Import patterns also changed. Our imports from developing countries increased from 33.4 percent to 41.4 percent; these increases occurred primarily in the form of oil from the Near East and, among developed nations, from West Germany and Japan which exported a variety of goods to the United States.

The distribution of trade by type of commodity also changed. The share of total exports increased in the category of food and feed grains, and declined in industrial supplies and materials; among imports, the agricultural proportion declined significantly while, especially during the late 1970s, the nation imported far more manufactured goods (for example, industrial supplies, capital goods, and automobiles). In 1978, there was a $29 billion deficit in manufactured goods compared to a $5.8 billion surplus in this category in 1967. However, the net balance of agricultural trade was nearly $15 billion in 1978. Therefore, our trade was increasingly with developing countries and exports were more likely to be agricultural products (and agricultural equipment) than previously. Of course, our imports of oil was a major factor in the trade picture during the 1970s.

The International Business Cycle. Another element in the consideration of international trade concerns the business cycle. In the 1960s, U.S. business cycles were somewhat "out of phase" with those of our industrial trading partners. That is, when the nation was in recession, the

Europeans were often enjoying expansions; when they were in recession, we usually had higher economic growth. In such a situation, cyclical growth of our trading partners (during U.S. recessions) would mean an expansion of U.S. exports and, therefore, more growth. Recessions abroad would have the opposite effect: our exports would be reduced and our growth would be slowed. The cycles that our economy went through had similar effects on the other industrial countries. Therefore, the stability of our domestic economy was enhanced by international trade.

There appears to have been more coincidence of cycles in the 1970s than in the 1960s. Much of this greater synchronization can be attributed to the rise in food prices in 1972 and the oil price increases in 1973–74 and 1979. Whether this synchronization will continue in the future is unclear, although the greater integration of the industrialized world might imply so. There are, however, differences in opinion among experts on this subject.[6]

If greater synchronization occurs in the future, then one can expect, all things equal, more domestic cyclical instability. As the U.S. economy expands in tandem with its trading partners, there would be a tendency for increasing export demand and, therefore, more growth. This growth, given underlying inflationary pressures as the expansion continues, would imply inflationary increases. Similarly, should a simultaneous downturn occur, the cumulative negative effects would be magnified. The shocks that might occur in the international economic system (for instance, through further oil price increases) would be transmitted from country to country. On the other hand, if the coincidence of international cycles does not continue, then less instability could be expected.

The 1970s have witnessed greater synchronization of international business cycles. Should this continue, domestic cyclical instability could result in the 1980s as domestic business cycles are exacerbated by international shocks and the transmission of instability through the international economy.

The possibility of continued cyclical synchronization can be seen in the forecasts of the Wharton-EFA World Model.[7] Data from 1977 to 1980 and forecasts to 1983 indicate the strong correspondence of the behavior of the time series over that period for the United States, Japan, West Germany, the less developed countries (LDCs), and the world.

The Changes in the International Terms of Trade. There have been important changes in the terms of trade facing this country. The increasing economic power of developing countries and some of our important developed nation trading partners, has made our position in the world economy less dominant than it was in the 1950s and 1960s. Two important issues are relevant. First, productivity of American workers has not grown as fast as that of laborers in other developed countries, although our absolute productivity (GNP per worker) is still higher. In particular, the newer plant and equipment of Japanese and West German factories has allowed them to compete more effectively against our manufacturers in the world market. According to Denison,[8] the average annual growth rate of U.S. manufacturing output per hour worked between 1973 and 1978 was 1.7 percent. During the same period, analogous figures for our industrial competitors were: Japan (3.5 percent), West Germany (5.1 percent), Canada (2.6 percent), and France (4.8 percent).

A second element in the changing terms of trade involves our competitive position vis-à-vis developing countries. Particularly with respect to labor-intensive production, the nation is at a disadvantage. Factory output in such sectors as textiles, wearing apparel, and shoes has declined relative to production in the LDCs, particularly Mexico, Taiwan, Hong Kong, and Korea. The shift of capital to these countries by American multinationals played an important role and is discussed further in the section on capital mobility.

Therefore, our competitive position with respect to our industrial trading partners and to industrializing less developed countries has deteriorated. This has put pressure on American workers with regard to economic security and, due to declines in the value of the dollar, increased inflationary tendencies in the economy.

In sum, the increasing interdependence of the United States within the world economy is significant. The growth of foreign trade, changes in its sectoral composition and our trading partners, the role of international business cycles on domestic stability, and our declining competitiveness in world markets, make for important challenges to American policymakers in the decade to come. Increased interdependence means that many of our producing sectors are more dependent on foreign buyers and sellers, that controlling the domestic economy is becoming more difficult, and that new methods must be developed to improve our competitive position. Finally, the importance of world trade has differential impacts on the regions and cities of this country, as discussed later.

The Effects of International Trade on U.S. Cities and Regions

Given the discussion of the previous section, what inferences can be drawn about the effects of international trade on our cities and regions? Clearly, some regions and business sectors are more sensitive to international conditions than others.

Sectors Influenced By International Trade. Two elements are important: the identification of export-oriented industries, and those that are affected by foreign imports.

Manufacturing has been historically an important source of export activity for the United States, although, as noted earlier, the share of manufacturing exports in international trade has declined in recent years.[9] However, there was still an absolute increase in manufacturing exports. The value of shipments for export rose from $16.5 billion to $83.1 billion from 1963 to 1976.

With regard to the patterns of export-related value of shipments and employment for 1976: of the 18.8 million workers in manufacturing, 1,173,000 (6.3 percent) were engaged in export or export-related activity. The major employing industries were nonelectrical machinery (295,000 employees), transportation equipment (203,000), electrical equipment (196,000), and chemicals (75,000). A lower proportion of export-related workers were employed in industries such as furniture and fixtures, apparel, textiles, and printing and publishing. Given the multiplier effects of export-oriented activity, the importance of this sector can be seen clearly.

Agricultural exports are also important components in our international trade. In terms of dollar value, the major exports are corn (for grain), soybeans, and wheat. For example, $1.2 billion of wheat was exported (64 percent of total wheat production) in 1978; corn exports were nearly $2 billion (27.5 percent of production) in the same year. The effects on nonmetropolitan regions of this important part of our international trade situation are discussed presently.

With regard to those industrial sectors that are most affected by imports, there are at least two related issues. First, what industries gain or lose employment due to trade? Second, what types of workers benefit or suffer from trade-related activity?

The Congressional Budget Office[10] (CBO) studied trade liberalization under the "Tokyo Round" Multilateral Trade Negotiations (MTN). The CBO found that industries that are relatively labor-intensive or make use of simple, well-known technologies would tend to suffer under the MTN. Firms producing textiles, apparel, footwear, leather products, steel products, and radio and television sets are included in this category. However, trade liberalization would increase employment in those industries that use highly sophisticated or new technology, such as semiconductors, computers, scientific instruments, electronic components, and aircraft; agricultural products (and agricultural machinery) would also be aided by freer trade.

Although the CBO study observed the effects of liberalized trade, the findings are consistent with other research indicating that, in general, imports hurt low-technology, assembly process industries. These industries have found it harder to compete with imports because of the higher wages paid to American workers compared, for example, to low-wage Korean or Mexican workers.

A production hierarchy has evolved in which high-technology, capital-intensive activity takes place in one set of places (e.g., Route 128 near Boston or "Silicon Valley" near San Jose, Calif.), and assembly work occurs in lower wage areas in the South and in developing countries. Therefore, not only is there a production hierarchy, but a geographical one as well.

From several studies, it is clear that the export sector's labor force tends to be more highly educated, younger, "whiter," and has a lower percentage of production workers than those employed in import-related activity.[11] Import sectors are more heavily unionized, contain relatively more female and nonwhite employees, and a lower proportion of part-time and older workers than is found in the export sector.

A final element in the consideration of international trade is energy. The amount of oil imports has increased dramatically in the past 20 years. The nation imported 1.8 million barrels of oil per day in 1960, a figure that grew to about 9 million barrels per day in 1979.[12] These figures represent a growth of imported oil as a percent of oil consumption from 19 percent to 47 percent, a dramatic indication of our dependence on foreign sources.

The sharp rise of oil prices in 1973–74 and again in 1979 has slowed economic growth and contributed to inflation.[13] For example, Hudson and Jorgenson[14] estimate that the 1976 GNP was 3.2 percent lower than it would have been in the absence of the 1973–74 oil price increases. They indicate that the price increases were a part of the reason for the mid-1970s recession.

Bjornstad estimates the effects of price increases on economic capacity in the context of President Carter's 1977 energy program.[15] For our purposes, it is interesting to note which industrial sectors are most affected by rising energy prices. Bjornstad indicates that the paper, chemical, and primary metals sectors are most sensitive to energy price increases.

Cities and Regions Influenced by International Trade. Having reviewed the major sectoral effects of international trade, the urban and regional effects of international trade must be considered next.

Manufacturing. The role of manufacturing exports in regional development can be seen by examining the percent of exports of the total value of shipments for each state. In nearly all states, the proportion increased between 1972 and 1976. The states that had the largest percentage of shipments devoted to exports in 1976 were: Alaska (23.5 percent), Washington (17.2 percent), and Connecticut (10.7 percent). On an absolute basis, the largest export-oriented states were California, Michigan, Illinois, Ohio, and New York, according to the *Annual Survey of Manufactures.* The ten states with the largest absolute amounts of export-related employment (62 percent of all export-related manufacturing) are located primarily in the northeastern-midwestern industrial belt, with Texas and California the exceptions to this generalization. The dominant sectors are in heavy industrial activity: transportation equipment, nonelectrical machinery, electrical machinery, and fabricated metals.

The 19 Standard Metropolitan Statistical Areas (SMSAs) with the largest amount of export-related manufacturing[16] are located mainly in the Frostbelt, again with some exceptions. Collectively, these SMSAs have a total of 438 thousand workers in export-related industry, about 37 percent all such workers in the country. These economies are dominated by the traditional manufacturing sectors.

Therefore, the Northeast and the North Central regions have the heaviest concentration of export-oriented manufacturing employment. Most of this employment is in the heavy manufacturing sectors, such as electrical and nonelectrical machinery, fabricated metal products, and transportation equipment.

Agriculture. Turning to agriculture, which is of growing importance in foreign trade, one finds a domination of midwestern and Sunbelt states. For example, corn (the leading agricultural export item) is grown mostly in states such as Iowa, Illinois, Indiana and Minnesota; the major wheat-producing states are Kansas, Montana, North Dakota, and Oklahoma. Other significant agricultural-export states are California, Idaho, and Texas.

Financial and business services. A third major export-related sector is in the financial and business service area. Firms in this business category serve the needs of multinational corporations both in banking and manufacturing and engage in direct trading activity themselves. Data concerning such activity are extremely difficult to isolate, but some proxy data have been developed by Stanback and Noyelle.[17] The long-term replacement of manufacturing activity by services is documented in this study. Stanback and Noyelle note that this is particularly true of the largest SMSAs. They emphasize the historical importance of managerial centrality in cities such as New York, Chicago, San Francisco, and Philadelphia. However, there has been considerable deconcentration of such activity in recent years to former "regional centers" such as Atlanta, Miami, Houston, and Phoenix.

Stanback and Novelle present data depicting what they call "complexes of corporate activity" (CCA), concentrations of corporate offices and corporate service firms. The authors show that, despite some decentralization, 45 percent of all CCA took place in the 20 largest SMSAs in 1976, compared to 50 percent in 1959. Significantly, there was a substantial change between 1959 and 1976 between the 10 largest and the next 50 largest metropolitan areas; the share in national CCA employment in the "top 10" of the CCA fell from 43 percent to 37 percent, while the share of the "11 to 60" group rose from 29 percent to 34 percent. Therefore, there has been decentralization within the hierarchy of cities.

Regionally, CCA is concentrated in the Mideast and Great Lakes areas; in 1976 the 15 largest SMSAs located in these regions accounted for about 60 percent of the CCA employment. Looking at data on the corporate headquarters of the *Fortune* "650," Noyelle and Stanback find that 297 were in 10 cities, of which all but Houston, Los Angeles, and San Francisco were in the Frostbelt.

Although these data do not precisely delineate export activity, it is clear that most of the international trade impact in the financial and services sector is in the largest SMSAs and in the Frostbelt. However, these regions have shown a declining share of such employment over time.

Foreign Investment in the United States

Manufacturing. Another consideration in the foreign trade picture with respect to cities and regions is that of direct foreign investment in the United States.[18] According to a study by the U.S. Department of Housing and Urban Development (HUD), most of the investment in new manufacturing plants by foreign corporations has been in the Southeast and the Far West, while the acquisition of existing firms was in the New England, Mideast, and Great Lakes regions. The HUD report also notes that more than half of the investment took place in states that had some economic distress, as measured by slow economic growth or low income levels.

In general, foreign firms seem to be building plants in the South where wages and unionization rates are low. In fact, about 20 percent of the new capital expenditures in the Southeast between 1969 and 1973 were undertaken by foreign investors.[19] The HUD report also looked at the location of foreign manufacturing investment in different cities. Using a measure of distress developed by the Urban Institute,[20] the report indicated that about 64 percent of foreign manufacturing investment was in distressed cities in 1974. Newer investments announced in 1977 and 1978, however, showed a decline in the proportion of investment going to such areas.

Banking. Another important portion of foreign investment is in the area of banking. Foreign banks have increasingly opened offices in U.S. cities, and have done so in a spatially concentrated manner. In 1978, 96 percent of the assets of foreign banks were in New York, Chicago, San Francisco, and Los Angeles. Foreign-owned banks accounted for one-third of all loans made in New York in the year ending in May 1978. This pattern is not surprising since the banks are financing trade and need direct access to customers who tend to agglomerate in these money-center cities.

Energy. Bjornstad[21] discusses the role of energy price increases on the major regions of the country. He compares the effects on economic activity under two scenarios: a continuation of current trends (called "Base") and those under President Carter's 1977 energy initiatives ("Init"). Using 1975 as a year for comparison, Bjornstad reports that the South West and North West had the lowest energy prices while New England and the New York/New Jersey regions had the highest prices. Under the Base case, prices of energy increased by 82 percent in the United States, versus a 77 percent increase under the Init situation by 1985; the slightly lower average price increase under the Init situation is due to increased reliance on coal in the Carter plan. However, there are substantial differences in prices among regions under the two situations. The largest increases occur in states that had the lowest prices in 1975, and the smallest increases take place in regions that started with the highest prices. Therefore, there is a leveling of energy price differentials across the country as a result of either policy scenario.

The result of this process on economic activity is of interest here. Bjornstad shows that all regions would experience declines in economic capacity due to increased energy prices. But the regions that currently have the lowest energy prices (and, therefore, a comparative advantage with respect to energy) lose the most economic capacity. Under the Base case, for example, the Southwest loses 10.1 percent of its capacity, while New York/New Jersey lose only 0.8 percent.

Therefore, the effects of energy price increases brought about, in part, by foreign economic actors (i.e., OPEC) and domestic deregulation policy would tend to attenuate regional advantages held by the southern and western regions in the mid-1970s. The regions with the highest energy prices suffer least from future increases in energy prices under either Init or Base.[22]

This section has highlighted the increasingly important role of foreign trade in U.S. cities and regions. While heavy manufacturing is the most important export-related sector, manufacturing employment in general and manufacturing exports as a proportion of all exports have been declining over time. The major impacts have been in the Northeast-North Central manufacturing belt and some of its large metropolitan areas. On the other hand, nonmetropolitan regions have gained because of increases in agricultural exports. The large metropolitan centers have been the principal beneficiaries of corporate headquarter activity (much of it international in orientation) and foreign branch banking. The Southeast has attracted a large proportion of the new manufacturing investment from foreign sources. Therefore, the urban and regional impacts of foreign trade are quite diverse.[23]

CAPITAL MOBILITY

Although the movement of labor across regional and international boundaries has been studied by demographers and others,[24] capital mobility has not been a subject of deep inquiry. Part of the reaon for this research imbalance is due to the lack of good data. However, the movement of financial and physical capital has recently become an important subject because of plant closings and slowdown in employment growth in many regions of the country. Barry Bluestone and Bennett Harrison[25] have completed an interesting analysis of disinvestment in plant and equipment in a wide range of industries for New England and, in a more limited manner, the remainder of the country. Their findings are related to some of the issues raised in the previous section.

The Nature and Process of Capital Movements

The notion of "capital shifts" or "industrial disinvestment" is often confused in the popular press and by some scholars with the closing of a plant and its "movement" to another area. However, the nature of disinvestment is much more subtle and complicated than mere plant movements. The actual physical relocation of a plant represents only about 2 percent of all private sector employment change. For this reason, as Bluestone and Harrison point out, the problem has been trivialized and dismissed by many.

However, there are other ways in which disinvestment can occur. First, companies can run down their physical capital without modernizing or replacing it; the savings, in the form of capital depreciation allowances, can be used for investments in other plants or, in the case of single-plant firms, for other kinds of investments. This occurs most often in the case of older plants that are allowed to deteriorate over time. Second, the plant may close. In this case, the equipment, land, and buildings may be sold. Third, multiplant (multistore, multioffice) corporations may shift equipment or skilled or managerial personnel from one plant to another over time. In such a case, the old plant stays in operation, at least for a while. Finally, there may be no relocation of the physical assets of a plant in the short run; however, the profits earned in one plant may be assigned to the corporate headquarters and then reinvested in a plant elsewhere. This is known in business circles as milking a "cash cow"—the draining of cash from a profitable plant for reinvestments elsewhere. All four patterns represent disinvestments of different kinds. Such drawing down on capital occurs most often in older plants and in older, industrial regions.

The Regional Effects of Capital Mobility

Movements of capital occur continuously and are part of the process of capitalist development. Some firms "die" and others are "born." Capital is moved from one line of production to another, or from one region (or nation) to another. Important for our consideration here is the differential effect of capital mobility among regions and some of the reasons behind this phenomenon.

According to Browne,[26] the growth of manufacturing capital stock for the United States was 3.7 percent per year between 1960 and 1976. However, the growth of capital among regions has been uneven. Over that period, the growth rates for the major regions of the country were as follows: Northeast (2.7 percent), North Central (3.1 percent), South (5.1 percent), and West (4.0 percent). In fact, the data indicate that, during the 1970s, the interregional gap in capital stock increase was widening.[27] For the 16 years in the Browne enumeration, the capital stock in the South grew at about twice the rate of the Northeast. The related effects on employment of course have been significant: the New England, Middle-Atlantic, and East North Central states that make up the Frostbelt lost 1.5 million manufacturing jobs between 1967 and 1976. At the same time, the Sunbelt states gained nearly 900,000 jobs.

Bluestone and Harrison document the nature of capital shifts, using data from the files of Dun and Bradstreet. They indicate the impact of capital shifts, as represented by start-ups or "births" of new firms and inmigrations of others, and the closings or "deaths" of existing firms and outmigrations of firms between 1969 and 1976. Plant closings eliminated 508,000 jobs in Massachusetts between 1969 and 1976; over one million jobs were lost in the New England region. However, during the period, new plants added 448,000 and 849,000 jobs in those regions, respectively. Of importance is the ratio of jobs destroyed to those created. It is shown that for every 100 jobs created in Massachusetts, 110 were lost (a ratio of 1.1). For New England, the ratio was 1.2.

Bluestone and Harrison also present a less detailed treatment for the entire country. The interregional shifts of capital are readily apparent: for every 100 jobs created in the Frostbelt, 111 are lost to plant disinvestment. For New York State, the ratio was 1.37, for example. The ratio for the South and the Mountain states is 0.8—for every 100 jobs created, only 80 are lost, leaving a net gain of 20 jobs.

It is even more interesting to observe the pattern of movement by type of ownership. Bluestone and Harrison argue that small, independently owned firms are more vulnerable to business cycles and adverse economic conditions than two other categories of plants—corporate branch plants and the branch plants of conglomerates.[28] The authors infer that a plant closing in the latter two categories is more likely to be planned as part of a corporate strategy, while a small firm closing can more reasonably be attributed to business failure. That is, there is often a corporate strategy for reallocating capital among areas or sectors.

In looking at employment change for New England and Massachusetts, Bluestone and Harrison find that (1) in most cases the average size of plants that closed was greater than of those that opened, no matter what kind of ownership; and (2) the rate at which conglomerates disinvested in New England was far greater than either for the corporate or the independent ownership forms. In fact, for 1969 to 1976, the ratio of job loss to job gain for conglomerates in all industries was 3.0 (300 jobs destroyed for every one 100 created), compared to 0.7 for corporations and 1.9 for independents. For the conglomerate sector, this represented nearly a 12 percent net loss in employment during that period.

It is important to understand that disinvestment is not a "northern" problem, since it is occurring, in one form or another, all over the country. If one examines Bluestone and Harrison's data for the larger manufacturing plants (those with more than 100 employees), interesting patterns emerge. First, not surprisingly, most of the plant closings occurred in the Northeast (about 39 percent). However, it is surprising that the South (28 percent of large plant closings) was worse off than the North Central states (24 percent). This pattern is even more startling if one calculates the probability of a plant that was in existence in 1969 being closed in 1976. If such "conditional probabilities" are estimated, large southern plants show the highest probability (0.34) of failure than any other region in the country; the Northeast (0.31), the West (0.30), and the North Central (0.25) all had lower figures. Therefore, a large firm existing in 1969 was more likely to close by 1976 in the South than in any other region.

The disinvestment in the South can be explained readily: the international economy. Much of this capital shift from the South must be occurring in the direction of foreign countries, especially low-wage, less developed countries.

Many firms moved from the North to the South over the past 40 years and continue to do so. This may be called the first interregional "jump" of capital. There have been a wide variety of reasons for this movement: lower wages, less unionization, lower taxes, better "business climate," and others. These shifts produced largely low-wage, low-skilled jobs in assembly line settings. With the relative growth of wages in the South, with some increase in unionization, and other factors, the owners of southern plants have begun to look for areas with still lower wages and an even more malleable work force. Therefore, firms are making, in effect, a second "jump" to LDCs. The continuing growth of multinational corporations and the simultaneous search for low-wage labor markets have led to what some have called the "export of jobs" to such LDCs as Mexico, Hong Kong, and Taiwan.

This loss of domestic jobs through foreign subsidiaries takes place in several ways. First, components that can be assembled by low-skilled labor are completed abroad, as in the semiconductor industry.[29] Another example is the automobile industry. In a 1980 interview, Lee Iacocca, president of the ailing Chrysler Corporation, complained about foreign car imports into the United States. However, the Chrysler Corporation itself imports 23 percent of all Japanese cars, and 3 of 10 Chrysler cars are made abroad. Moreover, the components of many "American" cars are made abroad. The Ford "Escort," the so-called "world car," is a classic example of the internationalization of the industry, reflecting a joint venture between American and foreign firms. Isuzu-General Motors and Mitsui-British Leyland are other examples of joint ventures in which capital flows across international boundaries. The worldwide division of labor has changed dramatically in the past decade, with product components made in several countries, assembled in other nations, and sold in still a third set of markets. The automobile industry is but one example.

Another example of job loss through the export of capital comes via "free trade" zones set up in Northern Mexico, Taiwan, Brazil, and elsewhere. In what have become known as "Little Detroits," component parts of autos are exported from the United States to newly built Mexican plants where assembly takes place; reexport occurs to the United States without customs duty on the parts. Thus, multinational corporations such as General Motors and Chrysler can take advantage of low wages in Mexico. Over 500 such plants (in many industries) exist in Mexico, employing about 110,000 workers.[30] Of course, the most usual form of international capital shifts is through direct investment, in which a U.S. firm buys an existing foreign firm or builds a new overseas plant.

The Social Costs of Capital Movements

Although the free movement of capital has been at the cornerstone of the American economy and ideology, some important social costs are attendant to such capital movements. Whereas the management goal of greater efficiency leads to movements of capital, the effects on workers who lose their jobs and communities that depend on plants must also be considered. For example, one need only point to the plant closings in Youngstown, Ohio, and Detroit, Mich. As these cities and states lose jobs and, with this loss, incur higher per capita public costs (for example, in welfare and unemployment benefits), the attractiveness of the area is lowered still further. The impact on workers is also significant. Jacobson shows the long-term earnings loss of workers in several industries after they are displaced from their jobs.[31] Automobile workers lose about 43 percent of their earnings over each of the first two years after losing their jobs; during the following four years, their annual loss is nearly 16 percent. In the steel industry, the analogous figures are 47 percent and 13 percent. Beyond income loss, the consequences of job loss on health (both physical and mental),[32] the increased tendency for sociopathic behavior (family violence, for example), and the increased crime rates are serious social costs that do not appear on corporate balance sheets.

Yet, capital mobility is, in and of itself, not "bad." It has been a necessary part of our economic development. The problem is one of both the speed of capital movement *relative* to labor mobility (the comment that "one can wire finance capital overnight to Hong Kong, but one cannot 'wire' a displaced worker" is apt) and the magnitude of capital shifts. Structural unemployment and distressed communities are often the products of this imbalance. The public consequences of such private actions must be considered more fully.

As indicated, capital mobility has been uneven and responsible for job loss in many communities. The issue is not strictly "regional," although the northern industrial belt has been hurt the most by disinvestment. It is "national" in that the role of interregional and international capital transfers affect all regions; it is "national" in that calls for limits on capital movements (which is discussed in Chapter XI) must be dealt with at the national level.

BUSINESS CYCLES, LONG-TERM GROWTH, AND URBAN AND REGIONAL CHANGE

With regard to business cycles and their differential effects on regions,[33] this section presents material on the employment and price changes that occur during cycles and how they vary among regions. Particular attention is paid to the last recession (1974–75). In addition, long-term trends of regional employment and population are noted. Changes in employment, unemployment, inflation, and other variables induced by national cycles are likely to differ among regions and cities. Following a review of several hypotheses concerning the reasons for differential cyclical behavior among regions, the results of previous studies of this subject are examined. Finally, long-term regional trends are considered.

Explanations of Regional Cyclical Behavior

Several hypotheses to explain differential regional responses to national business cycles have been put forward, including: (1) industry mix, (2) secular growth, (3) local labor market conditions, and (4) region size.

Industry Mix. The industry mix of a region has often been identified as a major cause of regional cyclical patterns. Thus, if a region is dominated by industries with high cyclical sensitivity, it will, in general, also behave in a highly cyclical manner.

Although it seems reasonable to believe, for example, that the domination of durable manufacturing in a region may play a cyclical role, there is also evidence that the relative importance of industry mix is declining. First, the regional concentration of industry has been decreasing due to the increasingly footloose nature of manufacturing and overall industrial decentralization nationally. That is, the spatial distribution of industrial activity is much more similar to that of population distribution than it was 30 years ago. The greater importance of services in the economy, of course, has meant a closer connection between population and jobs than previously. Second, a change in an industry at the national level is not necessarily a good predictor of change in the same industry at the local level because of differing local interindustry relationships among firms.

Third, firms in one industry in different regions are not homogeneous in nature. Their capital stocks may be of different ages, their capital-to-labor ratios may differ, and other factors may vary as well. Therefore, firms may react to changes in national demand in varying ways; some will be more resistant to recessions than others. The earlier discussion of capital mobility showed movement of capital from "older" (northern) regions to "newer" (southern) regions, indicating that the newer capital stock is in the South. The implications with regard to cyclical behavior is that capital shifts may exacerbate the interregional differences in business cycles. The northern regions experience more instability and the South less instability due, in part, to capital shifts.

Secular Growth. A second hypothesis to explain regional differences in cyclical behavior attributes them to local differences in secular growth. Two "secular growth" arguments are relevant. The first relates to the extent to which different regions respond to long-term national economic growth. This is determined in part by the income elasticities of demand for the region's products. Second, the internal nature of the regions experiencing different rates of long-term secular growth may vary. For instance, if a region is growing quickly, labor markets may be tight, labor hoarding may occur, and employment loss during a recession may be less than in slower growing regions. Often, fast-growing regions have significant shares of more efficient, low-cost plants. During national downturns, the region's plants are less likely to suffer production and employment cutbacks than less efficient plants which are often located in slower growing areas. Also, relatively more employment will be devoted to fulfilling local demand (e.g., new construction) in a growing area; the region, therefore, will be less susceptible to national recessions.

Finally, recessions might be resisted in fast-growing regions since migrants are attracted to them. The new migrants are a source of new investment demand; therefore, fast-growing regions often have larger expansions than slower growing ones. Thus, it would appear that high-growth regions would be more stable during downturns (i.e., employment loss would be less) and less stable during expansions (e.g., there would be more rapid employment growth) than slow-growth areas. Empirically, Borts[34] found that fast-growing regions had less severe cycles than their industrial mixes would predict *a priori.*

Local Labor Market Conditions. Several researchers have examined the role of local labor market conditions in regional cyclical behavior. Here, migration becomes significant because the availability of labor in a region is often important: an abundant labor supply reduces the need for labor hoarding and lowers a cycle's amplitude.

A second labor market factor relevant to the cycle is labor quality. Employers are less likely to lay off highly skilled workers during contractions. Therefore, in regions with a high proportion of highly skilled workers, other things equal, cyclical amplitude should be less than in areas dominated by a low-skilled labor force. Other local labor market phenomena may be important. These include relative wages and other factor costs (including energy), the labor force's demographic profile (e.g., age, sex, race), and institutional forces (e.g., unemployment assistance laws), which vary from state to state.

Region Size. The size of the region's labor market should affect labor mobility since there are more alternative local employment opportunities. As a result, larger areas will be less sensitive to fluctuations in economic conditions than smaller ones. The larger the region, the more stable its economy, according to this hypothesis.

It has been found, however, that both the local marginal propensities to consume and to invest (and the income created per dollar of local consumption and investment) will increase with region size. That is, the local multiplier should increase with region size as there is less dependence on exports in larger regions. This implies two contradictory results: (1) the larger the region size, the larger the multiplier and therefore the greater the degree of instability; and (2) the larger the region, the less the reliance on exports and the greater industrial diversity, implies more stability.

The Nature of Regional Cycles: Some Empirical Evidence

Some of the empirical research on the nature of regional business cycles are discussed below, with concentration on the amplitude and timing of regional cycles.

Amplitude. First, the amplitudes of regional cycles (that is, the difference between peak and trough) appeared to lessen over time, at least until the 1970s. In an early study of 33 states, Borts[35] found this to be so, and his results have been replicated by others. Second, regions differ in their sensitivity to national cycles.

Vernez *et al.*,[36] in a comprehensive study of all states and of over 100 labor market areas (LMA) for 1960–1975, found distinct regional patterns. Those states with the highest responsiveness to national employment changes were often dominated by durable manufacturing industries. For instance, a one percent change in national employment was associated with 1.6 percent change in Indiana, 2.3 percent in Michigan, and 1.4 percent in Ohio. Labor market areas showing high amplitudes were located in the East North Central region, the eastern portion of the West North Central (that is, the old Manufacturing Belt), the East South Central, and the Pacific Northwest. The authors also found that the smaller, primarily agricultural states exhibited the smallest cyclical amplitudes. These include Arkansas, Utah, Wyoming, and South Dakota; for South Dakota, a one percent change in national employment generated only a 0.41 percent change in state employment. Vernez *et al.* also indicate that some Middle-Atlantic states are relatively unresponsive to national cycles.

The findings of these and related studies show that: (1) there is a wide variation in cyclical amplitude among regions; and (2) that the northern tier states and LMA have larger-than-average cycles. Agricultural states are less sensitive to national cycles than those states in which manufacturing dominates.

Timing. Vernez *et al.* also viewed the timing of regional cycles and found that most regions and LMAs conformed closely to national employment changes. LMAs that lagged the nation were largely in the East North Central and Middle-Atlantic regions. By and large, the states that led the national cycle were in the West, Mountain, West North Central, and West South Central regions. The LMAs that led were in these regions and the South Atlantic.

Long-Term Regional Growth

National Growth. The past decade has witnessed considerably slower economic growth at the national level, especially after the oil crisis of 1973. For example, real GNP grew at an average annual rate of 3.77 percent between 1965 and 1973, but by only 2.62 percent between 1973 and 1978.[37] During the same time periods, labor productivity growth declined from 2.32 percent per year to 1.20 percent, and net capital stock growth was reduced from 3.67 percent per year to 2.05 percent. The slow economic growth rate, low labor productivity, and lack of significant new investment has led to higher levels of unit labor costs and increased unemployment.

Economists have had difficulty in analyzing the slower labor productivity growth. Denison, for example, can account for only 47 percent of the productivity decline between the 1948–73 and 1973–76 periods. Norsworthy *et al.* conclude that: "The 1965–1973 slowdown in largely unexplained by the factors we have considered. . . . The 1973–1978 slowdown is dominated by the effects of reduced capital formation."[38] Norsworthy *et al.* argue further that the rise of energy prices was part of the reason for the decline in capital formation during the late 1970s.

The slowdown in economic activity during the 1970s had differential regional effects. The slow-growing regions, especially those tied to manufacturing, experienced very slow growth and, in some cases, absolute declines during this period. However, the regional growth situation of the 1970s should be viewed in the context of longer term economic change among the regions.

Regional Change. Much has been written on long-term regional trends in the United States.[39] Several patterns have appeared over the past 20 years in the pattern of regional development. First, there has been a rather dramatic decline in employment and, in later years, population in the Northeast and North Central regions. Employment in the northern tier of regions has declined dramatically: the New England, Middle-Atlantic, and East Central regions had 66.7 percent of all manufacturing employment in 1950; this proportion fell to 58.8 percent by 1965 and to 51.1 percent by 1976. Therefore, in a quarter of a century those regions showed declines from two-thirds to one-half of the nation's manufacturing employment. The South and West have been growing at rates well above the national average since 1950, not only for manufacturing, but for all nonagricultural employment. Therefore, the current situation of low employment growth in the Frostbelt is not a new phenomenon. The decentralization of the service industry was just as significant. Much of the service sector is tied to population concentrations, which were also dispersing from the North to the South.

The reasons for this decentralization of industry and other economic activity are well known. First, of course, manufacturing has become more footloose and less tied to raw material sites than previously. Lighter weight goods have replaced heavier products and this has allowed the greater use of trucking rather than rail transport. As a result, the large, rail-oriented cities lost their transport cost advantage. Changes in communications technology made the separation of functions within a firm more feasible than in earlier economic history. For example, managerial functions have been increasingly separated from production and assembly, as I previously noted. The concentration of significant amounts of finance capital in the hands of large firms has allowed them to look for locations with low wages or relatively free of unions. Increasingly, this has meant that such locations occur in other countries. Energy costs, labor productivity, and other explanations of interregional cost difference have been put forward as explanations of location factors. The role of interplant resource reallocation by multiplant corporations is another important, albeit less familiar, factor.

A second important postwar trend involves the movements of population among and within regions. Much of this movement has been associated with the changes in the location of economic activity. The shift of population out of the Northeast has been increasing and significant. On a net migration basis, for example, the Northeast lost 224,000 people to the West and 438,000 to the South between 1965 and 1970; between 1970 and 1975, those figures increased to 311,000 (to the West) and 964,000 (to the South).

Interestingly, the intraregional distribution has changed in the 1970s. For the first time in decades, there was net inmigration to nonmetropolitan areas by about 1.5 million people between 1970 and 1975. Some of this movement can be considered "statistical" in that it merely reflected continuing decentralization of metropolitan areas; thus, some of this nometropolitan growth is a "spillover" across SMSA boundaries to adjacent nonmetropolitan countries. But this explains only part of the picture. There is considerable growth away from metropolitan areas, much related not only to retirement and recreation activity (especially in Florida, which captured a very large proportion of the Sunbelt's population growth during this period), but also to resource extraction and related employment and other manufacturing, especially in low-wage areas.

What do the long-term growth prospects of the national economy bode for urban and regional development in the next decade? Much of the answer to this question lies in answering a prior question: What will the U.S. economy be like in 1990?

LOOKING TO THE FUTURE

To set the stage for the discussion of policy options in Chapter 11, this section looks at the possible implications of the circumstances described earlier for the future of the U.S. economy. In making a range of forecasts, two tools are employed: "scenario" building and econometric modelling. It should be understood that the discussion that follows provides examples of ways of looking at the future. Other methods exist, but the two chosen methodologies are presented because they not only provide widely diverse methodologies, but also have the flexibility to yield a range of alternatives given different assumptions about the nature of societal change.

The Future Through Scenarios

Some interesting insights into the future of the industrialized world can be had by following the methodology of a recent study by the Organization for Economic Cooperation and Development (OECD) entitled *Facing the Future*[40] (also known as "INTERFUTURES"). This study observes the future of the OECD countries in terms of their interrelated economic functions, not only among themselves, but in relation to the LDCs.

"INTERFUTURES" Scenarios. After viewing the difficult structural problems facing the OECD nations, the INTERFUTURES report sets forth a set of long-range scenarios about alternative futures for these countries. The important questions raised by INTERFUTURES concern the physical limits to growth in terms of the supply and demand for commodities such as food, energy, and raw materials, as well as the environmental constraints on growth. INTERFUTURES concludes that

the major impediments to growth are primarily economic, social, and political—not physical—and discusses a set of "transitional problems" that must be solved. These problems include the impact of economic activity on the ecosphere, institutional and technological aspects of greater food production, the difficulties in increasing energy supply, and a set of sociopolitical issues facing individual countries and the industrialized nations collectively.

OECD countries also face problems with respect to macroeconomic growth. INTERFUTURES sees important technological developments in the fields of electronics, biology, new forms of energy, and the uses of the oceans and seas for productive activity. But the report is relatively pessimistic about the ability of the OECD countries to achieve the rapid growth of the 1960s due to such constraints as the lack of sufficient investment (including research and development), balance of payments problems, inflation, and the rigidity of international monetary system. Thus, moderate growth is forecast for the remainder of the century.

According to INTERFUTURES, there will also be a set of pressures on the structures of the advanced economies. Some strains are demographic: the world's population is predicted to grow to 12 billion by the year 2050 and to have an older age structure; in addition, labor force growth will slow in the 1990s. The OECD economies will have to adjust to continuing changes in intermediate and final demand for goods. That is, capital-to-labor ratios are likely to continue increasing; there will be faster rates of technological obsolescence, weak demand for consumption goods and housing, and greater demand for services. These are seen largely as intensification of current trends.

Importantly, there will be changes in international competitive positions as unit labor costs in developed countries have increased significantly since the late 1960s. This has changed the competitive positions among the most developed OECD countries. And, fundamentally, there is an important set of challenges from the Third World in the future that must be faced. INTERFUTURES sees the futures of the OECD and the LDCs as increasingly interdependent. The advanced nations must aid the LDCs that will be faced with important population and food demand pressures; the OECD nations are dependent on OPEC and other LDCs for oil and other raw materials. INTERFUTURES calls for a determination of coherent strategies with respect to the developing world in the areas of agricultural and industrial development, raw materials, and energy.

Given this kind of analysis about the nature of the world of the future, INTERFUTURES sets out six "scenarios" about the futures of the OECD that involve a wide range of assumptions and possible outcomes.

For example, what the study labels "Scenario A," the High-Growth case assumes a collective management of growth among the OECD countries, a consensus among the industrialized countries to pursue high-growth policies, increased trade liberalization, significant aid flows from the North to the South, and the increasing integration of the Third World into the world economy. This scenario envisions moderate growth until the year 2000, with the OECD averaging real growth of 4.3 percent per year over that period. Under this scenario, the United States grows more slowly than the average for OECD and the developing world increases its share of the world's output.

A very different view is given in Scenario D ("a fragmented world"), where increasing protectionism and a breakdown of free trade are assumed. OECD nations establish poles (or spheres of influence) with related LDCs. For example, the United States would establish stronger ties with Latin America; Japan would do the same with some nations of Southeast Asia. Growth declines in comparison with Scenario A.[41]

Possible Consequences of Scenario A for the U.S. and Its Regions. It is useful to trace through the implications for the nation and its regions of at least one of the INTERFUTURES scenarios; for example, the consequences of Scenario A, the high-growth scenario, following an interesting discussion by Sarbib and Lazin.[42]

According to INTERFUTURES, the role of the U.S., economy under all of the scenarios would decline relative to the rest of the world. For example, the country accounted for approximately 29 percent of the world's Gross Domestic Product (GDP) in 1975. Under Scenario A, our share would decline to 19 percent by the year 2000.[43] The proportion of GDP of Japan would rise from 7 percent to 10 percent and the GDP share of the Third World would increase from 22 percent to 31 percent. The slow rate of economic growth of the nation during the 1970s and early 1980s would, therefore, likely continue.

The report sees a possible restructuring of the U.S. economy which would entail the following developments: (1) increases in investment in pollution control technologies; (2) an increase in food production relative to its past share of exports and, perhaps, in proportion of GNP; (3) a liberalization of trade that will aid the developing countries to increase their export of products with high labor-to-capital ratios to the United States; (4) increased financial activity to service the increased international trade brought on by trade liberalization; (5) an increase in our emphasis on the production and export of high-technology items; (6) a fall in our share of the world's production of machinery and other manufactures from 31 percent to 19 percent by the year 2000; and (7) increased U.S. export of capital goods and finance capital because of the increasing capital needs of the relatively fast-growing Third World nations. INTERFUTURES concludes:

> The relative overall economic power of the United States is falling significantly. This relative decline, which reflects both the development of the rest of the world and the difficulties peculiar to the American society, is accompanied by considerable specific advantages of increasing importance: a technological lead in key sectors such as industrial electronics, and an abundance of agricultural, energy and mineral resources (not to speak of military factors). Although the USA is still the world's main economic power, its global position has ceased to be exceptional and because of the above duality it will not be easy for the United States, with the help of its partners, to find the way to cohesion and collaboration on a more equal footing within the developed world.[44]

The regional aspects may be inferred from this overall picture:

1. In connection with energy, trade liberalization will mean conservation through higher energy prices. This implies accelerated searches for conventional fuels, thus favoring the Southwest and Mountain states where considerable oil and coal reserves are available. The regions that are lacking in energy sources, such as the Northeast, will either have to rely on nuclear power or employ alternative energy sources such as solar, should the latter become economically feasible.

2. The industrial restructuring in this scenario would involve increased investment and production in several industries in which the nation has a comparative advantage. Electronics, computers, machine tools, aircraft, and hospital equipment are the most likely candidates. Regionally, the electronics sector is located mostly in the Sunbelt; many machine tool companies, however, are New England-based. The electronics industry may receive continued aid for research and development and production activities from the U.S. Defense Department, among other government agencies.

3. The relative decline of traditional industries would hurt largely the old Industrial Belt of the Northeast and Midwest in the production of textiles, shoes, leather, and other low-technology, high-labor content industry. However, because many of these firms have already moved to the South, the consequences of liberalized trade may be injurious to some southern states as well.

The restructuring of the automobile industry is but one example of other significant changes that must occur in the economy and probably bring with it somewhat more government "risk capital" in autos and other industries. That is, there may be government policies aimed at directing the economy into areas in which we have a comparative advantage. This may have regional consequences in terms of the location of these new governmentally inspired production units. For example, the government may use its leverage with respect to new industry to help locate industry in distressed areas. On the other hand, government may "follow the market" and not try to influence location patterns in this manner.

5. The continued development of agriculture would be carried out in the western states, primarily through agribusiness firms. However, there may be conflict with environmental groups over the use of pesticides that are economical for large-scale farming.[45]

In sum, the future as seen by INTERFUTURES' Scenario A implies a considerable intensification of some of our ongoing economic activity and a redirection of others. In an age of free trade, the nation cannot continue to compete in product lines without a comparative advantage. This, in turn, means the reshaping of some industries to become competitive in world markets.[46] With changes in industrial structure will come alterations in industrial location. In this free-trade scenario, new technology-based regions, financial centers, energy producing areas, and agricultural belts will gain employment at the expense of other regions.

Regional Consequences of Other Scenarios. Other scenarios put forward in INTERFUTURES would imply other configurations of economic activity and corresponding directions of urban and regional development. For example, the "protectionist" case (Scenario D) would require fewer financial services to engage in international trade; this would mean difficulties for cities specializing in such employment (for example, New York or San Francisco). Manufacturing production would have to be oriented toward some goods that currently are imported. Although space does not permit a full explication of these ramifications (or those of other scenarios), it is clear that the urban and regional picture would be different under Scenario D than under Scenario A.

The Future Through Model Forecasts

An alternative mechanism for looking at the future of the U.S. economy and its component regions is through the use of empirical models. This mode has been used for a wide variety of forecasting and policy analytic simulations, primarily at the nation level.[47] Such models have more recently been extended spatially in two directions: toward models of the world and to subnational areas.[48]

Although most models, especially econometric models, are used primarily for short-term forecasts, a long-term econometric model is of interest—the Wharton Annual Model. This large-scale econometric model contains over one thousand equations estimated from time series data and has a detailed input-output model imbedded within it. The Wharton Model of April 1980 made forecasts for the end of the decade, with great detail for industrial sectors, prices, employment, income by type, foreign trade, and other variables.

In the Wharton forecast through 1989, GNP is seen to grow at an average annual rate of 2.7 percent through 1985 and at 2.9 percent between 1985 and 1989. Following the 1980 recession, a mild rebound in 1982 and 1983 is forecasted. The inflationary pressures moderate through the end of the decade, although price increases remain high by historical standards; the average annual growth rate of the GNP price deflator is 7.0 percent between 1985 and 1989. Investment, particularly residential investment, remains fairly low. In part because the model forecast assumes that taxes would be cut to increase investment, some increase in productivity is expected.

The Wharton forecast shows particularly increased rates of output in farming, nonelectrical machinery, electrical machinery, chemicals, and services. These predictions are quite consistent with the notions advanced in the OECD Scenario A analysis. In the foreign trade sector, the major growth in exports is in the food and services commodity groups. Imports are expected to grow in the manufactured goods and services areas. Again, this is consistent with the previous analysis.

Given the relatively similar results from the Wharton Model and the scenarios method, the regional consequences of the former are likely to follow in a pattern similar to that of the scenario analysis. The banking and service centers and agricultural areas would likely gain under the model forecast, while the old Manufacturing Belt would continue to stagnate. Furthermore, it is possible to make regional forecasts from these national forecasts by "linking" the Wharton Model with a multiregion model such as that developed by Milne, Adams and Glickman.[49] This multiregion model was used to simulate the effects of national growth scenarios on nine Census regions. In addition, predictions were made given alternative assumptions about energy policy and other types of government action. Work continues in this area, although time did not permit new forecasts to be made. However, the methodology is fully developed for future research on the impacts of national economic activity and federal government policy on cities and regions.[50]

A Summing Up

In this section, two widely differing methodologies have been used to observe America's future. The scenario and the econometric modelling efforts showed surprisingly consistent results. However, it should not be concluded that they individually or collectively constitute a precise "forecast" of the U.S. economy at the end of this decade and beyond. They are merely suggestive of ways of viewing an evolving economy in a rapidly changing world system. Needless to say, the role of sets of cities and regions in this future is even more difficult to discern. However, the information provided here may provide a useful benchmark for future analysis. Both techniques indicate slow growth, relatively high inflation, and some cyclical volatility, when compared to the 1960s and early 1970s.

CONCLUSIONS

Several important elements to the previous discussion should be reiterated. First, the U.S. economy is much more "open" with respect to world trade than in the past, and the nation is much more highly interdependent with our trading partners. Second, the nature of trade has changed. Manufacturing activity is less important, while agriculture and financial dealings are more crucial. Third, the terms of trade facing the nation have deteriorated. We are less competitive in manufacturing than previously, both with respect to many of our industrial trading competitors and with less developed countries with low-wage labor. Fourth, there has been an increase in the synchronization of international business cycles during the 1970s which, if continued into the 1980s, has the potential to make domestic economic cycles more severe.

The effect of the changing international trade milieu on urban and regional development has been diverse. Manufacturing-based areas have lost employment due to a slowdown in the demand for manufacturing exports and through competition of foreign imports. Financial centers have gained service sector employment due to the importance of banking and other international trade-related services; many of these cities are the same ones that have lost manufacturing jobs over the past few decades—they tend to be large and are located primarily in the Frostbelt. Agricultural and mineral extraction regions have improved their relative positions in the economic hierarchy due to increased export demand for such products. In sum, the effect of international trade on American cities and regions has been diverse and, on balance, somewhat destabilizing. That is, cities have had to adjust to the rapidly changing economic parameters facing them.

The increasingly important role of capital mobility has been another destabilizing element facing some of our cities and regions. The evidence cited shows the movement of capital across regions and, with it, the loss of jobs and the economic dislocation of people and communities left behind. The capital shifts have important international dimensions as well, given the important role of multinational corporations.

Finally, the role of regional business cycles has been an important determinant of urban and regional change. It has been indicated that regional cycles are uneven across the nation with respect to timing, amplitude, and duration. Many of our most hard-pressed regions have found the effects of business cycles—in particular, the extreme one in the mid-1970s—an extra burden with respect to their economic health. International trade cycles and U.S. business cycles, should they become more severe in the 1980s, will continue to cause problems for many of our cities and regions in the future since a less stable national economy often means less stable regional economies.

These new trends will have profound effects on urban and other policymaking in the closing years of the century. Clearly, the *context* of government decisionmaking has been profoundly altered and made more difficult. Also, a set of issues at both the national and regional levels have emerged: how to achieve greater levels of economic growth, how to distribute income and wealth in a slow growing economy, the nature of institutions needed to guide the economy through the next few decades, and the nature of planning and policymaking at the local level in the future. These subjects have been referred to in Chapter XI.

ACKNOWLEDGMENTS

I thank Ian Dawson, Bennett Harrison, and Audrey Ryack for helpful comments on a previous draft and the National Science Foundation for partial financial support.

NOTES AND REFERENCES

1. Ralph C. Bryant and Lawrence B. Krause, "World Economic Interdependence," in Joseph A. Pechman, ed., *Setting National Priorities: Agenda for the 1980's*, Washington, D.C.: The Brookings Institute, 1980.
2. See, for example, Peter Mieszkowski and Mahlon Straszheim, eds., *Current Issues in Urban Economics*, Baltimore: The Johns Hopkins University Press, 1979; George H. Borts and Jerome L. Stein, *Economic Growth in a Free Market*, New York: Columbia University Press, 1964; Bennett Harrison, *Urban Economic Development*, Washington, D.C.: The Urban Institute, 1974; Edward M. Hoover and Raymond Vernon, *Anatomy of a Metropolis*, Cambridge, Mass.: Harvard University Press, 1959; William Alonso, *Location and Land Use*, Cambridge, Mass.: Harvard University Press, 1964; Walter Isard, *Location and Space-Economy*, Cambridge, Mass.: MIT Press, 1956; and David Harvey, "The Political Economy of Urbanization in Advanced Capitalist Societies: The Case of the United States," Baltimore: Johns Hopkins Center for Metropolitan Planning and Research, 1975.
3. For example, the proportion of imports in GNP was 6.2 percent in 1972 compared to 11.1 percent in 1979, according to Bryant and Krause, *op, cit.*, Table 3-1.

4. On a gross investment basis, U.S. private assets invested abroad amounted to $377 billion, about 5 percent of all private U.S. assets; see Bryant and Krause, *op. cit.,* Table 3-2.
5. See, U.S. Department of Housing and Urban Development, *The Impact of Foreign Direct Investment on U.S. Cities and Regions,* Washington, D.C.: U.S. Department of Housing and Urban Development, 1979.
6. Pigott, Sweeney, and Willett argue that the degree of coincidence among business cycles was higher in the 1950s than in the 1960s, for example. They say that there is no postwar trend toward more synchronization among countries, although they document the very high synchronization in the mid-1970s recession. This was due to external shocks, primarily the increase in oil prices. Thus, they argue that there is little reason to conclude that there have been fundamental or permanent changes that would imply continuing synchronization. Hargreaves-Heap provides similar results: there has been significant international synchronization in the postwar period, but there is no clear trend. See, Charles Pigott, Richard J. Sweeney, and Thomas P. Willett, "Aggregate Economic Fluctuations and the Synchronization of Economic Conditions Among Industrial Countries," *Revista Internazionale di Scienze Economiche e Commercial,* 25, 1978, pp. 409–433; and S. P. Hargreaves-Heap, "The Post-War International Business Cycle," *Journal of Economic Studies,* 6, 1979, pp. 106–127.
7. The Wharton-EFA World Model is an econometric forecasting model that links and predicts the economies of 34 countries and 7 regions. I would like to thank Professor Lawrence R. Klein, the principal architect the model, for providing these forecasts.
8. Edward F. Denison, *Accounting for Slower Growth: The United States in the 1970s,* Washington, D.C.: The Brookings Institution, 1979, and Denison, "Explanations of Declining Productivity Growth," *Survey of Current Business,* 59, August 1979, pp. 2–24.
9. Indication of the decline of U.S. manufacturing in world trade can be seen in data from the U.S. Department of Commerce, *Business America,* Washington, D.C.: General Printing Office, periodical. U.S. manufactures as a percent of world manufacturing exports fell from 25.3 percent in 1960 to 17.3 percent in 1977. Component industry changes over that time period were: nonelectric machinery (32.7 percent to 25.1 percent), transport machinery (33.2 percent to 23.8 percent), chemicals (29.6 percent to 21.1 percent), and electric machinery (28.2 percent to 23.2 percent).
10. Congressional Budget Office, *The Effects of the Tokyo Round of Multilateral Trade Negotiations on the U.S. Economy: An Updated View,* Washington, D.C.: U.S. Government Printing Office, 1979; and Congressional Budget Office, *U.S. Trade Policy and the Tokyo Round of Multilateral Trade Negotiations,* Washington, D.C.: U.S. Government Printing Office, 1979.
11. See, for example, Daniel J. B. Mitchell, *Labor Issues of American International Trade and Investment,* Baltimore: The Johns Hopkins University Press, 1976.
12. See Robert Stobaugh, "After the Peak: The Threat of Imported Oil," in Robert Stobaugh and Daniel Yergin, eds., *Energy Futures,* New York: Random House, 1979, Table 2-1.
13. See Robert Stobaugh and Daniel Yergin, "The End of Easy Oil," in Stobaugh and Yergin, eds., *op. cit.,* Chapter 1. For other accounts of the oil industry and the effects of energy on the economy, see Alfred D. Chandler, Jr., *The Visible Hand,* Cambridge, Mass: Harvard University Press, 1977; M. A. Adelman, *The World Petroleum Market,* Baltimore: The Johns Hopkins University Presss, 1972; Raymond Vernon, ed., *The Oil Crisis,* New York: Norton, 1976; and Edward A. Hudson and Dale W. Jorgenson, "Energy Prices and the U.S. Economy," *Natural Resource Journal,* 18, 1978, pp. 877–897.
14. Hudson and Jorgenson, *op. cit.*

15. David J. Bjornstad, *Changes in Economic Capacity at the Federal Region Level Due to NEP-1 Energy Price Changes,* Oak Ridge, Tenn.: Oak Ridge National Laboratory, 1980. The Carter Plan is described in Executive Office of the President, *The National Energy Plan,* Washington, D.C.: Executive Office of the President, 1977.
16. These SMSAs represent all metropolitan areas with more than one percent of total manufacturing export employment in 1976.
17. Thomas M. Stanback, Jr. and Thierry J. Noyelle, "Economic Tranformation in Selected American Cities: A Study of Processes with Implications for Development Policy," Conservation of Human Resources, New York: Columbia University, 1980 (mimeo).
18. U.S. Department of Housing and Urban Development, *The Impact of Foreign Direct Investment on U.S. Cities and Regions, op. cit.*
19. See HUD, *ibid.,* Table 4. Appendix B of the HUD study indicates that 52.7 percent of South Carolina's new manufacturing investment during 1969–73 was foreign. Tennessee, North Carolina, and Alabama also had very high proportions of foreign manufacturing investment.
20. See Harvey A. Garn, *et al.,* "Volume II, A Framework for National Urban Policy: Urban Distress, Decline and Growth," Washington, D.C.: The Urban Institute, 1977.
21. Bjornstad, *op. cit.*
22. The results reported by Bjornstad are similar to those obtained by William Milne, F. Gerard Adams, and Norman J. Glickman, "A Framework For Analyzing Regional Decline: A Multiregion Econometric Model of the United States," *Journal of Regional Science,* 20, 1980, pp. 173–189.
23. For discussions of "urban impact analysis," see Norman J. Glickman, ed., *The Urban Impacts of Federal Policies,* Baltimore: The Johns Hopkins University Press, 1980.
24. See, for example, Peter A. Morrison, "Population Movements and the Shape of Urban Growth: Implications for Public Policy," in John Friedmann and William Alonso, eds., *Regional Policy: Readings in Theory and Policy,* Cambridge, Mass.: MIT Press, 1975; Peter A. Morrison, "Emerging Concerns Over U.S. Population Movements in an Era of Slowing Growth," Rand Corporation Paper P-5873, Santa Monica, Calif.: The Rand Corporation, 1977; Daniel R. Vining and Thomas Kontuly, "Population Dispersal from Major Metropolitan Regions: An International Comparison," *International Regional Science Review,* 3, 1978, pp. 49–73; and Daniel R. Vining and Ann Strauss, "A Demonstration of Population Movement in the United States is a Cleaning Break with the Past," *Environment and Planning A,* 9, pp. 751–758.
25. Barry Bluestone and Bennett Harrison, *Capital and Communities: The Causes and Consequences of Private Disinvestment,* Washington, D.C.: The Progressive Alliance, 1980. Other studies on the same or related subjects include Ed Kelly, *Industrial Exodus,* Washington, D.C.: Conference on Alternative State and Local Public Policies, 1977; Geoffrey Faux and Robert Lightfoot, *Capital and Community,* Washington, D.C.: Project on Economic Alternatives, 1976; Jeremy Rifkin and Randy Barber, *The North Will Rise Again: Pensions, Politics and Power in the 1980's,* Boston: Beacon Press, 1978; Robert Aronson and Robert McKersie, *Economic Consequences of Plant Shutdowns in New York State,* Ithaca: New York State School of Industrial and Labor Relations, Cornell University, 1979; and Richard J. Barnet and Ronald Muller, *Global Reach,* New York: Simon and Schuster, 1974. For discussions of the role of international labor mobility, see Elizabeth M. Petras, "Towards A Theory of International Migration: The New Division of Labor," in R. Bryce-Laporte, ed., *Sourcebook on the New Immigration: Implications for the United States and the International Community,* New Brunswick, N.J.: Transactions Books, 1980; and Elizabeth M. Petras, "The Global Labor Market in the Modern World-Economy," paper presented at a Conference on International Migration Studies, Bellagio, Italy, 1979.

26. Lynn E. Browne, "Regional Capital Formation," *New England Economic Indicators,* Boston: Federal Reserve Bank of Boston, June, 1979.
27. For example, the ratio of the highest to lowest average annual growth rates among the nine Census regions was 1.6 between 1965 and 1970; the ratio grew to 2.3 between 1970 and 1976.
28. Bluestone and Harrison, following Dun and Bradstreet procedure, define branches and subsidiaries of multiplant firms that have the same Dun and Bradstreet identification number as the head office as "corporate." In legal terms, this means that only the home office can be sued in court. All other multiplant branches are considered "conglomerate" (that is, the branches have different D&B numbers and can be sued as separate entities). The authors indicate that this is not a perfect procedure, but they were bound by the D&B data system. See Chapter 2, footnote 7 of Bluestone and Harrison, *op. cit.,* for a more complete description of their typology.
29. For example, the Intel Corporation, a leading manufacturer of semiconductors, manufactures the "high tech" silicon chips in "Silicon Valley," Calif., but has the products assembled in the Caribbean and Southeast Asia. There were approximately 14,000 Intel employees in 1980, of which 12,000 were in overseas plants.
30. According to *The New York Times* article on the "Little Detroits" (March 3, 1980), branch plants of such corporate giants as IBM, General Electric, Westinghouse, and Zenith have located in the free-trade zones. In Juarez alone, there are 105 plants employing 37,500 workers.
31. Louis Jacobson, "Earnings Losses of Workers Displaced from the Steel Industry by Imports of Steel," Washington, D.C.: Public Research Institute, 1975.
32. See, Stanislaw Kasl and Sidney Cobb, "Blood Pressure Changes in Men Undergoing Job Loss," *Psychometric Medicine,* Vol. 32, 1970.
33. This section draws, in part, from Henry Coleman, Norman J. Glickman, David L. Puryear, and John P. Ross, "Business Cycles and Cities: Past Experience, Prospects and Policy Alternatives," written for *The President's National Urban Policy Report,* Washington, D.C.: U.S. Department of Housing and Urban Development, 1980. Other studies of regional cycles include: George H. Borts, "Regional Cycles of Manufacturing Industry in the United States, 1914–1953," *Journal of the American Statistical Association,* Vol. 55 1967; Cornelis P. A. Bartels, "The Structure of Regional Unemployment in the Netherlands: An Exploratory Statistical Analysis," *Regional Science and Urban Economics,* 7, 1977, pp. 103–135; Norman J. Glickman, *Econometric Analysis of Regional Systems: Explorations in Model Building and Policy Analysis,* New York: Academic Press, 1977; Raymond Fearn, "Cyclical, Seasonal and Structural Factors in Area Unemployment Rates," *Industrial and Labor Relations Review,* 28, 1975, pp. 424–431; Georges Vernez, Roger J. Vaughan, Burke Burright, and Sinclair Coleman, *Regional Cycles and Employment Effects of Public Works Investments,* Santa Monica, Calif.: The Rand Corporation, 1977; and Roger J. Vaughan, *Public Works as a Countercyclical Device: A Review of the Issues,* Santa Monica, Calif.: The Rand Corporation, 1976.
34. Borts, *op. cit.*
35. Borts, *op. cit.*
36. Vernez *et al., op. cit.*
37. Denison, *Accounting for Slower Growth, op. cit.*
38. J. R. Norsworthy, Michael J. Harper, and Kent Kunze, "The Slowdown in Productivity Growth: Analysis of Some Contributing Factors," *Brookings Papers in Economic Activity,* 2, 1979, p. 421.
39. See, for example, Peter Mieszkowski, "Recent Trends in Urban and Regional Development," in Peter Mieszkowski and Mahlon Straszheim, *op. cit.,* pp. 3–39; Allan K. Campbell, "Intra and Interregional Changes in Population and Economic Activity," presented at the L.B.J. School of Public Affairs, University of Texas at Austin, 1977

(mimeo); Seymour Sacks, *Trends in Metropolitan America*, Washington, D.C.: Advisory Commission on Intergovernmental Relations, 1977; Calvin L. Beale, "The Revival of Population Growth in Non-Metropolitan America," Washington, D.C.: U.S. Department of Agriculture, ERS-605, 1975; Roger Alcaly and David Mermelstein, eds., *The Fiscal Crisis of American Cities*, New York: Vintage, 1977; Charles L. Leven, ed., *The Mature Metropolis*, Lexington, Mass.: Heath-Lexington, 1978; William Alonso, "The Current Halt in the Metropolitan Public Phenomenon," mimeo, 1977; George Sternlieb and James W. Hughes, *Post-Industrial America: Metropolitan Decline and Inter-Regional Job Shifts*, New Brunswick, N.J.: Center for Urban Policy Research, 1975; and William H. Oakland, "Central Cities: Fiscal Plight and Prospects for Reform," in Peter Mieszkowski and Mahlon Straszheim, *op. cit.*, pp. 332–358.

40. Organization of Economic Cooperation and Development, *Facing the Future: Mastering the Probable and Managing the Unpredictable (INTERFUTURES)*, Paris: OECD, 1979. For a summary of this study, see OECD, "Facing the Future," *The OECD Observer*, No. 100, September 1979.
41. Between these two scenarios, there are four alternatives which span the range between Scenarios A and D.
42. Jean-Louis Sarbib and Steve Lazin, "The Future of American Cities and Regions in an Internationalized Economy: Two Scenarios," report to the U.S. Department of Housing and Urban Development, 1979 (mimeo). Note that this is not necessarily the most likely scenario. It has been chosen only for illustrative purposes. Also, although this is called the "high-growth" scenario, the economic growth rates inbedded in the scenario are quite moderate by historical standards. It is "high" only when compared to the other INTERFUTURES scenarios.
43. See OECD, *INTERFUTURES, op. cit.*, Table 21.
44. *Ibid.*, pp. 302–303.
45. Sarbib and Lazin, *op. cit.*, p. III-4.
46. For a study of industrial restructuring in the United Kingdom, see Doreen Massey, "Capital and Locational Change: The UK Electrical Engineering and Electronics Industry," *The Review of Radical Political Economics*, 10, 1978, pp. 39–54. A special issue of *Business Week* (June 30, 1980) on the "The Reindustrialization of America" discusses some proposals for the restructuring of U.S. industry.
47. See, Lawrence R. Klein, *Economic Fluctuations in the United States, 1921–1941*, New York: Wiley, 1950; Wassily Leontief, *The Structure of the American Economy, 1919–1939*, New York: Oxford University Press, 1951; Michael K. Evans and Lawrence R. Klein, *The Wharton Economic Forecasting Model*, Philadelphia: University of Pennsylvania Economic Research Unit, 1968; and James S. Duesenberry *et al.*, *The Brookings Quarterly Econometric Model of the United States*, Chicago: Rand McNally, 1965, for early examples of econometric and input-output models of the United States.
48. Models of the world economy have been built at The World Bank and at the University of Pennsylvania ("Project LINK"), the latter under the direction of Lawrence R. Klein. At the regional level, several models have been constructed for single regions and for multiregional systems. Examples include Norman J. Glickman, *Econometric Modelling of Regional Systems: Explorations in Model Building and Policy Analysis*, New York: Academic Press, 1977; F. Gerard Adams and Norman J. Glickman, eds., *Modeling the Multiregion Economic System: Theory, Data, and Policy*, Lexington, Mass.: Heath-Lexington, 1980; Kenneth P. Ballard, Richard Gustely, and Robert Wendling, *The National-Regional Impact Evaluation System: Structure, Performance and Applications of a Bottom-up Interregional Econometric Model*, Washington, D.C.: Bureau of Economic Analysis, 1980; Frederick Golladay and Robert H. Haveman, *The Economic Impacts of Tax-Transfer Policy*, New York: Academic Press, 1977; and Karen R. Polenske, *The*

United States Multiregional Input-Output Model, Lexington, Mass.: Heath-Lexington, 1975. For overviews of regional models, see Harry W. Richardson, *Input-Output and Regional Economics,* New York: Halsted, 1972; Norman J. Glickman, "Son of 'The Specification of Regional Econometric Models'," *Papers and Proceedings of the Regional Science Association,* 32, 1974, pp. 155–177; and Norman J. Glickman, "Using Empirical Models for Regional Policy Analysis," paper presented at a Conference on the Theoretical and Practical Aspects of Regional Development Modeling at the International Institute for Applied Systems Analysis, Laxenburg, Austria, 1980, forthcoming in Conference Proceedings, to be published by the North-Holland Publishing Co.

49. Milne, William, F. Gerard Adams, and Norman J. Glickman, "A 'Top-Down' Approach to Multiregion Modeling," in F. Gerard Adams and Norman J. Glickman, *op. cit.*

50. See Adams and Glicman, *op. cit.,* for a compendium of empirical approaches to analyzing the effects on regions of different growth policies and government policies on regions.

Chapter IX

REGIONAL ECONOMIC DECENTRALIZATION PROCESSES IN THE UNITED STATES AND THEIR POLICY IMPLICATIONS

John Rees

INTRODUCTION

During the 1970s, the United States experienced profound changes in its economic and regional structure—changes without parallel over the course of this century, with the exception of the Depression. Changes in the international economy had an impact on the national economy; in turn, these changes were manifested at various regional levels, both in the United States and in other developed countries. The OPEC price shock to the oil-dependent world economic system was a major causal factor in the inflation-recessionary spiral experienced in the United States and elsewhere. The slowdown of growth in the already slow-growing international economic system was an integral part of the "new international economic order" of the 1970s, where growth rates in developing countries were seen to converge on those of the developed world.

This slowed growth only exacerbated the productivity dilemma that the United States was already facing at the beginning of the 1970s [37]. "Productivity levels in the United States exceed those of France, West Germany and the United Kingdom, but United States' productivity gains between 1960 and 1976 were the smallest of the four countries" [62]. The United States experienced a particularly steep decline in productivity since 1973, but this is no coincidence, given the vicious cycle that tends to exist between inflation, productivity, and, hence, gains in real income.

Inflation affects productivity by putting a brake on capital investment, particularly on a peripheral item like research and development, which in turn is directly related to the rate of technological change and innovation. Productivity, in turn, affects inflation, particularly through labor costs, given that increases in labor costs amount to compensation increases minus productivity gains. This is a particularly important relationship when labor costs are greater than 50 percent of total business costs [88]. Hence, in the 1970s, the high degree of unanticipated inflation has weakened productivity growth, which, in turn, has contributed to inflation. Projections on world Gross Domestic Product according to Business Week (May 5, 1980) estimated that it is expected to rise at an anemic 2.3 percent in 1980 and 2.6 percent in 1981, with the western industrial nations showing a minimal 1.1 percent growth in 1980 and 1.6 percent in 1981.

Coinciding with this major slowdown in economic growth at the international and national levels, major changes were under way at the subnational level in the United States; the increased decentralization of economic activity from inner cities to suburban, exurban, or rural locations, and interregional shifts in economic growth between the Northeast and the South and West. The Great Recession of 1975—the low point of the economic slowdown—may be seen as the turning point in the dominance of the Manufacturing Belt in the American economy. The Belt's already aging industrial plant may have had wounds inflicted on it that will prove permanent, and other younger areas of the United States with different industrial structures may stand to gain even more at the expense of the older industrial areas (Rees 1979, Norton and Rees 1979).

This slowdown of growth in the national economy as a whole not only manifested itself at subnational levels, but also made the interregional allocation of resources, both by government and by industry, more conspicuous. When economic growth in a national economy approaches a zero sum game, interregional rivalries become more apparent as greater amounts of "political capital" can be generated at the local level.

The 1970s saw major changes in the international economy, in the national economic system, and at the subnational or regional scale. The changes are complex, not the result of one causal factor, but an interdependent number of causal mechanisms. Because of the interdependent nature of the world economic system, changes taking place at one level can manifest themselves at all levels. We were cognizant of this interdependence going into the 1970s. We are probably more cognizant of such interdependencies at the dawn of the 1980s because we failed to anticipate the types of changes that occurred in the 1970s, and the rapid impact of changes in one level of the system on other levels. One of the major policy concerns for the 1980s, therefore, has to be the anticipation of the impact of such changes and whether the kinds of changes seen in the 1970s will also be evident during the 1980s.

It is still a moot point whether the changes taking place in the 1970s were symptomatic of a long-term secular trend or whether they were the result of short-term cyclical fluctuations. Recently, it has become popular once again for economists to think in terms of Kondratieff-type long cycles of change. "It should be of little surprise that the long term swings in relative economic fortune have been newly rediscovered as the nation's aging industrial regions increasingly appear to be entering the negative phase of such cycles" [83:1]. Some neo-Malthusian economists contend that we have entered the downphase of one of these Kondratieff cycles that may result in a severe world recession or depression in the mid 1980s.

Others see the trends of the 1970s as cyclical fluctuations when the business cycle reached deeper levels. We know that the Manufacturing Belt was hit more severely than the rest of the country by the 1975 recession [1]. This should be expected, given that the capital stock of growing regions tends to be newer and incorporates more efficient technology relative to older slow-growing regions where firms first close their inefficient plants during temporary downturns. One might also expect a link between short-term cyclical changes in the economy and long-term structural changes, although empirical links between the two processes are difficult to verify [38]. Short-term trends, however, develop into long-term ones if the stop-go nature of U.S. business cycles continues in the 1980s as it did in the 1970s.

Against this background of major changes in the world economy during the 1970s, and the unanswered question whether they represent short-run or long-term changes, one must view changes in technology and regional economic structure within the United States. The processes of economic decentralization described in the first part of this paper cannot be viewed independently; each is implicitly linked to the other. Hence, any policies used to influence such changes cannot be derived independently, for one set of policies can have an impact on the goals of others. The history of policymaking in the United States is hardly replete with the anticipation of problems in comparison to the reaction to crises of various magnitudes. When dealing with future policy options that have interregional impacts, as the second part of this paper does, the anticipation of interdependency between various types of policy measures at a time of increasing interdependency between levels of the regional economic system becomes mandatory.

ECONOMIC DECENTRALIZATION TRENDS AND THEIR DETERMINANTS

The movement of economic activity, which implies the opening, closure, and relocation of businesses and jobs in the United States, can be seen to have taken place on at least four geographical scales in the post-1945 era. Because they can be interpreted as decentralization processes occurring at different *scales,* many causal mechanisms are common to all four.

The Movement From Inner to Outer City

Perhaps the most time-honored decentralization process—or at least the one most highly scrutinized in terms of urban policy—has been the exodus of industry and employment from central cities to suburban areas throughout the United States. As the country's population continued to grow and became more urbanized throughout the twentieth century, it was inevitable that in the United States, as in other developed countries, both businesses and population spill over the boundaries of existing cities. Conventional market mechanisms, such as the need for more space for industrial expansion, the attraction of cheaper land on the city periphery, together with an expanding transportation infrastructure and available labor pools, resulted in the exodus of manufacturing and later service industries from the inner to the outer city.

Suburbanization continued in the 1970s, as shown in Table IX.1. The central counties of the nation's largest metropolitan areas—those with one million population or more, where the central county itself included parts of many suburban cities—continued to show large absolute and relative losses of employment in manufacturing, construction, transportation-communication, and utility industries. Growth rates in wholesale and retail trade, finance, insurance, and real estate in these central counties only showed small gains relative to the suburban counties of large metropolitan areas. The process itself, however, has been documented well enough in this volume and elsewhere not to require further attention here [10, 36, 43, 16].

Suffice it to say, however, that the degree to which an urban policy for

Table IX.1. Employment Change in Central and Suburban Counties of Large Metro Areas, 1970–76

	Suburban Counties (Fringe of Large Metropolitan)		*Central Counties of Large Metro Areas (1,000,000 or more pop.)*	
	(% change)	*(absolute change)*	*(% change)*	*(absolute change)*
Number of Counties	123	123	48	48
Total Employment (Full and Part-Time)	16.74%	1,364,475	1.57%	459,355
Agriculture (Total Farm)	16.02	9,218	12.13	7,652
Agricultural Services, Forestry, Fisheries, etc.	26.32	8,290	32.23	17,577
Mining	12.14	3,376	26.84	21,800
Construction	2.31	9,614	(−) 13.80	(−) 157,742
Manufacturing	(−) 0.37	(−) 7,307	(−) 10.05	(−) 661,296
Transportation, Communication, and Public Utilities	13.59	47,268	(−) 7.45	(−) 146,932
Wholesale Trade	47.79	146,179	2.17	41,017
Retail Trade	26.96	338,782	5.44	215,132
Finance, Insurance, Real Estate	44.29	111,847	5.52	109,736
Services	35.71	426,019	13.98	762,061
Total Nonmanufacturing	22.22	1,371,782	4.95	1,120,651

Source: Compiled from Bureau of Economic Analysis data.

the 1980s should be concerned with the revitalization of existing areas (as implied in the urban enterprise zone concept), and whether this only implies the provision of artificial barriers to urbanization and the urban life-cycle process, is indeed a moot point at a time of scarce resources.

The Rejuvenation of Nonmetropolitan America

The decentralization process once limited to the intrametropolitan scale has now spread outwards. "Events once endemic to the metropolitan level, in particular employment decentralization, appear to have been attenuated to new spatial scales and are now working themselves out over the entire geography of the country" [82:231]. The growth of nonmetropolitan areas is a natural extension of the suburbanization process, particularly when it takes place adjacent to large metropolitan areas. This "spread effect" is indeed implicit in the definition of nometropolitan areas, given that the Bureau of Census uses two typologies: metropolitan areas (made up of central cities and suburbs on a county basis) and nometropolitan areas.

Unfortunately, this simplistic dichotomy is based on administrative jurisdiction rather than on functional characteristics like commuting fields and labor markets. It therefore may conceal many underlying processes. Suppose that a large metropolitan area continues its growth trends across its formally defined Standard Metropolitan Statistical Area (SMSA), then the growth would be classified as nonmetropolitan. Furthermore, the documentation of declining immigration into large urban areas that include the "spread effects" of these cities cannot be detected if intrametropolitan relocations are increasing and becoming exurban. To a degree, therefore, the term "counter urbanization" that has been applied to this process is a misnomer. In the same vein, this taxonomic issue also clouds the argument of those who advocate that the growth of nometropolitan America represents a "clean break with the past" [93].

Some convincing evidence does exist, however, that nonmetropolitan growth in the 1970s was under way in counties quite distant from large metropolitan areas [2, 60, 74]. Morrison and McCarthy [60] examined population changes in nonmetropolitan counties between 1960 and 1974 by type of economic specialty. During the 1960s, energy-extraction counties lost population while "recreation"- and "government"- oriented counties showed above average growth rates. Manufacturing-based counties showed above average growth rates in the 1960s, but not as much as might be expected given the tendency of branch plants (particularly in labor intensive industries) to filter down to low-wage nonmetropolitan areas [19]. "Nonmetropolitan areas added 1.8 million manufacturing jobs or 56% of the United States total increase between

1962 and 1978. But more than half of the gain had occurred by 1967 and most of the rest by 1974" [48].

In the early 1970s, energy-extractive counties, recreation-oriented areas, and particularly retirement-based counties showed above average growth rates, while growth rates in manufacturing- and government-oriented counties lagged behind. The relatively rapid growth rates in retirement- and recreation-oriented nonmetropolitan areas can be explained by the increased locational freedom of both elderly and working age groups of people. Given that many of these counties are not adjacent to SMSAs, *it suggests that economic base factors, rather than adjacency to metropolitan areas, account for nonmetropolitan growth rates in the early 1970s,* i.e., growth in amenity-rich nometropolitan areas is characteristic of the most remote locations in contrast to the trends of the 1960s. Irving Kristol summed up this feature of the 1970s when he stated that the nation was becoming "an urban civilization without cities" where nonmetropolitan areas have the technological capability of being functionally and culturally metropolitan [45].

The growth of amenity-oriented nonmetropolitan counties in the 1970s, coupled with the higher growth rates in manufacturing in such counties during earlier periods, is testimony to the increased diversification of the economic bases of these areas, *possibly providing the type of diversity that may enable these areas to sustain their economic growth in the future.* Table IX.2 shows absolute and relative increases in employment in U.S. nonmetropolitan counties by type of industry and size of place during the 1970–76 period (a longer time period than the one covered by Morrison and McCarthy [60]). The largest sectors of absolute growth were local services, retail trade, and manufacturing, respectively. The manufacturing sector, long regarded as the most propulsive sector in the economic growth process because of its relatively high productivity and multiplier effects, showed continued healthy growth in absolute terms, although these translate into small-growth rates. The high-growth rate of manufacturing in counties that included relatively small communities (between 2,500 and 20,000 inhabitants) is noteworthy.

Perhaps the most striking characteristic of nonmetropolitan economies over the 1970–76 period, however, is the growth in the wholesale trade sector, which showed the highest relative growth rate (65 percent). The large increases in the service sectors, in general, and in wholesale trade, in particular, seem to be a significant indicator of diversity in the evolving economic base of nonmetropolitan areas. Should this trend continue into the 1980s, given increasing accessibility caused by new developments in communication and transportation technology, one of the major barriers to the economic growth of nonmetropolitan America—a narrow economic base—may be overcome. Some recent research

Table IX.2. Change in Employment, 1970–76, By Size of Place

	Nonmetropolitan Counties (Absolute Change)				*Nonmetropolitan Counties (Percent Change)*			
	Total Nonmet	*Rural (<2,500)*	*Nonurban (2,500–19,999)*	*Less Urban (20,000–49,999)*	*Total Nonmet*	*Rural (<2,500)*	*Nonurban (2,500–19,999)*	*Less Urban (20,000–49,999)*
Number of Counties	2,384	814	1,250	320	2,384	814	1,250	320
Total Employment (Full and Part-Time)	2,535,618	257,326	1,274,837	1,003,455	12.06%	11.55%	12.73%	11.42%
Agriculture (Total Farm)	51,506	6,871	25,332	19,303	6.47	5.05	5.98	8.16
Agricultural Services, Forestry, Fisheries, etc.	12,831	(−) 2,022	(−) 3,294	18,147	12.41	(−) 17.27	(−) 6.53	44.00
Mining	90,848	15,737	56,511	18,600	26.98	39.33	29.16	18.08
Construction	126,404	14,042	68,119	44,243	17.92	21.95	21.55	13.60
Manufacturing	335,725	43,508	234,866	57,351	7.70	15.95	11.56	2.79
Transportation, Communication, and Public Utilities	64,909	7,597	31,418	25,894	8.41	13.60	8.93	7.11
Wholesale Trade	292,400	34,809	160,861	96,730	63.54	117.74	77.69	43.26
Retail Trade	436,750	24,989	175,211	236,550	18.06	12.39	15.67	21.53
Finance, Insurance, Real Estate	142,757	16,681	68,076	58,000	34.69	57.80	39.14	27.78
Total Services	470,311	54,961	202,061	213,289	18.51	25.50	17.26	18.47
Total Nonmanufacturing	2,199,893	213,818	1,039,971	946,104	13.20	10.94	13.03	14.06

Source: Compiled from Bureau of Economic Analysis data.

on the impact of the interstate highway system on demographic and economic change in nonmetropolitan areas does suggest, however, a very weak statistical relationship between proximity to interstate highways and employment growth by sector, particularly manufacturing and wholesaling [8].

Some regional contrasts in the growth process are shown in Table IX.3. Nonmetropolitan counties of the Northeast region showed declines in manufacturing and construction. The nonmetropolitan South, on the other hand, showed large absolute increases in manufacturing and construction, although decline occurred in the agricultural sector. The experience of the 1970s also shows that *many factors traditionally associated with economic distress* (low levels of urbanization, a southern nonmetropolitan location, service-based economies) *are now symptomatic of economic growth.*

Given the economic growth and increased diversity of nonmetropolitan areas of the United States in the 1970s, one crucial causal element in this change still remains unresolved, whether or not the search for economic opportunity still remains the dominant reason for migration. Earnings levels do not seem to explain the economic trends in the conventional way. Historically, wage rates would cause areas with high-wage industries to be more attractive to migrants than regions with low-wage industries; but data for the 1970s do not bear this out. "On the average, people are simply not moving to or between nonmetropolitan counties in a manner associated with the income level of areas, suggesting that many of them are not migrating for monetary motivations" [2:116]. However, a relationship that has been around since the Industrial Revolution and caused the growth of large U.S. cities and other parts of the world cannot be dismissed if the oscillations of the 1970s and early 1980s are vagaries that do not translate into long-term secular trends.

Phillips [68] in a recent review suggests that economic factors are not so unimportant in the resurgence of nonmetropolitan areas as they might initially appear. Her reasoning includes the fact that most migrants to nonmetropolitan areas are not retirees; most migrant household heads are employed when they move, and most increase their postmove earnings, while past evidence suggests that employment opportunities in nonmetropolitan areas have improved greatly in recent times. "While not the motivating factor behind the decision to move, it is likely that the existence of job opportunities in nonmetropolitan areas is an important factor facilitating households to act on their residental preferences for small town living" [68:28]. Further evidence concerning the 1970–76 period suggests that for most categories of nonmetropolitan

Table IX.3. Percent Change in Employment, 1970–76, By Region

	Nonmetropolitan Counties				
	Total Nonmet	*Northeast*	*North Central*	*South*	*West*
Number of Counties	2,384	117	878	1,040	349
Total Employment (Full and Part-Time)	12.06%	8.15%	10.00%	11.50%	23.46%
Agriculture (Total Farm)	6.47	11.09	31.95	(−) 8.64	11.06
Agricultural Services, Forestry, Fisheries, etc.	12.41	7.87	(−) 26.81	(−) .76	76.73
Mining	26.98	20.04	16.56	32.21	26.83
Construction	17.92	(−) 9.46	9.29	24.51	47.51
Manufacturing	7.70	(−) 5.60	6.12	10.96	22.79
Transportation, Communication, and Public Utilities	8.41	1.36	5.46	10.57	16.08
Wholesale Trade	63.54	34.94	80.13	52.88	80.09
Retail Trade	18.06	18.51	9.30	21.74	31.81
Financial, Insurance, Real Estate	34.69	21.05	31.27	39.18	46.05
Total Services	18.51	26.55	22.98	10.45	26.45
Total Nonmanufacturing	13.20	13.02	10.94	11.66	23.55

Source: Compiled from Bureau of Economic Analysis data.

counties when classified by size, the average annual rate of employment change exceeds that of population change [74].

Where employment change rates exceed population change rates by more than 2 percent, absolute and relative increases in per capita income are greatest (showing an 82 percent increase for all nonmetropolitan areas). Conversely, where employment change rates exceed population change rates by 0.5 percent, per capita income increases are lowest. It is clear, therefore, as might be expected from conventional neo-classical arguments, *the greater the gap between employment and population increases, the greater the potential for per capital income increases in those areas.*

Although the nonmetropolitan areas generally are portrayed by a healthy picture for the 1980s, this should not imply that such areas are immune from distress. In the past, metropolitan counties have tended to have higher overall levels of socioeconomic well-being than nonmetropolitan counties (see Table IX.4). In 1977, 11 percent of the total metropolitan population existed under the poverty level, ranging from 16 percent for central city to 7 percent for suburban residents, while 14 percent of the nonmetropolitan population remained in poverty [89]. The economic growth processes in nonmetropolitan areas in the 1970s therefore can conceal much poverty and distress. This is particularly the case since data on small cities and rural areas in general are not as sophisticated in their collection as they are for metropolitan areas [21].

Interregional Changes

No decentralization process has recently been given as much attention in the media and in the policy process as that occurring between the northern and eastern regions and the southern and western parts [67, 77, 95]. But much of what has been written may be the result of what has become known as "Newton's Third Law of Journalism" [22], where every overreaction leads to an equal and opposite overreaction. A partial reason for this attention is acceleration of the core-periphery movement during a critical time of the 1970s—when the national economic system as a whole was growing slowly. Another reason is that government funding patterns were seen as a cause of this decentralization process and that regional patterns of political representation would change as a result.

These interregional changes, however, are not new; they are only to be expected from theories that have been postulated to explain regional economic change [14, 25]. Such changes between regions at the subnational level can be the result of *national demand or market forces* at work, where cheaper production costs (particularly land and labor) in pe-

Table IX.4. Mean Indexes of Social Well-Being for Metro and Nonmetro Counties, by Region

County Group and Region	*Number of Counties*	*Socio-economic Status*	*Health Status*	*Family Status*	*Alienation*
			U.S. index = 100		
United States	3,097	100.0	100.0	100.0	100.0
Metro	612	115.7	106.1	99.3	99.2
Greater metro	175	122.6	108.6	102.4	97.8
Core	48	123.5	99.0	80.0	87.0
Fringe	127	122.2	112.1	110.8	101.9
Medium metro	258	113.9	105.3	99.4	99.8
Lesser metro	179	111.5	104.7	96.1	99.6
Nonmetro	2,485	96.1	98.5	100.2	100.2
Urbanized:					
Adjacent to SMSA	191	112.4	103.7	97.2	100.9
Not adjacent to SMSA	137	109.4	99.8	95.3	98.3
Less urbanized:					
Adjacent to SMSA	564	97.8	97.9	97.1	101.5
Not adjacent to SMSA	721	97.1	98.8	98.1	100.2
Totally rural:					
Adjacent to SMSA	246	87.3	96.4	99.1	100.0
Not adjacent to SMSA	626	89.2	97.7	107.7	99.4
Northeast	217	118.3	101.2	100.1	98.7
Metro	100	123.6	103.6	98.9	100.3
Nonmetro	117	113.8	98.9	101.1	97.2
North Central	1,055	107.5	107.5	112.0	101.1
Metro	178	122.3	110.1	108.8	100.5
Nonmetro	877	104.4	107.0	112.6	101.2
South	1,387	87.8	94.0	88.6	103.6
Metro	270	106.4	102.4	93.2	101.3
Nonmetro	1,117	83.3	92.0	87.4	104.1
West	438	111.6	100.2	107.6	86.8
Metro	64	124.0	113.8	99.4	84.6
Nonmetro	374	109.5	97.9	108.9	87.1

Source: P. J. Ross, H. Bluestone, and F. K. Hines, *Indicators of Social Well-Being for U.S. Counties*, ESCS Report, Washington, D.C.: U.S. Department of Agriculture, 1979.

ripheral regions entice industry and people into such areas. Such changes can also be the result of *planned adjustment* mechanisms, as suggested by accusations that the federal government has played a determining role in these regional shifts through the growth of military bases and military-industrial complexes, the expansion of the interstate highway system, the application of investment tax credits, and the like in the South and West. The interregional changes in the United States can be attributed more to *market forces* than to *planned adjustment* forces [64, 71, 73, 74] particularly in comparison to western Europe, where the role of central governments has been much stronger in similar types of regional changes [44, 35, 78]. These types of changes also should have been anticipated from what neo-classical economic theory indicates about unbalanced growth and factor mobility [96]. "Rising regional income disparities are typical of early development stages, while regional convergence is typical of the more mature stages of national growth and development" [99:199]. The "growth" of the South and West and the relative "decline" of the North and East can easily be interpreted as a process of *convergence* in income and economic welfare, a catching-up process where the regions within the national economic system tend toward equilibrium over time. This convergence process is dramatically illustrated in Figure IX.1, where per capita income trends are plotted by region over time.

In line with traditional economic perspectives, *a region's general economic health still depends to a greater degree on its performance in the manufacturing sector* [64]. When the components of manufacturing change are examined in detail, further clues are given to the causes and implications of these changes and the fact that they have been under way for some time. Table IX.5 shows that the decentralization of production workers (regarded as key employees in the manufacturing process) away from the Manufacturing Belt of the Northeast and Midwest has been under way at least since 1947. The impact of the decentralization of non-production workers (those involved in administration, sales, wholesaling, and other support functions) outweighed the losses in all but the New England states. This is not the case for the 1963–76 period, when absolute declines in manufacturing workers show up for the Manufacturing Belt as a whole. The relative loss of nearly one million production workers from the Manufacturing Belt and the periphery's gain of 1.2 million such workers over the 1947–63 period does emphasize the historical nature of the decentralization process. It also points to the recent political reaction as a rather late one, surrounded by concerns about the fate of the traditional industrial heartland and the voting power of its people.

Then again, such changes of employment and population at the subnational scale are hardly without precedence in the economic history of this country. Indeed it is the dynamism of such movements—the westward expansion in the 19th century and the movement from the South to the North (first of blacks, then of whites) earlier this century—that created the American character [94]. Danhof [15] reminded us some time ago of the recurring economic battles between North and South, and the perennial "conspiracy theory" implicit in these arguments. "Sectional conflict, which some heed to be inevitable, resulted in a conspiracy, deliberate or fortuitous, on the part of the North, the large national

Figure IX.1. Per capita Personal Income as a Percent of the U.S. Average, Selected Years, 1929–2000, BEA Regions

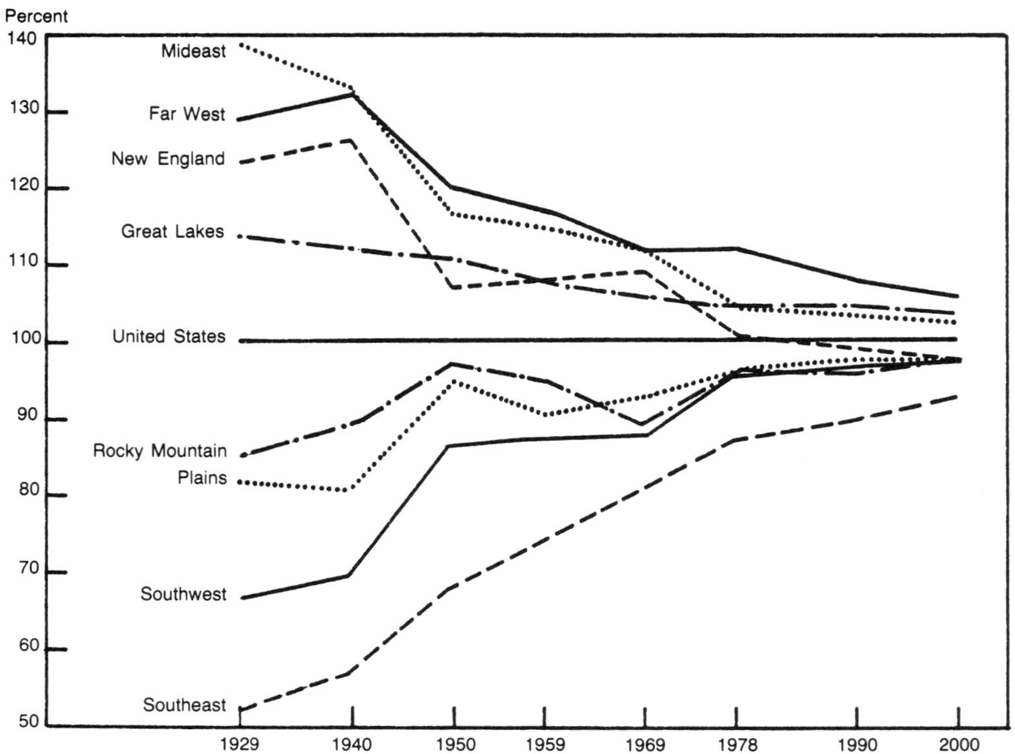

Table IX.5. Changes in Manufacturing Employment Type, by Region, 1947–76

Region	*1947–63* Change in Total Employment	*1947–63* Change in Production Workers	*1947–63* Change in Nonproduction Workers	*1963–76* Change in Total Employment	*1963–76* Change in Production Workers	*1963–76* Change in Nonproduction Workers
New England	− 50.2%	− 205.7%	155.5%	− 85.7%	− 141.9%	56.2%
Mid-Atlantic	121.3	− 399.1	520.4	− 573.9	− 568.6	− 5.3
East North Central	160.9	− 333.8	494.7	301.9	90.0	211.9
Manufacturing Belt	232.0	− 938.6	1170.6	− 357.7	− 620.5	262.8
West North Central	228.3	78.9	149.4	237.9	161.2	76.7
South Atlantic	600.9	320.3	280.6	609.7	397.3	212.4
East South Central	252.3	153.8	98.5	407.8	291.2	116.6
West South Central	313.8	169.3	144.4	488.2	327.4	160.8
Mountain	143.2	80.6	62.6	154.4	98.4	56.0
Pacific	884.4	444.8	439.6	266.0	182.4	83.6
Periphery	2422.9	1247.7	1175.2	2164.0	1457.9	706.1

Source: Compiled from Census of Manufactures data; adapted from Rees [72].

corporations or some financial groups, with the help of the federal government to thwart the South" [15:36]. The 1970s seem to have witnessed the birth of the 'conspiracy theory' in reverse, with the North accusing the South of obtaining preferential treatment (through the seniority system in Congress and the political allocation of resources) to fuel its economic growth process.

Another factor to emerge when one considers industrial changes over time is the role that *growth industries* have played in the growth of the South and West. The role of such growth industries, and their high technology bases, may indeed be a seminal factor in the long-term growth of these once-peripheral areas in the 1980s and beyond [71]. The higher growth sectors include electronics, machinery, chemicals and plastics, aerospace and scientific instruments—sectors that are also more technology-intensive. The leading growth industry in employment has been electronics. This sector has become the most propulsive in the current American economy in the same way that Rosenberg [76] views machine tools as the key sector of the industrial boom period of the late 19th century. Today, electronics provides key control functions in automobiles, apparel and printing machines, telecommunications, computers, aerospace, as well as in direct consumer markets (watches, calculators, and the like).

Previous research [64] has shown how these rapid growth industries have become more prevelant in the growing regions of the South and West rather than the stagnating areas of the North and East. The product cycle model of international economics [91] was used to explain the dispersal of innovative capacity from the Manufacturing Belt (the traditional heartland of American industry) to the South and West, using shift share analysis as a form of empirical verification. The product cycle argument, a derivation of Kuznets [46] law of industrial growth, postulates that products evolve through three distinct stages in their life cycles, and that each stage takes place in different geographical regions. The first or *innovation stage* occurs in established industrial regions (like the Manufacturing Belt), where a new product is introduced into new market areas through exports. A *growth stage* follows, during which demand expands to a point where interregional or foreign investment facilities become feasible and process technology can be standardized. The third or *standardized production* stage implies that production seeks out low-cost locations, especially peripheral areas where labor costs are reduced.

At the national level, therefore, the implications are that as the decentralization of production workers took place in the post-1945 era, certain external economies of scale (such as agglomeration economies, service industries, and localized linkage patterns) can build up in the periphery as local demand also grows, to a critical point where industrial growth and the generation of new products can take off in the peripheral areas. In essence, therefore, regions that have been the recipients of innovation (during the standardization phase) can become the generators of innovation (either through the spin-off of small firms from large firms or the migration of entrepreneurs).

It is not inconsistent with the above argument, therefore, that when one looks at the components of industrial change in large urban-industrial centers of the Southwest (like Dallas and Houston) during the 1960s and 1970s, the primary causes of increased manufacturing employment were the expansion of existing firms and the birth of new ones as opposed to relocations from the Northeast [70, 74]. Industrial growth in Dallas and Houston between 1960 and 1975 was not taking the form of branch plants set up from "external centers of control," but was the result of *indigenous growth* in the form of companies with headquarters within the region expanding locally and showing a greater degree of internal control over the regions' economic welfare. This analysis confirms the earlier work of Birch [6]—that firms relocating to and from areas play only a minor role in regional industrial change.

Birch's [7] more recent analysis of the 5.6 million business establishments listed in Dun and Bradstreet data over the 1969–76 period show some additional trends of interest. The rate of job losses due to the death and contraction of firms are fairly constant between regions, while most of the regional variations in job generation can be accounted for by the birth and expansion of companies. Birch also found that the propensity of companies (particularly manufacturing) to branch in the country as a whole did increase over time, and that the southern region still attracted more branches than the northern regions. More importantly, perhaps, small firms (those with 20 employees or less) generated most new jobs (66 percent) in the United States, a trend of considerable importance to the future economic health of the country, given that the National Science Board [63] found that smaller firms are also relatively more innovative than medium- or large-sized firms. Birch also sees a great deal of interregional control of industry in the United States.

> In manufacturing, the great majority of jobs generated in the South are controlled in the Northeast and North Central parts of the country. . . . Only in the service industries does each region tend to dominate its own territory, with the interesting anomaly that in this newest and most rapidly expanding sector of the economy, southern corporations are dominating northern and western establishments. *In branches, for example, southern headquarters generated almost as many service jobs in the Northeast as the northern firms did.* [7:18]

It is important to remember, however, that although Dun and Bradstreet data are the most reliable for the identification of enterprises and the role of different types of industrial organizations in the regional change process, their data have also been found to be "highly inaccurate" [35].

The question still remains: whether the interregional economic changes described in this section will continue as long-term changes, or appear as short-term cyclical fluctuations? Such changes may only represent the continuation of equilibriating tendencies (as suggested by Figure 1), but by definition these are long-term trends. *The salient question, therefore, becomes whether the technological seed-bed function of the Manufacturing Belt will continue to decline and that of the periphery will continue to increase,* forming the basis for a new regional divergence in the United States and a reversal of traditional regional roles? While Norton and Rees [64] have documented the continuous erosion of the Manufacturing Belt's function as a technological seed bed, Malecki's intensive study of research and development activities in different U.S. regions over time concludes that:

> Industrial Research and Development appears to be evolving away from a dependence on some large city regions, especially New York; it remains at the same time a very markedly large city activity. . . . The deconcentration of Research and Development from some of the major technological regions is difficult to extrapolate into more general trends. Many of the faster-growing areas of Research and Development activity are located in the Northeast despite signs of economic decline in other regional indicators. [50:32].

Long-run regional economic growth trends in the United States seem to depend on the compromise between two counterbalancing forces: the role of *innovation* or new developments, on the one hand, and the role of *inertia,* the continuation of existing patterns under differing conditions, on the other.

A developed region such as the Manufacturing Belt possesses many economic and political control factors that act as ratchet effects against decline. Furthermore, the new growth regions have recently been experiencing rates of inflation well above the national average both in labor costs and land costs, factors in which these regions had a clear advantage in the past. In accordance with neo-classical arguments postulated earlier, this factor, in itself, can act as a brake on the growth process in the South and West. At the same time, cuts in the growth rates in the Manufacturing Belt working through Philips' curve-type relationships at the regional level may restore advantages to the northern and eastern states over the longer term [68].

The International Decentralization Process

Another decentralization process that has been going on since the 19th century is American industrial investment abroad. This process has implications for possible employment losses within the United States and for the transfer of technology, and has been the subject of considerable scholarly attention [92, 17, 39, 27, 97].

Gilpin [27] argues that the proliferation of foreign direct investment (f.d.i.) from the United States is a denial of investment in the domestic economy in the same way as the United Kingdom's history of portfolio investment had earlier allocated scarce resources away from the British economy. This assumes that if f.d.i. had not taken place, domestic investment would have, which is not necessarily the case. Gilpin further argues that the low interindustry movement of capital in the United States in the 1960s (despite the rise of conglomerates), combined with cheaper production factors abroad, caused companies to increase their f.d.i. American investment abroad did escalate during the 1960s to the point that Servan-Schreiber [81] classified it as the world's third economic power when he warned Europe of the dangers of the American challenge. By 1970, the output of American overseas subsidiaries was approximately $200 billion, representing several times the amount of goods that American companies exported abroad, and the ratio of foreign sales to export continues to grow rapidly. The United States has become more of a foreign investor than exporter. Moreover, approximately 25 percent of all American exports are really intracorporate transfers [27:185].

Table IX.6 shows the general distribution of foreign direct investment *from the United States* as well as f.d.i. *in the United States* (also known as reverse investment) in the 1970s. This was an era when the foreign investment climate (under fluctuating exchange rates) was quite different to the situation of the 1960s. Using the most recent available data [79], American companies invested over $168 billion abroad in 1978, with over 40 percent of this involving manufacturing facilities. The developed countries received over 70 percent of this f.d.i., with the European market the largest receiver followed by Canada. A slightly larger share of American f.d.i. went to developing countries in 1978 compared with 1973, with most of the increase going to countries in Latin America, historically the largest receiver of American investment abroad. Certain companies in a few sectors, particularly electronics and apparel, have established assembly plants in the cheap-labor havens of Southeast Asia (Hong Kong, Singapore, and the like), but one result has been inflationary pressures on wages there also. In 1978, only 9 percent of total Amer-

Table IX.6. Foreign Direct Investment Patterns

	American Investment Abroad (Billions of Dollars)				
	1973	*%*	*1978*	*%*	*Change 1973–78 %*
Total	$101.3	100	$168.1	100	66
Manufacturing	44.4	44	74.2	44	67
Developed Countries	72.2	72	120.7	72	67
Canada	25.5	25	37.3	22	46
Europe	38.3	38	69.7	42	82
Other	8.4	8	13.8	8	64
Developing Countries	22.9	22	40.5	24	77
Latin America	16.5	16	32.5	19	97
Other	6.4	6	8.0	5	25
	Foreign Investment in the United States (Billions of Dollars)				
	1973	*%*	*1978*	*%*	*Change 1973–78 %*
Total	$ 20.6	100	$ 40.8	100	98
Manufacturing	8.2	40	16.3	40	98
Canada	4.2	20	6.2	15	48
Europe	13.9	67	27.9	68	101
United Kingdom	5.4	26	7.4	18	37
Japan	0.2	1	2.7	7	1250
Other	2.3	11	4.1	10	78

Source: Adaped from R. B. Scholl, "The International Investment Position of the United States," *Survey of Current Business*, 1979.

ican direct investment in manufacturing in developing countries went to these pockets of economic growth in Southeast Asia, which amounts to less than one percent of all American investment abroad.

Because of the plight of the dollar in the 1970s, rising U.S. interest rates relative to those of other countries, the economic slowdowns resulting in reduced capital needs abroad, and the general volatility of exchange rates, the 1970s saw an increase in *reverse investment*—foreign companies investing in the United States. Table IX.6 shows that the amount of reverse investment as a proportion of American investment abroad increased from 20 percent in 1973 to 24 percent in 1978, while the total amount of f.d.i. in the United States nearly doubled in current dollars between 1973 and 1978. The net international investment position of the United States was still $77 billion in 1978, with total American assets abroad amounting to $450 billion and foreign assets in the United States totaling $373 billion [79]. Table IX.6 also shows which countries were responsible for the greatest increases in f.d.i. in the United States during the 1970s. While the relative amount of foreign investment in U.S. manufacturing remained the same between 1973 and 1978, Canadian investment in the United States declined, as might be expected from the downturn in the Canadian dollar. On the other hand, European investment in the United States increased over 100 percent during the 1973-78 period, while Japan showed the largest relative growth in investment in the United States, although from a very low base in 1973.

Given the large increase in foreign investment in the United States during the 1970s, the allocation of those investments are important to consider relative to the current interregional changes in business investment going on in the country. In a detailed study of foreign investment in the United States, McConnell [56] found that foreign companies were asking which existing U.S. corporations should be acquired rather than where in the country their investments should be located. "Such a change in motivations increases the likelihood that the foreign firm will invest in an area where established manufacturing activities exist, rather than in newer, less developed industrial areas which may be increasingly attractive to American corporations" [56:8]. McConnell found that a state's share of total f.d.i. in 1976 *increased:*

- As the number of manufacturing establishments with more than 20 employees per capita *increased;*
- As the state's urban population as a percent of total state population *increased;*
- As a state's social well-being index *declined;*
- If the state was located in the traditional Manufacturing Belt;
- As direct expenditures per capita of state and local government *increased;*
- As federal aid per capita to state/local governments *decreased;* and
- As the number of employees in manufacturing per capita *decreased* and
- As total retail sales per capita *decreased.*

In summary, *foreign direct investment in the United States in 1976 was concentrated in the traditional Manufacturing Belt.* In addressing changes in the locational preferences of foreign investors between 1974 and 1978, McConnell did see some changes; foreign investors showed a strong preference not only for locations in the Industrial Heartland, but also for eastern coastal states of the South, and for Texas and California (key growth states within the southern rim).

> Foreigners were investing in nationally growing industries, but they were making such investments in regions where these growth industries were declining in terms

of value-added investments by American domestic corporations. This pattern reflects a *lagging response* by foreigners to regional shifts in the structure of American manufacturing. [56:18]

This increased flow of reverse investments to the United States is largely predictable from international economic theory. Much of this investment from abroad is defensive and can be explained by oligopoly theory—that the large flows of foreign investment from the United States by firms in oligopolistic sectors was bound to be reacted to by oligopolistic firms from other countries. Assuming no dramatic rise in the value of the dollar in the early 1980s, this "non-American challenge" seems destined to increase in the 1980s. Franko [22] stated that the American dominance of multinational companies was at its peak in 1968, and was destined to decline in the new slow-growth economic order of the 1970s.

> Whatever else the quadrupling of oil prices by OPEC did, it gave a tremendous boost to the demand for energy-saving products and processes, and resource-short Europe and Japan had them first. Innovations in the United States have historically been biased toward labor saving products which are energy and material intensive . . . continental Europe in particular has had to cope a lot longer than the United Stated with scarce resources. [22:98]

Such a trend has important implications for the role of high-technology industries in international investment processes in the 1980s, i.e., the comparative advantage may be with labor-using more than labor-saving industries. Although the traditional definition of technology-intensive industries in the United States has implied the substitution of capital for labor, the innovations generated (as in the electronics industry) in themselves have created numerous new jobs. Franko [22] also leaves us with a consoling factor—that this new order among multinationals may mean more acceptance of American companies abroad. "A France with a few major direct investments in the United States in the early 1960's would be much more restrictive against United States investments in France than can today's France, which has a good many American subsidiaries . . . who may themselves have a French connection" [22:98]. In retrospect therefore, these complex, changing processes of foreign investments have the potential of having considerable impact on the economic health of the United States during the present decade.

Common Causes Behind Economic Decentralization Involving the United States and Other Industrialized Countries

The four decentralization processes discussed in this paper are complex, but they appear to have many common features. One undoubtedly is the amount of economic determinism that lies behind these contemporary geographical shifts, somewhat analogous to forces behind such shifts in the past. The kind of economic determinism currently at work is considerably different, however, given the types of technologies existing today. Communication and transportation technology has created much greater degrees of locational freedom for people and industry, which have been particularly manifest in the growth of nonmetropolitan areas in the 1970s. These new technologies are also products of new industries (like electronics and chemicals) that have mushroomed in the post-1945 era in the South and West, away from the traditional heartland of American industry.

The shifts that have taken place, however, are quite consistent with theories developed to explain regional economic change. All four trends described earlier reflect the "filtering down" theory of industrial location, which maintains that:

> In national perspective, industries filter down through the system of cities, from places of greater to lesser industrial sophistication. Most often, the highest skills are needed in the difficult early stage of mastering a new process, and skill requirements decline steadily as the production process is rationalized and routinized with experience. As the industry slides down the learning curve, the high wage rate of the more industrially sophisticated innovating areas become superfluous. The aging industry seeks out industrial backwaters where the cheaper labor is now up to the lesser demands of the simplified process. [85:8]

This concept of *industrial filtering* is consistent with the conventional equilibrium tendencies of neo-classical economics and is closely related to the notion of the product cycle explained earlier in an interregional context, a concept initially derived to explain decentralization trends at the international level. Indeed, the interpretation of interregional industrial shifts using the product-cycle concept [71, 64] is an *extension* of the industrial filtering argument. It argues that growth centers in peripheral areas are the recipients of innovations via branch plants, and that at a subsequent time threshold, such areas can generate their own innovations. This internal generation of innovations from growth centers in peripheral areas takes place only after sufficient decentralization of production has accumulated to generate external economies in the form of agglomeration economies, the development of a service infrastructure, localized linkage patterns, and incubating environments (often generated by one or two lead firms) that lead to the birth of new companies.

The economic explanations behind these decentralization processes are further confirmed when one looks at the experience of other industrialized countries during the 1960s and 1970s [93, 32]. A recent study of decentralization tendencies in western Europe concludes that:

> During the latter part of the period studied (1950–1975) the beginning of the movement away from metropolitan cities can be discerned in those countries in

> which urbanization had progressed furthest. While the trend in some countries may reflect mainly the movement from large cities to the suburbs, in others it appeared to indicate a growing preference for residence in non-metropolitan cities. In the latter countries, urban growth seemed to be taking place more and more in towns of intermediate size and in the hinterland of industrial centers. . . . In the highly industrialized countries industry can be expected to move increasingly from the large cities to towns of medium size or even into the country." [18:273]

In the British context, Keeble reminds us: "Whether at the inter-regional, inter-subregional or inter-urban scales, by the late 1960's and early 1970's, manufacturing activity in Britain was rapidly declining in most larger existing industrial centers while growing equally rapidly in most smaller, non-industrial locations" [44:286]. In the same vein, Hamilton suggests links between structural and regional changes in the United Kingdom very similar to those seen in the United States: "Both inter- and intra-regional diffusion of the *growth industries* from Midland and Southeastern England is an integral part of the process of structural modernization throughout Britain" [33:156].

A major difference in causal mechanisms behind these decentralization processes in Europe compared to the United States must be the role of government policy, given that most countries of western Europe have developed a more explicit set of regional industrial policies than the United States [35, 44]. In the British context, regional development policy since the 1930s has had a complex and varied history subject to rapid fluctuations in the intensity of policy measures (such as the Regional Employment Premium and the Selective Employment Tax), the scale of financial inducements for firms to establish branches in peripheral areas, the extent of areas affected, and the result of change in the macroeconomy under different government administrations.

General support [59, 44] can be found, however, that government policy had a significant influence on the location of industry in the United Kingdom, and that job creation was low when regional policies were weak and high when regional policy was strong. One can easily be skeptical, however, about the perceived success of these policies, (which included grants up to 35 percent of total building costs and 45 percent of capital equipment costs for firms setting up in designated Development Areas) when one asks the question: success at what cost? The perceived success of regional policy in Europe may indeed be a Pyrrhic victory when one assesses what market mechanisms may have accomplished in the absence of such policies. Given the increasing flirtation of the American government with urban policy and a broader regional policy in recent years, there are many lessons to be learned from a careful evaluation of policy measures used in Britain and the rest of Europe, particularly when powerful market forces seem to have accomplished a high degree of regional economic equality in the United States.

Despite the commonality of causation postulated behind the decentralization processes that have taken place in the United States and elsewhere, some questions remain about certain symptoms of these processes. Hansen recently reminded us of some of these when he asked "whether manufacturing decentralization abroad may not have the same consequences for industrial employment in the South as decentralization to the South had for manufacturing employment in the old United States industrial heartland?" [35:9]. Hansen shows that export-related manufacturing activities in the South lag well behind those of the United States as a whole; the South is not competing that well in the international sphere. One explanation of this presumably lies in the greater local consumption of goods produced in the South, and the fact that southern exports are interregional more than international [70].

Hansen also shows that in the 1970–76 period, only 25 percent of new manufacturing jobs in the South were in historically low-wage sectors, whereas high-wage industries accounted for 42 percent of all new southern manufacturing jobs during the same period. Such a trend may appear counter to Thompson's industrial-filtering argument [85], but not when put into the context of the product-cycle argument that areas receiving innovation can become the generators of innovation, hence implying higher wage occupations and sectors. Despite the upgrading of southern manufacturing, the region is still relatively specialized in those activities that compete directly with low-wage manufacturing abroad [35:12]. Yet the pattern of American investment abroad does show that most of the investment still flows to the developed countries, particularly Europe, which makes the attractions of cheap labor in less developed countries appear weak in comparison with the marketing opportunities of the developed world. These are some of the anomalies that make the definition of gainers and losers in regional terms for the 1980s a complex and difficult issue.

The Gainers and Losers in the 1980s

From a national and international perspective, there is nothing dramatic to suggest as yet that the fate of the 1980s will be much different from that of the 1970s. In 1980, the nation witnessed another recession that may end up with a double, rather than single, dip formation. Given that the U.S. economy remains hostage to a large degree to international economic and political forces, the stop-go pattern of inflation and recession resulting in low rates of productivity gains and economic growth generally seems destined to continue into the 1980s. Because of this, it would seem that the *decentralization trends* described earlier would continue along similar lines, although with varying intensities.

At the urban-regional scale, Berry's prognostication may well be accurate:

> The time-eliminating properties of long distance communication and the space-spanning capacities of the new communication technologies are combining to concoct a solvent that has dissolved the agglomeration advantages of the industrial metropolis. . . . There is no reason to believe that aging industrial cities will be able to revitalize unless they are able to develop a post-industrial high technology or service activity base [4:18].

Furthermore, historians may well look back at the 1970s as the decade when regional income convergence occurred for the first time in U.S. history. Because of this convergence process accompanied by current inflation rates greater than the national norm in the growth regions, one may expect the rates of growth in the South and West to slow down by the late 1980s. From a policy perspective,

> . . . one of the ironies of current public policy as viewed from a New England perspective is that allocation formulas for public funds and other federal aids for regional economic transitions are becoming more favorable and available to New England just as the worst of its own transition problems may be at an end [57:114].

So much of the regional economic performance of the United States, as well as economic performance at the national level, still seems to depend on the international arena and the capacity of the international economic order to break out of the vicious cycle of inflation and low-productivity growth. Meanwhile, the developed world is continuing in its evolution as a consumer-oriented, postindustrial society where employment growth rates in service sectors are higher than those in the manufacturing sectors. In this regard one has to be wary of the evolution of what the French economist Jean Fourastié called a "tertiary crisis," where a shift in the labor force from the secondary to the tertiary without technological change would result in economic stagnation. "Tertiary activities benefit less from technological change than either primary or secondary activities. And it is technological change broadly defined which produces rising real incomes" [58:25]. The economic agenda of the United States and the developed world as a whole, therefore, depends to a large degree on the extent to which the growth of the service sectors (particularly financial, communication, and data-processing services) can serve as an *accelerator effect* to induce further innovations within the manufacturing sector. It is imperative, therefore, that policy-makers concerned with the future U.S. urban and regional development prospects also be concerned with the innovation capacities of various economic sectors. In essence, urban policy at the federal level has to be integrated with national science policy and any new efforts in the direction of "reindustrialization" and economic recovery.

LINKS BETWEEN SCIENCE POLICY, INDUSTRY POLICY, AND URBAN-REGIONAL POLICY

Industry Policy

Government assistance to industry has grown steadily in range and volume as most developed countries have expanded. Such assistance or cooperation between private and public sectors has gone under the title of "industry policy," "sectoral policy," or "industrial adaptation policies" in various countries [61, 66, 26]. Although the United States has refrained from applying "industry policy" of the kind applied in western Europe and Japan, it cannot convincingly be argued that American industry does not receive any aid from the state. For example, research and development contracts, and military contracts in limited sectors (such as aerospace), can be viewed as implicit forms of industry policy, as can certain tax incentives and other indirect forms of financial assistance and the provision of services (such as employment training) rather than financial benefits. Given the general productivity dilemma described earlier, coupled with the decline of certain basic industries in the traditional American industrial heartland, there is a need to consider the adoption of more explicit forms of industry policies in the United States.

Given the evolving interest in industry policy recently [11, Schwartz in this volume], policymakers are faced with the gigantic tasks of defining the *goals* of industry policy and then choosing *appropriate instruments* of industry policy, as in the initial evolutionary stages of an urban policy for the country.

Any goals established for industry policy need to recognize the limitations of Keynesian demand management in controlling inflation and eliminating regional and sectoral differentials in the economic recovery process. Given that current sources of national economic problems are not in the national ability to *consume* but in the capacity to *produce*, these goals should address certain supply-side problems of the economy: supply shortages as in energy and basic metals, capital formation, and what Schwartz and Choate [11] called "structural stress points" in the economy. Industry policy also "denotes a shift from a pre-occupation with macro-economics to the micro-economic dynamics of market and business development" [41].

What are some of the *potential instruments* of industry policy? Policies can be targeted toward specific industries or they can be designed to affect all sectors. *Industry specific* policies could include: research and development subsidies aimed at developing new products or processes in specific growth industries, training programs targeted similarly, changing regulations that prohibit entry in particular sectors, and public-private joint ventures. The more general policies would include tariff-measures, antitrust adjustments, and small business development incentives.

If industry policy is to develop seriously in the United States over the next decade, several other issues need to be addressed. One surely is Disraeli's reflection on the lessons of history: what we learn from history is that we do not learn from history. Most other countries have some sort of industry or sectoral policy. For example, British sectoral policy was established with the Science and Technology Act of 1965 and expanded by the Industry Act of 1972. There, the Department of Industry permits company-specific assistance for electronics, textiles, ceramics, and leather; while research and development subsidies are available in the microelectronics sector, as witnessed by the creation of Inmos. Both growing and declining industries are targets of U.K. industry policy, although more investment has gone into declining sectors. On the other hand, the mighty MITI of Japan (the Ministry of International Trade and Industry) has, as its fundamental goal, the responsibility for ensuring that Japanese industry competes successfully in world markets. This, as a recent survey in *The Economist* (February 7, 1980) indicates, implies selective intervention, including subsidies to particular industries and chosen companies—*industrial targeting at the company level.* "The American Congress (still more the British Parliament) hurries to protect industries making things that are already beaten by imports. They are precisely the industries which Japan hurries to kill" [*Economist,* February 7, 1980: 27].

Industry policy, therefore, can be of three main types (as suggested by Bell [3]):

1. *Defensive*—protecting the existing level of employment and production in a particular sector from unfair trade policies and from unpredictable changes in the economic environment;
2. *Stabilizing*—providing for an orderly adjustment to excess capacity by reducing capacity until it corresponds to demand once again; and
3. *Positive*—providing assistance in capital diversion to more viable use, for example, replacing declining sectors with growth-inducing high-technology sectors.

Given that one of the built-in tendencies of policymaking is to be reactive rather than anticipatory, *there are implicit dangers in defensive strategies that include the subsidy of declining industries,* like steel and textiles. This is a strategy that has hardly helped the economic performance of other countries. If sectoral policy implies targeting, then at a time of declining productivity and scarce resources, it would make more sense to *protect the growth sectors,* like aluminum and microprocessors, particularly when major international competitors (Japan and Germany) have a more direct public-private sector link.

A second caveat to be considered in an industry policy is the link with other policies: fiscal, monetary, trade, regulatory, and regional policies. The intersectoral impact of current changes in monetary policy, for example, are very poorly understood. Industry policy would indeed be dangerous if it did not take into account the regional concentration of industry. Indeed, industry policy that is not integrated with urban and regional policy seems to be counterintuitive. An industry policy toward the steel industry would largely restrict its impact to the Great Lakes states and to cities such as Pittsburgh, PA, Youngstown, OH, Gary, IN, and Buffalo, NY. An industry policy involving electronics, an industry perceived to be footloose but still highly clustered spatially, would have to take account of the initial seedbed in New England (the Boston area in particular), which has since lost out to California (particularly "Silicon Valley") and other growth points such as Dallas and Phoenix in the southern rim. To date, however, little if any industry-specific policy has been integrated with distressed area policies represented by Economic Development Administration, HUD's Community Development Block Grant and Urban Development Action Grant regions or the Title V commissions.

Yet, the experience of other countries does show that sectoral and regional policies can be integrated fairly successfully. France has probably the most successful history of coordinating industrial and regional development policy. DATAR—the Delegation for Territorial and Regional Management—has a form of public-private sector cooperation where public investment is negotiated directly with the private sector [35]. West Germany is moving toward an *innovation-based regional policy* [20], where national science, sectoral, and regional policies will be tightly integrated. There, innovation-based regional policy and regionalized innovation policy amount to the same thing. Some of the concepts implicit in the links between national science, industry, and regional policies seem to be worthy of further examination in the context of the United States.

The Links Between Innovation Policy and Urban-Regional Policy

Two types of science or innovation policies are usually recognized in contemporary industrial societies: one characterized as *demand pull,* and the other as science or *technology push* [23, 84, 49]. Supporters of the demand-pull theory suggest that market demand, e.g. the current demand for advanced software in service sectors, is the dominant influence on innovative activity. Proponents of the science-push or supply theory suggest that internal developments within science and technology determine changes in output and how it is produced. It would seem that the current status of nuclear energy, computers, aircraft, space technology, and communication systems are all the result of technology-push policies of government. It is assumed that such supply-push policies would also stimulate the breakthroughs needed for various synthetic fuel technologies, coal gasification, and more advanced communication systems.

Because of the relative success of technology-push policies in the past, as in the case of NASA, and because of the high risks associated with innovation, many have argued that governments should subsidize technological development to a greater degree. Not all agree, however. Hill and Utterback [37] suggest that governments should encourage innovation *by increasing the risk* that a company will fail if it does not innovate. Linking their arguments to the relationship between innovation potential and market structure, they suggest: "Rivalry among firms in an industry is essential to stimulating risk-taking, technological innovation and productivity advance" [37:17]. Policies to enhance competition include:

1. Encouraging new entrants by increasing the availability of venture capital. (This can hardly be questioned due to the low rates of new capital formation in the United States in recent years compared, say, with Japan, where capital formation has been much higher.)
2. Modifying the structure of existing industries by prohibiting corporate mergers above a certain size.
3. Avoiding the protection of U.S. firms from foreign competition, given that firms minimizing risks also have fewer incentives to innovate.

These views, although in the minority, point out some counter arguments that have to be faced if science and industry policies are to be integrated at the national or regional scale. To integrate these policies further with regional policy, other issues have to be addressed. One of the more important of these concerns the *differing theories involving research on innovations and their diffusion.*

Researchers concerned with regional economic development have rested larely on three models in their study of the diffusion of innovations: *the hierarchical diffusion model* [4], *contagious or neighborhood diffusion* [75], and *nonhierarchical, spatially noncontinuous transmissions* [69]. The first type suggests that, given the research and development base and larger markets of big cities, innovations are most likely to be adopted first in large cities, and then diffuse to other components of the urban system. Stability in the geographical innovation patterns results in a stable system of urban centers, whose hierarchical nature becomes better articulated over time. In the second type, spatial diffusion patterns are hierarchical but tend to spread out evenly over space. The last type emphasizes the importance of nonlocal interurban (rather than intra-regional) linkages that support large city growth through the multilocational organizational structures of large companies. Although all three claim to be explanations of differences in the spatial diffusion process, they only answer the "how" question and not the "why" question.

Economists, despite their case studies and array of independent variables, have been more concerned than regional scholars with the "why" question directly. Economists concerned with the diffusion of innovation relate to two different models: *industry diffusion* and *firm diffusion* models. The work of Mansfield [52], Gold [31], and Nasbeth and Ray [62] falls mostly into the former type, with emphasis on the sectoral and technical environment in examining the innovation process. Variables of importance include market structure, firm size, age of capital stock, and learning effects. The firm-specific diffusion models on the other hand are mostly the products of organizational theorists [47] and emphasize the internal characteristics of companies as innovation determinants. Studies by economists usually include both the external and internal influences on innovation [53], *but locational variations in industry- and firm-specific characteristics are completely ignored.*

There is some consensus, however, that each innovation diffusion model applies to particular types of processes and all are therefore relevant to policy analysis concerned with the spatial diffusion of innovations. Martin and Swan [55], in addressing the problems of determining regional technological lags and their regional policy implications using examples from limited sectors in Canada, conclude: ". . . if an innovation originates in an industry where the process of diffusion is governed by market structure, regional characteristics can largely be ignored. On the other hand, if an innovation is diffused according to the urban hierarchy, the regional factor becomes preponderant."

Most urban and regional policies to date do not include the increased importance of innovation policy at the national level, nor do they reflect the innovation diffusion theories discussed earlier: The European Economic Community (EEC) may be representative of a new generation of regional policies in this regard. Ewers and Wettman [20] recently discussed the *institutional options* open to government to integrate innovation-oriented urban-regional policy into industry policy. The policy options include:

1. Integrating innovation-related policies into traditional regional policy programs, e.g. subsidizing new product/process technologies in particular regions.

2. Regionalization of existing national research and development (R&D) incentives, although most are biased toward large-scale technology and larger firms. Understanding the problems of small- and medium-sized firms, particularly in peripheral regions, has been given low priority so far in the R&D process.
3. National R&D policies could be designed to have calculated regional impacts.
4. Focussing on *implementation procedures,* given that most national R&D policies favor the urban-industrial core regions of their existing countries (see Malecki [50] and Goddard [29]). This assumes, fairly correctly, that policy implementation procedures tend to be more efficient in core rather than peripheral regions.
5. Decentralize to regional or state levels the implementation of R&D policies. This option is particularly viable if small firms more readily respond to policies at the local level than at the national level.

An innovation-oriented urban-regional policy should also include the following:

First, strategies should be directed toward small- and medium-sized firms. Oakey [65] recently suggested that technological change for small firms is a far less traumatic process due to a more modest scale of operation and greater market adaptability. Such a strategy targeted toward smaller companies would amount to what the Regional Commission of the European Economic Community regard as "the mobilization of indigenous potential," given that small firms in a given region are more likely to be locally owned than larger firms.

Second, large urban areas are destined to continue as centers of innovation relative to peripheral areas, and most small firms cannot be viewed as potential sources of numerous new technologies. Hence, *policy at both the federal and state level has to focus more on the diffusion process interregionally, intersectorally, and on an inter-firm basis.* Given that the timing of adoption is critical, policies would have to focus on the timing of diffusion in order to integrate small and medium firms into the job-creation process at an *early,* not a *late,* stage. Regional advisory centers, technological assistance centers for small firms (involving universities to a greater degree), would, therefore, be in order in peripheral areas.

Thirdly, more questions need to be answered on the relationships between industrial innovation and urban-regional change. This includes:

1. Further empirical clarification of the *industrial seed-bed process* as it takes place interregionally and intraregionally, i.e., further understanding of the indigenous growth process. One important ingredient of the industrial growth process is the spin-off effect—how large firms serve as incubators for the birth of new firms. There

are signs that the diffusion of new technology may be highly related to personnel movements between firms in the same and related sectors. But verification of this is limited. Most generalizations about the process refer to the work of Cooper [12, 13] on the spin-off process in the San Francisco area. Nowhere in his work are the detailed results of his survey research recorded; yet vast generalizations are adopted (e.g., small firms have higher spin-off rates than large firms). Cooper's seemingly casual empiricism has been accepted in the literature, although we may be perpetuating myths on the topic.

2. Because researchers concerned with the geographical diffusion of innovations have been primarily concerned with consumer products and not industrial innovations, further information is needed on the interregional diffusion of product and process innovations in manufacturing.
3. Also, the regional impacts of what Schon [80] called "*innovation by invasion*" need clarification. Innovation by invasion takes place when a technologically retarded, mature industry is invaded by more advanced, developing growth industries. The impact may not simply be employment losses in the former and employment gain in the latter. During a period of technological substitution, as is taking place in the Manufacturing Belt today, the defensive efforts of established firms may cause the old technology to attain much higher levels of performance and sophistication than those previously accomplished. Utterback [90] has shown evidence for this form of *technological rejuvenation.* Intuitively one assumes that such responses will be futile, unable to prolong industrial life cycles indefinitely. Yet there may be ratchet effects implicit in certain established technologies that enable them to fight off competition from new rival processes. *The impact of such a rejuvenation effect would have important implications* for the continued growth of the Manufacturing Belt.

In conclusion, therefore, an industrial policy for the United States may be long overdue if American industry is to compete effectively with that of other countries and if the United States is to benefit from the greater amount of public-private sector coordination apparent in other countries. Such industry policy is needed to protect the comparative advantage of its key growth sectors (like electronics), although it may not be as wise to subsidize declining industries. The *innovation potential* still inherent in the nation's large cities needs more encouragement in an urban policy for the 1980s. Small companies in particular have to be protected to a greater degree, e.g., by increasing access to venture capital. The incubator environment found lacking in the nation's large cities may have to be nurtured by specific policy measures in the future, if the innovation potential of this country's large urban systems is to be fully realized. In short, therefore, the United States seems *to warrant a closer examination of an innovation-based urban-regional policy that focuses on the mobilization of indigenous potential across all types of cities in all regions.* Whether the political barriers to the implementation of such policies prove to be too great in the cold light of political structures at the dawn of 1983 remains another issue.

REFERENCES

1. Advisory Commission on Intergovernmental Relations, *The Intergovernmental Grant System as Seen by Local, State and Federal Officials,* A-54, Washington, D.C.: U.S. Government Printing Office, 1977.
2. Beale, L., "The Recent Shift of United States Population to Nonmetropolitan Areas, 1970–75," *International Regional Science Review,* Vol. 2, 1977.
3. Bell, M., "The National Economy, Industry Policy and Regional Development Policy," Paper presented to Atlantic Economic Society, Bahamas, 1980.
4. Berry, B.J.L., "Hierarchical Diffusion: The Basis of Development Filtering and Spread in a System of Growth Centers," in N.M. Hansen, ed., *Growth Centers in Regional Economic Development,* New York: Free Press, 1972.
5. ———, "Inner City Futures: An American Dilema Revisited," *Transactions Institute of British Geographers,* 1980.
6. Birch, D.L., and Allaman, P.M., "Components of Employment Change for Metropolitan and Rural Areas in the United States," Cambridge, Mass.: MIT-Harvard Joint Center for Urban Studies, 1975.
7. Birch, D.L., "The Job Generation Process," paper prepared for the U.S. Department of Commerce, Economic Development Administration, Washington, D.C., 1979.
8. Briggs, R., "The Impact of the Interstate Highway System on Nonmetropolitan Growth," Office of University Research, Department of Transportation, Washington, D.C., 1980.
9. Brown, L. A. *Innovation Diffusion: A New Perspective,* New York: Methuen, 1981.
10. Bryce, H.J., ed., *Small Cities in Transition: The Dynamics of Growth and Decline,* Cambridge, Mass.: Ballinger, 1977.
11. Choate, P. and Schwartz, A.A., *Revitalizing the U.S. Economy: A Brief for National Sectoral Policy,* Washington, D.C.: Academy for Contemporary Problems, 1980.
12. Cooper, A.C., "Entrepreneurial Environment," *Industrial Research,* 1970.
13. ———, "Spin-offs and Technical Entrepreneurship," *IEEE Transactions on Engineering Management,* 1971.
14. Cumberland, J.H., *Regional Development: Experiences and Prospects in the United States of America,* The Hague: Mouton, 1971.
15. Danhof, C.H., "Four Decades of Thought on the South's Economic Problems," in M.L. Greenhut and W.T. Whitman, ed., *Essays in Southern Economic Development,* Chapel Hill: University of North Carolina Press, 1964.
16. Department of Housing and Urban Development, *The President's National Urban Policy Report 1980,* Washington, D.C.: U.S. Government Printing Office, 1980.
17. Dunning, J.H., *Economic Analysis and the Multinational Enterprise,* London: George, Allen and Unwin, 1974.

18. Economic Commission for Europe, "Labor Supply and Migration in Europe: Demographic Dimensions 1950–75 and Prospects," Geneva: United Nations, 1979.
19. Erickson, R.A. and Leinbach, T.R., "Characteristics of Branch Plants Attracted to Nonmetropolitan Areas," in R.E. Lonsdale and H.L. Seyler, eds., *Nonmetropolitan Industrialization,* Washington, D.C.: Winston, 1979.
20. Ewers, H.J. and Wettman, R.W., "Innovation Oriented Regional Policy," *Regional Studies,* 1980.
21. Fischer, P., "Patterns of Distress and Growth in Suburban and Nonmetropolitan Cities," Paper prepared for the President's National Urban Policy Report, Washington, D.C.: U.S. Department of Housing and Urban Development, 1979.
22. Franko, L.G., "Multinationals: The End of U.S. Dominance," *Harvard Business Review,* 1978.
23. Freeman, C., "The Determinants of Innovation," *Futures,* 1979.
24. Friedland, R., Piven, F. and Alford, R., "Political Conflict, Urban Structure and the Fiscal Crisis," in D. Ashford, ed., *Sage Yearbooks in Politics and Public Policy,* Beverly Hills, Calif.: Sage, 1977.
25. Friedmann, J. and Alonso, W., *Regional Policy,* Cambridge, Mass.: MIT Press, 1975.
26. Gerstenfeld, A., ed., *Technological Innovation: Government-Industry Cooperation,* New York: Wiley, 1979.
27. Gilpin, R., *U.S. Power and the Multinational Corporation,* New York: Basic Books, 1975.
28. Glassberg, A., "Organizational Responses to Municipal Budget Decreases," *Public Administration Review,* 1978.
29. Goddard, J.A., *The Mobilization of Indigenous Potential in the UK,* Report to the Regional Policy Directorate of the European Economic Community, 1980.
30. J. Goddard, "Industrial Innovation and Regional Economic Development in Britain" Commission on Industrial Systems, International Geographical Congress, Japan, 1980.
31. Gold, B. *et al., Evaluating Technological Innovations: Methods, Expectations and Findings,* Cleveland, Ohio: Case Western Reserve University, 1979.
32. Gordon, P., "Deconcentration Without a Clean Break," Vienna: International Institute for Applied Systems Analysis, 1978.
33. Hamilton, F.E.I., "Aspects of Industrial Mobility in the British Economy," *Regional Studies,* 1978.
34. Hansen, N.M., *Public Policy and Regional Economic Development: The Experience of Nine Western Countries,* Cambridge, Mass.: Ballinger, 1974.
35. Hansen, N., "The New International Division of Labor and Manufacturing Decentralization in the United States," Presidential Address, Southern Regional Science Association, 1980.
36. Harrison, B., *Urban Economic Development,* Washington, D.C.: Urban Institute, 1974.
37. Hill, C.T. and Utterback, J. M., eds., *Technological Innovation for a Dynamic Economy,* New York: Pergamon Press, 1979.
38. Howland, M., "The Business Cycle and Long Run Regional Growth," in W. Wheaton, ed., *Inter-regional Movements and Regional Growth,* Washington, D.C.: Urban Institute, 1979.
39. Hymer, S., *The International Operations of National Firms: A Study in Direct Investment,* Ph.D. dissertation, Cambridge, Mass.: MIT, 1960.
40. James, F., "Economies of Central Cities," Paper presented for President's National Urban Policy Report, Washington, D.C.: U.S. Department of Housing and Urban Development, 1979.
41. Jasinowski, J.J., "The Case for an Industry Policy," Speech given to National Association of Manufacturers, 1979.

42. Jusenius, C.L. and Ledebur, L.C., *A Myth in the Making: The Southern Economic Challenge and Northern Economic Decline,* Washington, D.C.: Office of Economic Research, Economic Development Administration, 1976.
43. Kain, J.F., "Implications of Declining Metropolitan Population on Housing Markets," in G. Sternlieb and J.W. Hughes, eds., *Post-Industrial America: Metropolitan Decline and Inter-Regional Job Shifts,* New Brunswick: The Center for Urban Policy Research, 1975.
44. Keeble, D., *Industrial Location and Planning in the United Kingdom,* London: Methuen, 1976.
45. Kristol, Irving, "An Urban Civilization Without Cities," *The Washington Post,* Dec. 3, 1972.
46. Kuznets, S., *Secular Movements in Production and Prices,* Boston: Houghton Mifflin, 1930.
47. Lawrence, P.R. and Lorsch, J.W., *Organization and Environment: Managing Differentiation and Integration,* Cambridge, Mass.: Harvard University Press, 1967.
48. Lonsdale, R.E. and Seyler, H.L., *Nonmetropolitan Industrialization,* Washington, D.C.: Winston, 1979.
49. Maier, H. and Haustein, H.D., "Innovation, Efficiency Cycle and Strategy Implications," Austria: International Institute for Applied Systems Analysis, 1980.
50. Malecki, E.J., "Locational Trends in R and D by Large U.S. Corporations, 1965–77," *Economic Geography,* 1979.
51. ______, "Dimensions of R and D Location in the United States," *Research Policy,* 1980.
52. Mansfield, E., *Research and Innovation in the Modern Corporation,* New York: Norton, 1971.
53. Mansfield, E. *et al., The Production and Application of New Industrial Technology,* New York: Norton, 1977.
54. Martin, C. and Leone, R., *Local Economic Development,* Lexington, Mass.: D.C. Heath, 1977.
55. Martin, F. and Swan, N., *The Inter-regional Diffusion of Innovations in Canada,* Ottawa: Minister of Supply and Services, 1978.
56. McConnell, J.E., "Foreign Direct Investment in the U.S.," *Annals,* Association of American Geographers, 1980.
57. Meyer, J.R. and Leone, R.A., "The New England States and Their Economic Future," *American Economic Review,* 1978.
58. Miernyk, W.H., *The Changing Structure of the Southern Economy,* Conference Paper, Southern Growth Policies Board, 1976.
59. Moore, B. and Rhodes, J., "Evaluating the Effects of British Regional Policy," *Economic Journal,* 1973.
60. Morrison, P.A. and McCarthy, K.F., "The Changing Demographic and Economic Structure of Nonmetropolitan Areas in the United States," Santa Monica, Calif.: Rand Corp., 1979.
61. Mukherjee, S., *Restructuring of Industrial Economies and Trade with Developing Countries,* Geneva, Switzerland: International Labor Office, 1978.
62. Nasbeth, L. and Ray, G.F., *The Diffusion of New Industrial Processes: An International Study,* Cambridge, Mass.: Cambridge University Press, 1974.
63. National Science Board *Science Indicators 1976,* Washington, D.C.: U.S. Government Printing Office, 1977.
64. Norton, R.D. and Rees, J., "The Product Cycle and the Spatial Decentralization of American Manufacturing," *Regional Studies,* 1979.
65. Oakey, R., "An Analysis of the Spatial Distribution of Significant British Industrial Innovations," discussion paper, University of New Castle, UK, 1979.
66. Organization for Economic Co-operation and Development, *Policies for the Stimulation of Industrial Innovation,* Vol. II, Paris, 1978.

67. Perry, D. and Watkins, A., "People, Profit and the Rise of the Sunbelt Cities," in D. Perry and A. Watkins, eds., *The Rise of the Sunbelt Cities,* Urban Affairs Annual Review, Beverly Hills: Sage, 1977.
68. Phillips, R.S., "Geographic Redistribution of Population and Employment in the United States since 1970," paper prepared for President's National Urban Policy Report, Washington, D.C.: U.S. Department of Housing and Urban Development, 1979.
69. Pred, A., "The Interurban Transmission of Growth in Advanced Economies: Empirical Findings Versus Regional Planning Assumptions," *Regional Studies,* 1976.
70. Rees, J., "Manufacturing Change, Internal Control and Government Spending in a Growth Region of the USA," in F.E.I. Hamilton, ed., *Industrial Change: International Experience and Public Policy,* Longman: London, 1978.
71. ———, "Technological Change and Regional Shifts in American Manufacturing," *Professional Geographer,* 1979.
72. ———, "Regional Industrial Shifts in the U.S. and the Internal Generation of Manufacturing in Growth Centers of the Southwest," in W. Wheaton, ed., *Inter-regional Movements and Regional Growth,* Washington, D.C.: Urban Institute, 1979.
73. ———, *Government Policy and Industrial Location in the United States,* report prepared for Special Study in Economic Change, Joint Economic Committee, U.S. Congress, Washington, D.C., 1980.
74. ———, "Economic Development Trends in Non-metropolitan and Suburban Communities," report prepared for President's National Urban Policy Report, Washington, D.C.: U.S. Department of Housing and Urban Development, 1980.
75. Rogers, E.M., *Diffusion of Innovations,* New York: Lee Press, 1962.
76. Rosenberg, N., "Technological Change in the Machine Tool Industry 1840–1910," *Journal of Economic History,* 1963.
77. Sale, K., *Power Shift,* New York: Random House, 1975.
78. Sant, M., *Regional Policy and Planning for Europe,* Lexington, Mass.: Saxon, 1974.
79. Scholl, R.B., "The International Investment Position of the United States," *Survey of Current Business,* 1979.
80. Schon, D.A., "Innovation by Invasion," *International Science and Technology,* 1967.
81. Servan-Schreiber, J.J., *The American Challenge,* London: Penguin Press, 1967.
82. Sternlieb, G. and Hughes, J.W., "New Regional and Metropolitan Realities of America," *Journal,* American Institute of Planners, 1977.
83. ———, *Revitalizing the Northeast,* New Brunswick: Center for Urban Policy Research, 1978.
84. Stroetmann, K.A., ed., *Innovation, Economic Change and Technology Policies,* Stuttgart: Burkhausen Verlag, 1977.
85. Thompson, W.R., "The Economic Base of Urban Problems," in N. Chamberlain, ed., *Contemporary Economic Issues,* Irwen, Ill., 1969.
86. Thurow, L., *The Zero Sum Society: Distribution and the Possibilities for Economic Change,* New York: Basic Books, 1979.
87. Thwaites, A.T., "Technological Change, Mobile Plants and Regional Development," *Regional Studies,* 1978.
88. U.S. Department of Commerce, Bureau of Census, *Census of Manufactures,* Washington, D.C.: U.S. Government Printing Office, 1977.
89. ———, *Current Population Reports* (p-23), Washington, D.C.: U.S. Government Printing Office, 1978.
90. Utterback, J.M., "Business Invasion by Innovation," paper presented to International Institute on Applied Systems Analysis, Vienna, 1978.
91. Vernon, R. "International Investment and International Trade in the Product Cycle," *Quarterly Journal of Economics,* 1967.

92. ______, *Sovereignty at Bay,* New York: Basic Books, 1972.
93. Vining, D.R. and Strauss, A., "A Demonstration that the Current Deconcentration of Population in the United States is a Clean Break with the Past," *Environment and Planning,* 1977.
94. Watson, J.W., "Image Geography: The Myth of America in the American Scene," *British Association for the Advancement of Science,* 1970.
95. Weinstein, B.L. and Firestine, R.E., *Regional Growth and Decline in the United States,* New York: Praeger, 1978.
96. Wheaton, W.C., *Inter-regional Movements and Regional Growth,* Papers in Public Economics, Vol. 2, Washington, D.C.: Urban Institute, 1979.
97. Wilkins, M., *The Maturing of Multinational Enterprise,* Cambridge, Mass.: Harvard University Press, 1974.
98. Whelan, R., "City Dependency, Federal Budget Cutbacks, and City Responses," paper presented at Midwest Political Science Association, 1980.
99. Williamson, J.G., "Regional Inequality and the Process of National Development: A Description of the Patterns," *Economic Development and Cultural Change,* 1965.

Chapter X

REVITALIZING CITIES THROUGH NATIONAL SECTORAL POLICIES

Gail Garfield Schwartz

The time has come for a major change in national development policies. In the past, the U.S. economy was growing and development policies were designed to address the distribution of economic benefits. The debate over appropriate policy to deal with economically lagging regions and subregions, including cities, centered on the places-versus-people question. The Federal government sought ways to promote the physical and economic development of places and at the same time, to ensure that disadvantaged people—those left out of the mainstream of economic prosperity—were aided in finding employment and maintaining a decent standard of living.

The economic circumstances that produced past policies no longer prevail. The U.S. economy is not growing. The primary question is no longer how to distribute income and jobs. Instead, a much more complex question must be answered: how to ensure that enough jobs and income will be produced to support the society. Economic equity is very hard to achieve when the pie is shrinking.

In the current situation, many cities are in chronic economic decline because the industries that have provided support in the past are inefficient, obsolete, and noncompetitive. Cities cannot be revitalized unless the industries within them are strengthened. But many practices of the private sector and much public policy are antithetical to this goal.

There are two sets of causes of urban economic decline. One is the decreasing attraction of older congested urban space for certain economic activities, given the less expensive and more attractive nonurban options. These spatial characteristics are conditioned by the complex interjurisdictional arrangements in many metropolitan areas. They are not dealt with in this paper.

The other cause is structural change in the economy. Changing technologies, changing markets, and changing resource needs are interrelated. In many industries, American firms are not meeting the challenge of structural change successfully. They are not producing the right goods of the right quality in sufficient quantity at competitive prices. As a result, they are losing out in domestic and foreign markets. They are laying off workers, or failing to hire new workers. Plants or portions of plants are closing. And many firms are disinvesting, which means that their competitive position will grow weaker, not stronger. Therefore, if the many cities affected by these conditions are to revive, one of three options must be pursued:

- The industries that presently support their economic base must be reinvigorated;
- Other substitute industries must take their place; or
- The residents must leave to seek employment in communities where industries are growing.

Most public attention has been focused on the demise of the automobile and steel industries, primarily because these are the traditional backbone of the economy. Whereas historically one in every six workers was employed in the automotive sector, now an estimated one in 12 workers earns his/her living from that sector. Domestic automobile production has been stagnant for three years. Production dropped 8.6 percent in the first half of 1981 while imports threatened to take 30 percent of domestic sales,[1] despite pressures placed on Japan (the nation's major competitor) to restrict sales to the United States.

In part due to reduced demand from the automotive sector, steel production has also been moving downward, although more contrary upswings occurred over the past five years in this industry. Nevertheless, domestic producers' share of the U.S. steel market has been and is falling, while imports for the past five years have received 15 to 19 percent of domestic sales annually.[2] In other key manufacturing industries, such as aluminum, transport equipment, machine tools, and semiconductors, production has not met the growing domestic demand. Imports rose even while millions of Americans remained unemployeed in these and other key industries.

Beginning in 1978, and continuing at an accelerating pace through 1981, retrenchment in two key sectors alone—autos and steel—brought economic disaster to more than 40 communities throughout the nation. While these industries are most heavily concentrated in the Great Lakes States, plant closings and layoffs have affected steel communities in California, Illinois, Indiana, New York, Ohio, Pennsylvania, and West Virginia. In 1979 and 1980, Ford Company shutdowns alone affected 35,000 workers in 13 communities, 10 of which were major cities, and Chrysler Corporation's 100,000 workers were deployed in 18 cities in 8 states. Cities with older industrial bases, especially those dependent on the steel industry, the tire industry, and the automobile industry, are not confined to the Northeast and Midwest. Like their northern counterparts, communities in the South such as Birmingham, Alabama are in fiscal as well as economic trouble. Not only are their older industries in decline, but also new investment has not taken place, working people have continued to move away, and the costs of maintaining public infrastructure and providing municipal services have been spread across a shrinking local tax base.

The Federal government responded during the 1970s by spreading the fiscal burden to nonlocal taxpayers through general revenue sharing and grants in aid. But in 1981, with the election of a conservative President and a conservative majority in the House of Representatives, there was a massive reduction of federal support for the urban fiscal base. States and localities were challenged to cope alone with a problem over which they have little, if any, power—namely, the demise of the local economy.

THE URBAN IMPACT OF THE AUTOMOTIVE CRISIS

A closer look at the automotive sector illustrates how changes in one component of the sector affect changes in other components, and how the effects of these changes are distributed over the nation's cities. In 1979, domestic motor vehicle manufacturers operated 300 facilities employing 900,000 production workers in 147 cities and towns in 26 states. Auto vehicle employment was heavily concentrated in 30 urban areas, ranging from 212,000 in Detroit, with 73 facilities, to 4,800 in San Francisco, and Okalahoma City, with one facility each (see Table X.1). Clearly, with as much as one-quarter to one-third of their workforce dependent on one industry, such cities are on shaky economic ground. Add

Table X.1. Cities in Which the Motor Vehicle Industry Employs 10 Percent or More of the Work Force

City	*Percent*
Anderson, Ind.	46%
Kokomo, Ind.	34
Flint, Mich.	33
Saginaw, Mich.	25
Kenosha, Wis.	24
Janesville, Wis.	16
Ann Arbor, Mich.	15
Detroit, Mich.	12
Lansing, Mich.	11

Source: U.S. Department of Transportation, Transportation Systems Center, unpublished report, Washington, D.C., 1979.

the fact that the industries that feed the motor vehicle industry also are concentrated in or near the same cities, and the problem is compounded. In a six-state region—Illinois, Indiana, Michigan, Minnesota, Ohio, and Wisconsin—every dollar lost through decreased auto production causes another estimated $1.73 loss to the regional income.[3]

An estimated 81,000 employees in the steel industry depend on the motor vehicle industry according to the Transportation Systems Center. They live in Gary, Indiana; East Chicago, Indiana; Cleveland, Ohio; Baltimore, Maryland.; Dearborn, Michigan; and several other cities. Iron foundries employ additional thousands of workers for auto-related production, particularly in Saginaw and Detroit, Michigan, and Cleveland, Ohio, but also in Pontiac and Flint, Michigan: Tonowanda, New York; Defiance, Ohio; and many smaller cities.

Increasing amounts of aluminum are used in automobiles to reduce weight and increase mileage. Plants supplying aluminum to the industry are located in Listerhill, Alabama; Evansville, Indiana; Toledo, Ohio; Massena, New York; Ravenswood, West Virginia.; and several other communities. Auto assemblers plan to open their own aluminum foundries to integrate castings into the production process. To the extent this is done in places like Kokomo, Indiana, or Toledo, Ohio, jobs may be added to the local economy. However, the city's dependence on one sector would also increase.

Plastics plants are also operated by automobile firms in Flint and several other Michigan towns; Sandusky, Ohio; and Michigan City, Ind. The motor vehicle industry buys about 5 percent of the output of the plastics products industry, which comprises 8,000 plants in scores of cities and employs 390,000 persons. Plastics, like aluminum, are increasingly used to reduce auto weight, and a healthy auto industry would help expand the plastics industry.

Automobile tires used to be made in 27 cities. Seven plants in five cities closed in the 1978–80 period. Akron, Ohio, lost 1,400 jobs; Los Angeles lost 2,000 jobs, and Detroit lost 2,000 jobs as a result. To be sure, tire plants were planned or opened in other communities in other states, such as North Carolina, but the net number of jobs in the industry nationwide declined.

One very important component of the automotive sector is the manufacturers of auto parts. Together, firms in these industries employ an estimated 2 million persons, more than twice as many as the auto assembly industry itself.[4] This $50 billion annual market is served by roughly 2,000 firms, which are currently in even deeper trouble than auto manufacturers themselves.

The changes in automobile design hastily and belatedly initiated by domestic producers in 1980 naturally altered the type of parts needed and therefore created a need for heavy new capital investment to make new parts. One estimate places this figure at $70 billion during the 1980s.[5] But many parts suppliers cannot command the needed capital, especially as nearly one-half of the firms employ fewer than 20 persons. Especially while high interest rates prevail, such firms will operate with obsolete equipment and will be exceedingly vulnerable to competition from overseas firms. As a result, imports are estimated to rise to 15 percent of the domestic auto parts market by 1991, more than 2.5 times their 1980 share. Imports of auto parts in 1990 are expected to reach $7.5 billion, more than twice the value of exports.[6] A loss of 400,000 jobs could be associated with such an event, most of which would be in cities or metropolitan areas.

Electronic devices are ever more important elements of modern automobiles. Sensors and actuators control fuel use and emissions; engine control computers make the engine work efficiently. Facilities making the equipment in many U.S. communities will have to compete successfully with high-quality Japanese products.

There can be no doubt that cities dependent on industries linked to the automotive sector are in trouble since over 30 percent of the motor vehicles sold in the United States are foreign models. The unemployment rates in these communities are as high as 17 percent (see Table X.2).

The more important point, however, is that like other sectors, the automotive sector has been in trouble for many years. Instead of helping the industries to become competitive, government has encouraged them to be lax in responding to the exigencies of the market. While the Federal government tried to help the cities' fiscal base through grants

Table X.2. Proportion of Employment in Durable Goods Manufacture 1977 and 1980, and Unemployment Rates for Five Auto-Dependent Cities

	Percent of Nonagriculture Employment in Durable Goods Manufacture		*Percent of Durable Goods Manufacture in Transport Equipment*		*Unemployment Rate*
	1977	*1980*	*1977*	*1980*	*1980*
Anderson, Ind.	46%	39%	NA	NA	16.6%
Gary, Ind.	35	32	4	6	9.2
Detroit, Mich.	28	25	50	47	11.7
Flint, Mich.	41	36	76	77	6.9
Saginaw, Mich.	37	32	47	47	11.8
United States	NA	13	NA	6*	7.1

* Proportion refers to automotive transportation equipment only.

Sources: U.S. Department of Labor, Bureau of Labor Statistics, *Supplement to Employment and Earnings, State and Areas, Data for 1977–80,* Washington, D.C.: U.S. Government Printing Office, September 1981; and U.S. Department of Labor, Bureau of Labor Statistics, *Employment and Earnings,* Washington, D.C.: U.S. Government Printing Office, May 1981.

and general revenue sharing, and tried to help unemployed workers through trade adjustment assistance and other remedial programs, it was pursuing other policies that virtually guaranteed trouble for urban economies.

HOW FEDERAL POLICIES INFLUENCE INDUSTRIAL PERFORMANCE

The poor performance of key industries has persisted through a period of chronic inflation and high unemployment. For nearly seven years, the United States has tolerated inflation and unemployment rates at levels unthinkable a decade ago. Both rates have been consistently higher than those in other advanced industrial nations, even though those nations likewise were held hostage to inflationary OPEC price increases, and even though slow growth now plagues some of them as well. In periods of slow growth, U.S. inflation stays above 8 to 9 percent. In periods of economic acceleration, more than 5 percent of those who want to work have remained jobless, and an uncounted number of discouraged workers go unregistered.

In some industries, uncompetitiveness is due to low productivity resulting from failure to reinvest and modernize. But this failure may have been caused by one or several factors. For example, in the aluminum industry, investment was curtailed during the 1970s by lack of an assured energy supply at a reasonable cost. In the steel industry, requirements for meeting technically specified pollution control goals diverted a substantial proportion of capital investment (about 18 percent) out of actual production, thus reducing the ratio of output to input.[7] In some industries, notably the passenger car industry, poor management and poor market decisions were evident, and the industry failed to keep up with technological advances. Poor quality control has plagued some industries, especially the electronics industry.

In most sectors, it is safe to say, a little of everything is involved, with the result that productivity is falling and firms have difficulty selling their products at competitive prices. Profits are depressed, capital is short, and the temptation to use cash reserves to acquire profitable subsidiaries, rather than retool and reorganize for more efficient production, has been very great, particularly in the steel and machinery sectors. In sum, U.S. industries have increasingly focused on short-term profitability rather that long-term planning to gain market share in highly competitive industries.

These efforts have been aided by government policies, which have been both inconsistent and ignorant of their systemwide effects. In general, industry-specific attention has been confined to trade and regulatory policies, while the differential effects of fiscal, monetary, and manpower development policies went largely unnoticed. While the sum effects of all these contradictory policies contributed to the decline of industries in urban areas, urban development policies generally ignored the industry-wide approach in favor of project-by-project approaches. The net result was that many economically weak firms were assisted by various subsidies, and few beneficiaries helped their communities through added jobs or increased tax payments.

The following discussion highlights the way in which major policies influence the costs of conducting business, and hence, the ability of firms to compete successfully for markets, expand production, and increase employment.

Fiscal Policies. The cost structures of firms are most directly affected by fiscal policies through tax rates, tax credits, and exemptions. Subsidies to private enterprise in 1980 probably exceeded $200 billion, and the 1981 tax bill could add substantially to that figure.[8] In the United States, some sectors, such as the housing construction sector, traditionally are subsidized directly, while other sectors, such as transportation, are subsidized indirectly through highway construction and other means. Investments in some sectors are encouraged by direct and indirect subsidies, especially by tax shelters; this is a way of attracting capital to sectors defined as vital to the national interest. However, the consequences for other sectors are seldom considered and seldom measured before legislation is passed.

Tax measures also have cumulative impacts on places. Several studies have indicated that investment tax credits encourage firms to locate where land is less expensive—outside of cities. The same can be inferred with regard to accelerated depreciation for new plant and equipment, enacted in 1981.

By late autumn 1981, it was clear that the hastily drafted and ill-considered 1981 tax bill would have an effect on capital flows, which some economists predicted but politicians chose to ignore. It would encourage jockeying by profitable firms to minimize their federal tax liability, regardless of whether or not the consequences contributed to greater efficiency in unprofitable or profitable industries. Conoco, for example, was able to reduce its corporate income tax liability to almost nothing by acquiring the tax credits and deductions of unprofitable firms. This game of fiscal musical chairs might have netted out to a form of sectoral policy favoring steel, railroads, and the other unprofitable industries that Congress intended to help, had those firms used the cash gained to invest in productive equipment.

Monetary Policy. Both the amount and distribution of public and private investment are influenced by monetary policy, although its impact on capital flows to particular sectors of the economy is seldom, if ever, assessed in advance. Some sectors are known to be more sensitive than others; the construction and automobile sectors, for example, respond very rapidly to shifts in the cost of credit. Other sectors may also be affected differently, according to factors such as their debt-to-equity ratios and the rate of obsolescence of their equipment. At present, no systematic analysis is conducted of the sectoral effects of shifts in monetary supply (or interest rates) before those shifts are promulgated.

Regulatory Policy. Some industrialists and economists have declared regulatory policy a prime culprit in boosting the costs of conducting business, ignoring the fact that in many instances, regulation can increase a firm's profits by forcing it to greater efficiencies. Many firms in many industries also testify that regulations protect their reputations and their products. Certainly, regulations have spawned new manufacturing opportunities (such as pollution control equipment), have encouraged innovation (such as in biotechnology), and have created new jobs. When regulating or deregulating, it is necessary to look at the costs associated with change throughout the linked industries, not merely in the immediate subject industries. Rather than viewing deregulation as the sole alternative to the costly application of environmental standards, other approaches—such as loans or grants to encourage compliance, to conserve resources, and to limit the hardship to struggling firms—might be far more efficient in achieving all short- and long-term objectives.

Trade Policies. To protect domestic industries, trade policies are increasingly being applied. Yet, protectionist pressures are inversely related to the performance of domestic firms. Barriers to imports are useful only if they are implemented as part of an overall effort to increase productivity in the domestic industry. By the same token, trade adjustment assistance, which provides aid to workers in industries adversely affected by imports, is appropriate, provided that the assistance facilitates structural adjustment, either by encouraging greater efficiency in firms in the affected industries, or by moving workers from low-demand to high-demand industries or sectors.

In the past, this has not been the case, in part because retraining programs only receive a small fraction of available funds. While nearly 500,000 workers have benefitted monetarily from trade adjustment assistance, only 10,000 participated in retraining; there is little evidence that structural readjustment has resulted. This is partly due to reluctance of workers to relocate and/or retrain—a reluctance that should erode as alternatives diminish. But in large part this situation is due to failures of policy and of political will.

While adversarial means dominate America's adjustment responses, the nation will continue to spend billions of dollars pressing weak cases for protectionism—as in the 1981 steel industry bid for a trigger price at a time when domestic earnings were up—while at the same time failing to rationalize our production goals and processes.

Manpower and Training Policies. An estimated $11 billion annually has been spent on manpower and training programs over the past decade. Some funds have been directed at the hard to employ who may have never worked; much less has been directed at older workers needing retraining to qualify for jobs in new occupations and/or in new industries. The effect of this expenditure on the employment and employability of urban residents has been minimal, although most mayors and other urban officials welcome the funds.

During Fall 1981, the Reagan Administration proposed to reduce all federal funding for manpower training to a mere trickle, as well as threatening to reduce federal aid to education drastically. The rationale was that states and local governments were best able to meet the education and training needs of their own residents.

This rationale does not bear up under closer examination. According to the Bureau of Labor Statistics, 80 percent of the available jobs will require postsecondary education by 1990. A shortage of 2.5 million skilled workers is anticipated by the Department of Labor.

If one looks beyond the funded programs to the economic goals of federal expenditure, the picture is much clearer. There are major sectors of the economy experiencing acute labor shortages: the machinery sector is one of them, with an estimated gap between need and supply of some 35,000 workers per year, according to U.S. Department of Labor forecasts. Yet employers in the machinery sector complain that job applicants are not equipped with the basic skills required to become qualified apprentices. Computational skills are needed to manipulate the modern digital equipment that machinists use; the same skills are needed by auto workers to control robots.

Other occupations are similarly short of personnel. In nearly every metropolitan area, the demand for computer programmers and systems analysts far exceeds the supply. Word processors and executive secretaries are desperately needed in major cities like New York City, Washington, D.C., and Chicago. Thus, the problems are (1) to set curricula that are relevant to the job opportunities that will be available, and (2) to finance training that is too expensive for firms to support individually because of costly essential equipment. Again, the answer lies in industry-specific approaches, bringing together the ultimate employers, the manpower training establishment, and the educational establishment to plan the needed steps.

Federal financing will still be needed to implement a successful manpower training program, for the simple reason that the communities that are least able to attract industries that provide jobs for the residents given their present level of skills are also the least fiscally able to finance the skills improvement that is needed by residents to leave and search for jobs elsewhere. Yet, manpower training is the best possible expenditure of taxpayer dollars, because development of the labor resource in all communities will help to improve their competitive position in a technologically advanced economy. Of all the investments possible, a massive education and training program, for both the unemployed and those workers requiring retraining, would best encourage higher productivity in all industries and offset the perceived differentials between older industrial cities and nonmetropolitan areas as locations for high-technology and service industries.

Area Development Policies. These policies, including urban policy, are designed to bring regions or subregions to a higher level of income and employment. The means include subsidies for land assembly and investment in public works, social infrastructure (such as schools, day care centers, hospitals, and clinics), and human resources (such as job training programs). Such programs were first aimed at cities in 1954 and were supplemented by the 1965 Public Works and Economic Development Act. The high point of national concern about urban revitalization was reached during the late 1970s, when the Carter Administration worked diligently to turn a hodgepodge of programs into a coherent urban development policy. But events overtook intentions, and too little was accomplished.

BRITAIN AND THE ENTERPRISE ZONES

Perhaps the most blatant example of the simple, quick and wrong solution is the "import" from Britain still being debated in 1983: the urban enterprise zone. This program would amass federal tax and local incentives to encourage private investors to fund projects or to locate in inner city areas that they otherwise would not consider, provided that a substantial number of jobs are made available to the hard-to-employ residents of the areas. The notion that a large dose of incentives could liberate pent up entrepreneurship in economically devastated urban areas is very appealing. Yet, when so many other more attractive locations for investment are available, there is reason to question whether the zones would be cost effective and whether they would be equitable. Drawing the boundaries for eligibility is difficult. Ensuring that they do not create major distortions in producer costs within a particular industry in a community is almost impossible.

The attention that the enterprise zone proposal gained in the United States underscores once again the need to examine the systemwide effects of policies to assist particular places when such policies work through the private sector. A national economic development policy, supported by complementary policies in the housing, transportation, and social services, is needed—a policy that recognizes the vital linkages among encouraging economic growth in the nation as a whole, stabilizing and revitalizing our cities, and providing opportunities for meaningful work for all Americans.

REVAMPING URBAN PROGRAMS

If one expects an increase in jobs or in the average income in cities that have received substantial federal assistance in economic development, relative to those that have not, one will be disappointed. Most studies that try to assess the significance of particular incentives to industrial location come up with inconclusive or contradictory results that do little to enhance policy decisions. Although many industrial facilities have been constructed with the aid of government investment, a good many—perhaps as much as two-thirds of the industrial parks assisted by the Economic Development Administration—stand vacant.

That this should be so is not surprising. The principle of recent urban policy has been that the worst-off communities should get the most assistance from the Federal government. Yet, the worst-off communities may be those in which the existing industrial structure is totally obsolete. The only viable strategy for such cities may be to revamp the industrial mix and to spend public effort on helping the strong rather than marginal enterprises.

The various urban-oriented policies—from Urban Renewal through Model Cities through the Community Development Block Grant—have had one common outcome, however: the allocation of scarce dollars to places inevitably created a political battle over eligibility formulas, and never allowed policies and programs to address the underlying cause of unemployment or underemployment in any beneficiary place—noncompetitive industries. Annually, the merits of political formulas have been debated to identify eligible areas and to distribute their entitlements to Federal aid. Whether the Sunbelt or the Frostbelt is being "shortchanged" by these formulas becomes more important than whether economic growth goals are being served. Rural and urban, metropolitan and nonmetropolitan communities vie for what they see as their "fair share" of Federal assistance.

Sectoral policies can help lay to rest the perennial dilemma of how to "target" urban programs. By first treating the problems of industries and sectors, and considering their distribution over the landscape as but one among many aspects, government—in cooperation with labor and management—can encourage economic growth without making artificial, and sometimes arbitrary, distinctions among eligible places.

SECTORAL STRATEGIES

During the past few years, terms such as "industrial policy" and "industrial revitalization" have been offered as solutions to the problems of declining productivity and shrinking economic growth. These terms are ill defined and unsuited to the problems at hand.

The term "sectoral strategies" is intended to emphasize both a subject of concern and a process for dealing with it. The first meaning of "sectoral" is that the economy is composed of many interrelated industries.

Problems in any part of the chain of linked industries may be caused by various conditions, such as shortages of raw materials or reduced demand for the final product, but the repercussions will be felt at every point in the chain. Thus, it is in the rational self-interest of all linked industries to anticipate problems and opportunities so that they may be handled in a strategic manner.

The second meaning of the word "sectoral" is equally significant, extending beyond "industry," in its common definition. "Industry" usually refers to manufacturing, transportation, and wholesale distribution. Yet, the growth sectors of the future will not necessarily be confined to industry, but will include other services, such as financial planning, consulting, legal services, engineering, and computer programming. These service industries—part of the knowledge revolution—are a growing element of the U.S. export base. Most importantly, they link human or knowledge services to the manufacturing sector. For example medical research breakthroughs create opportunities to develop and market new scientific instruments, and the manufacture of new instruments creates opportunities to conduct new experiments and research. Thus, the modern economy is not easily divided into traditional segments, and the term "sectoral" is used to connote cross-sector interrelationships that are becoming increasingly significant.

By definition, a "strategy" presumes a known objective, a knowledge of the resources available to meet that objective, and an understanding of the costs associated with applying any given combination of resources. "Reindustrialization" is not a strategy, but rather a simplistic, misleading prescription for economic renewal. It implies that an infusion into the old mix of industries of a double dose of economic vitamins such as tax cuts and accelerated depreciation is all that is necessary. On the contrary, the remedy for our economic ills is selective, strategic treatment for selected elements of the economy.

The sectors chosen for treatment should not be restricted to those that include the mature manufacturing industries, like the automotive and steel sectors. Emerging sectors (such as biochemicals) that link services (patient care) with manufacturing (of specialized instruments or computerized control systems) will provide future job opportunities and will boost the Gross National Product. The mature sectors are bound to shrink if they are to be winners in a keenly competitive world market. But the emerging sectors will spawn many new jobs in both blue- and white-collar occupations. An undersupply problem already exists for programmers, and the need will grow for electronic engineers, systems analysts, technicians, assemblers, sales persons, and marketing experts in these volatile sectors.

PRODUCTIVITY, MARKET SHARE, AND URBAN JOBS

If the nation is to develop and implement a comprehensive sectoral growth strategy, two unpalatable facts must be accepted: (1) greater competitive advantage in any one set of linked industries does not necessarily lead to more jobs in all of those linked industries; and (2) all places will not benefit equally from structural adjustments.

Again using the automotive sector as the example, the single most important key to improved international competitiveness is the robotization of the industry. During 1980–81, General Motors (GM) took the lead in investing in computer-controlled multifunctional equipment capable of completing many different and repetitive tasks with virtually no human supervision other than programming the machine. This development has resulted in the shutdown of major plants for long periods of time. The Baltimore plant, for example, was closed for up to a year for major remodeling, but sagging auto sales led to the indefinite postponement of the multimillion dollar investment despite the down time. According to GM officials, productivity was expected to increase a minimum of 10 percent per hour after the investment. Yet, engineers report that output on the auto assembly line can rise 50 percent following "state of the art" robotization.[9] Thus, unless sales increase very substantially, job shrinkages will be inevitably associated with rationalization and modernization.

The traditional, understandable, yet shortsighted responses to such a situation have been for labor to demand guarantees against joblessness and for labor and management to demand protection from foreign competition during the transition to greater efficiency. But the interdependencies among industries are largely ignored, as are the opportunities to substitute new jobs in new industries for lost jobs in mature industries.

Using again the example of the automotive sector, the obvious industry to be developed quickly is the manufacture and programming of robots. Automotive robots are expected to constitute a $100 million market in 1981, and the market will double in a very short time.[10] Yet, evidence shows that U.S. firms are not able to meet the domestic market; as a result, foreign competitors, such as Japan and Sweden, will offer stiff competition. Although foreign firms may establish plants in the United States, which would be desirable, it would be even more desirable for U.S. shareholders to receive a portion of the benefits of robot production.

DEVELOPING SECTORAL STRATEGIES

A sectoral approach demands a new process. To receive the most from economic opportunities associated with changing domestic and world markets, business, government, and labor must jointly identify and strengthen the competitive edge of U.S. firms in key sectors. Not only must the nature of the relationships between business and government, and between labor and management, change, but also the relationships between management and management must change. More candid, more forward-looking communications will be essential if market targets are to be established, resources efficiently allocated, and interindustry frictions reduced in the interest of greater productivity throughout the economy.

Using the automotive sector example, there is a revolution occurring in the autoparts industries; leading firms are opting to produce high-technology components (such as autoelectronics) as well as traditional engine and suspension components. Auto manufacturers, at least for the present, perceive greater economies in buying rather than producing these parts. Historically, however, relationships between parts suppliers and manufacturers have not always been smooth; contracts have been short, and suppliers have not been given what they considered sufficient information for advance planning. Now, suppliers report that they are able to sign three-year contracts, which assists them in their resource planning. Some are skeptical, however, that when manufacturers' profits improve, their willingness to outline production plans three years into the future will decline.

Changes in labor management relationships have already occurred in some major industries. Auto unions and others have foregone promised increases in wages in the interest of improving profits and attracting new capital to their employer firms. There is a willingness on the part of many labor leaders to modify American unionism's traditional adversarial attitude toward management, symbolized by the President of the United Auto Workers Douglas Fraser, taking a seat on the Board of Directors of the Chrysler Corporation. On the plant floor, there are more frequent efforts to bring workers into the decisionmaking process, through quality circles and other mechanisms.

These trends are not widespread and are not universally welcomed by either labor or management. There remains a traditional and pervasive antagonism, just as there remains a traditional and pervasive distrust of big business on the part of many individual citizens. Yet, although in 1979 it was considered outrageous to suggest that American enterprises could profit by emulating the practices of Japanese, German, or Swedish firms in developing mutuality of interests, in the 1980s this option is regularly discussed in the media.

To accomplish the recommended change in direction, the first step is to identify the sectors to receive policy priority. Their selection is a political, as well as an economic, process.

Leadership need not—and should not—come from the federal government, in every sector, although it is the one institution that has access to all the data needed to analyze and forecast market conditions and resource availability. The government should act as resource agency and mediator. It should not take the role of definitive planner.

The basic process required within each sector is for business and labor leadership and government to come together using a new form of collective bargaining. In the bargaining process, each party would commit itself to reducing costs and increasing efficiency. Government policies and programs would be conceived and implemented in relation to the extent of commitment on the part of labor and management. There would be no "bailouts," because government's partnership position would be negotiated in exchange for an economic return: more jobs, more taxes, a share of the profits, or some other benefit. The overall objective in all industries would be to reduce costs, increase efficiency, and position the industry for long-term market penetration rather than short-term profits.

How this general strategy is worked out will depend on the industry and the quality of its leaders. There is no single model to emulate. The importation of the Japanese Keidanren or the German Quality Circles is not proposed here, although no doubt much could be learned from each. On the contrary, the model must be inherently American—that is, the collective bargaining mode. Americans would not tolerate a paternalistic institution such as inspires the Japanese, no matter how beneficial the results might appear. They also would not tolerate an authoritarian system, no matter how brisk and efficient it may appear. The collective bargaining tradition of hard-fisted, tough-minded assertion of rights, goals, and intentions is not antithetical to cooperation; it merely sets the boundaries within which agreement must be reached.

Government, on its own, needs to take some particular steps to improve its stance vis-à-vis industries and sectors. All new legislation should be reviewed to determine differential impacts on specific industries and in specific places. Scenarios should be drafted to anticipate the probable magnitudes and directions of change in affected industries and sectors, both with and without the proposed law.

To accomplish this goal, government is but one of three equal partners. A consultative system with the private sector for each sector is needed. The suggested vehicle for this system is industry production committees composed equally of business, labor, and governmental representatives. The committees would highlight problems and opportunities far enough in advance to take appropriate action. The concept has its roots in the new nationalism of Teddy Roosevelt, followed by the National Recovery Administration (NRA) (but without NRA's powers over prices, wages, and profits), and later by the World War II production boards.[11] Such a public-private partnership is far more feasible today because telecommunications make it possible for the different actors to communicate with one another easily.

There is no promise that sectoral growth strategies will benefit all communities equally. Nor is there a promise that they will support all places at the same level as did past policies. Some communities that in the past were relatively well off may benefit from sectoral strategies. Some past federal subsidies might be diverted from communities that have a long history of impoverishment. But by creating more job opportunities in new industries and expanding job opportunities in the service industry, sectoral strategies will support full-employment goals. The preparation of a skilled labor force needed to fill the new jobs, and assistance for workers to find and secure those jobs, will be an integral element of the sectoral approach.

Because of their particular mix of economic resources, some communities may grow as particular industries find them suitable for expansion or new start-ups. There is a limit to the reasonable cost of trying to create similar attractions in other communities. Yet, if this is not attempted at all, the alternative is impractical: to move hundreds of thousands of people, most of whom may not wish to relocate, to places of economic growth that may not wish to accept them and would then be faced with the problems associated with too-rapid growth.

CONCLUSION

Structural economic change—which has a devastating effect on cities with large concentrations of residents employed in the industries undergoing structural change—is beyond the reach of municipal or state governments. It responds to international and national economic forces, and to local differentials in resource availability (over which government has very little control). It follows, therefore, that a different approach to dealing with structural change and its impact on cities is required.

The usual macroeconomic policy choices are monetary, fiscal, and incomes policies. The usual choices have left the nation with an unemployment rate that has not dropped below 7 percent in five years and with the highest inflation record of any advanced industrial nation.

One reason usual choices do not work is that they ignore the differential impact of macropolicies on major industries and sectors of the economy. These effects, distributed to places according to the relative concentration of affected industries, are among the causes of urban problems. To deal with urban economic decline, it is necessary to first deal with sectoral problems and the effect of national policies on sectoral competitive advantages in the world market context.

Sectors, or interdependent chains of linked industries, are the proper targets of economic policies. Strategies that make it possible for all firms in those sectors to compete on equal terms with the same benefits from government would enhance urban economic development goals. They would prevent special benefits from flowing to the least efficient firms in a sector, as has happened time and again under previous economic development programs. The Chrysler bailout, the huge loan to Wisconsin Steel (a firm that subsequently declared bankruptcy), would not be permitted under a sectoral strategy, because every firm that took advantage of the taxpayers' subsidies would offer something greater in exchange than the mere promise to repay the loan. In other words, investments of taxpayers' dollars would be treated as an investment of private dollars: the public would look for tangible and competitive returns.

All sectoral strategies would not be equivalent, however. Some sectors are declining and need to retrench with minimum dislocation. Others are stagnant and need to improve efficiency and to expand markets. Others are growing and need to control costs and to ensure market share.

Major industries on which the nation's phenomenal economic performance formerly depended are facing radically different competitive conditions, while, at the same time, new industries are promising growth potential and new job opportunities in new occupations. It is clear that direct efforts to strengthen specific industries could possibly do far more for the places in which they are concentrated, or in which they might locate, than traditional approaches have been able to.

NOTES AND REFERENCES

1. The 30-percent figure is estimated by the author on the basis of *Ward's Automotive Report* and other trade association data. The U.S. Department of Commerce reports in unpublished data that U.S. car sales in 1981 were 6,400,000 units down a mere 3 percent from low-sales record of 6,600,000 units during the 1980s. Truck and bus sales in the United States in 1981 were 2,300,000 units, of which 1,750,000 were domestically

produced. Domestic truck and bus production was down 32.6 percent from 1980. For both passenger cars and trucks and buses, sales have dropped while imports have risen, yielding a rapidly rising import penetration rate. In 1981, imports of cars were 26.5 percent of domestic sales and imports of trucks and buses were 19.5 percent of total domestic sales. In both cases, import penetration is felt most strongly in the smaller vehicles. 1981 was the worst of the last three years, all of which were dismal for U.S. producers. For trends, see U.S. Department of Commerce, *U.S. Industrial Outlook, 1981*, Washington, D.C.: U.S. Government Printing Office, 1981, pp. 316–323.

2. Domestic shipments in 1981 are estimated by the U.S. Department of Commerce (unpublished data) at 89 million tons, up slightly from 1980 figures. However, shipments at the end of the third quarter were 68.9 million tons. Commerce Department data on apparent domestic steel consumption for 1981 was 81.2 million tons, and imports were 17.9 percent of this total. But the American Iron and Steel Institute, to support its lobbying for barriers to imports, placed the import penetration rate at 25 percent. Thus, import penetration was somewhat less in 1981 than in 1980 and 1979. Nevertheless, in a world market in which both advanced industrial nations and developing nations are determined to produce steel, the United States faces dwindling markets and stiff competition, necessitating reorganization of the entire domestic industry. See Gail Garfield Schwartz and Pat Choate, *Being Number One: Rebuilding the U.S. Economy*, Lexington, Mass.: Lexington Books, D.C. Heath, 1980, pp. 50, 80–83, 95–98.
3. Richard Buxbaum, *Appendix A to Stimulating the Economy of the Great Lakes States*, Columbus, Ohio: The Academy for Contemporary Problems, December 1977, p. 6.
4. There is no Standard Industrial Classification Code for Motor Vehicle Parts. Components like pistons, rings, valves, starters, etc., are distributed among several machinery industries and electronic industries. The figures in the paragraph are derived from trade associations and corporations themselves, as reported in Arthur D. Little, *The Changing World Automotive Industry Through 2000*, Cambridge, Mass.: A.D. Little, Inc., January 1980; and *Business Week*, June 15, 1981, pp. 114c-d.
5. U.S. Department of Transportation, *A Transportation Agenda for the 1980s*, Washington, D.C.: U.S. Government Printing Office, 1981, p. 7.
6. Arthur Andersen and Company, February 1981, as reported in *Business Week, op. cit.*, p. 114c.
7. Industry and Trade Administration, U.S. Department of Commerce, *U.S. Industrail Outlook with Projections to 1983 for 200 Industries*, Washington, D.C., 1979, p. 175.
8. In 1974, the last year in which a comprehensive study was undertaken, the figure was $75 billion. Joint Economic Committee of the Congress, *Federal Subsidy Programs*, Washington, D.C.: U.S. Government Printing Office, 1974. In 1980, federal investment tax credits were $16 billion. Deductions for manpower training were $15 billion.
9. A $1 increase in labor hourly wages justifies the purchase of 1,000 robots, according to the Chairman of General Motors (*The New York Times*, Nov. 15, 1981, p. E3). The payback period for an industrial robot on a two-shift per day basis is 1.28 years, but robots can work three shifts a day for eight years (Joseph F. Engelberger, *Robots in Practice*, AMACOM, 1980, p. 12).
10. *The New York Times*, Nov. 15, 1981, p. F9.
11. See Arthur Schlesinger, Jr. *The Coming of the New Deal: The Age of Roosevelt*, Boston: Houghton, Mifflin, Chapter 6.

Part III

Looking Ahead: National Urban Policy Conflict, Consensus, and Choice

Chapter XI

NATIONAL URBAN POLICY IN AN AGE OF ECONOMIC AUSTERITY

Norman J. Glickman

INTRODUCTION

This chapter presents some notions about the future of national urban policy. There are two basic objects: first, to provide an overview of what may be the *context* in which urban and social policymaking will take place, and second, to outline some *policy responses* to the conditions in which we will likely live during the next decade. As noted in Chapter VIII, the next 10 to 15 years can be viewed as a period of unprecedented challenge to both industrialized and developing countries of the world. This challenge results from dramatic changes in the international division of labor, slower economic growth, structural change (both economic and demographic), inflation, and other economic and social phenomena that occurred in the past two decades.

This period can be called the "age of economic austerity." The term "austerity" is used to mean not only a very slow-growing economic "pie," but also a set of social and political tensions that evolve from the difficulties of societies making decisions about the pie's division among individuals and regions. In what Thurow [110] calls the "zero-sum society" and Barnet [10] refers to as "the lean years," every decision to aid some region or group of people means taking resources from others; when our economies were growing, the nation could afford to "buy off" those hurt by actions taken for the "national interest." This is no longer possible. To provide jobs to workers in the Mezzogiorno, employment opportunities in Milan will likely be reduced.

Efforts to legislate fiscal relief for New York City have involved interregional political battles. The fight over resources also involves counterdemands by workers and employers over the division of production activity. Although this is not a new phenomenon, it has resulted in new calls by businesses for the relaxation of safety, pollution, and other regulations; aid to spur investment and productivity (in the form of government subsidies and by "speed up" on the production line); and other measures. Workers, on the other hand, resist efforts of firms to reduce real wages, lobby against cuts in social expenditures, and fight against plant closings and "runaway" shops. As high unemployment and severe inflation ("stagflation") continue, these frictions will be exacerbated. The list of issues involving the problem of redistribution of resources within slow growth (or steady state) economies is very long indeed.[1] Unfortunately, democracies are not adept at making redistribution decisions during periods of slow growth.

Slow growth in industrialized nations is related to the increasing internationalization of national economies, where the flows of capital, labor, and goods cross national boundaries and make decisionmaking by national governments more difficult than ever before. National governments have less control over their economies than they would in less interdependent situations. In addition, the amplitudes of national business cycles have increased, and the greater degree of international synchronization of business cycles during the 1970s has made economic stability more difficult to achieve, because cycles are transmitted from nation to nation. Stagflation was with us for most of that decade, and the 1980s have started with low growth as well. No longer is there significant trust in the efficiency of Keynesian demand-management techniques in solving cyclical and long-term growth problems.

As a result of this set of difficult problems, the state is perceived often as being less capable of formulating coherent social and economic policy than during the 1960s. In turn, there have been political actions that have led to the relative reduction of social expenditure programs in the areas of urban development, welfare and income maintenance, infrastructure, and others. This has certainly been true in Great Britain and the United States (see Pascal and Menchik [89] on "fiscal containment" efforts in the United States). Simultaneously, but not independently, there is an increasingly strong set of demands from the business community for a more free-market orientation of our economies and further reductions in redistributive programs. This has resulted, in the past few years, in reductions in the share of social spending relative to other kinds of public and private consumption.

The effects of the reduction in social programs on urban policy will be extensive. In many countries, there has been an ongoing reevaluation of regional policy, in part because of real failures of past policies and in part because of the changing economic and political situation of the 1980s. There is a discernable decline in interest in cities and regions as a focus of policy relative to 10 years ago, especially with regard to interregional redistribution policies.

Some recent trends in the international division of labor, capital mobility, business cycles, and long-term growth, and their relationship to urban and regional development and policy, are summarized in the next section followed by a review of some policies that have been followed in developed countries to manage urban development and assess their present and future applicability. Next are sketched some possible directions for urban policy in future years, given the new "austere" situation in which we are likely to live. This policy prescription is tentative—no "Master Plan" is offered—and departs from traditional urban policy notions of the past. Suggestions for urban policy are linked to domains long considered primarily nonurban: income maintenance, employment creation, industrial, macroeconomic, and other policies. That is, to the extent possible, "people" and "place" elements of policy are connected; on this subject, see Edel [32] and Norton (Chapter VII). The final section contains some suggestions for future research.

This chapter also differs from many previous works in urban policy in that it does not reflect the primarily microeconomic approach to regional development that has characterized this field. In viewing regional change and the location of economic and social activity, we have, I believe, spent too much time on somewhat narrowly defined endeavors in land use, transportation, agglomeration economies, and the like. Although these studies have often served us well, this chapter looks at some more (literally) global issues that have been badly neglected but are of increasing importance in today's world. With the rapidly changing structure of the world economy and the other factors mentioned, the traditional location factors are less important than previously. For example, national business cycles are likely to have more effect on regional change than, say, interregional differences in transportation costs.

Some emphasis is also placed on the nature of a "just" or "good" society. The chapter draws from modern urban political economy and posits a set of ideas that may be controversial and provocative of further work in this field.

STRUCTURAL CHANGE, THE WORLD ECONOMY, AND REGIONAL DEVELOPMENT

In Chapter VIII three phenomena that affect the growth and development of American cities and regions were analyzed: international trade, capital mobility, and business cycles and long-term economic growth. Although these subjects are rarely considered by urban policymakers or analysts, the impact on the development process of trade, capital shifts, and cyclical behavior can be substantial.

International Trade

Several trends in the relationship between the United States and the rest of the world should be noted. First, the level of U.S. international trade has increased dramatically in the past 25 years. There has been a greater degree of interdependence among industrialized nations and between those nations and developing countries.

Second, the composition of trade has changed over time. The nation exports proportionately less manufactured goods and we have increased our proportion of exports in agriculture, agricultural equipment, high technology devices, and financial services. We import relatively more manufactured goods (especially those that result from labor-intensive processes) and oil.

Third, there has been a greater synchronization of our business cycles, with those of our trading partners during the 1970s. Should this trend continue, domestic business cycles could become more severe in the future.

Fourth, the terms of trade between the United States and other countries has deteriorated. This has resulted in the decline of the dollar in international money markets and increasing foreign trade deficits. The nation has had more difficulty maintaining its competitive position with industrialized countries in items such as steel and automobiles and with developing countries in textiles, apparel, and shoes.

Given the rapidly changing world situation, the effects on American cities and regions (including nonmetropolitan areas) were traced in Chapter VIII. Given the decline of sales of heavy manufacturing goods in the international markets (for example, transportation equipment, nonelectrical and electrical machinery, and chemicals), the traditional Industrial Heartland of the Northeast and Midwest will likely have continuing employment problems. Also, the increase of agricultural exports has aided farming areas, especially those specializing in grains; these areas include the rural Midwest and the West. However, some of the large cities that have lost manufacturing jobs over the past 30 years, are gaining service jobs that are related to international trade and the servicing of multinational corporations. These are highly concentrated in the largest metropolitan areas, many in the Northeast. At the same time, investment by foreign nationals in this country has tended to favor the South, particularly for new manufacturing investment. Firms in the Northeast that have been acquired by foreign firms have not benefitted greatly from infusions of modernization funds. Much foreign investment has occurred in areas suffering from high unemployment and low income.

Effects of the Internationalized Economy. In all, there has been a marked shift of production sites of industries requiring low-wage labor in assembly-line settings (for example, textiles, shoes, and semiconductor assembly) from developed to less developed nations through international capital flows. This has been made easier by two technological factors. First, the wide range of communications technology has allowed corporations to decentralize operations nationally and internationally; such technological factors include computers, containerized shipping, jet cargo carriers, and others.

The second set of factors concern innovations that promote the continued standardization of production tasks—that is, the ability to divide production into ever more simple components in an effort to lower labor costs through the "deskilling" of labor and to maintain control over the work force.[2] Therefore, a new international division of labor has been evolving in which production sites and workers are increasingly interchangeable to a given firm. Due to the changing nature of work, a textile worker in Manchester, England, is less distinguishable from one in Lisbon or Singapore than previously, but receives a higher wage. Therefore, the movement of textile plants to low-wage countries has been occurring. As a result of technical developments and the greater importance of multinational corporations (MNCs) in organizing these widely dispersed activities, less developed countries (LDCs) have become sites for factories previously located in developed countries.[3] We now have, what Barnet [10] has called "The Global Factory,"[4] where production can occur in many places. Using an extended metaphor, Barnet says:

> Viewed from space, the Global Factory suggests a human organism. The brain is housed in steel-and-glass slabs located in or near a few crowded cities—New York, London, Frankfort, Zurich, and Tokyo. The blood is capital, and it is pumped through the system by global banks assisted by a few governments. The financial centers New York, London, Frankfort, and Tokyo . . . . function as the heart. The hands are steadily moving to the outer rim of civilization. More and more goods are now made in the poor countries of the southern periphery under direction from the headquarters in the North, and most are destined to be consumed in the industrial

> heartland with the new postindustrial look. . . . A new division of labor is taking place across the planet, and as a consequence the smoke, sweat, and tears that have always accompanied the process of industrialization are shifting to the new production centers of Asia, Africa, and Latin America. [10:239]

This change in the international division of labor reflects significant shifts in comparative advantage and terms of trade among nations, as well as the technological and organizational factors (e.g., MNCs). There have been important political changes too. First, there has been a transformation in the balance of economic and political power within the industrialized world, brought on, in part, by the decline of the American imperium beginning in the 1960s. Simultaneously, with the growing strength of the economies of Japan and the Federal Republic of Germany (largely rebuilt after World War II), an overvalued dollar, and related factors, the United States began to show significant trade-related problems in the 1960s which worsened in the 1970s. It is important to remember another phenomenon within the industrialized world: the relationship between the high-income countries of the Organization for Economic Cooperation and Development (OECD) and the middle-income nations such as Portugal, Greece, Ireland, and Turkey. The latter have played a role similar to some LDCs, serving both as export platforms for foreign firms and as exporters of labor ("guest workers") to their richer neighbors.

Second, there has been the important growth in strength of portions of the developing world; the emergence of OPEC as a powerful force has, of course, been apparent since 1973. In addition to the capital-exporting oil nations, many other countries have industrialized rapidly: the Republic of Korea, Hong Kong, Brazil, and Mexico are among them. On the other hand, many LDCs continue to stagnate, suffering from the burdens of oil price increases and foreign debt; see World Bank [123] for a discussion of this.

The Global Factory has had differential impacts on the various regions of the United States.[5] Although no detailed analysis of the experience of other countries is given here, it is clear from secondary sources, and inferences drawn from them, that uneven impacts are felt in other nations as well. For example, the increased competition in the automobile industry has resulted in plant closings in Coventry, England and elsewhere; Manchester, too, has lost employment to overseas competition from Portugal, for example. Many of the current economic and political struggles within the European community involve trade matters.

The problem for policymakers at the national and regional levels is clear: the flow of capital and merchandise across international borders leaves less leverage for the state to direct and manage the economy.

Planning and policymaking at the national level—as practiced in social democracies—ends at the national frontier. At the corporate level, however, this may not be true, as MNCs are able to organize their resources in space on a global level.

Interregional Capital Shifts

The problem for regional policymakers is made even more difficult because of the frequent movements of capital within national boundaries. Efforts to aid declining regions may be thwarted by private market activity that goes in other directions. With the freedom of capital to move at a rapid rate in a wide variety of directions, the ability to make urban policy is limited, as indicated in the discussion on the international scale. Less well-documented are the more traditional and more frequent movements of capital at the subnational level.

In Chapter VIII, the effects of capital shifts on urban and regional change were demonstrated, drawing heavily from the work of Bluestone and Harrison [20]. First, industrial disinvestment, the result of capital shifts, occurs in several ways. These include the failure to modernize equipment, the removal of skilled personnel and equipment, the reinvestment of profits in other locations, and the closing of the plants. Second, there has been the shifting of capital facilities from older northern plants to newer southern factories or offices. As a result, the capital stock in the South grew twice as fast as that of the Northeast between 1960 and 1976. For every 100 jobs created by new plants in the North, 111 were lost due to plant closings and other kinds of disinvestment. In the South, 80 jobs were lost for every 100 added through new capital investment.

However, among larger manufacturing plants, the South was the most likely among all regions to have a plant closing between 1969 and 1976. Labor-intensive manufacturing that was drawn to the South in the 1950s by the availability of low-wage labor is probably now being relocated in developing countries in the Caribbean and South Asia. It was also shown in Chapter VIII that conglomerate, multinational firms were more likely to relocate than either independently owned or corporate firms as part of a planned strategy to reinvest capital in both other lines of production and in other regions and countries.

The public policy consequences of unfettered capital mobility are twofold. First, at the local level, there are significant social costs in terms of the disruption of communities, high public expenditures for unemployment compensation, earnings losses for workers, and considerable physical and mental stress for the unemployed. The problem relates to the relative speed of movement of capital relative to labor—workers cannot move as fast as capital and often are reluctant to relocate from areas where they have deep family and other ties.

The affected communities cannot often find replacement industries. "Planning for decline," which has been a frequently used term in local communities, is the essence of the "age of economic austerity." Firms tend to play communities against each other to gain tax breaks, greater public services, and the like. Walker [122] has called this "lumpengeography" as firms try to create the spatial equivalent of Marx's "reserve army" in the form of cities bidding against each other for new jobs. Although this term is not completely consistent with Marxian terminology, the image is correct.

The mobility of capital also constrains urban policymaking at the national level. Programs to aid distressed areas, for example, cannot be implemented effectively if the private sector deems such regions "unsuitable" for one reason or another. Although it is argued that "efficiency" dictates that capital remain free to locate wherever profits are highest, the efficiency implied by such arguments does not include the social costs borne by both people and places. The market failure implied by the dislocation attendant to capital shifts must be remedied by public policy. Given the internationalization of capital flows, it will be difficult to formulate appropriate responses under the set of institutions that now exist.

Business Cycles and Long-Term Growth

A third set of forces that make policymaking difficult is the differential responses of regions to national economic growth—both over the course of the business cycle and in the long run. In essence, the issue is the differential "elasticities" of regional economies with respect to the national economy. From a growing literature on the subject, we see the ways in which regions respond to national economic change depend on a wide variety of factors: industrial mix, internal regional secular growth, local labor market conditions, and region size.[6]

Regions differ greatly in their long-term growth patterns.[7] The U.S. northern tier states have suffered relative (and sometimes, absolute) decline, especially in the 1970s. The decades-long migration from South to North has been reversed as has the even longer trend of nonmetropolitan decline (for a review of the migration experience of 20 industrialized nations, see Vining, Pallone, and Yang [121] and Chapter IV). Vernez *et al.* [118] have studied long-term and cyclical change in U.S. regions for the period 1960–75. They show the experience of states and labor market areas with respect to their cyclical responsiveness, timing, and conformity to national cycles as well as their long-term growth characteristics. The northern belt (New England, Middle-Atlantic, East North Central, and West North Central) had a cyclical pattern that conformed closely to the nation and had very low secular growth. The East North Central, which has much durable goods manufacturing, was very responsive to national cycles (that is, it varied greatly). The western and southern regions had fairly low conformity with the national cycles and a varied picture with respect to responsiveness and secular growth.

Independent of national policy, regions have their own characteristic responses with regard to cycles and long-term growth. So, for example, a tax cut to spur investment for the nation would have a very different effect in Phoenix than in Philadelphia; on this subject, see Petersen and Muller [90] and Chapter VIII. Efforts at broad-scale macroeconomic policy would therefore have very mixed effects across regions. Again, given the discussion of the international transmission of business cycles above, the degree to which national governments can control national cycles and provide effective countercyclical aid to regions is questionable.

A Summing Up

This section has raised some questions for analysts and policymakers about the nature of some problems facing them in the future. Given the increasing internationalization of national economies, rapid and frequent capital shifts, business cycles, and long-term economic growth patterns, the ability to influence events in individual regions and the national system of regions is more limited than often believed. The power of the private market is very strong compared to that of the state. Given this, what can be done? Can policies be devised to aid cities and regions in need of positive intervention? What might these policies be like? Answers to these questions are given later. First, it is important to summarize the experience of social democracies in formulating national urban policy to date.

EXPERIENCES WITH NATIONAL URBAN POLICY

National urban policies have been attempted in one form or another in nearly all industrialized nations and much has been written on the subject.[8] Some of the major goals and strategies of some major industrial nations, with particular emphasis on the United States, are briefly outlined here.

Goals and Strategies

The major phenomenon confronting countries has been "uneven spatial development" (see Walker [122]). That is, there have been lagging regions, such as the Mezzogiorno (southern Italy), the Midi (southern France), Wales, Appalachia, and Kyushu (southwestern Japan), that have been the object of development policies. On the other hand, there have been regions deemed overdeveloped that were the subject of decentralization policies: the Paris Basin, Tokkaido Megalopolis, and the Rhine Valley. Therefore, various strategies were devised to bring better balance to national multiregion systems.

Four principal objects of national urban policies have been: (1) aid to distressed regions, (2) reduction of interregional income inequalities, (3) greater economywide efficiency through the reduction of structural unemployment in backward areas (for example, those regions with declining agriculture or mining sectors), and (4) reducing high concentrations of population in major metropolitan areas.

The major strategies adopted included growth poles; the French *métropoles d'équilibre* and the Japanese "New Industrial Cities" and "Special Areas," for example, aimed at generating further development around them and lessening the concentration in larger metropolises. Richardson [95] has written extensively on this subject. A second strategy involved the decentralization of public investment away from the core cities and regions. As demonstrated in the case of Japan [39], governmental rhetoric often runs well ahead of action. Despite pronouncements of the intent to spur decentralization in the mid-1950s, public investment continued to be concentrated in the Tokkaido Megalopolis until the early 1970s. A similar argument has been made by Prud'homme [92] about France. Given the relatively small budgets of planning agencies (such as France's DATAR), the ability to provide large amounts of public infrastructure in remote areas is limited as well.

A third strategy was to restrict activity in highly built-up areas; OECD [83] provides an overview of the policies followed in several countries. For example, the United Kingdom has been using a system of Industrial Development Certificates (IDC) since 1948; IDCs are required for industrial development outside of designated "development areas." In Italy, where the growth of the South (Mezzogiorno) has been the major object of national policy, firms must apply to CIPE before making new investments; the object of the legislation is to limit capital investment in congested areas and to aid the South. In the Netherlands, attempts to restrict development in the Randstad include higher taxes for investment in large buildings, building licences, and compulsory notification of intention to build.

Fourth, there have been a set of financial incentives, particularly to encourage manufacturing relocation. According to OECD [88] the most frequent financial incentives are investment grants, loan guarantees, the provision of land and sites, manpower training, direct loans (both subsidized and market rate types), aids to manpower mobility, and other fiscal concessions (e.g., tax abatements).

A Brief Evaluation

Clearly, the orientation in these countries is largely toward a "place" conception in urban development policy, rather than a "people" one. Attempts have been made to target limited development funds to certain distressed areas, while the retrictive policies are more often used to slow the development of highly concentrated regions. Often, however, the attempts at targeting are lost in the political arena, as legislators in non-aided areas attempt to attract funds for their constituencies. Therefore, the original eight French *métropoles* were superseded by a very large number of small- and medium-sized centers; in Japan, the process of concentrating resources on a relatively small number of regions was thwarted by the political process, as the number of regions receiving aid was increased. In the United States, attempts to highly target urban programs, such as Model Cities, the Community Development Block Grant (CDBG) and Urban Development Action Grants (UDAG), have not been as successful as many would like. In the cases of all of these countries, extensions of aid to more and more cities and regions have occurred, therefore watering down the already small budgets for development aid. There simply has not been enough money to finance adequately so many areas.

A second problem with regional policy has been the relative lack of power of governmental efforts relative to the power of the market. This, of course, is the major theme of this chapter. In the efforts cited, there is little that the state can do to encourage production in an area that has been abandoned by the private market. Effects to "lead" the market by providing infrastructure, tax incentives and other devices are more often than not mere subsidies for capitalists who would have located in a given region anyway; on this subject, see Bluestone and Harrison [20] and Harrison and Kanter [46].

Third, there have been few attempts (or, at least, not very successful ones) to reorient the location of the service sector, although much of this sector has been mechanized and decentralized [23]. Given the primacy of this sector in most advanced economies, there seems to be room for innovative planning activity. However, the nature of services' location factors make the control of the service sector difficult. For example, efforts to control office building in Paris, Tokyo, and London have not been very effective in stemming speculative building in those cities.

Fourth, there has been little success in integrating people-oriented programs with the place policies that have formed the core of national urban policies. In most countries, income transfers and other social programs are large relative to strictly urban expenditures. Effective attempts to coordinate urban programs with a larger set of social policies (e.g., employment, industrial, health, and welfare) are not obvious in many countries. Of course, the integration of urban programs with monetary and fiscal policy has been even more difficult to achieve, despite evidence of the important impacts of these latter policies on cities and regions. Much of the problem can be attributed to bureaucratic fragmentation and much to serving urban lobby groups. However, a conceptual gap exists in policymaking circles that explains part of the problem: the inability to integrate these sides of the same (or similar) social issues involving people and places in distress.

Case Study: The United States

The history of U.S. urban policy is somewhat different than that of most other developed countries. It was not until 1978 that the nation formulated a "national urban policy," although there were efforts to aid cities before that time. In fact, U.S. urban policy has long been an amalgam of often conflicting policies at the federal and other government levels. Much of the urban policy has as its background the War on Poverty, begun (although never effectively waged) by the federal government, beginning in the 1960s. Much of the increase in social spending that occurred in the late 1960s and early 1970s created institutions and programs that helped people and places, although the latter was emphasized; an example of a "place" policy was the Model Cities program, later abandoned, that originally tried to target funds to poor communities.

Another element in U.S. national urban policy was the set of revenue sharing programs established under President Richard Nixon's "New Federalism" banner: the general revenue sharing and the CDBG programs are examples of policies that distribute federal funds to localities largely "without strings" for spending according to local needs.

A third part of the urban policy picture came in the form of a wide variety of programs from several U.S. departments: food stamps (Agriculture), income maintenance programs and health programs (Health and Human Services), mass transit and highway building (Transportation), and many others. Therefore, in viewing U.S. national urban policy, one must take into account a wide range of programs in different agencies. In addition, the federal system of government also requires an examination of state and local programs to understand fully urban policy.

The Urban and Regional Policy Group [115] and the U.S. Department of Housing and Urban Development [113] collectively reported on the first attempt at a formal national urban policy (NUP). After more than a year of deliberation among federal agencies and with the public, President Jimmy Carter announced the policy in March, 1978.[9]

First, the policy called for extensive cooperation between the public and private sectors in order to rebuild the cities that, many believe, have been long abandoned by capital. Second, the policy had a significant (although, not exclusive) place orientation. Third, the NUP provided relatively little new money to implement its programs—about $2.5 billion.[10] Fourth, the policy emphasized the streamlining of many existing programs, the involvement of states and localities, and a set of Presidential Executive Orders that, whether effective or not, would not appear as budgetary commitments. Among the Executive Orders was one requiring "urban and community impact analysis" of proposed new federal programs; for a compendium of papers on this subject see Glickman [43].

Independent of the specific recommendations of the NUP,[11] the policy was not implemented successfully. Many of the key programs were never enacted, in part due to poor legislative relations and bill drafting, but also because of the resistance of the Congress to much of the package. In austere times, Congress tends to look carefully at new social programs. Although a National Consumer Cooperative Bank, loan guarantees to New York City, and funds for urban parks, education and mass transit were approved, many of the NUP's major elements were rejected. Among the programs never approved were the National Development Bank (which was to provide financial assistance for firms located in distressed areas) and the supplemental fiscal assistance program for countercyclical aid to cities.

However, there are matters related to the NUP that are more important than the rationale for the package or its implementation. As I noted above, the national urban policy for the United States or any other country must be viewed within the context of other social programs. Aid to cities may be increased, but this will not give relief to many urban dwellers if other programs are cut or abolished. For example, if welfare payments do not keep pace with inflation, then those receiving such aid will be worse off;[12] if transit funds are reduced at the same time housing funds are raised, what is the net benefit to cities?

In order to view the total social and urban spending picture, a set of broad-based social programs are defined and their trends are calculated over time. Although, of course, this or any other set of programs is defined somewhat arbitrarily, those selected are related most closely to urban life and to the urban poor: (1) commerce and housing credit; (2) transportation; (3) community and regional development; (4) education, training, employment, and social services; (5) health; (6) income security; and (7) general purpose fiscal assistance. These U.S. budgetary categories represent a wide variety of activities that may be called (for simplicity) "social and urban" spending.[13]

This time series is plotted in two forms in Figure XI.1. The solid line represents the real percent change in this group from fiscal year (FY) 1973 to FY 1981. The trend after FY 1975 is downward, with negative real percent changes registered in FY 1979 and FY 1981.[14] The dashed line represents the changes in the total "social and urban" figure after subtracting intergenerational transfers in the form of social security payments and federal employee retirement funds. This leaves the current set of social and urban spending programs that are not intergenerational transfers but also not strictly tried to cost of living adjustments as is Social Security. The two time series yield quite similar patterns, except that the decline in social spending on the "net" basis is even more precipitous.

The overall conclusion to be drawn from Figure XI.1 is one of the social austerity which has been occurring in the late 1970s and is projected for the early 1980s. Figure XI.2, which measures "social and urban" spending as a percent of total federal outlays, shows a similar picture: increases in the share going to social programs until the mid-1970s, followed by a decline (or, at minimum, a leveling off) in the second half of the decade.

To refine further the measure of "urban" spending, the work of Goldsmith and Derian [44], who attempted to measure more strictly "urban" expenditures by examining detailed line items in the U.S. Budget Appendix, has been revised and updated. Once again, the Goldsmith and Derian definition of what is "urban" is as arbitrary as my revisions.[15]

Figures XI.3 and XI.4 give parallel information to that provided for the broader definitions of "social and urban" spending presented in Figures XI.1 and XI.2. There has been a dramatic decline in the growth rate of "urban" expenditures after 1978, the year of the announcement of the national urban policy (Figure XI.3) and a fall in urban spending as a percentage of federal outlays (Figure XI.4).

With the announcement of the first national urban policy, we witnessed *declines* in spending on urban programs. While spending alone will not bring about a better urban life, those who dismiss social spending as "throwing money at problems" are also incorrect; the decline in such programs has had serious effects on urban fiscal and social conditions. At a time when unemployment is rising in cities, especially among

Figure XI.1. Percent Change in Real Social and Urban Outlays FY1973–FY1981

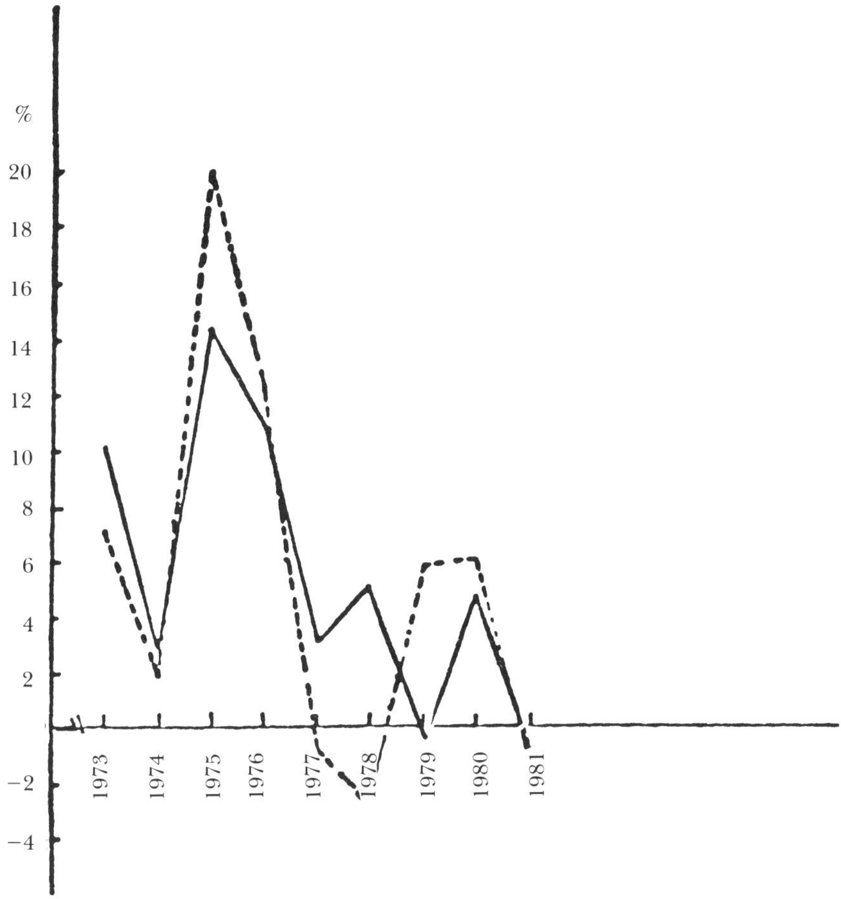

KEY:
—— Percent Change in Real Total Social and Urban Outlays
------ Percent Change in Real Social and Urban Outlays Net of Retirement Programs

minorities and youth, when the fiscal problems of New York are spreading to other cities (including some industrial suburbs), when the physical infrastructure is decaying and the role and security of cities in our future society is unclear given the factors discussed earlier, the national role in urban development is being reduced. Given this situation, it seems that a new way of thinking about urban and social policy must be put forward. A "new" NUP model must take into consideration the instability of econ-

Figure XI.2. Social and Urban Outlays and a Percent of Federal Outlays

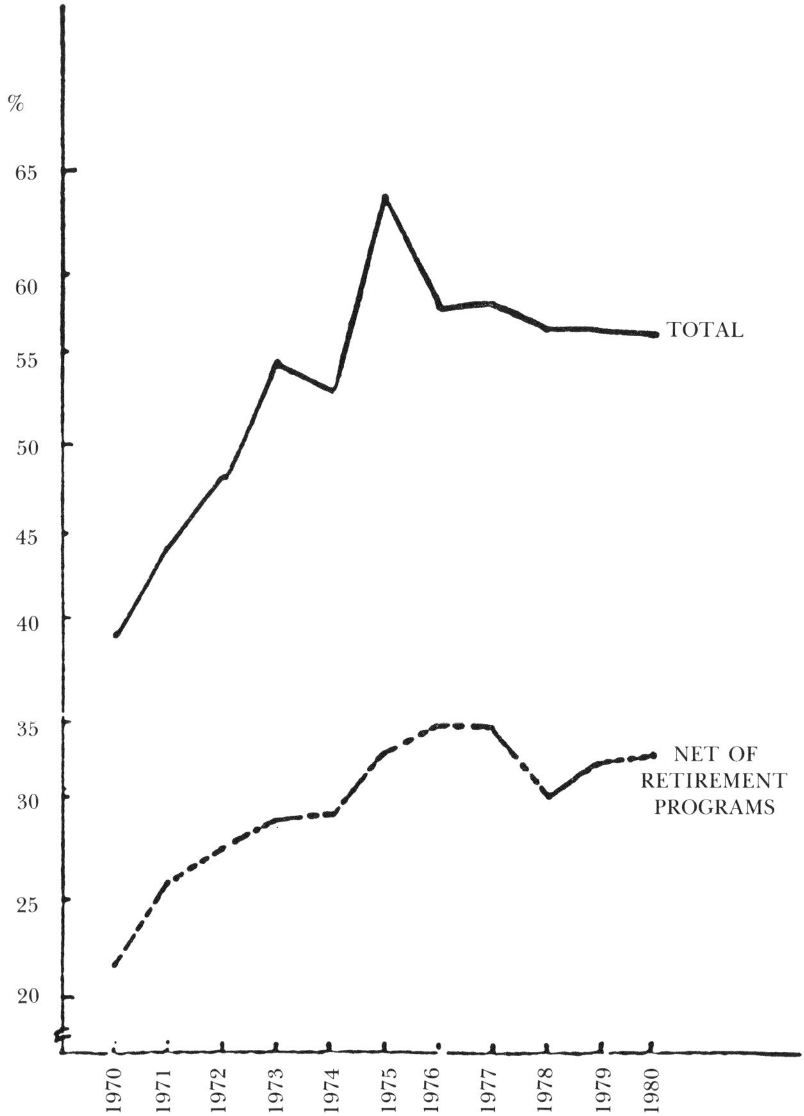

Figure XI.3. Percent Change in Real Urban Outlays FY1973–FY1981

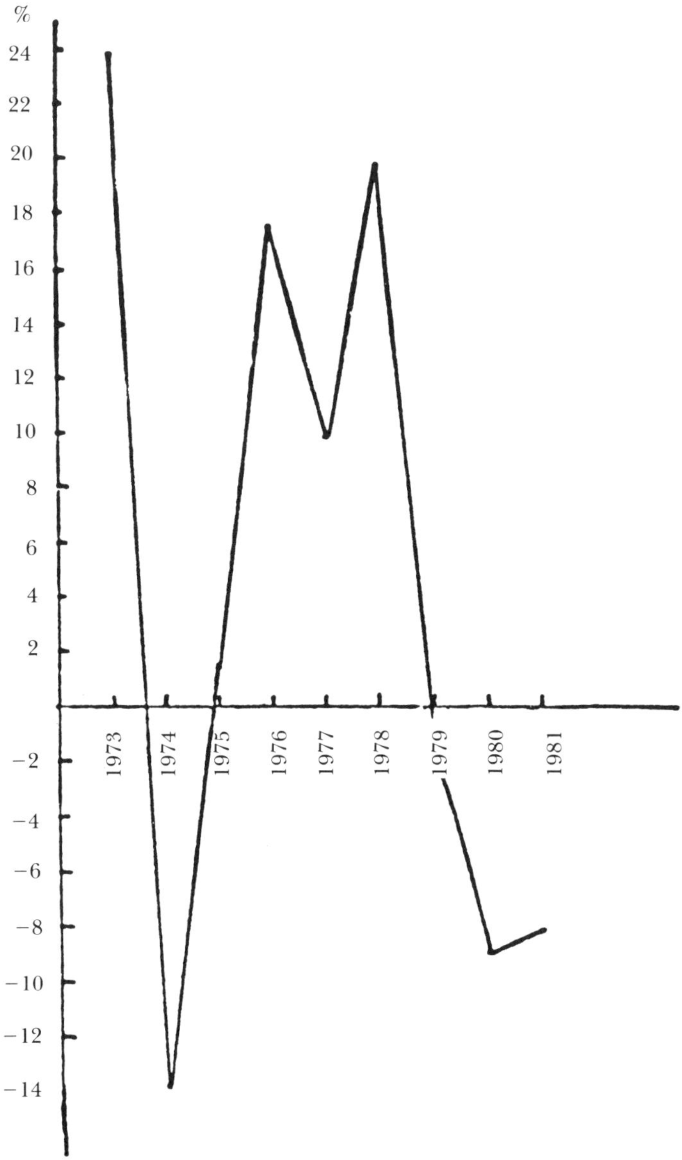

Figure XI.4. Urban Outlays as a Percent of Total Federal Outlays

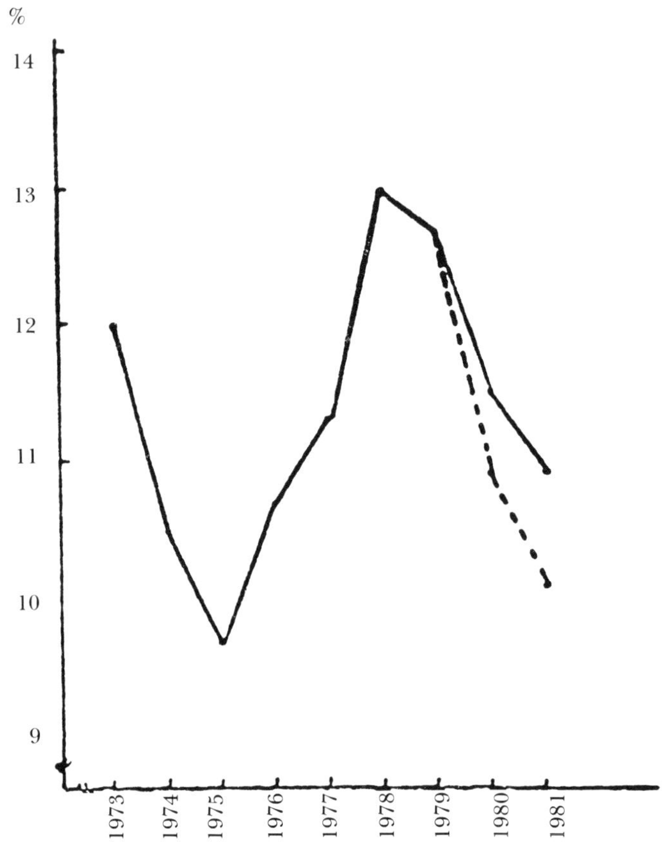

KEY:

—— Original Budget

------ Revised 1980 and 1980 Budgets

omies, the economic and political austerity, and the uneven success of previous urban policy efforts in many countries.

In a real sense, urban policy has been wrong-headed—it has attacked the symptoms of the urban malaise rather than root causes. And it has done so with so little social and urban spending that a "failure of policy" was guaranteed. A truly comprehensive policy would look at cities and their people in a more coherent manner and be placed within the context of our society's changing nature. To do so requires an understanding of the workings of capitalism and the restructing of it that is needed in the future.

AUSTERITY AND THE NEED FOR A NEW NATIONAL URBAN POLICY FRAMEWORK

A new set of parameters facing policymakers at both the national and regional level have been outlined. The increasing internationalization of trade and capital mobility have contributed to the slowdown in economic growth and inflationary trends in many industrialized nations. There have been political and economic power shifts between the North and South and within the developed world. We now see a set of declining industries and regions and, with them, cries for special aid and protection.

According to most forecasts of the next 10 years, the stagflation of the late 1970s will continue. Therefore, many industrialized nations will have a very slowly growing "pie" in the future. In addition, if the deep recessions that occurred in the 1970s linger long into the 1980s (and if the cycles are synchronized internationally), then the pie may be more like a collapsing soufflé, subject to alternate booms and collapse, as Heilbroner [51] has argued persuasively.

The major attempts to deal with the macroeconomic problems facing our economies have been through demand management techniques, which have not worked very well. The battle against inflation has been fought largely by increasing unemployment, as the 1980 policy-induced U.S. recession exemplifies. As Bosworth points out, "the fundamental problem for economic policy was that control of demand did not translate in a simple and direct way into control of inflation" [22:38]. In part because of external shocks, especially in oil and food prices, and, in part, because of sticky industrial prices, Keynesian demand-management techniques have become relatively ineffective. General demand has not been responsible for our inflation, much of which is due to price rises in particular sectors (oil, food, etc.). To reduce overall inflation would require very large declines in prices in other sectors or extremely high unemployment. The United States opted for the latter. Attempts to reduce inflation by creating idle capacity and unemployment has further exacerbated the low growth of productivity and produced more inflation, according to Thurow [110]. The attendant social costs of high unemployment are a very high price to pay for such a limited impact on inflation.

Case Study: Industrial and Regional Decline

Many of the regional problems of the 1970s have at least part of their origin in the internationalization of capital and capital shifts. An example is the auto complex and the Industrial Heartland.

Combining employment loss in key industries and the effects of the 1980 recession, the midwestern states have suffered massive unemployment during recent times. According to the U.S. Department of Transportation, automobile production has fallen rapidly and has had a dramatic differential impact on a few states. There were about 910,000 workers employed directly in the auto industry in 1979 and an additional 1.4 million employed by direct suppliers. The total of 2.3 million workers represents about 11 percent of all manufacturing workers in the country, without including indirect and induced employment connected with the industry. Because of the increased competition from abroad and the inability of the U.S. auto industry to anticipate the demand for smaller cars, there has been a precipitous decline in employment in the industry: about 300,000 workers have been laid off, many of them permanently. The impact of these layoffs has been felt most directly in a few states: Michigan, Ohio, Indiana, Illinois, and New York. Unemployment in Detroit and other auto-dependent cities was at 20 percent in mid-1980.

But the situation for the Industrial Heartland is even worse than these figures imply. The requirement to redesign cars, as well as the decline in domestic sales, has caused large numbers of layoffs in two related industries—steel and rubber. The steel industry has had many problems, some independent of its linkages with the auto industry, particularly with regard to its unwillingness to modernize over the past 20 years. As a result, European and Japanese steel firms have captured a large portion of the U.S. steel market. However, the energy-saving requirement that lighter automobiles be built (and, therefore, use less steel) has meant that the demand for steel has fallen even more sharply, especially among plants with older, open-hearth furnaces. Most of these older mills are located in the Midwest and Northeast as well; Michigan, Illinois, Indiana, Ohio, and Pennsylvania are the main states with open-hearth furnaces. Sheet steel mills, which produce most of the steel for the auto industry, are located in many of the same states.

Were that not enough, the tire industry is also in serious trouble, again because of foreign competition (U.S. tiremakers did not anticipate the increased demand for radial tires while foreign firms produced radials). As a result, plants were closed in a number of states, including Ohio, Michigan, California, and Pennsylvania. Although the spatial concentration of tires is not as great as that of autos and steel, the impact on the older Industrial Belt is evident.[16]

The Importance of Integrating Sectoral and Regional Analysis

This case study is presented because it highlights a number of important general issues relating to the future of industrialized economies and to regional policy: the importance of integrating regional and sectoral analysis. First is the issue of declining regions that have large proportions of old and declining industries. Clearly, the decline in the Midwest of the auto and related sectors, has had secondary effects on workers in other industries and in the public sector. Second, there is the policy question of what to do about these industries and their workers. Can disinvestment be undertaken in what the Japanese call declining "sunset" industries and a smooth transition be made to more promising "sunrise" industries? "Reindustrialization" and "positive adaptation" are terms that we see often these days, referring to the restructing of our economies to changing economic conditions (see, for example, [26], Schwartz and Choate [103], OECD [78, 87], Massey [74], and others for discussions of these concepts). Furthermore, what will be the role of retraining, relocation, and reemployment of workers displaced during the transition period?

Third, and related, is the issue of protectionism; in all three industries discussed here, tariff and nontariff barriers have been requested and granted. Will protectionist policies be followed, given growing sentiment for such programs? Protectionism could have catastrophic global consequences, as the 1920s and 1930s have shown.

Fourth is the internationalization and sectoral diversification of these industries. Automobile manufacturing, in particular, has taken on an increasing international flavor. U.S. firms have set up production facilities in a number of countries (as have other car producers, such as Volkswagen), and undertaken joint production ventures with foreign automakers in order to take advantage of lower wages, to escape unionism, and to penetrate foreign markets. One-fourth of Chrysler's cars are imported from Japan, and that company is using part of the proceeds from its recent "bail out" to build a large plant in Mexico. This is interesting in light of Chrysler's demands for import reductions of foreign autos. Ford, has retrenched greatly in the nation in order to pursue its strategy of building a "world car." In steel, investments of retained earnings have been made in other sectors, rather than in the badly needed modernization of the steel industry itself. Therefore, to what extent can policy be adjusted to the realities of increased international trade and greater importance of MNCs?

Fifth, the auto case represents an example of the problems of redistributive policy in a slow-growth economy. Should the state be called on to "bail out" a declining and badly managed firm with the scarce resources at its disposal? If aid is forthcoming, what sort of *quid pro quo* should be demanded by the electorate. For example, in return for loans or grants to the automobile industry, should the government receive equity in the corporations? Should it demand a reorientation of the industry in terms of its product mix (for example, more mass transit production), environmental quality (more fuel efficient, less polluting cars), and related issues? In addition, what should the new relationship be between the state and the workers in the industry; between the workers and the companies?

Sixth, what general societal tensions are created by sectoral and regional decline? The auto companies want protection from foreign imports, contrary to the professed free-trade policy of the United States. If protection is given, will there be retaliation by other countries? If so, what will happen to American farmers if additional trade barriers are placed on U.S. agricultural products? Implicitly, should farmers subsidize auto workers? Or, more generally, should consumers pay higher prices for autos to protect a failing industry? What should be done for the regions that are heavily dependent on declining industries? With rising unemployment, what is the impact on minorities, youth, women, and foreign workers? In effect, what are the opportunity costs of subsidization?

Since it is likely that the restructuring necessary to create a better economic environment will create pressure for aid to other industries in all developed countries, we must be able to respond in a rational manner. In order to do so, the nation must increase productivity, devise compensation schemes for the "losers," rebuild our cities, and find ways to finance these programs. Therefore, we must invent new institutions and think very differently about future urban policy within the context of overall social policy.

The Nature of a New Social Contract

Given the situation in which we find ourselves, it is clear that a new set of institutions must be established to undertake a set of difficult tasks—to reorganize and rationalize industry, to increase productivity, to rejuvenate and aid distressed cities and regions, and to find compensation mechanisms for people and places that will be disrupted and dislocated by the changes that occur. This will be difficult, and the institutions to be established must, in a real sense, be representative of all major interest groups. The nation needs a new "social contract" in order to carry this out.

A broad-based, democratic restructuring of the economy is in order to solve some of our major economic problems. In the past, the capitalist system has undergone major restructurings (in the 1840s, 1890s, and 1930s, for instance) after which new institutions emerged. It is probably time for a new reordering of our economy. The proposals advanced herein differ sharply from those evolving from corporate groups and their media representatives [26], which look to a corporation-dominated system. The view here is that such action would be undemocratic and would not change many of our fundamental economic problems. Certain key institutions with sound governing principles must be established. These institutions (and the accompanying programs) should aid in the reordering of our society that must be done.

There has been discussion about so-called "tripartite committees," consisting of representative of labor, business, and government, that could be formed to play a major role in industrial restructuring and other functions. This is probably a good idea, but tripartite committees (TCs) must be sufficiently broad based to include many previously excluded from high-level decisionmaking: minorities, the poor, and others. On the other hand, such groups must not be so large as to be unwieldy. TCs must operate at the national, regional, and community levels, depending on the particular job at hand. There should be an agreed set of governing principles in the form of a social contract among the parties and, implicitly, for the society as a whole. It is recommended that the following principles be adopted at the national level.

1. *The establishment of economic democracy;*
2. *A commitment to full employment;*
3. *The rejuvenation of communities;* and
4. *Equity in the public and private sectors.*

The principle of *economic democracy* is probably the most important and controversial. It is ingrained in our ideology, though not our practice. To achieve true economic democracy, the redistribution of economic power (and with it, political power) within society must be attained. At present, control of the economic structure, capital, and, through this, the workplace is highly concentrated.[17] Most workers do not have any important share of ownership of capital (except for their pension funds) or the means of production and, therefore, their working conditions are controlled by others. A movement toward economic democracy would give the majority a stake in the future of our society that they do not have now.

The *full employment* principle should be broadly conceived and be central to all social policy decisions. This refers not only to an open-ended ("entitlement") employment program of all able-bodied workers, but also to the full utilization of capital and community resources as well.

The *rejuvenation of communities* means the revitalization of the cultural and physical stock of cities and their neighborhoods. It also implies decentralized power, and, in a sense, is the spatial analog of economic democracy. It would require the establishment and promotion of institutions at the local level—including cooperatives, neighborhood associations, and community development corporations. Finally, there should be decentralized control of public services and energy. In particular, the development of alternative energy programs based in communities and under democratic control could be made available in future years.

Equity in the public and private sector concerns several related issues. First, in the public sector it implies a more fair tax system. Although, as Thurow [110: Chapter 7] points out, the tax and transfer system prevents the market solution from creating an even more unequal income distribution, people with equal incomes are not treated equally under the present system. Second, we must try to remove discrimination in the private sector, with regard to minorities, women, and others, in both work and housing opportunity. This is consistent with the principles of full employment and economic democracy.

Programmatic Recommendations

Having set down some general principles, some ways in which they might be implemented are discussed.

Economic Democracy.

As noted above, economic democracy is a very difficult condition to achieve, in part because of the nature of capitalism and in part because it means different things to different people. Following Carnoy and Shearer [28:3], economic democracy could mean "the transfer of economic decision making from the few to the many." In simple terms, it comes down to the democratic control of capital, which is fundamental to the recommendations in this chapter.

Such a transformation would be far reaching indeed. The nature of the work process, technology, the product mix, the income and wealth distributions, and other basic elements of the capitalist system would be altered. Such a system would not be implemented without great struggle, at the workplace and at the ballot box. But it may be necessary in order for capitalism to survive at all. For as workers see their jobs destroyed by automation or plant closings, as their working lives are made miserable by speed ups and dangerous work sites, the social tensions within the society will increase, even in one with as little class consciousness as the United States.

But there is another important reason for broad support for economic democracy: it will likely make "the system" work better. When workers see that they have a true stake in their jobs, they may work harder and more carefully. Productivity could rise, output increase, and a bigger economic pie could result (this, of course, is an empirical question).

Note, it would be a somewhat different "system," but it would likely be a more just one. It is not at all clear that economic democracy is "antiefficient," as some of its critics have argued.

What will an economically democratic society look like? First, there will have to be a change in the manner by which investment decisions are made. With workers and government representatives on TCs, different types of investments would be made. Healthy plants would not be closed because they did not fit the corporate strategy. Technology that is more under the control of the individual worker, allowing greater room for individual effort, would be put in place. Work rules would be different. Perhaps, the output mix would change, and more socially useful products would be manufactured.

But at the heart of economic democracy must be the restructuring of the work site and relations between workers and management, so that employee creativity can be tapped and jobs enriched. Changing ownership to TCs or even worker-managed firms will not necessarily mean democracy at the workplace unless management-worker relations are changed. One means of greater worker control could come through the effective use of union pension funds (now more than $500 billion) to purchase equity in firms, as Rifkin and Barber [97] have advocated.

Full Employment.

The lack of a firm political commitment to full employment has been with us for a long time. The Humphrey-Hawkins Equal Opportunity and Full Employment Bill was passed, although in a much watered-down form. However, the Humphrey-Hawkins Bill provides a goal of full employment and a framework for "democratic, nationwide, and decentralized planning." Humphrey-Hawkins can be used as a vehicle for further efforts to attain full employment. From the base of this legislation, there are several, related measures that could be taken to achieve full employment.

Reindustrialization.

First, there is an overriding need to increase economic growth and productivity. The term "reindustrialization" has been used as a catch-all to mean several things: disinvestment in failing industries and the shifting of resources to more promising ones; increases in productivity by granting tax credits for capital investment and research and development (R&D) expenditures; more government spending for research and development, particularly basic and process R&D; fewer government regulations, particularly in the areas of the environment and occupational health and safety; austerity in the sense of the primacy of capital goods production over consumption goods production and quality-of-life improvements; also, the social spending austerity. Some in the business community call for "give backs" by labor (that is, giving up working condition and wage gains achieved in the past); a few call for indicative central planning or governmental equivalents of corporate investment committees in order to channel resources from one sector (or region) to another. (Although the term "planning" is usually avoided, reindustrialization is really microeconomic sectoral planning at the national level.) The retraining of workers is also part of this general strategy. The efforts of the Japanese Ministry of International Trade and Industry (MITI) are generally given as an example of how reindustrialization should be organized.

While the reindustrialization strategy is important, the details of such an effort must be carefully planned. Implicit in the strategy is its "efficiency" orientation—we must give up most other national goals to spur the economy to greater economic heights. Although not part of the "no growth" camp, I sense that reindustrialization without other elements (noted below), and without careful safeguards for the "losers" in the process, is not as good a policy as its proponents claim. We must, as Rawls [93] has said, adopt "a principle of redress" for those who are dislocated.

For example, these proposals clash directly with redistributional goals of the society, both interpersonal and spatial. Cameron [27], in reviewing the relationship between the British "Industrial Strategy" and regional policy, indicates that regional policy becomes less important. This is especially true since, at least in the UK, many of the so-called "super sectors" and others chosen for expansion tend to increase work activity "in place" rather than by relocating in the development areas designated for regional development. Reindustrialization will probably increase interregional disparities among regions, not reduce them. In addition, resources devoted to industrial development cannot be used for interregional (or interpersonal) redistribution.

Reindustrialization could lead to interpersonal inequities. The calls for general investment tax credits and a host of anti-regulation proposals would mean that much of the burden of adjustment would likely fall on workers and consumers. Many of the suggested "reforms" are, in fact, highly regressive.[18] The drive for efficiency would inevitably mean less societal equity.

Another issue regarding reindustrialization is its control. Who will make these important investment and restructuring decisions? If such decisions are taken in a democratic manner, as I have advocated with respect to the TCs, then there is a possibility for reasonable and just action. If control remains essentially unchanged (or is shifted to the state), without important worker participation, reindustrialization would not be beneficial to most of the people.

If the government (through the TCs) provides financial and other aid for business firms as part of reindustrialization schemes, it should demand partial ownership and a say in the direction of the product mix; for example, in the bailout of Chrysler, a TC could require some production of mass transportation equipment as part of the company's restructuring.[19] The notion of ownership by government is not new, of course, as governments in many European countries own all or part of companies (for example in Italy, France, and West Germany).

Public enterprise must be a central part of a democratic reindustrialization strategy.[20] First, public enterprise can serve as an important yardstick by which to measure pricing and output policies of other firms in an industry. Might not a public auto or oil firm have made a difference in those highly oligopolistic industries? Public enterprise would, therefore, have significant antitrust benefits as well, since it would enhance competition by acting as a check on oil firms. Second, more public ownership could be obtained through a reconstituted Reconstruction Finance Corporation (RFC) (structured along TC lines) that could purchase shares in firms in several industries and place public members on the corporate boards. Another task of a new RFC would be the financing of new enterprises, in part through a set of public-private partnerships, cooperatives, and worker-managed firms. Such a policy could be spatially targeted, with funds earmarked for ventures in distressed regions. An important example of public enterprise could be in the energy field. Former Senator Adlai Stevenson III proposed a Federal Oil and Gas Corporation, which would develop energy on publicly owned lands. For futher discussion of public enterprise, see Carnoy and Shearer [28], Shepherd [105], and Holland [54, 55].

Therefore, reindustrialization is an important, but flawed, notion. Clearly, nations need to retool and adapt to a changing economic climate. But in terms of equity/redistribution issues and in the control of the restructuring process, serious questions must be answered. In any event, reindustrialization must take place in conjunction with other policies, some of which are discussed in the following pages. As it relates to urban policy, reindustrialization is unlikely to produce jobs in depressed areas. The more productive regions will likely become even more economically strong. Interregional income redistribution may be inconsistent with reindustrialization.

Guaranteed Jobs.

A second part of a full-employment program should involve a guaranteed job for all willing and able to work. This could be accomplished by a number of mechanisms, including public service employment, wage subsidies to private firms, and other mechanisms. Public service employment (PSE) has been used in several countries, including the United States. PSE has the advantage of serving public needs directly where the private market does not function properly. To the extent that it can be targeted to the previously unemployed and, importantly, be linked to job training programs, it can be a good tool for increasing employment in cities. In the United States, Operation Mainstream, the Work Incentive Program (WIN), and the Comprehensive Employment and Training Act (CETA) are examples of programs that involved PSE. In addition, PSE can be spatially targeted.

Another kind of direct job creation program involves wage subsidies to the private sector; on this subject, see, Haveman [47, 48, 49] and Haveman and Christainsen [50]. The advantages of wage subsidies are significant.[21] First, they are likely to increase employment in a relatively noninflationary way. Wage subsidies can attract workers into the labor force (many of whom have given up searching for employment) and employ them, with the potential GNP of the nation rising. Second, because wages are lowered, there may be a marginal decrease in the rate of inflation. This may help in terms of international competitiveness.

Third, a wage subsidy scheme can be easily targeted to youths, minorities, cities in distress, regions, community development corporations, small business, etc.[22] Employment of the targeted group can increase total employment in the economy. The incentives for firms would be to substitute the subsidized labor for other labor and capital. Such programs, therefore, encourage labor-intensive processes. Since wage subsidies are flexible, they can fit into a spatially targeted urban policy motif. Sweden, for example, has a regionally based wage subsidy arrangement to aid firms locating in designated areas, as do the Netherlands and the UK.

Fourth, these programs are good substitutes for income maintenance programs. They can help gain employment for those hard-core unemployed who would otherwise be receiving welfare payments. Fifth, wage subsidies seem to be more effective at employment creation (in terms of jobs per dollar of expenditure) than many alternative devices such as general public spending. Although there are questions about the net effect of these programs (there is the likelihood of displacement of other workers) and the often cumbersome mechanics of wage subsidy programs, many observers find them potentially important. Wage subsidies are helpful to reach both equity and efficiency goals.

Employment subsidies and public service employment are much more effective if combined with training programs. Training ought to increase the long-term employability of many workers, when put in an on-the-job training atmosphere.

Mobility grants are another component of a good full-employment program. Subsidies to cover job search, moving costs, and related items are helpful in "bringing people to jobs." Most of U.S. urban policy history has been to bring jobs to people. Sweden, among other European nations, has long provided such subsidies, which can reduce structural unemployment.

Macroeconomic approaches.

A third major category of employment creation involves the macroeconomy. Given the other measures advocated here, a combination of moderately expansionary fiscal policy combined with low-interest monetary policy will provide a good investment climate. However, the nation should employ selective (not general) tax cuts to spur R&D and investment in particular industries, in conjunction with democratic reindustrialization strategies. Credit subsidies to firms in depressed areas could be provided to encourage investment (although such may not be effective), and a strongly targeted countercyclical and long-term grants program to communities in distress should be instituted. For instance, a permanent, standby countercyclical fiscal assistance program should be instituted to replace the antirecession fiscal assistance (ARFA) program that has lapsed. A "trigger mechanism" that would take account of differences in regional responses to business cycles should be developed. Perhaps the program should be set in motion by movements of a "lead economic indicator" such as construction activity at the local level (rather than a "coincident indicator" such as the unemployment rate, as has been the case in the past) and a change in GNP or the unemployment rate at the national level. A capital infrastructure program should also be put into effect, both as a countercyclical and long-term device. It is important to have standby programs so that they can be implemented quickly; the legislative process has been so lengthy in the past, that such programs have generally begun to operate after recessions have ended. It is unfortunate that as part of the "austerity" recently imposed, the Carter Administration withdrew its support for such measures, as well as for labor-intensive public works.

Incomes Policy

A necessary component of any full employment program that is relatively noninflationary is an incomes policy. Although nearly every social democracy has had incomes policies of one form or another, the United States has had only voluntary wage-price guidelines during peacetime. They have never worked well, in part because their administrators (especially in the Nixon Administration) never believed in them. There is a need for long-term controls of wages and prices in order to maintain stability and equity in the system. Several proposals have been made, including the tax incentive plan (TIP) which works through the income tax system (see Seidman [104]). Firms are penalized with higher taxes when they grant wage increases (or raise prices) above some previously determined level. A strong incomes policy should be instituted as part of any social contract.

Rejuvenation of Communities

There are several things that could be done to rejuvenate distressed communities. First, there must be greater local control of capital, as outlined above. In particular, the control over multiplant and conglomerate investments must be shared with communities. This means, in the absence of any fundamental societal changes, enactment of laws to protect workers from sudden and unreasonable plant closings or employment cutbacks.

In the United States, several states and the Congress (H.R. 5040—the Ford-Riegle Bill, the National Employment Priorities Act of 1979) have been considering legislation that would require disclosure by firms of the intent to close, of severance pay, of continued health insurance coverage, of increased rights of workers to transfer to other plants, and of payments into a community development fund. These policies amount to an "exit tax" on firms.[23] The fund would be used to retrain workers, attract new industry, replace worn-out infrastructure, and other development-related programs.

Other efforts have been made by workers to assume the ownership of their firms. This has recently happened with the Rath Packing Company in Iowa where workers will buy shares in the company; within two years, the workers will have majority ownership. Although there has been a mixed experience with worker ownership in the United States, it has worked when the firm was reasonably healthy to begin with and when the worker/owners had technical assistance in management functions.[24] Worker-owned firms could maintain employment when a conglomerate wanted to close a profitable firm in a particular community.

Other things need to be done. National-level funding must be found to replace decaying infrastructure in cities. There is a tremendous shortage of rental housing, especially for the poor and elderly; this results, in part, from the advantages of home ownership imbedded in the income tax laws that make home ownership more attractive. In fact, the largest U.S. housing subsidy program existing is not in HUD but in the Internal Revenue Service, through the interest and local tax writeoffs allowed by law. Renters should have equal treatment for equity purposes.

Fiscal policy should be reoriented so as to provide more countercyclical and long-term aid to regions and cities in need. Targeted employment subsidies, noted in the previous discussion, should be instituted on a spatial as well as personal basis. That is, cities with high levels of unemployment and greater numbers of the poor should be eligible to receive greater subsidies. National-level public facilities, public employment programs, and procurement should also be more highly targeted.

Targeting is a very difficult political issue in the age of economic austerity since each region wants a bigger share of the national budget. As a result, we often see programs that were relatively highly targeted in their earlier stages, become less targeted when other cities and regions fight for less their "fair share." This has recently happened to HUD's Urban Development Action Grants program. It will take strong political leadership to keep targeting at respectable levels in the future.

Equity in the Public and Private Sector

The final set of suggestions involve equitable treatment of individuals in both the public and private sectors. On the public side, there is considerable room for long-overdue tax reform. The tax and transfer system now in effect has a slight redistributive character—that is, the distribution of after-tax income is somewhat more equitable than the before-tax distribution. As Thurow [110:156–157] indicates, the distribution of income has remained constant over the past 30 years; for example the lowest quintile of families had 5.0 percent of total income in 1947, compared to 5.2 percent in 1977. But, according to Thurow, this constancy masks an increasingly unequal market distribution of income: the lowest 60 percent of the population is losing ground to the richer 40 percent. The poorer families in our society have managed to keep pace because of income transfer payments and increasing female labor force participation rates. However, both of these props to the income of the poor may be ending. First, labor force participation rates of upper income women are now rising faster than previously. This fact, plus the slowdown in income transfer programs, means that there will likely be a more uneven distribution of income in the future. Given the zero-sum society in which we live, the difficulties in making redistributive decisions to reverse such trends will be very difficult indeed.

Clearly, one must also devise a tax system which is fair; our present system certainly is not. Besides the obvious loopholes that exist for the rich, current laws do not treat equals in the same manner. There are great dispersions of effective tax rates around mean tax rates paid by people with the same income. In addition, there has been a recent trend toward a more regressive tax system: sales, payroll, and other regressive taxes have increased in importance relative to more progressive taxes.

Several things could be done to improve the workings and equity of the tax system. First, the corporate income tax should be abolished and the taxes on corporations should be shifted to the shareholders of the corporations. There are some good reasons for this: the corporate income tax is now generally passed on to consumers in the form of higher prices and is probably, in effect, a sales tax in the long run.[25] Its abolition would shift some of the tax burden to primarily upper income stockholders from lower income consumers. Also, since there would be a doubling of after-tax returns to corporations, the managers of private corporations (or the TCs) would have an incentive to invest in new plant and equipment. At present, the tax laws are biased in favor of debt capital instead of equity capital. A change in the system would reverse this and probably increase investment and productivity. The total amount of taxes collected would likely increase, along with employment. In all, then, both equity and efficiency considerations would argue for the abolition of the corporate income tax.

A second area for tax reform would be the estate tax. Here, the ability of the rich to avoid such taxes is well known. At present, estate taxes amount to only about 0.2 percent of net wealth and therefore the tax has little impact on the distribution of wealth. Thurow [110] has shown that little wealth is accumulated over generations, but occurs largely from "one shot" successes. Therefore, increasing the effective levy on the estate tax would increase tax revenues to be used for other purposes, such as investment or redistribution, without significantly reducing incentives to innovate or save.

In general, the nation should try to restructure the tax system in order to reduce taxes that are inflationary (sales, value added, payroll, for example) and substitute taxes that would be more equitable and increase investment opportunity.

Another area for new legislation concerns income maintenance. The current set of programs to aid the poor is inequitable and self-defeating, perpetuating a poverty underclass. Negative income tax programs have been proposed (including Nixon's "Family Assistance Program" and Carter's "Program for Better Jobs and Income"), but none have been enacted. It is important to put a national floor on income (adjusted for interregional cost-of-living differences).

In the private economy, equity must be increased through efforts to end discrimination in work and housing. "Equal pay for equal work" must become more than a slogan. We have discrimination laws that have been evaded by private employers and not enforced by government agencies. The same is true in the housing market: many studies have shown that blacks pay more for equivalent housing than whites; often, women are denied credit and therefore access to the housing market. Little new legislation is needed here, only effective enforcement of existing laws. This would have the effect of enhancing the economic democratic ideal and the equal opportunity efforts long in effect in the United States.

Institutional and Political Change

Some wide-ranging notions about social and urban policy have been outlined in the previous sections. What does this mean for a social democracy such as the United States and others?

First, it would require some fundamental changes in institutions. The triparite commissions that would make democratic decisions would mean a very different way of "doing business." At the national level, a high-level TC would be required to make long-term planning decisions in order to help guide the national economy. This would have to be more than "indicative planning" that has been discussed. In many cases, investment and resource allocation would have to be made outside the market. This would likely be true in the energy and resource areas where, as Barnet [10] has shown, the Global Factory system has near-monopoly control over many critical resources. As noted above, corporate planning extends across borders, and a strong countervailing force in the form of a national planning TC must be in place.

A second set of institutions should be established at the regional level. Regional TCs (and TCs for local firms and communities) would be necessary in order to carry out a set of decisions made at the national level and to influence national decisionmaking according to disparate local needs. "Top-down" planning alone would not be democratic.

A third issue to be discussed involves appropriate compensation for those displaced by the change ahead. We must provide large-scale aid to communities hurt by planned disinvestment and to workers and owners whose livelihoods are reduced. A "fair" compensation scheme would mean setting some standard relative to the national median income for those who cannot work and a changed market system of wages that would provide long-run equity and good jobs. This would be a difficult task, but it is crucial in order to mobilize the populace for the acceptance of the dislocation that will come.

URBAN POLICY IN THE 1980s: THE TASK AHEAD

A broad scheme for future social policy in the United States has been outlined. What does it mean for urban policy? Some suggestions are aspatial in nature—recommendations for aid to people rather than places—but others have explicit or implicit place orientations. The latter include targeted wage and capital subsidies, capital infrastructure grants, "exit taxes" on capital, targeted public service employment, countercyclical and long-term grants to local governments, tax incentives for rental housing and for the rehabilitation of housing, and others. However, the main recommendations involve an integration of place policies and people programs: full employment programs, mobility grants, changes in tax code, and others. My message is that the 1980s will require much effort to improve and expand a set of social programs that have bettered the lives of many of the poor and that have been reduced in the past few years through austerity. Only with economically healthy individuals will we have a vibrant and healthy society and cities.

So, what is to be done? For our profession, more research should be undertaken. We need to know more about the urban and regional impacts of international trade, capital mobility, and business cycles. As noted, there has been little done to date in these areas. Second, the outline of the social contract needs to be made more substantial: the organization of tripartite committees, the nature of the full-employment programs (i.e., reindustrialization, guaranteed jobs, wage subsidies, etc.), and the other recommendations that seem reasonable. Third, we need to extend the analysis of the practicality of some recommendations, particularly with regard to cost[26] and the effects on income distribution. Fourth, what will be the future population and employment distributions as a result of market and policy forces? Finally, we may have to become more active in the political arena: the role of academics in directly influencing policymaking is limited, as Aaron [1] has told us. But under the new set of circumstances facing the world, it is possible that political leaders will turn to us for answers to some very difficult questions.

ACKNOWLEDGMENTS

The research reported here was supported in part by funds from the U.S. Social Science Research Council—American Council for Learned Societies, the U.S. National Science Foundation, U.S. Department of Housing and Urban Development, and the President's Commission for a National Agenda for the Eighties. I have also had the benefit of discussions on some of the issues raised in this paper with Robert J. Brand, André Farhi, William Goldsmith, Elizabeth Friedman, Bennett Harrison, Robert H. Haveman, Maryellen R. Kelley, John O'Donnell, Yvonne Scruggs Perry, David L. Puryear, and Thomas A. Reiner. The views contained in this chapter are mine and do not necessarily reflect those of the aforementioned organizations or individuals.

A longer version of this paper appeared in Peter Nijkamp and Piet Rietveld, ed., *Cities in Transition: Problems and Policies,* Alphen aan den Rijn, The Netherlands: Sijthoff and Noordhoff, 1981. Thanks are extended to the publisher and the editors for permission to publish this revised version. For the convenience of the reader, I have included the original set of references. There is some overlap between the material in first two sections of this chapter with parts of Chapter 8. I have retained the material in this chapter for purposes of continuity of the argument.

NOTES

1. Thurow [11] provides an interesting review of several important issues facing the United States, and other nations. Burton and Murphy [25] have discussed planning issues within this political climate.
2. For accounts of the nature of the work process, the "deskilling" of labor, and the changing technology to mold it, see Braverman [23], Edwards [33], and Noble [77].
3. The establishment of "export platforms" or "free-trade zones" in LDCs has led to a large amount of employment creation in some; for example, there are over 400,000 export-related workers in Brazil and 700,000 in Hong Kong alone, although not all are working in "export platforms." On export platforms and the relationship between the U.S. and Mexico, see Baird and McCaughan [6]. For a study of international trade and LDCs, see Keesing [65].
4. I do not contend that MNCs are *the* cause of many of the problems discussed here. If MNCs did not exist, other institutions would be invented to undertake their functions. Nor are MNCs new to the 1970s; think of the British East India Company that was operating in the 18th century. However, the scale and importance of MNCs in the past 20 years has qualitatively changed the nature of international trade. For interesting, and often conflicting, accounts of the functions and importance of MNCs, see Barnet [10], Barnet and Müller [11], Vernon [119], Bergston, Horst, and Moran [17], and Jegan and Wilbur [63].
5. There is a substantial interest in the United States in the subject of "urban impact analysis" which is a new federal government effort to gauge the effects on jurisdictions of proposed new national programs. See Glickman [40, 41, 42], Barro [12], Petersen and Muller [90], Vaughan [117], and others. Little in this field has been done on the subjects covered in this chapter and Chapter 8; the Congressional Budget Office [111, 112] has studied the effects of the "Tokyo Round" Multilateral Trade Negotiations, but relatively little emphasis was placed on the regional effects in that work. Balassa [7] has viewed the effects of the Tokyo Round on LDCs.
6. The findings for the United States indicate that industry mix has become somewhat less important as a determinant of regional cyclical change, because spatial decentralization and the greater share of services has made regions more alike; durable goods-dominated regions, however, continue to show greater amplitude than other regions. Agricultural regions had the least sensitivity to national economic cycles. There appears to be a wider variation among regions in their amplitude than in their timing.
7. There have been many studies of long-term regional growth patterns for several nations. Recent ones include Mieszkowski [75], Alcaly and Mermelstein [2], Leven [70], Sternlieb and Hughes [107], and Glickman [39].
8. See, for example, Clawson and Hall [29], Glickman [39], Hansen [45], Allen and Maclennon [3], Maclennan and Parr [73], Emanuel [34], Sundquist [108], OECD [80, 81, 82, 84, 85, 88], and others.

9. For discussions of the U.S. national urban policy, see Vining [120], Bearse [15], Goldsmith and Derian [44], Hirschhorn [53], Inman [58], Kain [64], Allman [4], Sternlieb [106], and others.

10. Sternlieb [106] characterized the tension between people and place orientation in terms of the fable of "Ballaam's ass" (the animal tethered between two piles of food who starves to death since he cannot decide which pile to eat first) and says: "Thus the issue of the regeneration of the city as place versus the care and feeding of its unfortunates creates only immobility." In discussing the policy process and what he regards as rather meager results, Sternlieb quips: "Leviathan hath labored mightily and has brought forth a mouse." Many other commentators were not much more charitable.

11. The policies were divided into nine "policy clusters' as follows: (1) improvements in local planning and management capacity and in the administration of ongoing programs; (2) fiscal assistance to highly distressed jurisdictions; (3) greater involvement of the states in aiding their cities; (4) more participation by community groups; (5) improvements in cultural and physical infrastructur;e (6) incentives for development efforts by the private sector; (7) aid to the long-term unemployed; (8) increased opportunities for the disadvantaged; and (9) improvements and expansions of health and social service programs.

12. An interesting example concerns welfare payments in New York City, which have not been increased since 1974. Therefore, recipients have had a real cut in payments of about 50 percent due to inflation. This policy has been a perverse example of the adage "to do nothing is to do something." There is a reduction in the incomes of a portion of the population by purposeful governmental inaction. It is fairly clear that if the New York City Council were asked to vote a 50 percent cut in welfare allowances, they would refuse to do so. It would not, after all, be "humane" to cut the stipends of the poor! Yet, by not doing anything to raise welfare payments, the city council has done precisely the same thing.

13. As noted in the text, the categories are given by the U.S. Budget and are not meant to be exact definitions of the "social and urban" spending undertaken by the federal government. For example, much of "transportation" group does not effect urban areas (or may have negative effects) and excluded activities such as "agriculture" (which administers the Food Stamp program) may have an effect on urban or social life. These categories were chosen on a common sense basis. The long-term trends with other combinations are similar with respect to the points made in the text with the present set.

14. The FY 1981 figures are calculated based on the government's proposed budget as amended in March 1980 and by the Congress thereafter. The deflator used for 1980 and 1981 in these calculations is from forecasts of the Wharton Econometric Forecasting Model.

15. For the Goldsmith-Derian [44] definitions of urban programs, see their Appendix Tables B-D. I have added several other programs, such as the Anti-Recession Fiscal Act, EDA Title IX, CETA, the Job Opportunities Program, and some other programs, to their list. Although the figures change, the overall result is not very different.

16. Although it is difficult to get an accurate picture of the other auto subcontractors and suppliers, the Department of Transportation estimates that approximately three-quarters of the suppliers are in Michigan, Ohio, Illinois, New York, and Pennsylvania.

17. About 80 percent of the wealth in the U.S. is held by the top quintile of the population, according to Thurow [110:168]; 1 percent of the families in the United States hold about 53 percent of the corporate sotck. These figures imply (although they do not "prove") a control of economic life by a relatively small minority of the population.

18. The ideological nature of this set of proposals should not be underestimated. Not only do economists and members of the business establishment accede to the "less is more" credo of those like Paul Volker (Chairman of the Federal Reserve System), so do a large number of American workers. *Business Week,* tells its readers "some people will obviously

have to do with less . . . so that the economy as a whole can get the most mileage out of available capital. . . . Indeed, cities and states, . . . and the consumer will all get less than they want because the basic health of the country is based on the basic helath of its corporations and banks. . . Nothing that this nation, or any other nation, has done in modern economic history compares in difficulty with the selling job that must now be done to make people accept the new reality." (October 12, 1974, as quoted by Bluestone and Harrison [20]). When I read such pronouncements, I fear that the burdens of reindustrialization will not be shared equitably.

19. A counterexample to the Chrysler case is that of Volkswagon, which faced problems of retooling and redesign similar to Chrysler's in the early 1970s. With the cooperation of the West German government (which owns about 20 percent of VW) and the banks that held loans, VW engaged in vigorous restructuring that was ultimately successful. Toyo Kogyo (the manufacturer of Mazda cars) was also restructured in the mid-1970s with the aid of the Japanese government.

20. It must be understood that the mere substitution of the state-as-owner for the private capitalist will not necessarily change basic intrafirm relations; if work remains hierarchical and undemocratic, then one important potential of public ownership will be undermined. In France and Italy, public enterprises have tended to bemore progressive in labor relations than old-line firms, according to Carnoy and Shearer [28, Chapter 2]. With a TC structure, a democratic organization of work could be attained. Such a restructuring of work relations is one of the ways in which these proposals may be distinguished from those of the business community.

21. There are several types of wage subsidies. Some go to employers as a percentage of the firms wage bill or in relation to the number of new workers that the firm hires (known as "marginal employment subsidies"). Other schemes involve certifying certain workers as eligible (based on various unemployment or poverty characteristics) with the subsidy going directly to them. The marginal wage subsidy idea is discussed here.

22. There are numerous examples of wage subsidy schemes in Europe, many of which began as temporary countercyclical measures but were later extended. These include the ABM Program (FRG), Incentive Bonus for Job Creation (France), 30 Percent Wage Bonus Plan (The Netherlands), and the Premium Employment Program (Ireland). See, Haveman and Christainsen [50] for a discussion of these and other programs.

23. There has been extensive experience with plant closing legislation in Europe. Sweden in particular has had a long-standing worker relocation program and policies to replace jobs in the affected community through public enterprise and grants and loans for new private firms. In the FRG, disclosure of intended plant closings must be made, along with public access to corporate data regarding the rationale for closing.

24. There were over 1,000 employee stock ownership plans (ESOPs) in effect in 1979; in about 100 firms, workers held majority ownership. Bluestone and Harrison [20: Chapter 8] say that productivity wages and employee satisfaction were reported to be higher (along with higher profitability) in such companies.

25. There is disagreement over the overall incidence of the corporate income tax. Thurow [110] believes that in the long run it acts as sales tax that is eventually paid by consumers.

26. I have done some preliminary work on the costs of some of these ideas and ways of raising revenues to implement them. Revenues can be increased by several mechanisms: part of the windfall profits tax on oil firms, reductions in "tax expenditures" (such as the exclusion of income earned abroad by citizens, deferral of income by DISCs and of controlled foreign corporations, interest on state and local industrial development bonds, greater taxation on capital gains), increases in the estate tax, and a minimum tax on personal services. These revenues, plus "bracket drift" if the personal income tax were not

indexed, would produce well over $125 billion dollars per year in new funds. Additional monies could be raised by reducing defense spending. To put these figures in perspective, about 5 million workers (the difference between the current 8 million unemployed and a reasonable estimate of full employment) could receive wage subsidies for between $25 and $30 billion. The other funds could be used for additional R&D, income maintenance, and related programs. Bluestone and Harrison have made some estimates of revenues to be raised for a full-employment program that they outline.

REFERENCES

1. Aaron, Henry, *Politics and the Professors: The Great Society in Perspective,* Washington: The Brookings Institution, 1978.
2. Alcaly, Roger and David Mermelstein, *The Fiscal Crisis of American Cities,* New York: Vintage, 1977.
3. Allen, Kevin and M.C. Maclennan, *Regional Problems and Policies in Italy and France,* London: Allen and Unwin, 1970.
4. Allman, T.D., "The Urban Crisis Leaves Town," *Harper's Magazine,* December 1978.
5. Alonso, William, *Location and Land Use,* Cambridge, Mass.: Harvard University Press, 1964.
6. Baird, Peter and Ed McCaughan, *Beyond the Border: Mexico and the U.S. Today,* New York: North American Congress on Latin America, 1979.
7. Balassa, Bela, *The Tokyo Round and the Developing Countries,* Washington: The World Bank; World Bank Staff Working Paper No. 370, 1980.
8. Barkin, David, "Confronting the Separation of Town and Country in Cuba," in William K. Tabb and Larry Sawers, eds., *Marxism and the Metropolis,* New York: Oxford University Press, 1978, pp. 317–337.
9. Barnet, Richard J., "Planning," in Marcus G. Raskin, ed., *The Federal Budget and Social Reconstruction,* New Brunswick, N.J.: Transaction, Inc., 1978, pp. 109–135.
10. ———, *The Lean Years: Politics in the Age of Scarcity,* New York: Simon and Schuster, 1980.
11. Barnet, Richard J. and Ronald Müller, *Global Reach: The Power of the Multinational Corporations,* New York: Simon and Schuster, 1974.
12. Barro, Stephen, M., *The Urban Impacts of Federal Policies: Vol. 3, Fiscal Conditions,* Santa Monica, Calif.: The Rand Corporation, 1978.
13. Bartels, Cornelis P. A., "The Structure of Regional Unemployment in the Netherlands: An Exploratory Statistical Analysis," *Regional Science and Urban Economics,* 7, 1977, pp. 103–135.
14. Bartke, Istvan, Viktor Kulcar and Gyorgy Perczel, "Regional Development, Planning and Research in Hungary," Institute of Economic Planning, National Planning Office, Budapest, Hungary (mimeo), 1977.
15. Bearse, Peter, "Influencing Capital Flows for Urban Economic Development: Institutions or Institution Building?," *Journal of Regional Science,* 19, 1979, pp. 79–92.
16. Beier, George, Anthony Churchill, Michael Cohen, and Bertrand Renaud, *The Task Ahead for the Cities of the Developing Countries,* Washington: The World Bank; World Bank Staff Working Paper No. 209, 1975.
17. Bergston, C. Fred, Thomas Horst, and Theodore H. Moran, *American Multinationals and American Interests,* Washington: The Brookings Institution, 1978.
18. Bjornstad, David J. *Changes in Economic Capacity at the Federal Regional Level Due to NEP-1 Energy Price Change,* Oak Ridge, Tenn.: Oak Ridge National Laboratory, 1980.
19. Bluestone, Barry and Bennett Harrison, "Economic Development, the Public Sector,

and Full Employment: An Outline for a Plan," in Marcus G. Raskin, ed., *The Federal Budget and Social Reconstruction,* New Brunswick, N.J.: Transaction, Inc., 1978, pp. 405–466.

20. ———, *Capital and Communities: The Consequences of Private Disinvestment,* Washington: The Progressive Alliance, 1980.
21. Borts, George H., "Regional Cycles of Manufacturing Industry in the United States, 1914–1953," *Journal of the American Statistical Association,* Vol. 55, 1967.
22. Bosworth, Barry, "Economic Policy," in Joseph A. Pechman, ed., *Setting National Priorities: Agenda for the 1980s,* Washington: Brookings Institution, 1980, pp. 35–70.
23. Braverman, Harry, *Labor and Monopoly Capital: The Degradation of Work in the Twentieth Century,* New York: Monthly Review Press, 1974.
24. Browne, Lynn E., "Regional Capital Formation," *New England Economic Indicators,* June 1979.
25. Burton, Dudley and M. Brian Murphy, "Democratic Planning in Austerity: Practices and Theory," paper read at a Conference on Planning Theory, Ithaca, New York (mimeo), 1979.
26. *Business Week,* "The Reindustrialization of America," Special Issue, June 30, 1980.
27. Cameron, Gordon C., "The National Industrial Strategy and Regional Policy," in Duncan Maclennan and John B. Parr, eds., *Regional Policy: Past Experiences and New Directions,* Oxford: Martin Robinson, 1979, pp. 297–322.
28. Carnoy, Martin and Derek Shearer, *Economic Democracy: The Challenge of the 1980s,* White Plains, N.Y.: M.E. Sharpe, 1980.
29. Clawson, Marion and Peter Hall, *Planning and Urban Growth,* Baltimore: The Johns Hopkins University Press, 1973.
30. Coleman, Henry, Norman J. Glickman, David L. Puryear, and John P. Ross, "Business Cycles and Cities: Past Experience, Prospects and Policy Alternatives," written for the *President's Urban Policy Report,* Washington: U.S. Department of Housing and Urban Development, 1980.
31. Colosio, Donaldo, "Urbanization and Economic Development in Mexico," WP-79-19, Laxenburg, Austria: International Institute for Applied Systems Analysis, 1979.
32. Edel, Mathew, "'People' versus 'Places' in Urban Impact Analysis," in Norman J. Glickman, ed., *The Urban Impacts of Federal Policies,* Baltimore: The Johsn Hopkins University Press, 1980, pp. 175–191.
33. Edwards, Richard, *Contested Terrain: The Transformation of the Workplace in the Twentieth Century,* New York: Basic Books, 1979.
34. Emanuel, A., *Issues of Regional Policies,* Paris: OECD, 1973.
35. Fajferak, Anton, "Regional Economics and Policy in Centrally Planned Economy," Krakow, Poland: Academy of Economics, mimeo, 1977.
36. Faux, Geoffrey and Robert Lightfoot, *Capital and Community,* Washington: Project on Economic Alternatives, 1976.
37. Fearn, Raymond, "Cyclical, Seasonal, and Structural Factors in Area Unemployment Rates," *Industrial and Labor Relations Review,* 28, 1975, pp. 424–431.
38. Friedmann, John, *Urbanization, Planning and National Development,* Beverly Hills, Calif.: Sage, 1973.
39. Glickman, Norman J., *The Growth and Management of the Japanese Urban System,* New York: Academic Press, 1979.
40. ———, "Urban Impact Analysis: Its Role in Federal Decisionmaking," paper read at the meetings of the Association of Public Policy and Management, Chicago, Ill., and forthcoming in *Conference Proceedings,* John P. Crecine, ed., 1979.
41. ———, "International Trade, Capital Mobility, and Economic Growth: Some Implications for American Cities in the 1980s," a report to the President's Commission on

a National Agenda for the Eighties (mimeo). Reprinted as Chapter VIII of this volume.

42. ———, "Methodological Issues and Prospects for Urban Impact Analysis," in Norman J. Glickman, ed., *The Urban Impacts of Federal Policies,* Baltimore: The Johns Hopkins University Press, 1980, pp. 3–32.
43. ———, *The Urban Impacts of Federal Policies,* Baltimore: The Johns Hopkins University Press, 1980.
44. Goldsmith, William W. and Michael J. Derian, "Is There An Urban Policy?" *Journal of Regional Science,* 19, 1979, pp. 93–108.
45. Hansen, Niles M., ed., *Public Policy and Regional Economic Development: The Experience of Nine Western Countries,* Cambridge, Mass.: Ballinger, 1974.
46. Harrison, Bennett and Sandra Kanter, "The Political Economy of States Job—Creation Business Incentives," *Journal of the American Institute of Planners,* October 1978, pp. 424–435.
47. Haveman, Robert H., "Direct Job Creation: Potentials and Realities," DP #570-79, Institute for Research on Poverty, University of Wisconsin, Madison, 1979.
48. ———, "The Potential of Targetted, Marginal Employment Subsidies: Economic and Institutional Issues," paper prepared for the OECD (mimeo), 1980.
49. ———, "Toward Efficiency and Equity Through Direct Job Creation," *Social Policy,* Vol. 11, No. 1, 1980. pp. 41–50.
50. Haveman, Robert H. and Gregory B. Christainsen, "Public Employment and Wage Subsidies in West Europe and the U.S.: What We're Doing and What We Know," DP #522-78, Institute for Research on Poverty, University of Wisconsin, Madison, 1978.
51. Heilbroner, Robert L., *Beyond Boom and Crash,* New York: Norton, 1980.
52. Herman, Stanislaw and Jerzy Regulski, "Regional Research and the International Economic Integration," paper read at the 17th European Congress of the Regional Science Association, Krakow, Poland (mimeo), 1977.
53. Hirschhorn, Larry, "The Urban Crisis: A Post-Industrial Perspective," *Journal of Regional Science,* 19, 1979, pp. 109–118.
54. Holland, Stuart, *The State as Entrepreneur,* London: Weidenfeld and Nicolson, 1972.
55. ———, *The Socialist Challenge,* London: Quartet Books, 1975.
56. Hoover, Edgar, *Introduction to Regional Economics,* New York: Alfred A. Knopf, 2nd Ed., 1974.
57. Hudson, Edward A. and Dale W. Jorgenson, "Energy Prices and the U.S. Economy," *National Resource Journal,* 18, 1978, pp. 877–897.
58. Inman, Robert P., "Federal Policy and the Urban Poor," *Journal of Regional Science,* 19, 1979, pp. 119–129.
59. International Monetary Fund, *Balance of Payments Yearbook,* Washington: International Monetary Fund, 1980.
60. Isard, Walter, *Location and Space-Economy,* Cambridge, Mass.: M.I.T. Press, 1956.
61. Japan Economic Planning Agency, *New Economic and Social Seven-Year Plan,* Tokyo: Economic Planning Agency, 1979.
62. Japan National Land Agency, *The Third Comprehensive National Development Plan,* Tokyo: National Land Agency, 1979.
63. Jegen, Mary E. and Charles K. Wilbur, eds., *Growth with Equity: Strategies for Meeting Human Needs,* New York: Paulist Press, 1979.
64. Kain, John F., "Failure in Diagnosis: A Critique of Carter's National Urban Policy," Policy Note P78-2, Cambridge, Mass.: Department of City and Regional Planning, Harvard University, 1978.
65. Keesing, Donald B., *Trade Policy for Developing Countries,* Washington: The World Bank; World Bank Staff Working Paper No. 353, 1979.

66. Kelly, Ed, *Industrial Exodus,* Washington: Conference on Alternative State and Local Public Policies, 1977.
67. Korcelli, Piotr, "Aspects of Polish National Urban Policy," in Harry Swain, ed., *National Settlement Strategies: East and West,* Laxenburg, Austria: International Institute for Applied Systems Analysis, 1975, pp. 49–63.
68. ______, "Metropolitan Development in Poland and Implications for America," in Charles L. Leven, ed., *The Mature Metropolis,* Lexington, Mass.: Heath-Lexington, 1978, pp. 91–106.
69. Kuklinski, Antoni, ed., *Regional Development and Planning: International Perspectives,* Leyden, The Netherlands: Sijthoff International Publishing Co., 1975.
70. Leven, Charles L., ed., *The Mature Metropolis,* Lexington, Mass.: Heath-Lexington, 1978.
71. Linn, Johannes F., *Policies for Efficient and Equitable Growth of Cities in Developing Countries,* Washington: The World Bank; World Bank Staff Working Paper No, 342, 1979.
72. Lösch, August, *The Economics of Location,* New Haven: Yale University Press, 1954.
73. Maclennan, Duncan and John B. Parr, *Regional Policy: Past Experience and New Directions,* Oxford: Martin Robinson, 1979.
74. Massey, Doreen, "Capital and Locational Change: The UK Electrical Engineering and Electronics Industries," *Review of Radical Political Economics,* Vol. 10, No. 3, 1978, pp. 39–54.
75. Mieszkowski, Peter, "Recent Trends in Urban and Regional Development," in Peter Mieszkowski and Mahlon Straszheim, eds., *Current Issues in Urban Economics,* Baltimore: The Johns Hopkins University Press, 1979, pp. 3–39.
76. Milne, William, Norman J. Glickman, and F. Gerard Adams, "A Framework for Analyzing Regional Decline: A Multiregion Econometric Model of the United States," *Journal of Regional Science,* 20, 1980, pp. 173–189.
77. Noble, David F., *America By Design: Science, Technology and the Rise of Corporate Capitalism,* Oxford: Oxford University Press, 1977.
78. Norton, R.D., "Reindustrialization and the Urban Underclass," Chapter VII of this volume.
79. OECD, *Policies for Promoting Industrial Adaptation,* Paris: OECD, 1976.
80. ______, *Regional Problems and Policies in OECD Countries: Volume I,* Paris: OECD, 1976.
81. ______, *Regional Problems and Policies in OECD Countries: Volume II,* Paris: OECD, 1976.
82. ______, *Regional Policies: The Current Outlook,* Paris: OECD, 1977.
83. ______, *Restrictive Regional Policy Measures,* Paris: OECD, 1977.
84. ______, *Regional Policies and the Service Sector,* Paris: OECD, 1978.
85. ______, *Regional Problems and Policies in Portugal,* Paris: OECD, 1978.
86. ______, *Facing the Future: Mastering the Probable and Managing the Unpredictable,* Paris: OECD, 1979.
87. ______, *The Case for Positive Adjustment Policies,* Paris: OECD, 1979.
88. ______, *The Role of Industrial Incentives in Regional Development,* Paris: OECD, 1979.
89. Pascal, Anthony H. and Mark D. Menchik, "Fiscal Containment: Who Gains? Who Loses?," Santa Monica, Calif.: The Rand Corporation Paper R-2494/1-FF-RC.
90. Peterson, George and Thomas Muller, "The Regional Impact of Federal Tax and Spending Policies," Working Paper 0000-06-05, Washington: The Urban Institute, 1977.
91. Petras, Elizabeth M., "Towards a Theory of International Migration: The New Division of Labor," in R. Bryce-Laporte, ed., *Sourcebook on the New Immigration: Implications*

for the United States and the International Community, New Brunswick, N.J.: Transactions Books, 1980.

92. Prud'homme, R., "Regional Economic Policy in France," in Niles M. Hansen, ed., *Public Policy and Regional Economic Development: The Experience of Nine Western Countries*, Cambridge, Mass.: Ballinger, 1974.
93. Rawls, John, *A Theory of Justice*, Cambridge, Mass.: Harvard University Press, 1971.
94. Renaud, Betrand, *National Urbanization Policies in Developing Countries*, Washington: The World Bank; World Bank Staff Working Paper No. 347, 1979.
95. Richardson, Harry W., *The Economics of Urban Size*, Farnborough, Hampshire: Saxon Hous, 1973.
96. ———, *National Spatial Strategies in Developing Countries*, Washington, D.C.: The World Bank; World Bank Staff Working Paper No. 252, 1977.
97. Rifkin, Jeremy and Randy Barber, *The North Will Rise Again: Pensions, Politics and Power in the 1980s*, Boston: Beacon Press, 1978.
98. Rodwin, Lloyd, "Regional Planning in Less Developed Countries: A Retrospective View of the Literature and the Experience," *International Regional Science Review*, 3, 1978, pp. 113–131.
99. Sakashita, Noburo, *Methods of Regional Economic Analysis*, Tokyo: Japan Economic Planning Agency; in Japanese, 1976.
100. Sarbib, Jean-Louis and Steve Lazin, "The Future of American Cities and Regions in an Internationalized Economy: Two Scenarios," a report to the U.S. Department of Housing and Urban Development (mimeo), 1979.
101. Sawers, Larry, "Cities and Countryside in the Soviet Union and China," in William K. Tabb and Larry Sawers, eds., *Marxism and the Metropolis*, New York: Oxford University Press, 1978, pp. 338–394.
102. Sawyer, M., "Income Distribution in OECD Countries," *OECD Economic Outlook Occasional Studies*, Paris: OECD, 1976.
103. Schwartz, Gail G. and Pat Choate, *Revitalizing the U.S. Economy: A Brief for National Sectoral Policies*, Washington: The Academy for Contemporary Problems, 1980.
104. Seidman, Laurence, "Tax-Based Income Policies," *Brookings Papers in Economic Activity*, 2, 1978, pp. 301–361.
105. Shepherd, William G., *Public Enterprise*, Lexington, Mass.: Heath-Lexington Books, 1976.
106. Sternlieb, George, "Sailing Directions for Urban America: Beating, Reaching, and Running," *Journal of the American Institute of Planning*, 1978, pp. 335–337.
107. Sternlieb, George and James W. Hughes, *Post-Industrial America: Metropolitan Decline and Inter-Regional Job Shifts*, New Brunswick, N.J.: Center for Urban Policy Research, 1975.
108. Sundquist, James L., *Dispersing Population: What America Can Learn from Europe*, Washington: The Brookings Institution, 1975.
109. Thurow, Lester C., *Generating Inequality*, New York: Basic Books, 1975.
110. ———, *The Zero-Sum Society: Distribution and the Possibilities for Economic Change*, New York: Basic Books, 1980.
111. U.S. Congressional Budget Office, *The Effects of the Tokyo Round of Multilateral Trade Negotiations on the U.S. Economy: An Updated View*, Washington: Government Printing Office, 1979.
112. ———, *U.S. Trade Policy and the Tokyo Round of Multilateral Trade Negotiations*, Washington: Government Printing Office, 1979.
113. U.S. Department of Housing and Urban Development, *The President's National Urban Policy*, Washington: U.S. Department of Housing and Urban Development, 1978.

114. ———, *The Impact of Foreign Direct Investment on U.S. Cities and Regions,* Washington: U.S. Department of Housing and Urban Development, 1979.
115. Urban and Regional Policy Group, *A New Partnership to Conserve America's Communities,* Washington: U.S. Department of Housing and Urban Development, 1978.
116. Vaughan, Roger J., *Public Works as a Countercyclical Device: A Review of the Issues,* Santa Monica, Calif.: The Rand Corporation, 1976.
117. ———, *The Urban Impacts of Federal Policies: Vol. 2, Economic Development,* Santa Monica, Calif.: The Rand Corporation, 1977.
118. Vernez, Georges, Roger J. Vaughan, Burke Burright, and Sinclair Coleman, *Regional Cycles and Employment of Public Works Investments* Santa Monica, CA: The Rand Corporation, 1975.
119. Vernon, Raymond J., *Storm Over the Multinationals: The Real Issues,* Cambridge, Mass.: Harvard University Press, 1977.
120. Vining, Daniel R., Jr., "The President's National Urban Policy Report: Issues Skirted and Statistics Omitted," *Journal of Regional Science,* 19, 1979, pp. 69–77.
121. Vining, Daniel R., Jr., Robert L. Pallone, and Chung Hain Yang, "Population Dispersal from Core Regions: A Description and Tentative Explanation of the Patterns in 20 Countries," Working Paper No. 26, Department of Regional Science, Philadelphia, Pa: University of Pennsylvania, 1980.
122. Walker, Richard A., "Two Sources of Uneven Development Under Advanced Capitalism: Spatial Differentiation and Capital Mobility," *Review of Radical Political Economics,* Vol. 10, No. 3, 1978, pp. 28–37.
123. World Bank, *World Development Report, 1979,* Washington: The World Bank, 1979.

Chapter XII

URBAN AND ECONOMIC ADJUSTMENT TO THE POSTINDUSTRIAL ERA

Donald A. Hicks

Among the subtle tyrannies imposed by the calendar is the compulsion we feel every time a new decade rolls around to gaze across the landscape of the years ahead and "take stock" before plunging ahead. This is akin to the "stop, look, and listen" response triggered as we approach a railroad crossing. Frequently—some would say, fortunately—little comes of this decennial ritual, and we settle back into familiar routines almost before the urge itself is spent. As the gates to the 1980s were flung open, however, a number of events and eventualities commingled to justify an extra measure of caution from even the most surefooted among us.

Many of the nation's largest and oldest cities—long portrayed as caught in a vice-like distress that could be alleviated, if at all, only by summoning sufficient political will and spending sufficient tax dollars—continued their relentless trek to lower levels of population and employment. Likewise, the nation's economy exhibited such a bewildering array of seemingly conflicting symptoms that traditional remedies were only half-heartedly administered, since the aggravation of one symptom was certain to accompany the hoped for amelioration of another.

Fewer than 1,000 weeks remained in the century. To generations of Americans for whom the Depression of a half-century ago was but an arrid historical event, American economic supremacy, rising levels of general affluence, and the context of unprecedented growth that made it all possible were likewise being relegated to the history books. It all seemed to be coming apart. Through the late 1970s, the anxieties were building for countless Americans who sensed that the promises were becoming frayed and the dreams were clouding over. As the 1980s approached, and a general election along with them, the political response was predictable. Urban "revitalization," economic "reindustrialization," and spiritual "renewal" became the symbolic currency of the 1980 election—an alliance of backward-looking political responses formidable enough to make us wonder whether too many policymakers and political pundits were not traveling to work on subways while sitting on seats facing backwards. With medical metaphors stretched taut to help us embrace the enormity of the "ailments" afflicting two of the dominant and defining features of modern America—her cities and her economy—we were bombarded on all fronts with the supposed necessity of making one last stand to save our "dying" cities and resuscitate our moribund economy.

The crisis mentality that had influenced our thinking and tinkering in urban affairs for so long had infected at last our understanding of our economic problems. For an election year, such mindsets are not without their virtues. They tend to quicken the pulse and deepen resolve; unfortunately, they do far less than we might imagine to help us understand the significance of the urban and economic crossroads we find ourselves at. As the 1980 election loomed, the task of nurturing noninflationary growth—economic recovery—began to be communicated as a need to "reindustrialize," mistakenly suggesting to many some sort of retracing of steps back to the days when our cars and our hopes for an ever more prosperous future were stamped "Made in the U.S.A."

Predictably, the circumstances that define urban and economic life in the United States have come to be treated more as matters of *allocation* than *adjustment.* This should not surprise us, though, since the role for public policy is grander in the former—that of leader—and more humble in the latter—that of shepherd. And so it was that following Reagan's landslide victory, taming the budget and strategies of capital formation eclipsed a larger concern for accommodating America's exit from a century-and-a-half-long industrial era with all that that passage implies for economic activity and its geographical locations.

THE TWIN TRANSFORMATIONS: THE CITY AND THE ECONOMY

The Industrial Era of the past century and a half had unfolded hand-in-glove with a period of massive and rapid urbanization. Indeed, the 19th century became the great city-building era of our national history. Economic transformations such as the exit from a centuries-long agrarian era have a way of sculpting in general terms the outlines of new settlement systems that they require. Within the bounds set by the structure and organization of the economy and the technological capacities available, the individual and institutional preferences reflected in social and cultural life are free to leave their stamp and to provide the finer details for those settlements. The dense and compact arrangements within our older central cities reflect the viscissitudes and constraints imposed by the era in which they experienced the bulk of their growth. What often comes as a surprise to many is that this process is continuous, rather than lurching and episodic. In the past decade, our awareness of the growth in tandem of the population and the economy that had commanded the spotlight since World War II was rapidly yielding to an often grudging acknowledgment of the changing structure and distribution of the population and economic growth. The implications for where and how we lived and worked became more and more telling.

As the 1970s wore on, a phenomenal dispersal of the population and economic activity began to synchronize across several spatial scales. Reinforcing a now century-old process of suburbanization were two important developments. First, the long-term convergence among multistate regions continued to work itself out as a result of differential relative growth rates. The difficulty of deciding whether this constituted the "decline" of the Industrial Heartland or the "catching up" of historically peripheral regions—the South in particular—fueled intermittent regional squabbles in Congress and in the press. Second, for the first time since the early 19th century, growth rates in nonmetropolitan and rural areas exceeded those in metropolitan areas. Furthermore, this non-metropolitan resurgence appeared to be taking hold in all regions of the nation.

In the aggregate, then, we were seeing a dramatic deconcentration of population throughout the urban system. As a result, these several trends operating synergistically were having an appreciable impact on the urban-industrial arrangements and mix of economic activities and opportunities bound to them that had prevailed since before the Civil War. Together these trends were now dealing the combination of blows to the larger pattern of urban settlement that had through the 1950s and 1960s been reserved for older central cities alone.

Table XII.1 lists by region the major metropolitan areas of the nation. Between 1970 and 1980, 15 of our largest and oldest metropolitan areas experienced net population declines. All are located in the Northeast and Midwest—the old Industrial Heartland. Table XII.2 reports the population trends over the same decade for the nation's central cities larger than a quarter million population. While selected central cities in all regions lost population, the pattern was most dramatic and pervasive through the Industrial Heartland. Finally, Table XII.3 reports the degree to which the central cities of the nation's major metropolitan areas gradually lossened their grip on the population of the metropolitan areas that they anchored. The declining proportion of the population in these central cities has been a pattern as uniform as it has been the predictable result of the way in which metropolitan areas are defined and grow.

Debates over the condition of the nation's industrial cities and the larger economy reveal certain similarities. Fearful of being thought to genuflect to existing economic and demographic trends and denying their aura of inevitability, we are more readily urged to seek their restoration than abide their transformation. Yet, the difficulties besetting our nation's flagship cities and the larger economy are indeed better understood as transformations than as lamentable degeneration and decay. That the city and the larger economy are transforming is less problematic than our perception and reaction to these eventualities. Calls for revitalization on both fronts are animated by the urge to engineer a future that looks reasonably similar to what has gone before, if not to recapture the glories of the past. And it is the past, as Alvin Toffler reminds us in *The Third Wave,* that has a well-defined and entrenched political constituency which dwarfs that of those who seek to anticipate the future rather than back into it.

The nation's economy, like the gangling giant that it is, can be seen to be shifting its weight slowly from one foot to another—manufacturing to services—as the larger nation beyond the network of older cities itself emerges from the industrial era and is forced to adjust to new energy, demographic, and technological opportunities and limitations. Still the most productive economy in the world, these structural adjustments leave the older muscle-bound manufacturing sectors not so much withering as receding to share center stage with a faster growing service sector. To be sure, as the economic center of gravity shifts, the effects are felt most acutely in older cities, which are better wired politically than other places to sense and broadcast the painful adjustments accompanying their transformation. While the nation's economy is not yet service-dominated, increasingly our cities are. Yet, there should be nothing new or particularly disturbing about these cities being in the cross

Table XII.1. Population Trends for Metropolitan Areas Over 500,000 By Region, 1970–80

Metropolitan Area	*1980 Population*	*1970 Population*	*Percent Change 1970–80*
Northeast			
New York, NY-NJ	9,080,777	9,973,716	−9.0
Philadelphia, PA-NJ	4,700,996	4,824,110	−2.6
Boston, MA	2,759,800	2,899,101	−4.8
Nassau-Suffolk, NY	2,603,817	2,555,868	1.9
Pittsburgh, PA	2,260,919	2,401,362	−5.8
Newark, NJ	1,963,600	2,057,468	−4.6
Buffalo, NY	1,241,434	1,349,211	−8.0
Rochester, NY	970,313	961,516	0.9
Providence-Warwick-Pawtucket, RI-MA	917,962	908,887	1.0
Albany-Schenectady-Troy, NY	794,298	777,977	2.1
Hartford, CT	726,036	720,581	0.8
Syracuse, NY	642,547	636,596	0.9
Allentown-Bethlehem-Easton, PA-NJ	637,109	594,382	7.2
Northeast Pennsylvania	629,912	621,882	1.3
New Brunswick-Perth Amboy-Sayreville, NJ	594,984	583,813	1.9
Jersey City, NJ	555,483	607,839	−8.6
Springfield-Chicopee-Holyoke, MA	530,373	541,752	−2.1
Midwest			
Chicago, IL	7,057,853	6,974,755	1.2
Detroit, MI	4,344,139	4,435,051	−2.0
St. Louis, MO-IL	2,344,912	2,410,884	−2.7
Minneapolis-St. Paul, MN-WI	2,109,207	1,965,391	7.3
Cleveland, OH	1,895,997	2,063,729	−8.1
Milwaukee, WI	1,392,872	1,403,884	−0.8
Cincinnati, OH-KY-IN	1,392,394	1,387,207	0.4
Kansas City, MO-KS	1,322,156	1,273,926	3.8
Indianapolis, IN	1,161,539	1,111,352	4.5
Columbus, OH	1,088,973	1,017,847	7.0
Dayton, OH	826,891	852,531	−3.0
Toledo, OH-MI	791,137	762,658	3.7
Akron, OH	660,233	679,239	−2.8
Gary, IN	638,945	633,367	0.9
Grand Rapids, MI	601,106	539,225	11.5
Omaha, NE-IA	566,140	542,646	4.3
Youngstown-Warren, OH	529,887	537,124	−1.3
Flint, MI	521,541	508,664	2.5
South			
Washington, DC-MD-VA	3,045,399	2,910,111	4.6
Dallas-Fort Worth, TX	2,964,342	2,377,623	24.7
Houston, TX	2,891,146	1,999,316	44.6
Baltimore, MD	2,166,308	2,071,016	4.6

(continued)

Table XII.1. (Continued)

Metropolitan Area	*1980 Population*	*1970 Population*	*Percent Change 1970–80*
South			
Atlanta, GA	2,010,368	1,595,517	26.0
Miami, FL	1,573,817	1,267,792	24.1
Tampa-St. Petersburg, FL	1,550,035	1,088,549	42.4
New Orleans, LA	1,183,606	1,046,470	13.1
San Antonio, TX	1,070,245	888,179	20.5
Fort Lauderdale-Hollywood, FL	1,005,507	620,100	62.2
Memphis, TN-AR-MS	909,767	834,103	9.1
Louisville, KY-IN	901,970	867,330	4.0
Birmingham, AL	834,067	767,230	8.7
Oklahoma City, OK	829,584	699,092	18.7
Nashville-Davidson, TN	828,540	699,271	18.5
Greensboro-Winston-Salem-High Point, NC	823,285	724,129	13.7
Norfolk-Virginia Beach-Portsmouth, VA-NC	799,853	732,600	9.2
Jacksonville, FL	736,343	621,827	18.4
Orlando, FL	694,645	453,270	53.3
Tulsa, OK	678,627	549,154	23.6
Charlotte-Gastonia, NC	632,083	557,785	13.3
Richmond, VA	630,965	547,542	15.2
Greenville-Spartanburg, SC	562,934	473,454	18.9
West Palm Beach, FL	551,961	348,993	58.2
Austin, TX	532,811	360,463	47.8
Tucson, AZ	531,896	351,667	51.2
Raleigh-Durham, NC	525,059	419,254	25.2
Wilmington, DE-NJ-MD	523,386	499,493	4.8
West			
Los Angeles-Long Beach, CA	7,445,721	7,041,980	5.7
San Francisco-Oakland, CA	3,226,867	3,109,249	3.8
Anaheim-Santa Ana-Garden Grove, CA	1,925,840	1,421,233	35.5
San Diego, CA	1,859,623	1,357,854	37.0
Denver-Boulder, CO	1,615,442	1,239,545	30.3
Seattle-Everett, WA	1,600,944	1,424,605	12.4
Riverside-San Bernardino-Ontario, CA	1,538,066	1,139,149	35.0
Phoenix, AZ	1,511,552	971,228	55.6
San Jose, CA	1,290,487	1,065,313	21.1
Portland, OR-WA	1,236,294	1,007,130	22.8
Sacramento, CA	1,010,989	803,793	25.8
Salt Lake City-Ogden, UT	935,280	705,458	32.6
Honolulu, HI	762,020	630,528	20.9
Oxnard-Simi Valley-Ventura, CA	529,425	378,497	39.9
Fresno, CA	507,005	413,329	22.7

Source: U.S. Bureau of Census News Release, *Population of Standard Metropolitan Statistical Areas and Standard Consolidated Statistical Areas by Rank Size, 1980 and 1970*, Washington, D.C.: U.S. Government Printing Office, March 1981.

Table XII.2. Population Trends for Central Cities of 250,000 and Over, By Region, 1970–80

City and State	*1980 Population*	*1970 Population*	*Percent Change 1970–80*
Northeast			
New York, NY	7,071,030	7,895,563	−10.4
Philadelphia, PA	1,688,210	1,949,996	−13.4
Boston, MA	562,994	641,071	−12.2
Pittsburgh, PA	423,938	520,089	−18.5
Buffalo, NY	357,870	462,768	−22.7
Newark, NJ	329,248	381,930	−13.8
Midwest			
Chicago, IL	3,005,072	3,369,357	−10.8
Detroit, MI	1,203,339	1,514,063	−20.5
Indianapolis, IN	700,807	736,856	−4.9
Milwaukee, WI	636,212	717,372	−11.3
Cleveland, OH	573,822	750,879	−23.6
Columbus, OH	564,871	540,025	4.6
St. Louis, MO	453,085	622,236	−27.2
Kansas City, MO	448,159	507,330	−11.7
Cincinnati, OH	385,457	453,514	−15.0
Minneapolis, MN	370,951	434,400	−14.6
Toledo, OH	354,635	383,062	−7.4
Omaha, NE	311,681	346,929	−10.2
Wichita, KS	279,272	276,554	1.0
St. Paul, MN	270,230	309,866	−12.8
South			
Houston, TX	1,594,086	1,233,535	29.2
Dallas, TX	904,078	844,401	7.1
Baltimore, MD	786,775	905,787	−13.1
San Antonio, TX	785,410	654,153	20.1
Memphis, TN	646,356	623,988	3.6
Washington, DC	637,651	756,668	−15.7
New Orleans, LA	557,482	593,471	−6.1
Jacksonville, FL	540,898	504,265	7.3
Nashville-Davidson, TN	455,651	426,029	7.0
El Paso, TX	425,259	322,261	32.0
Atlanta, GA	425,022	495,039	−14.1
Oklahoma City, OK	403,213	368,164	9.5
Fort Worth, TX	385,141	393,455	−2.1
Tulsa, OK	360,919	330,350	9.3
Miami, FL	346,931	334,859	3.6
Austin, TX	345,496	253,539	36.3
Charlotte, NC	314,447	241,420	30.2
Louisville, KY	298,451	361,706	−17.5
Birmingham, AL	284,413	300,910	−5.5
Tampa, FL	271,523	277,714	−2.2

(continued)

Table XII.2 (Continued)

City and State	*1980 Population*	*1970 Population*	*Percent Change 1970–80*
South			
Norfolk, VA	266,979	307,951	−13.3
Virginia Beach, VA	262,199	172,106	52.3
West			
Los Angeles, CA	2,966,763	2,811,801	5.5
San Diego, CA	875,504	697,471	25.5
Phoenix, AZ	789,704	584,303	35.2
San Francisco, CA	678,974	715,674	−5.1
San Jose, CA	636,550	459,913	38.4
Seattle, WA	493,846	530,831	−7.0
Denver, CO	491,396	514,678	−4.5
Portland, OR	366,383	379,967	−3.6
Honolulu, HI	365,048	324,871	12.4
Long Beach, CA	361,334	358,879	0.7
Oakland, CA	339,288	361,561	−6.2
Albuquerque, NM	331,767	244,501	35.7
Tucson, AZ	330,537	262,933	25.7
Sacramento, CA	275,741	257,105	7.2

Source: U.S. Bureau of Census News Release, *1980 Census Population for Cities of 100,000 and Over by Rank Order*, Washington, D.C.: U.S. Government Printing Office, June 1981.

hairs of larger scale adjustments. For as long as we have had cities, they have always been required to make the bulk of such adjustments, though seldom out from behind the veil of overall national economic expansion, as they have been doing in recent years.

Because inherent in the impulse to revitalize older cities is a danger that the recovery of the larger economy will be imperiled, it is perhaps less important what we do about these difficulties than how we come to think about them. In both instances the results are worth waiting for, cannot be deferred, and threaten to be unappreciated because of the considerable dislocations that are required during this period of transition.

This nation has a surprisingly well-developed conventional wisdom about her cities, what is happening to them and why and what needs to be done, that has been handed down over the decades largely intact—with additions, but seldom with substitutions. Not only have our more distressed cities been thought to be "dying," population and employment decline come to be considered unequivocably undesirable, concentrated development judged to be good, and dispersed lower-den-

Table XII.3. Central City Population as Percentage of SMSA, By Region, 1970–80
(Listed in Order of 1980 Population)

Metropolitan Area	*Central City Proportion of SMSA 1980*	*Central City Proportion of SMSA 1970*	*Percent Change 1970–80*
Northeast			
New York	77.9	68.2	9.7
Philadelphia	35.9	40.4	−4.5
Boston	20.4	23.3	−2.9
Midwest			
Chicago	42.6	48.2	−5.6
Detroit	27.7	36.0	−8.3
Indianapolis	60.3	67.1	−6.8
Milwaukee	45.7	51.1	−5.4
Cleveland	30.3	38.3	−8.0
Columbus, Ohio	51.9	68.3	−16.4
St. Louis	19.3	29.3	−10.0
Kansas City, Mo.-Kans.	33.9	40.4	−6.5
South			
Houston	55.1	62.1	−7.0
Dallas-Fort Worth	30.5	54.3	−23.8
Baltimore	36.3	43.7	−7.4
San Antonio	73.4	75.7	−2.3
Memphis	71.0	81.0	−10.0
Washington, D.C.	20.9	26.4	−5.5
New Orleans	47.1	56.7	−9.6
Jacksonville, Florida	73.5	100.0	−26.5
Nashville	55.0	82.9	−27.9
El Paso	88.7	89.7	−1.0
Atlanta	21.1	35.7	−14.6
West			
Los Angeles-Long Beach	39.8	40.0	−0.2
San Diego	47.1	51.3	−4.2
Phoenix	50.6	60.1	−9.5
San Francisco-Oakland	21.0	23.0	−2.0
San Jose	49.3	41.9	7.4
Seattle-Everett	30.8	37.3	−6.5
Denver-Boulder	30.4	41.9	−11.5

Source: U.S. Bureau of Census, News Release, *1980 Census Population for Cities of 100,000 and Over by Rank Order*, Washington, D.C.: U.S. Government Printing Office, April 1981; and *1970 Census of Population, General Population Characteristics, U.S. Summary* (PC (1) B1), 1972; Table 1967. Reported in Appendix D, in *American Federalism in the 1980's: Changes and Consequences;* Cambridge, Mass.: Roundtable on Governments, Lincoln Institute of Land Policy, August 1981, pp. 75–76.

sity development ("sprawl") bad, but also federal policy responses thought best are those that are well funded and restorative. Well-intentioned candidates for national political office tirelessly pose for ritual photographs in the South Bronx in an effort to convince voters that the fate of urban America somehow hinges on what we allow to happen there. Suggestive of an urban Masada complex, these visual images prod us to resolve that it is in such desperate locations that we should take our stand against forces that would unravel our cities.

It is against such a grim backdrop that the moral authority for these cyclical prescriptions for more targeted federal resources is highlighted. Seeing is believing. Unfortunately, much of what we know has become flawed by what we believe. Our perceptions of cities and their circumstances are often captured by misleading images and communicated with inappropriate metaphors. Believing is seeing. By 1980, it was time to challenge the conventional wisdom that was at the heart of a quarter century of federal urban policy. This was required not because it was known to be wrong, but because it had grown rigid; it stifled debate about issues long thought to be decided, and it promoted policies that were poorly articulated with the urban circumstances of the 21st century.

There is a sense in which cities as we perceive them simply do not exist, if indeed they ever have. For Americans, cities have served as pegboards on which to hang any symbol or image that was wished. While at any one time a city is different things to different people, we do not easily permit a city to become different things over time. Yet, like it or not, the essence of a city is change; since cities are constantly changing, the ways in which we view them should also change. Today, without too much effort the life that only older industrial cities once offered can be lived nearly anywhere thanks to the accessibility-enhancing developments in transportation and communication. Though the communities in which we are embedded for work and play are scattered across a far-flung territory, they can be relatively easily stitched together at will when we either step out or "reach out and touch someone."

Although our industrial cities are fascinating amalgams of symbol and substance, in a strictly material sense the city never has been more than the physical trace of existing economic arrangements, technological capabilities, and social preferences. As such, our older cities provide telltale evidence of the degree to which we have pressed back the limits of space, time, scarcity, and prejudice while expanding accessibility across places and among peoples. Multistory factory buildings, large single-family residences in segregated housing patterns, and the convergence of transportation routes to, from, and around a central core all tell us more about the prevailing cost of energy, the state of the art in linking technologies, and the historical intergroup competition for city space at the time these cities experienced the bulk of their expansion than do they serve as inherent standards against which the form or function of tomorrow's urban settlements should be judged.

Today we are witnessing the gradual dissolution of the industrial era city as we have known it. What the notion of the city will be for the 21st century is being defined at least two decades early. The city is being redefined in the same sense and for the same essential reasons that new lifestages (e.g., preschooler, teenager, "swinging singles," and senior citizen) and household types (e.g., single parent and blended families) accompanied the maturation of the industrial era. Similarly, the transforming city is a predictable response to changing demographic, economic, and technological realities. While the image of the city's form is etched into our consciousness, it is the city's functions that will always be its *sine qua non.* Recently that range of functions has been narrowing; in time its form will adjust to the new roles that cities will come to play for the larger society. That changes in city form are more visible than changes in city function, and that the latter pace the former in the transformation process, may trick us into responding inappropriately.

Older central cities are no longer the anchors of the national economy in the ways that they have been in the past century. As the industrial era recedes, central cities that blossomed prior to World War II have been left behind as only one of several alternative sites inside and outside metropolitan areas for the productive activities of the nation. Cities are perhaps less usefully understood as places than as environments conducive to the flourishing of certain activities, and ever less conducive to the nurturance of others.

The city of the 21st century will still be of vital importance to the life of the nation, but it will step back to join the ranks of an increasing variety of places both peripheral to and distant from historical population and industrial centers. The industrial era did much to move the productive core of the nation's economy into the central city; today that core has fragmented into a handful of competing segments, and much of the nation's productive capacity and her people flourish outside the nation's large, and especially central, cities.

The future urban center will probably retain only a small range of the wide spectrum of manufacturing activity that was once located there. The maturation of production technologies and their historical locations will diminish the importance of goods production and enhance the prospects for the flourishing of the full range of services production. For this next act, the city will need to exchange old props for new ones. Increasingly, the urban centers will be defined more by who and what is left behind than by who or what is arriving. The transformed local economic base will reflect the outmigration of much manufacturing along with the blue- and white-collar work forces vital to the functioning of the factory. Retained will be those white- and blue-collar workers who are required to run and service the offices that define the expanded service economy. A new, leaner municipal service package that is reconstructed and hopefully better articulated to the needs of the retained individual and corporate residents and temporary visitors to conferences, conventions, and cultural events will have evolved. Limited upgrading of neighborhood housing and shopping areas in selected areas will be attractive to the narrowing range of middle-class households who prefer life downtown, and will be discouraging to others.

REINDUSTRIALIZATION AND THE REAPPRECIATION OF MANUFACTURING[1]

Much of the impetus behind the call for reindustrialization can be traced to the characteristic ways in which structural changes in the nation's economy have been perceived. In a report prepared by the Senate Democratic Task Force on the Economy, it was estimated that the loss of U.S. competitiveness in a changing international marketplace translated into $125 billion in lost production and more than 2 million industrial jobs. In the past decade, the U.S. share of the world market shrank by nearly a quarter.

The often distinct fates and fortunes of the handful of major segments into which the larger national economy has evolved clearly belies the tremendous interdependence that once characterized the larger economy. Particular consternation has been generated by the seemingly irrevocable decline of manufacturing as a proportion of total employment. This happened despite the fact that even this hard-pressed segment of the economy continues to grow, albeit at a slower rate than historically. Not only has manufacturing output nearly tripled in the past three and a half decades, but employment has also increased by a third over the same time span. This pattern of output pacing employment indicates rising levels of productivity. Even though 9 of 10 new jobs since the mid-1970s have been in the services, one of five American workers is still employed in either direct or indirect production in manufacturing industries.

The perceived "decline" of manufacturing in the U.S. is an implication drawn from considerable myth and misunderstanding. While major structural changes in the national economy are being registered in both industry mix and labor force composition, much of the reaction to these changes have focused on the apparent diminishment of this nation's goods-producing capability. The glacial shift to services in the overall economy and the more rapid shift to services in central city economies that define for many the essence of our postindustrial future have conspired to obscure important changes in that sector of the economy that transforms raw materials into finished products. Concern in recent years over high rates of inflation and interest rates, unused industrial capacity, and structural unemployment as well as low rates of productivity advance and capital formation may well have caused too many to equate the changes working themselves out within the sector with demise and decline. Yet, it would be a monumental mistake to write off prematurely the very large contributions that the sector will make to the era ahead.

While the nation is indeed exiting the urban-industrial era that has reigned for the bulk of the past two centuries, we are today not so much jettisoning one set of productive arrangements as witnessing their vulnerability to structural and spatial realignment brought on by recent technological developments in such fields as aviation, electronics, computers and microprocessors, genetic engineering and related science-based transformative activity. Employment generation in high-technology industries accounted for approximately three of every four new manufacturing jobs in the past quarter of a century. Therefore, a fuller appreciation of the coming postindustrial era must include the realization that accompanying the expansion of the service sector is the promise of a "new industrial" sector in which traditional and derivative goods-producing industries assimilate a flurry of technological innovations—both product and process—that will improve their competitiveness and productivity. However, no unitary and compact New Industrial Heartland is likely to emerge that will in any way resemble the structural and spatial features of the original one. Not only will the new jobs created look different than the old ones but they will adhere far less to the locational dictates that governed the first industrial era.

Thus while much of the dislocation associated with the transformation of the larger economy is centered in the manufacturing sector—especially the automobile industry which accounts for 1 of 12 manufacturing jobs—and while employment growth rates in the service sector eclipse those in manufacturing, we cannot easily equate economic growth with economic health, nor can we assume that the heady expansion of the service sector diminishes in the least the importance of manufacturing now or in the years ahead. Discussion of the passing industrial era should not blind us to the enduring importance of the manufacturing sector, whose adjustment involves slower rates of growth, not absolute decline.

PRODUCTIVITY DECLINE AND ECONOMIC RESILIENCE

The U.S. economy is the most productive in the world despite the fact that our growth rate of labor productivity lags behind those of several other industrialized nations. In the century prior to the 1973 oil embargo, the average growth rate of productivity was about 2.4 percent per year. Against that historical background, the 3.2 percent growth rate realized between 1948 and 1965 (after emerging from World War II as the world's dominant superpower) looks to be not only an historical anomaly itself, but also an overly severe standard against which to judge the more recent performance of the nation's economy. Nonetheless, the 0.6 percent average growth rate of the last half of the 1970s looks puny indeed and cannot fail to catch the eye of even the most casual observer. Yet, as to what it might mean, that is a different matter.

Ironically, this recent preoccupation with declining productivity has served for many as ample evidence of the palsied and arthritic condition of our national economy. Too often obscured from view is the fact that in several of our most beleagured industrial sectors (e.g., steel), labor productivity is still the highest in the world, thanks largely to shifts within the industry itself. Older steel plants have been increasingly automated and newer smaller plants have emphasized the production of speciality steel. The capital requirements for shifts of this sort may be a far more sensible focus than productivity itself as the nation seeks economic recovery.

Wisely, when dealing with adult human beings, we equate health with resilience and endurance rather than with rate of growth; perhaps we should do the same when evaluating the economy. A case can be made that, if anything, our national economy has shown a remarkable agility in responding to all manner of disturbances since 1965, even though it failed to grow very much. Of particular significance has been the ability of the national economy to absorb unprecedented millions of new labor force entrants who have higher levels of education but low skill and experience levels. The building shock waves of the baby boom and the re-entry of millions of women into the labor force reversed the labor scarcity of previous decades and encouraged the substitution of labor for capital. With that *ad hoc* substitution came dampened labor productivity. Still, even though the labor force expanded an average 1.3 percent per year between 1973 and 1979, the rate of growth of capital stock only slowed—it did not decline.

Viewed from another perspective, as the relative price of energy increased through the later 1970s, the substitution of labor for energy was the predictable consequence. Thus, while labor productivity declined, energy productivity increased. The greater significance of labor costs as compared to energy costs when considering the total of production costs diminishes the importance of this increased energy productivity, to be sure. Nonetheless, the larger point is that even while increased energy productivity only partially compensated for reduced labor productivity, it did cushion somewhat the economy's wrenching adjustment to skyrocketing energy prices. The entire latter half of the past decade witnessed the wringing out of many of the most energy profligate industries; some of those adjustments necessitated a period of lowered labor productivity to compensate for the rate at which new energy price levels were escalating.

As demographic metabolism proceeds and the bulge of new workers wends its way through the labor force, the relative cost of labor in post-baby boom cohorts will likely begin to rise again, the growth rate of capital stock should pick up, and the productivity increases historically realized through the substituiton of capital for labor should return. The introduction of robotics into factories will continue to be accompanied by the introduction of word processors and "smart" appliances into offices. Therefore, such a responsiveness by the nation's economy to rapidly changing relative costs and supplies of factors of production may have limited labor productivity in the short term, but it did so while at the same time providing new jobs at record rates and conserving energy. It may be important not to overlook evidence of such resilience when diagnosing and prescribing for a slow-growth economy.

Beyond this, however, not only may the decline in rates of productivity be overly emphasized as the crux of our economic problems, but also higher rates of productivity may not be much of a solution. Indeed, some have suggested that our problems will not be solved by simply being more productive, since in some cases we may have reached the upper limit, beyond which it is unrealistic to expect to squeeze more productivity out of the economy by simply increasing capital equipment. The reason for this relates to the organization of industry today. The proportion of workers engaged in direct production has dropped so rapidly during the late industrial era, and the proportions of workers shifted to overhead and support roles has increased so rapidly, that increasing the efficiency of the former group probably cannot be accomplished fast enough to counter the drag effect of the latter group. It may be the organization of productive activity itself more so than the ratio of capital to labor that bogs down our efforts to increase our industrial efficiency.

Finally, our flirtation with productivity as an economic cure-all needs to be conditioned by consideration of its impact on employment. As the experiences of older mainline manufacturing industries such as automobile and steel illustrate, difficult adjustments to stronger international competition have resulted in greater productivity on the factory floor. Part of the price paid for this adjustment has been the creation of legions of employees who have been rendered obsolete, redundant, and expendable. Increased productivity is certainly desirable, but it must be part of a larger process wherein capital is directed not only to reorganize and retool mainline manufacturing, but also to stimulate business expansion and creation to ensure that the larger transformation generates new jobs as it eliminates older ones. In the chorus for reindustrialization there are many voices; when the call for greater productivity drowns out these other voices, their song may no longer be worth listening to.

THE REAGAN ADMINISTRATION'S "SHADOW" URBAN POLICY

There is a sense in which the fate and fortune of urban America is no longer tied so closely as it has been historically to the fates and fortunes of her older cities. Residential preferences, as well as the locus of business births and expansions, increasingly favor locations peripheral to, or at considerable distance from, existing metropolitan areas. In the past decade, several of our largest metropolitan areas declined in population for the first time; further, nearly 60 percent of new manufacturing growth between 1962 and 1978 was found in nonmetropolitan areas. As with most changes besetting the nation in recent decades, these realities are mixed blessings, wherein the disadvantages are more easily discerned than the advantages.

The circumstances that define our national system of settlements are far too diverse to be easily comprehended with generalizations; yet it is safe to say that urban America—its capital, jobs, people, income, and innovative capacity—has been spreading out for decades. Just as clearly, the thinning out of our larger, older, more compact and central urban settlements has been accompanied by the reconcentration of wealth, vitality, and optimism in new central locations at the periphery of older metropolitan areas and in regions peripheral to the older Industrial Heartland of the Northeast and Midwest. The new urban America, no longer conterminous with the nation's network of older industrial cities, does not have less vitality than before, but the nation's older industrial cities do. Unfortunately—though predictably—there has been little political support forthcoming for the greater appreciation of these social and economic developments.

As the third year of the Reagan Presidency unfolds, not only have we not heard an explicit urban policy enunciated, but also we can be fairly certain that one will not be. This is consistent with the newly prevailing view in many quarters that the federal government should pay more attention to assuring that national economic growth takes place at all than that it takes place in specific, historical locations. In short, the proffered federal initiatives that promise urban implications do not constitute an urban policy at all, but rather bespeak a more general commitment to a program of economic recovery and revitalization. Thus, stability and predictability in our monetary policy, easing of the burden of federal mandates on localities and regulations on business, a disciplined budget through spending cuts as a precursor to a balanced budget, and tax cuts for businesses and individuals are believed to provide the more potent remedy for all manner of urban distress than religious reliance on traditional place-specific policies and programs, from urban renewal to Community Development Block Grants, that have accumulated since the early 1960s.

The Reagan Administration's economic recovery program might well be viewed as the *de facto* urban policy for the rest of the century. The two major tax reduction proposals—a hefty cut tilted toward higher income households to be phased in over three years, and accelerated depreciation schedules for business—promise to return untold billions to individuals in after-tax disposable income (estimated by loyalists to be a quarter trillion dollars before the next Presidential election in 1984!) and after-tax returns on investment for business.

Lurking within these supply-side economic theories, political values and sentiments for limited government, and rosy scenario taxing and spending projections are the makings of a "shadow" urban policy, the likes of which we have not seen since the federal government first assumed during the Depression a major responsibility for the nation's cities and those who reside in them. This shadow urban policy implies that we must be able to produce wealth before we can redistribute it; that in a transforming American economy, all places, not just places of historical importance, are able to contribute to aggregate national growth and productivity; that shifts in people, jobs, capital and income out of older cities and even entire regions should not necessarily be resisted since they raise the wealth of the entire nation, enhance our international competitiveness, save jobs for the nation, inhibit inflation, as well as create new larger scale urban entities that have enhanced economic, if ever less political, integrity.

Further, it suggests that the best way to relieve distress in our older and larger settlements is not to overreact to the transformation of local and regional economies and the shrinkage of certain local populations and economic bases. "Health" at the local level may well be expected to be achieved at new, often lower levels of population and employment.

The emphasis is being shifted away from federally prompted subnational development efforts and toward national economic policies that have as their aim the creation and maintenance of an attractive investment climate conducive to steady and long-term economic growth, to higher rates of job creation, and to low rates of unemployment, poverty, and dependence.

Wary local officials across the land decry the intention of seeking traditional urban policy goals via macroeconomic policy, charging that it is naive to think that overall national economic vitality will automatically redound to the benefit of specific local economies. In this they are largely correct. The shadow urban policy of the Reagan Administration contains no guarantees that the locus of restored economic vitality will be or can be the nation's historic urban centers. Given that the health of all places is ultimately dependent on the health of the national economy, economic policies that entail inadvertent and unavoidable antiurban impacts (e.g., accelerated capital recovery programs and business tax cuts) may be preferable to those that make the strength of the national economy secondary to, or the implied sum of, the strengths of specific local and regional economies. If the city is the be "fixed," it will be fixed as a consequence of the same market economic and demographic forces that led to its having been "broken." The probable efficacy of a more interventionist federal political economic role in that process is too easily overstated, oversold, and ultimately believed.

URBAN ENTERPRISE ZONES: AN INNER CITY STRATEGY FOR THE EIGHTIES?[2]

And so it is that the nation appears to be opting for urban revitalization by means of national economic revitalization rather than vice versa. It is somewhat curious, then, that to date the only explicit urban policy initiative that has received limited Administration backing has been the notion of an urban enterprise zone. While it is still too early to tell whether this is not simply the latest in a long line of place-sensitive antidistress remedies whose ability to garner political support from politicians will exceed its ability to achieve its longer term intended economic results, it does appear that we see for the first time an administration differentiate its implicit urban policy intentions from an explicit inner city strategy.

The enterprise zone concept is essentially the free trade zone notion that flourishes in the Far East rewrapped as a British import, which on its home turf is relatively recent in origin. It has been heralded in recent months as embodying precisely the blend of free enterprise mechanics and targeted focus that is needed to achieve political consensus between conservative economic advisors and turf-conscious politicians. Touted as the unassuming—albeit lean and one-legged—centerpiece of the Reagan-era shadow urban policy, it is curiously enough both supply side in theory and surgical in implementation. However, despite its ideological acceptability and its "fit" into the intellectual lineage of place-specific policies since the late 1960s, upon closer examination of the enterprise zone, there may be less there than meets the eye.

The premise is that jobs so desperately needed by inner city residents—particularly poor youth lacking readily marketable skills—do not exist because the enterprises that have traditionally generated them—particularly small businesses—have been suffocating under the combined weight of regulations, zoning restrictions, and taxation. The proposed policy response is the reduction of the differential cost of doing business that exists between the targeted neighborhood and nearby alternative locations. The policy levers to be pulled would include reduction of property and business taxes and Social Security deductions; suspension of regulations requiring a whole host of building codes, permits, and licenses; and curtailment of the restrictions imposed by zoning ordinances. The goal is to create a *zone sanitaire* within which existing enterprise will be encouraged to stay, new enterprise will be encouraged to germinate, and the supply of housing—particularly rental units—will not be artificially dampened.

The idea has merit. It correctly draws attention to the considerable disadvantages of doing business in most older central cities, and its principle objective is the creation of jobs. It is even more attractive in that it invites active participation of state and local governments in the generation of private sector, rather than public sector, employment. However, there are some nettlesome implications that should be considered. No one implication is necessarily a fatal flaw; taken together they may rein in any unbridled optimism about the potential success of the urban enterprise zone concept.

For all the delicate chemistry of substance and symbols, the notion of an enterprise zone should receive far closer scrutiny than it has thus far. The concept may represent much less of a break with the past than is now thought. Indeed, the enterprise zone concept may be simply the logical and latest "next step" in a succession of place-oriented urban policy concepts that overemphasize the necessity of achieving specific policy outcomes in specific places. While the details of Anglo-American cross-cultural transplantation have not yet been fully worked out, the cautions that are advised here are not those that stem from such difficulties. Rather, we would do well to ask a more fundamental question. Does the adoption of this kind of surgical place-oriented public policy discount at its peril the fact that the fortunes of specific places will—and probably should be encouraged to—fluctuate over time? The nation should be cautioned to understand that cities must be permitted to reflect changing technological capabilities and social circumstances, rather than be constrained by an attempt to preserve under glass any particular historical combination of them.

The strength of cities is tied to their ability to reflect and accommodate change, not fend it off. Expansion and contraction are unavoidably arrayed across the geography of city centers and their satellite neighborhoods and are the inevitable local accompaniments of a transforming national economy and society. While we may wish that this were not so, we should have learned by now to pause before making official promises that it can be otherwise.

Despite its well-intentioned focus on business nurturance, the enterprise zone concept overemphasizes the role of economic factors and underemphasizes the role of essentially noneconomic factors that contribute significantly to the rather amorphous and much ballyhooed notion of "business climate." This may well be more of a concern for the larger established firm serving regional or national markets than it is for the smaller enterprise whose locational options are more constrained. Nonetheless, factors such as fear of crime, congestion, limited accessibility, lack of widely diversified support services during and after the workday, and ease of parking all influence the attractiveness of doing business in a particular area.

The "greenlining" envisioned has as its principle aim the nurturance of small businesses. While it may be true that small businesses are the main generator of new jobs in our economy, they are also the most likely to falter. The precariousness of their existence is due to many factors beyond the costs of doing business including inexperienced management, dependence on diversified labor pools and hypervulnerability to swings in the national economy. Since small businesses come in so many shapes and sizes and their needs are so diverse, they often are the most difficult to assist through governmental bureaucratic actions—surgical or otherwise.

Emphasis on rewriting codes, regulations, and tax policies may be evidence of having assigned undue importance to what government does or can cease doing. It is more likely that the absence of sufficient jobs in a particular area is attributable to larger-scale structural changes in local, regional, national and international economies. Changing technological requirements in the production and marketing processes may outweigh public policies (zoning, regulation, taxation) in explaining why older local businesses have closed their doors and business expansion has occurred in other locations. Further, the majority of businesses in the U.S. are small, and many make only a slim profit, if any. More favorable tax treatment of enterprises whose tax liability is miniscule in the first place will not be much of a boon.

The notion of an enterprise zone is the ultimate example of our belief that we can target and treat a jurisdiction—albeit ad hoc in this case—as a self-contained entity, relatively isolatable from its social and economic moorings. Any chance for sustained economic and social health is substantially reduced the longer the rules of the market economy are suspended in deference to the remedies of the political economy. The promise of steady, sustained vitality of a designated enterprise area is dependent on the manner in which the rules that apply to everyone else are eventually reimposed. There may be an inevitable temptation to delay the long-term social and economic integration of the enterprise zone with the larger community and to postpone the reexposure of the area to the market forces that apply elsewhere.

Experimentation of this sort within a bounded territorial unit may underemphasize the fragile bonds of interdependence that exist with surrounding neighborhoods. Ironically, businesses in nearby distressed areas that have not been designated as enterprise zones may be encouraged to relocate under the protective canopy of suspended market rules and government regulations and thereby leave a trail of lost jobs and associated social costs in their wake. The net effect would be the simple redistribution of opportunity, rather than the creation of it. Relationships disrupted within the zone may cause undue hardship on areas just beyond its boundaries. We underestimate the systemic character of the local urban economy at our own peril.

Regrettably, the urban enterprise zone concept does little to sensitize local officials to the need for "planned disinvestment." There is little incentive to develop policies to help older industrial communities, in particular, adjust to long-term population and employment declines derivative from larger patterns of regional change and the transformation of central city economies. It delays the development of a local politics of shrinkage and contraction and postpones the day when local public officials can finally dare to encourage discussion of how their community might work to scale down with a minimum of civic anxiety and pain. While shifts in assignment of certain traditionally public services (sanitation, security, fire) to the private sector are sometimes conceived of as an accompaniment of the urban enterprise zone strategy, the political temptation to have a distressed neighborhood designated an enterprise zone rather than be a candidate for purposeful disinvestment in redundant and expensive public service infrastructure (water and sewer branches, traffic control, street lighting) may also be as overwhelming as it is regrettable.

Identifying areas for designation as potential enterprise zones will almost surely proceed according to political dynamics, rather than for reasons having to do with any realistic expectation that the building blocks of a revitalizable area are in place. "Worst-first" strategies are all too often the response to the urgent political requirement that public monies, however limited, be spent where circumstances are the most dire; sacrificed in the process is the more economically rational logic that public monies be spent where they have a reasonable chance of doing the most good—in places showing incipient rather than advanced decline. Such is the familiar fate of preventative measures. We must add to this the confession that our knowledge concerning what makes a location a likely prospect for reclamation and rejuvenation is sketchy at best.

The explicit and implicit "place" orientation—while it makes sense politically—may make little sense economically or socially. The historical decline of the significance of "place" is a condition of modern society that we have difficulty building into our analysis of public policies and our conduct of political affairs. Remedying presumed deficiencies in places for the sake of remedying disadvantages facing people may be an indirect policy strategy that encourages unwarranted faith in the logic that aid to distressed places benefits distressed people. Our understanding of the linkages and causal chains in local economic development is rudimentary at best and may even be less trustworthy the smaller the areal unit that is our focus and target.

The urban enterprise zone notion is not immune to the charge that it is a quintessential example of "social engineering." For some, the suspension or weeding out of regulations, lowering of taxes, and the like suggests a reliance on a less fettered market process. For others, it is viewed as the creation of a business climate that is artificial and unable to be supported by the operation of the larger urban economic and political system. Inner city business climates have evolved and costs of business and residence are likely as they are for reasons having more to do with the opportunity and necessity associated with larger scale technological and economic change than with manipulable public policies. Urban enterprise zones conceived of as economic fantasy islands may simply delay the impacts of market forces and power shifts rather than assist a community to adjust to and withstand their impact and to survive and even perhaps to thrive.

Areas that are targeted for designation as urban enterprise zones are likely already in the process of evolving to the point that they can perform new functions for the larger community. This process is consistent with trends in countless central cities that are transforming to play equally vital, if narrower, roles for the larger region. The building construction boom in many of our older downtown areas attests to the fact that we are between acts in an urban historical drama of epic proportions.

Also, as may always be the case, there will be difficulty knowing to what extent the outcome induced by public intervention really differs from what would have occurred in its absence. That such intervention may disrupt a process that would have yielded directly a more easily sustained economic activity than that yielded indirectly is a possible and likely outcome. If it makes sense to suspend some aspect of governmental presence because it dampens job creation or economic growth, then we should consider suspending it entirely and disavow the search for advantages for some communities relative to others.

Like all similar forms of government intervention, the implementation of the urban enterprise zone as a cornerstone in any federal urban policy may raise unrealistic expectations about what can be accomplished in the long run. Political strategies of this sort are often judged more by the promises made to gain support for them than by more reasonable criteria. Above all, responsible policy actors in coming years must resist the temptation to promise more than government in the past has shown the capacity to deliver.

The enterprise zone concept has embedded in it a logic of special concern for those who study the special fates of people in special places. Implicit is the commitment to respond to the plight of the urban underclass by job generation in-place. Yet, uncritical reliance on an inner city strategy of this sort deflects interest in the positive aspects of encouraging and facilitating the mobility of unemployed or underemployed workers. On a larger scale, this is important because the mobility of labor is restricted in ways that the mobility of capital and the jobs it creates are not. While we should have no illusions about the universal relevance of relocation to the plight of the unemployed and unemployable in our inner cities, our best intentions are hobbled when we fail to appreciate that people-to-job sequences, more so than jobs-to-people policy strategies, have played the major role in linking individuals and households to economic opportunity in our recent and distant past. At the same time, while we may be properly skeptical of finely-tuned local economic development strategies that seek to create jobs or lure them to the people who need them, we should take care not to replace one myth with another. Jobs and a better life do not await everyone at journey's end. The linkage between distressed people and distressed places can be unraveled not only by reducing the barriers to mobility that hinder some, but also by assisting people to increase their relevance to the local and regional job markets transforming around them. Where retraining and relocation assistance fail to make inroads into the circumstances that enmesh the urban underclass, then a sensible blend of social welfare policies should be available as a last resort. All manner of "bootstrap" theories aside, there will continue to be an intractable portion of the urban destitute for whom employment as a linkage to the economy is not feasible. Their welfare and dignity will continue to be assured only by the safety net about which we have heard so much in the past two years.

THE FEDERAL ROLE IN A NEW URBAN-INDUSTRIAL AMERICA: A SUMMARY

The restructuring of the nation's economy throughout the 20th century has been accompanied by (and has even required) the shifting of local and regional economic bases throughout the land. The bulk of what we have experienced as "urban" and "welfare" crises in the past two decades are the consequences of this economic transformation. Much of this restructuring has occurred in response to technological developments for which we should be thankful in large measure. Much has also been in response to a restructuring international economy, which ever prods us to remain responsive and flexible while it expands opportunities for consumers in other countries to purchase our goods and services. The price of no longer being insulated from the building competitive pressures of the international marketplace includes the bracing realization that historical urban places must often exchange an older range of functions for newer, if more limited, ones. Likewise, newer urban forms, even long denigrated ones such as "sprawl" itself—along with the values with which we have propped up our stated desire for more concentrated arrangements—will command our recognition as well as our respect. In both form and function, neither Rome nor New York nor Detroit are eternal after all. Finally, our very notions of social welfare, and how we may ensure some acceptable minimum for all people, may have to transform to reflect the changing promises and problems presented by the passing of the industrial era.

In the end, as we consider what the national governmental response should be to the evolving industrial economy and the industrial cities that used to house its main engines of growth, we must ask ourselves whether or not the best transition policy might be something other than a spatially sensitive urban or regional policy that proceeds by playing off regions and localities against one another. Perhaps a better transition policy is a sensible blend of macroeconomic and social welfare policies whose goal is to insulate people primarily, rather than places, from the coming changes. Increasingly, our political organization is mismatched to the scale of our economic life. Perhaps once again we will be concerned more with the functioning of the national economy and the access of our citizens to it than with first translating those responsibilities into an endless series of anachronistic spatial conflicts.

In any event, the variety of perceptions of the economy and the city that have been translated into public policies illustrate our inability to let go of increasingly inappropriate settlement patterns and economic arrangements that are being rendered obsolete. Despite the fact that evidence exists for the continuing responsiveness of the economy and the demography to each other and to technological innovations—if less clearly to our explicit public policies devised to influence each—it is becoming clear that the standards necessary to anticipate and judge the emerging new urban-industrial arrangements will have to be different from those of the waning urban-industrial era which is now taking leave of us.

NOTES

1. The author gratefully acknowledges the research assistance of and helpful discussions with Ms. Bahar Norris of the graduate program in Political Economy at The University of Texas at Dallas.
2. This section is heavily dependent on testimony "An Inner-City Strategy for the Eighties? Urban Enterprise Zones" by the author in *Hearings Before the Senate Subcommittee on Intergovernmental Relations*, Washington, D.C.: U.S. Government Printing Office, February 1981.

REFERENCES

1. "American Renewal," *Fortune*, March 9, 1981, pp. 71–101.
2. "America's Restructured Economy," *Business Week*, June 1, 1981, pp. 55–100.
3. Forrester, Jay W., "Why More Productivity Will Not Solve Our Problems," *Business and Society*, Fall 1980, pp. 10–18.
4. Hershman, Arlene and Mark Levenson, "The 'Reindustrialization' of America," *Dun's Review*, July 1980, Vol. 116, No. 1, pp. 34–43.
5. Hicks, Donald A., "Place-Sensitive Public Policies in the Eighties," Testimony before the Joint Economic Committee, U.S. Congress, in hearings on *The Economic Report of the President: Regional Balance and Economic Policy*, Washington, D.C.: U.S. Government Printing Office, January 1981.
6. Joint Economic Committee, U.S. Congress, "The Regional and Urban Impacts of the Administration's Budget and Tax Proposals," Washington, D.C.: U.S. Government Printing Office, July 31, 1981.
7. Office of Technology Assessment, *U.S. Industrial Competitiveness: A Comparison of Steel, Electronics, and Automobiles*, Washington, D.C.: U.S. Government Printing Office, 1981.
8. Pascarella, Perry, "The Case for Industrial America," *Industry Week*, January 12, 1981, pp. 51–58.
9. President's Commission for a National Agenda for the Eighties, *Urban America in the Eighties: Perspectives and Prospects*, Washington, D.C.: U.S. Government Printing Office, 1980.
10. "Revitalizing the U.S. Economy," *Business Week*, June 30, 1980. pp. 56–105.
11. Schmid, Gregory, "Productivity and Reindustrialization: A Dissenting View," *Challenge*, January-February 1981, pp. 24–29.

12. Schwartz, Gail Garfield and Pat Choate, "Revitalizing the U.S. Economy: A Brief for National Sectoral Policies," Washington, D.C.: Academy for Contemporary Problems, 1980.
13. Senate Democratic Task Force on the Economy, *Report of the Subcommittee on Industrial Policy and Productivity,* (mimeo), August 4, 1980.
14. Stanfield, Rochelle L., "Economic Development Aid-Shell Game or the Key to Urban Rejuventation?" *National Journal,* March 21, 1981, pp. 494–497.
15. Toffler, Alvin, *The Third Wave,* New York: Morrow, 1980.

Index